OL' STROM

An Unauthorized Biography
of STROM THURMOND

Jack Bass *and* Marilyn W. Thompson

LONGSTREET
Atlanta, Georgia

OL'
STROM

To Nathalie Dupree
-J.B.

To Andrew McKinley Thompson
-M.W.T.

Published by LONGSTREET PRESS, INC.,
a subsidiary of Cox Newspapers,
a subsidiary of Cox Enterprises, Inc.
2140 Newmarket Parkway
Suite 122
Marietta, Georgia 30067

Printed in the United States of America

2nd printing, 1999

Library of Congress Catalog Card Number: 98-066360

ISBN: 1-56352-523-2

Jacket design by Jill Dible
Book design by Burtch Hunter

Photo credits: Modern Political Collection, University of South Carolina (front cover, 166); Jack Bass (6, bottom of 175); Strom Thurmond Collection at Clemson University (24, 72, 96, 134, 138, 148, 161, 162, 164, 165, 167, 170, 171, 172, 173, top of 174,184, 218, 312); *Life* magazine (118); Associated Press (163); Vic Tutte (168, 169); Armstrong Williams (bottom of 174, top of 175); South Carolina State 1948 yearbook (272). Cartoon credits: Robert Arial (172, 176, 326); Doug Marlette (246).

ACKNOWLEDGEMENTS

We are indebted first to Strom Thurmond for living a life whose richness, longevity, and historic impact combine to make it worth telling. Sen. Thurmond told us in the fall of 1997 that he was getting many requests for book interviews, turning them all down, and could not make exceptions.

Although he was therefore unavailable to respond to specific questions and issues raised in research for this book, each of us separately has interviewed him in-depth on more than one occasion in the past. His voice is present throughout this book.

In addition, historian James G. Banks and Thurmond biographer Nadine Cohodas both generously provided transcripts of many hours of interviews with Thurmond. She also made available extensive additional research material collected for her book, *Strom Thurmond and the Politics of Southern Change*. Banks, whose 1970 dissertation on Thurmond at Kent State University — "Strom Thurmond and the Revolt Against Modernity" — stands out as a scholarly study of his career to that point, and Bass have corresponded and discussed the subject on and off for more than twenty-five years.

Jack Bass covered Thurmond between 1963 and 1973 as a South Carolina-based political writer who also served as correspondent for a number of national publications. This critical decade included Thurmond's switch to the Republican Party, his kingmaker role in Richard Nixon's winning the 1968 Republican nomination for president, and Thurmond's central role in that campaign. This period also covered Thurmond's second marriage and the start of his becoming a family man, and it marked the beginning of his reaching out politically to black South Carolinians.

Marilyn Thompson conducted extensive interviews in the early 1980s, first in preparation for a series on Thurmond for *The Columbia Record*. Thurmond gave her access to his gubernatorial papers at the South Caroliniana Library at the University of South Carolina. At the urging of Thurmond protégé Lee Atwater, she began research on a Thurmond biography and wrote more than twenty chapter drafts for an unpublished book manuscript. She owes a debt of gratitude to her former editors, Thomas McLean and Gil Spencer, and to her editors at *The Washington Post*. She also thanks Bob Thompson and her children, Cory and Andrew, for their support, and her sister, Leigh Myzk, for assistance.

Special appreciation is due the archivists at the Strom Thurmond special collection at the Robert Muldrow Cooper Library at Clemson University, the Caroliniana Library and its Modern Political Collection at the University of South Carolina, the South Carolina Historical Society, and the Southern Historical Collection at the University of North Carolina at Chapel Hill. Joe Cross of the U. S. C. Law School Library staff provided especially valuable assistance in locating court records.

Emily Newman at *The Charlotte Observer* and Dargan Richards at *The State* in Columbia, S. C., were especially helpful in providing access to the rich archives of those two newspapers. Other valuable assistance came from researcher Ginny Everett at *The Atlanta Journal and Constitution* and from researchers Margot Williams and Alice Crites at *The Washington Post*.

Special thanks to cartoonists Robert Arial of *The State* and Doug Marlette of *Newsday* for use of their work.

The University of Mississippi provided research support for this project to Bass as a member of the faculty there. Additional help came from graduate assistant Parrish Baker. The Freedom Forum provided Bass a faculty research grant.

Publisher Chuck Perry of Longstreet Press invoked the discipline of a tight deadline, gave full commitment to a priority production schedule, and provided the review of a skilled editor.

Literary agent Ron Goldfarb encouraged this project from its inception and performed professional responsibilities with efficiency and dispatch.

Most of the scores of persons interviewed are mentioned in footnotes throughout the book. Special thanks among them goes to Harry Dent, for sharing insights developed from an intimate relationship with and knowledge of Strom Thurmond that dates back to his unsuccessful 1950 Senate campaign.

Among those who read and commented helpfully on portions of the manuscript are Dan Carter, Orville Vernon Burton, Allen Tullos, Laura Kalman, James G. Banks, and Jack Nelson. Nathalie Dupree, the wife of Jack Bass, provided useful critiques of the manuscript as it developed and spousal support replete with a breadth that only fellow authors can fully appreciate.

✛ ✛ ✛

CONTENTS

CHAPTER ONE

✛

Introduction

Striding rapidly, Strom Thurmond headed toward a cluster of legislators at the edge of the racecourse for the Carolina Cup. The spring steeplechase serves as a huge outdoor cocktail party for Camden's Yankee "horsy set" and South Carolina's social elite. It was the year Thurmond turned seventy, fathered his first son, and ran for his fourth term in the Senate. A seasoned political reporter, standing beside the legislators and holding a cup of boozy good cheer, spotted the senator heading their way.

Directly in Thurmond's path sat a large pile of fresh horse manure. As he neared the clump of still-moist droppings, he established eye contact with the group. Watching closely, the reporter suppressed the flicker of a wicked smile. At the last moment, without looking down or breaking his stride, Thurmond deftly side-stepped, greeted the men, and vigorously shook their hands.

For reporter Kent Krell, a native of England with an appreciative eye for his adopted state's eccentricities, the scene remained vivid a quarter century later as an image of Strom Thurmond's finely calibrated political antennae and his innate capacity to both sniff danger and move adroitly to avoid it.[1]

With his dyed orange-red hair transplants and shambling gait, Thurmond in his mid-nineties daily sets records as the United States Senate's oldest and longest-serving member. He may seem to the knowledgeable observer in New York or Washington as an old seg and irrelevant relic. But in his native South Carolina, whose voters returned him to the Senate in 1996 for an eighth six-year term that will end just after his 100th birthday, ol' Strom retains a larger-than-life mystique.

There's Strom the politician and there's Strom the searing individualist. Like the fruit in a blueberry and peach cobbler, the two combine inseparably to make him America's most enduring twentieth century political figure. The tales of "colored offspring," his penchant for young wives, and a legend for lechery provide a larger-than-life overlay of ribald rascality. But ordinary citizens love him. He speaks the common man's language. He is the rare politician who seems to relate to and care about everyday people. Strom is the master of retail politics.

"He took small county politics and applied it on a statewide basis," explained Butler Derrick, a Democrat who served twenty years in Congress with Thurmond and grew up in his hometown of Edgefield. "He's always ready to help someone. Politics is a matter of addition, not subtraction, and he's the one who wrote the rule on that."[2]

Thurmond's political legacy is found not in the annals of legislative achievement, but in redefining America's political culture. As the segregationist Dixiecrat candidate for president in 1948, he won four Deep South states and shook the foundations of the Democratic "solid South." This psychological break opened the path for two-party development in the region. Elected to the Senate in 1954 in an unprecedented write-in campaign, he switched parties ten years later to campaign across the South for presidential candidate Barry Goldwater. This symbolic act, after Goldwater voted against the landmark Civil Rights Act of 1964, for the first time helped attract large numbers of the most racially conscious white Southerners into the GOP. It helped lay the foundation for a race-flavored "Southern strategy" that altered the character of the party of Abraham Lincoln.

In 1968 Thurmond became kingmaker for Richard Nixon, first holding the South for him against Ronald Reagan to win the nomination for president at the Republican national convention, and then in thwarting Alabama Gov. George Wallace's third-party drive. Thurmond already had led the charge that blocked Justice Abe Fortas from becoming Chief Justice after Earl Warren. As Thurmond foresaw, President Nixon's appointments to the Supreme Court would begin its movement to the right.

Once when a speechwriter used the word "afraid," Strom handed the text back to him with the comment, "I've never been afraid of anything." His record in both military and political combat proves it.

In electoral politics, Thurmond is the proven master. As a child he learned how to shake hands from the legendary race-baiter Pitchfork Ben Tillman. He's done it so long and so often in South Carolina that he is able to detect a glint of recognition in someone's eyes and greet them with "So good to see you again." The ordinary citizen thinks, "He remembered me."

His political mastery, however, is based not on show, but substance. The four corners of its foundation are: (1) political boldness, which reflects both courage and an unsurpassed instinct for timing; (2) a refusal to keep an enemy, which dissipates opposition; (3) a willingness to take a firm stand on issues, which generates respect; and (4) a record of legendary constituent service, which creates goodwill.

Thurmond's effrontery at pork barrel politics is almost breathtaking. After voting against almost all federal legislation aimed at improving health care, education, housing, and other domestic spending programs not involving the military, Thurmond sought every federal dollar he could get for South Carolina, with a press release seeking credit for every grant made to the state.

For Thurmond, politics represents total commitment that's part of his being. Ordinary citizens trust him. A textile worker in overalls once explained he would vote for Thurmond "because he stands up for what he believes in — even when he's wrong."[3]

Thurmond's political foundation is reinforced by a quiet and simple religious faith, values rooted in family pride and loyalty, and a fierce determination to win that is reflected in a lifelong passion for physical fitness. On his sixty-fifth birthday, he performed before a group of reporters in his Senate office, doing a hundred push-ups.

Until Gov. George Wallace of Alabama came along, no one symbolized resistance to civil rights for African-Americans more than Thurmond. In the Senate the former Dixiecrat set a filibuster record against the 1957 Civil Rights Act. That record still stands. But when the tide of changing constitutional law forced the American South to abandon the state-enforced system of rigid racial segregation that served as the model for South Africa, Southerners changed their behavior. Changes in attitude followed. Strom Thurmond moved with the tide.

He abandoned his ship of "states rights" opposition to civil rights progress and swam into the mainstream. He voted in 1982 to extend the Voting Rights Act he had bitterly opposed. He became a champion of traditionally black colleges. He supported legislation to make the birthday of Martin Luther King, Jr., a national holiday. He reached out, politically and personally, to blacks in South Carolina, recognizing that they too had become constituents who should get service from his office. And he recognized most of all that blacks now voted.

Thurmond treats the public's money like it's his own. When he became chairman of the Senate Judiciary Committee, Thurmond personally approved every expenditure of funds — down to buying a box of pencils.

Dennis Shedd, his trusted staff director who became a federal trial judge, never forgot his first presentation as a young staffer in Thurmond's Senate office. Shedd had carefully read and absorbed an in-depth, four-page article in a Sunday issue of the *Washington Post* that analyzed complex issues about nuclear energy. When he came in Monday morning, Thurmond asked him to read the article, written by a noted scientist, and brief him. Shedd saw it as an opportunity to display his brilliance.

A few minutes later he told Thurmond he was ready, and the senator said to go ahead. After less than thirty seconds, Thurmond stopped him and asked, "Is he for it or against it?"

Shedd explains, "He just wanted to know if the man was for nuclear energy or against it. I learned a very important lesson."

When he became top aide, Shedd told other staffers that in briefing the senator they needed to be prepared to do it in fifteen seconds. "I told them, 'If you can't tell him in fifteen seconds, you don't understand it well enough yet. And if he wants to hear more, or ask questions, be prepared to talk for up to an hour.'"[4]

Miss Hortense Woodson, for decades the keeper of the flame of local history in Strom's hometown of Edgefield, knew him since he was a little boy coming into church with his father and his mother. "He hasn't changed," she once told a writer for *The New York Times Magazine*. "Everything he's done has been done to the full. There's no halfway doings about Strom."[5]

So, what's Thurmond's weakness, his character flaw? The biblical book of Ecclesiastes may have had Strom in mind with its observation: "Vanity, vanity, all is vanity." He often appears "out of it" because, as one former aide explained, he's too vain to wear a hearing aid.[6] Thurmond tells witnesses who sit too far from the microphone at Senate committee hearings, "Talk into the machine. Talk into the machine."[7]

At Clemson University, Strom's alma mater, the floor of an entire building is dedicated to the Strom Thurmond collection. A former staffer in his Senate office said that "everything — even napkins from a reception" are collected and sent to Clemson.

Full-time archivists organize the material — speeches, correspondence, newspaper and magazine articles, and endless photographs. During months of cataloging photographs, an archivist said that eleven cubic feet of them were discarded.

In South Carolina his name seems everywhere — buildings, highways, a lake. And more.

The marker over the grave of his universally admired first wife, Jean Crouch Thurmond, includes two long lines, engraved in granite, that identify her as:

THE WIFE OF A LAWYER-GOVERNOR-
PRESIDENTIAL CANDIDATE-UNITED STATES SENATOR

1. Telephone interview with Kent Krell, March 3, 1998.
2. Bass telephone interview with Butler Derrick, July 24, 1998.
3. *The Charlotte Observer*, October 29, 1972, p. 1-B.
4. Interview with Dennis Shedd, August 11, 1997.
5. *The New York Times Magazine*, October 6, 1968, p. 85.
6. Confidential interview.
7. Interview with Sam Nunn, 1998.

Strom Thurmond statue on the courthouse square in Edgefield.

CHAPTER TWO

✢

The Boldness of an Edgefield Man

Two crusty farmers in overalls ruminate with cheeks stuffed with tobacco along Edgefield's busy main street, their eyes fixed on passing cars like Wimbledon tennis fans watching a mesmerizing rally at center court.

After silently watching an unfamiliar, dented Dodge with Georgia license tags, one spews a stream of brown tobacco juice onto the sidewalk and turns to the other with a joke.

"Hey," he says, pausing long enough to wipe with rumpled handkerchief the sweet juice in the corner of his mouth. "J'you hear the one about Strum and the 'bortion bill?"

"Nope," says the other, his eyes never leaving the road.

"Well . . . Strum's up in his office, up thar in Washington, one day and the secretary comes in and sez, 'Senator, thar's a lady on the phone wants to talk to you.' Well, Strum's kind of busy, doncha know, and he looks up from his desk and growls, 'What she want?' The secretary says, 'Well, senator, sez she wants to talk to you 'bout the 'bortion bill.' Strum didn't even look up. Just as natural as anything he yells out to the secretary, 'Just tell her to pay it and I'll reimburse her.'"

If "Strum" had been there, he would have chuckled with them, relishing as he always has the off-color references to his sexual prowess. He left his hometown, for the most part, in 1947, when he went to Columbia as Edgefield's tenth homegrown governor.[i] But his

---

i. The ten governors are named on a stone marker on the courthouse square: Andrew Pickens (1816-18), George McDuffie (1834-36), Pierce Butler (1836-38), James H. Hammond (1842-44), Francis Pickens (1860-62), Milledge L. Bonham (1862-64), John C. Sheppard (July-Dec. 1886), Ben Tillman (1890-94), John Gary Evans (1894-96), and J. Strom Thurmond, 1947-51). Many of their family names still command respect in Edgefield County.

presence still lived in the county seat town of 2,500 that created him and shaped his view of the world. There is no escaping him.

Walk across the square and there, facing the stately courthouse in which his and his father's portraits hang, is a life-size statue of Strom himself. Sculpted by Maria Kirby-Smith, an artist with Edgefield connections, local wags called it "Strom's last erection" after it went up in 1984. (Fifteen years later he would have another erection — a statue of him would join other South Carolina luminaries on the State House grounds in Columbia — men such as John C. Calhoun and James F. Byrnes, Wade Hampton and Pitchfork Ben Tillman.)

Kirby-Smith expressed certain feelings, however, when she included a cockroach on Thurmond's left rump, hidden beneath his overhanging suit jacket. After a Columbia newspaper story about the bug, the statue was a tourist attraction until Bettis Rainsford (the entrepreneurial Harvard-educated chairman of the statue committee whose Edgefield roots precede the Revolutionary War) sent in a construction worker with a blowtorch to remove the metallic insect.

Thurmond remains part of the town's humor, part of its folklore, part of its glory. His life symbolizes its past.

From Roosevelt New Dealer to death-sentencing state judge, from progressive governor to Dixiecrat segregationist, from successful write-in candidate to Senate filibuster champion, from a penchant for young wives to stories of "colored offspring," from party-switching Democrat to Republican kingmaker for Richard Nixon, from civil rights antagonist to supporter of a Martin Luther King holiday, from a D-Day crash-landing in a glider behind German lines at Normandy to a liberator role at Buchenwald, from a direct challenge of George Wallace to dismantling the Warren Court, and from death-house seduction to patting Sally Quinn's ass, Thurmond lived and survived with the boldness of an Edgefield man.

Blood ran thicker and honor ran hotter in Edgefield, a county more Faulknerian than William Faulkner's and seared by a history of explosive political violence. As Thurmond once explained, his father probably would have been elected governor except "one time he had to kill a man."[1]

When four percent of all indictments in South Carolina were for murder, in Edgefield it was eight percent.[2] An early twentieth-century merchant remembered eighteen bloody murders committed in front of his store.³ Courage, endurance, and impetuous action provided the seeds for romance and tragedy. Those twin components of Southern history, like the shell of a soft-boiled egg, encase the human yoke of Edgefield. The wind still blows there, but the lingering memory has not gone.

The Southerner's deep-rooted sense of place is reflected in the invariable first question asked of a stranger in Edgefield. "Whar' you from?" If the answer is New Jersey or Chicago, the response may well be, "Oh," — followed by silence that may reflect suspicion or simply disinterest. If the visitor is from Texas or Tennessee, however, the questioner may tell of a friend or relative who moved there. If the stranger is from anywhere in South Carolina, a clerk might ask, "Who's your daddy?" And the response may set the place of one's social rank. South Carolina's late poet-philosopher James McBride Dabbs compared the process to two strange dogs sniffing one another.

Among deep-rooted white families in the state, one indication of status is the presence of many blacks sharing the same surname. It indicates that one's forebears were prosperous slave owners. Modjeska Monteith Simkins, who became known as "the matriarch" of the civil rights movement in South Carolina and married the son of one of Edgefield's top black political leaders during Reconstruction, said she was always greeted on the street in her native Columbia as "cousin" by one of the city's most prominent white attorneys.⁴

At the southeast corner of Edgefield's courthouse square, a large mural — on the outer wall of a building next to the Ten Governors Café — greets visitors. It displays a quote boasting that Edgefield has produced "more dashing, brilliant, romantic figures, statesmen, orators, soldiers, adventurers, and daredevils than any other rural county in America." W. W. Ball, the knowledgeable editor of the *News and Courier* in Charleston, wrote it in 1932 not as extravagent exaggeration, but as mere observation.⁵

Around the corner past the Thurmond statue and the courthouse and adjoining the aged three-story hotel that was once the finest boarding house along the well-traveled Dixie Highway, sits the home of the state's oldest newspaper, the weekly *Edgefield Advertiser*, established in 1836. When Thurmond was born in 1902, it was the voice of literate thought and culture in frontier territory, reporting on the latest trends in everything from Paris fashion to social and economic developments in Washington.

The *Advertiser* served as the community's public-spirited conscience. Its motto proclaimed: "We will cling to the pillars of the temple of our liberties and if it must fall we will perish amidst the ruins." William Walton Mims, the editor since 1937, lives by that motto. His father and grandfather were editor and publisher for a combined sixty-three years before him. When Thurmond was elected in 1954 to the U. S. Senate as a write-in candidate, Mims ran a front-page replica of the ballot, with an arrow pointing to a line with Thurmond's name hand-written on it. For years, a framed copy of that front page hung prominently displayed in Thurmond's Washington office.

"I don't know anything good about him," Mims told the authors in 1998. "My view of Thurmond is he is Satan's agent for South Carolina. He is my mortal enemy."[6]

When the Thurmond statue was unveiled in the square, some remarked on its slightly reddish hue, and Mims was heard to remark it was because Thurmond was such a communist.

A gentlemanly eccentric whose soft voice belies the terror of his pen, Mims closets himself in a dark, cluttered back office to write long, rambling editorials intended to expose Thurmond's villainous ways. Many townspeople dismiss him as "a nut," but few question his honesty. Embroiled since 1970 in a feud that began over location of a county water system and since has involved years of litigation, he seems not to care what they think.

On October 14, 1970, using his largest headline type to display BIGGEST SCANDAL IN COUNTY'S HISTORY, Mims linked Thurmond and county planners to a "shocking" affair that "has the elements of conspiracy and the appearance of a fraud against the best and long-term interests of this county." Soon thereafter, his newspaper suffered a total advertising boycott.

After seeking unsuccessfully to pry loose plans for the $5 million water and sewer system, Mims became outraged when he learned that instead of covering all of Edgefield County as a federally designated "redevelopment area," the system would be concentrated in the county's southern part.

The majority black and poor white population in economically depressed Edgefield County would be neglected, Mims contended, and the main water line would be located near land owned by Thurmond's brother and moneyed supporters, with primary benefit to the neighboring and more prosperous Aiken County trade area.[7] Thurmond fired back that Mims owned land in the area of Edgefield County he wanted to include.

Butler Derrick, a state legislator before his election to Congress in 1974 and a son-in-law of Mims at the time of the dispute over the water system, said funding for the project included revenue bonds, which required that it initially serve the area of greatest population density. An oversized trunk line to draw water from the Savannah River was installed, Derrick said, to allow expansion into other parts of the county, which he said has occurred. Derrick said Thurmond wasn't involved in the "so-called boycott."[8]

In 1972 Mims ran as a write-in candidate against Thurmond in what the senator called "a scurrilous campaign." Mims ran large headline type down the length of his front page accusing Thurmond of having "COLORED OFFSPRING WHILE PARADING AS A DEVOUT SEGREGATIONIST." The editor repeated his charge in a sworn deposition given to back his case in a federal lawsuit. Mims said he could substantiate the charge with taped conversations he had with Edgefield blacks who knew the details of the birth. The line of questioning was dropped abruptly.

After securing a lawyer from the prestigious Arnold & Porter law firm in Washington to represent him in a six-year court fight, Mims won a judgment of $151,500 in damages in a restraint of trade verdict against local businessmen, together with attorneys' fees and costs of $101,333, for a total of $252,833.

His attorney, David Bonderman, stated to the authors that he "never saw any evidence of Thurmond's involvement in the Mims dispute, although it is obvious that the ringleaders were all Thurmond supporters." Mims, however, believed that Thurmond's Washington office directed the boycott efforts by telephone. Mims said his attorney advised him against making Thurmond a named defendant in the case because "all the jurors will have voted for him in elections, and they won't go against him." Mims said he was offered $450,000 to consolidate his newspaper with the *Citizen-News*, owned by Bettis Rainsford, whom Mims views as "Thurmond's commissar in Edgefield County."[9]

Mims's large two-story home on the Dixie Highway burned to the ground, his newspaper never regained retail advertisers, and almost all the veterans whom he supplied subsidized room and board were withdrawn from the hotel he owns next door to the newspaper office.

Thurmond is known for refusing to keep a political enemy, and Mims acknowledged the senator has called him. But the editor refused Thurmond's entreaties, saying, "I'll never forgive him until he apologizes to the people of Edgefield County."

A century after a post-Reconstruction, mass migration of 5,000 blacks from Edgefield to Arkansas, Edgefield County African-Americans won a landmark lawsuit in 1984 requiring single-member districts rather than at-large voting for County Council. The case was decided by the U. S. Supreme Court. Blacks temporarily won a 3-2 majority of the seats and appointed lead plaintiff Thomas C. McCain as county manager.

U. S. District Judge Joe Anderson, then a Democratic state legislator from Edgefield in his early 30s with a House district almost 50-50 black and white, recalled the appointment "created a lot of concern in the white community. To everyone's pleasure things went along very smoothly and the county council worked well together." McCain remained as county manager for about ten years, even after the council majority shifted to 3-2 white.

"Race relations really settled down and smoothed out and were very harmonious after that litigation played out," Anderson said. As a legislator, he found Thurmond — an old family friend (Anderson's father, as a Clemson student, made a gavel that was a replica of one used by John C. Calhoun and presented it to Thurmond when he became a state circuit judge in 1938) — quite helpful in getting federal support for projects in Edgefield. Anderson marveled at the senator's attention to personal politics. "I would come home from Columbia, having been there three days in the General Assembly, and go home to find someone who had a problem or an illness or death or something and called to express my sympathy and find that Senator Thurmond had beat me to the punch by two days. He really stays on top of the details."

He said that Thurmond was "just revered" in Edgefield.[10]

Strom's widowed sister Mary Tompkins, a retired school teacher, continued to live an active life in Edgefield, serving as her brother's eyes and ears, her home filled with Strom and family memorabilia.

Rainsford worked closely with the new biracial political structure in developing his business enterprises, including a leveraged buyout of Delta Woodside, a textile firm, but says that Thurmond's political influence played little role.[11] Many in

Edgefield, however, wonder about that.

Mims and others contend that Rainsford uses his newspaper to promote his own interests. Rainsford without doubt has emerged as the "big man" in Edgefield. He spearheaded an effort to locate a federal prison in Edgefield County. The project, which provides more than 400 jobs, got strong support from Thurmond.

Mims continued to write long, rambling stories of Rainsford's financial activity. The October 30, 1996, *Advertiser*, for example, linked a loan to Rainsford by Chase Manhattan Bank to a new world order in which the Rockefellers used "their wealth for world power" and "picked presidents for years" — from Richard Nixon (with the help of Thurmond) to Bill Clinton.

Mims's universe centers on Edgefield, the town and the county. In a gentle voice that reflects his gentrified upbringing, Mims explains, "Unless you understand Edgefield from way back, you won't understand Thurmond. Edgefield has had a religious theme. The great Southern Baptist Convention was conceived here in the central Savannah River area by Dr. William Bullein Johnson, pastor of the First Baptist Church here who became its first president.

"And there was, thereafter, a long succession of brilliant, devoted, old-fashioned type preachers. They had an intellectuality about them that was unusual and that was, as I understand it, not the same in other places.

"And then you had [William] Travis and [James] Bonham, the heroes of the Alamo. The way I understand it, they revived in this country a patriotic fever, and these people from the Old Edgefield District, they exemplified, they brought to light what had been the character of our people since the Revolution. The background there was religious and patriotic.

"The most brilliant lawyers — and this is really what formed the nucleus intellectually and religiously and almost every other way — the most brilliant lawyers began to gravitate to Edgefield in search of the Holy Grail, because there was *something here*. There was something here that you just didn't find anywhere else."[12]

William Jennings Bryan Dorn, the silver-throated former Third District congressman for twenty-six years from neighboring Greenwood County, whose own Edgefield roots run deep, explained, "You would never understand Edgefield and the background that goes through all these people, unless you understand the violence, the emotionalism of the people. They fought duels. George McDuffie was a congressman from this district one time,

13

and he was always into a duel.

"Preston Brooks was a congressman. He whipped the 'H' out of Senator Sumner on the floor of the Senate. That brought on the Civil War probably as much as anything. They said it was inevitable, and it probably was, but one of the immediate causes of the Civil War was Preston Brooks whipping Sumner.

"And then you would have big shootouts there, like Abilene and Dodge City, occasionally in Edgefield. I even remember yet hearing the old-timers talk about it.

"It had a lot of anti-Negro feeling. Edgefield has been noted for that kind of violent politics. As for Senator Thurmond's seeming radicalism on the race issue, it was not radical for Edgefield. That's the tradition of that area and the heritage of those people. And Senator Thurmond grew up in that area, his daddy managing campaigns for Ben Tillman, who would call the aristocrats everything in the book and then something else, you know. Cussed 'em out on the platform.

"Ladies didn't vote. In those days, with no women involved, things would get so hot they had bodyguards at the political meetings and all this kind of doings."[13]

Talking about Edgefield's history, Strom himself once said, "Back in Edgefield County everybody would fight." With a laugh, he added, "Fighters and lovers."[14]

As Thurmond indicated, the passion in that history spilled over into sex. Francis Pickens, a wealthy Edgefield planter who served as congressman and ambassador to Russia before becoming South Carolina's Civil War governor, protested sharply before the Civil War about a woman's claim that he had fathered her illegitimate son. He paid support despite his doubts of being the father, but said, "If a man's character depends upon maids or low women, he would indeed be damned in this world as well as the next."[15]

Fellow Edgefield District planter James H. Hammond had taken the woman's claim, but as governor he maintained discreet silence over charges he had seduced four nieces, the daughters of Wade Hampton II. To do otherwise would compromise the honor of his four nieces, he said, then charged that was precisely what their father did in exposing the incident. In a letter to a brother, Gov. Hammond said he believed the people of South Carolina would be with him: "They would not mind it a pin's worth if it was known I had seduced all of Hampton's daughters."[16]

South Carolina legislators didn't impeach Gov. Hammond.

Although exiled for awhile from state politics after the nieces incident, Hammond subsequently was elected by the legislature to the United States Senate.

Sexual liaisons also crossed racial lines, even among the elite. Hammond, for example, openly maintained a slave mistress, and in his diary noted telling a legitimate son to take special care of a specific slave because he was the son's half brother.[17]

Before the Civil War, some free persons of color in Edgefield — roughly one percent of the African-American population there and usually of mixed racial parentage — married whites. South Carolina did not adopt laws against interracial marriage until after Reconstruction.

But the end of slavery didn't mean an end of white-black sexual liaisons. Lucy Holcome Pickens, a Texas beauty less than half the age of fifty-five-year-old Francis Pickens when she married him, was joined in Edgefield after his death by her brother and his male friend. Both of them took former slaves as lifelong partners, who bore them children. The children grew up in the Pickens family mansion in Edgefield and played with neighborhood white children.[18]

Blacks achieved full political parity during Reconstruction and held many offices in Edgefield, creating a climate for social and economic opportunity. They also became attorneys, clerks, business partners with whites, bakers, and shopkeepers. The period was by no means peaceful, however, with gangs of white bushwhackers attacking and killing black men in widespread violence throughout the county.

Many black families moved into Edgefield, for reasons of both opportunity and safety. When Edgefield whites regained power in ending Reconstruction, however, occupational choices for black men became restricted again to traditional agricultural roles, as sharecroppers or laborers. By 1880, residential segregation created black sections in Edgefield, with many households headed by females, who found work as domestics. These poor sections of town received little in public services and would remain in place at the end of the twentieth century.[19]

A few blocks east of the square, the weight of history is felt in the quiet of Willowbrook Cemetery, behind First Baptist and Trinity Episcopal churches. Hortense Woodson, the Edgefield historian, lived across the street from the cemetery for most of her ninety-four years. She died in 1990. On her tombstone, not far from the oversized Thurmond family plot, is engraved the full text of her four-stanza poem, "The Spirit of Edgefield," written to be sung to the tune of "The Bells of St. Mary's."

The final stanza reads:

OLD EDGEFIELD, DEAR EDGEFIELD
THY CHILDREN ALL LOVE THEE,
THY GREAT MEN, THY GOOD MEN,
WHEREVER THEY BE,
TURN BACK TO THE SCENES OFT
REMEMBERED IN STORY
THY CHILDREN ALL COME BACK,
COME BACK
TO THEE, TO THEE

With its markers of 150 Confederate soldiers and the inter-marrying families of the six governors buried there, the dead generals and other heroes, and the faded Confederate battle flag flying from the pole erected decades earlier by the Edgefield Chapter of United Daughters of the Confederacy, the cemetery will serve as Strom Thurmond's final resting place.

The faint echoes of Edgefield's violent past are heard here, too. Marking the grave of Preston Smith Brooks (a great, great grandfather of the sculptress Maria Kirby-Smith) is a marble obelisk extolling that he "WILL BE LONG, LONG REMEMBERED AS ONE IN WHICH THE VIRTUES LOVED TO DWELL." His crippling assault in 1856 on Massachusetts Sen. Charles Sumner, delivering thirty blows that "wore out my cane completely," followed Sumner's speech casting dishonor on Brooks's aged Edgefield relative, South Carolina Sen. Andrew Pickens Butler.

Brooks resigned his seat and was reelected in a special election, with barely a dissenting vote. He died shortly thereafter of a respiratory illness, at thirty-seven.[20]

Buried next to the crowded Brooks family plot is General Matthew Calbraith Butler. The handsome co-leader with General Martin Witherspoon Gary (the Bald Eagle of the Confederacy) in the violent Redshirt campaign of 1876, Butler was a man who, after a foot was blown off by a cannon ball in the Civil War, would return to battle with one foot, mounted on his horse.

The adjacent plot is that of Francis Pickens, the early Civil War governor. Beside his marker is that of his spirited daughter, Frances Eugenia Olga Neva, born March 14, 1859 in St. Petersburg, Russia. Known as Douschka (Little Darling), she is celebrated in Edgefield as "the Joan of Arc of South Carolina."

At seventeen she rode on her horse from nearby Oakley Park at the front of 1,600 Redshirts who terrorized blacks in the 1876 campaign and stole the election for Wade Hampton III, the "redeemer" governor who ended Reconstruction rule. (A man so powerful physically that he wrestled bears in the swamps of the Mississippi Delta that bordered Hampton plantations there, he was the namesake for Scarlett O'Hara's little boy.)

M. C. Butler's portrait adorns a wall at Oakley Park, Gary's five-columned, two-story plantation home on the edge of town that today stands as the Redshirt Shrine. An upright display case there exhibits one of the original red shirts, made of homespun cloth dyed with the juice of poke berries. At the bottom of the same case sits an authentic carpetbag, a suitcase made of carpet in which the mythical Yankee interlopers carried their belongings when they joined turncoat Southern scalawags and the freed slaves during Reconstruction. In the words of United Daughters of the Confederacy tour guide Amelia Reese in 1998, this period was "worse than the war for the people."

Organized racial violence by Edgefield whites became widespread in 1876. In July at Hamburg, the site of present day North Augusta, a confrontation occurred between black militia and a white mob. After two blacks and one white were killed by gunfire, forty black militiamen surrendered. Five known political activists were picked out and executed to avenge the death of the white man. It became known as the "Hamburg Massacre."

Ben Tillman, who as a teenager wasn't drafted for the Army during the Civil War because he had lost an eye in an accident, had become a leader in the white rifle clubs that organized and participated in the violence. He later wrote that Generals Gary and Butler had agreed to pursue a policy of "terrorizing" local blacks "by letting them provoke trouble and then having the whites demonstrate their superiority by killing as many as was justifiable."[21]

On September 17, Butler's men had killed more than a hundred blacks at Ellenton when joined by Tillman and roughly forty men under his command. The arrival of federal troops saved other blacks from being massacred.

Two of Tillman's men, however, were selected to execute Simon Coker, a black state senator from Barnwell. Upon being informed that he had only a few minutes to live, Coker replied, "Here is my cotton house key; I wish you would please send it to my wife and tell her to have our cotton ginned and pay our landlord rent just as soon as she can." Asked if there was anything else, Coker said he "would like to pray" and dropped to his knees in prayer.

Tillman described what happened next: After a few moments, one of his men said, "'You are too long'. . . . The order 'aim, fire,' was given with the negro still kneeling." Tillman continued, "It will appear a ruthless and cruel thing to those unacquainted with the environments. . . . The struggle in which we were engaged meant more than life or death. It involved everything we held dear, Anglo-Saxon civilization included."[22]

On election day, Gary's Redshirt patrols prevented blacks from voting in Edgefield. Yet the county's vote exceeded by 2,000 the voting age population as recorded by the 1870 census. Without Edgefield's fraudulent vote inflation, Hampton would have lost to incumbent Republican Daniel Chamberlain.

In a two-tier campaign, Hampton himself had personally pledged to protect the rights of the freedmen. Rule 12 of Martin Witherspooon Gary's 33-rule "Plan of the Campaign" stated, however, "Every Democrat must feel honor bound to control the vote of at least one negro, by intimidation, purchase, keeping him away or as each individual may determine how he may best accomplish it."[23] Gary's Redshirt supporters spread the use of violence, intimidation, and fraud beyond the confines of Edgefield. More than a century later, one observer concluded that no Southern county regained white domination with "more fanaticism and brutality than Edgefield."[24]

Hampton's contested victory provided a key element in the Compromise of 1877, in which Republican Rutherford B. Hayes got the electoral votes of South Carolina and two other Southern states to win the presidency by a single electoral vote. In exchange the South got an end to Reconstruction. Political control returned to white Democrats, with an understanding that the states rather than the federal government would gain the right to set policy on racial matters. The echo of that understanding would reverberate in Strom Thurmond's 1948 Dixiecrat "states rights" campaign rhetoric.

Tillman would emerge as the state's new political leader, beginning as the spokesman for aggrieved farmers. But the farmers revolt in South Carolina never shared the radical goals of the larger Populist movement, which in other Southern states often involved a biracial coalition. Tillman's virulent racism precluded that possibility.

As governor, he established Clemson and Winthrop as land grant colleges for men and women. He used his influence to displace aristocrats Wade Hampton and M. C. Butler from the United States Senate. In those days before popular election of U. S. senators, the legislature elected them, and Tillman himself succeeded Butler.

The historian Francis Butler Simkins, Tillman's faithful biographer and an Edgefield native who grew up next door to the Thurmond home, considered Tillman's act against Hampton "a ruthless violation of cherished traditions."[25]

A crude, profane man with one eye, in the Senate Tillman played demagogue in defending lynching, the ultimate weapon for controlling blacks after their loss of political rights to vote or serve as jurors had reduced them to virtual bondage. "Whenever the Constitution comes between me and the virtue of the white women of the South," he told the United States Senate in 1902, "I say to hell with the Constitution!"

Although the number of rapes of white women did not increase after the Civil War, he vividly described the scene of the southern woman vulnerable to rape by black men, "her chastity taken from her and a memory branded on her brain as with a red-hot iron to haunt her night and day as long as she lives." Arguing that the rapist had "put himself outside the pale of the law, human and divine," he raged, "Kill! Kill! Kill!"[26]

A popular speaker on the national Chatauqua circuit, Tillman has been rumored as having told Thomas Dixon the story that became his best-seller 1905 book, *The Clansman*,[ii] from which D. W. Griffith made America's first talking movie, "Birth of a Nation." That film helped create a searing national image of the black man as the lustful beast described in Tillman's speeches.

A story of the film's power was told by Benjamin Mays, the mentor of Martin Luther King, Jr. as president of Morehouse College in Atlanta. Mays grew up not far from Bryan Dorn in Greenwood County and as a child hid under Dorn's grandfather's house during a race riot. As a student at Bates College in Maine,

---

ii. *The Clansman* was the second book in a trilogy Dixon wrote about Reconstruction. Tillman may well have been a source, but Dixon's biographer, Raymond Allen Cook, reports that he sifted through more than five thousand pamphlets and books for source material. (Raymond Allen Cook, Thomas Dixon: His Books and His Career, dissertation, Emory University, 1953, pp. 79-80.)

Mays said, he faced little discrimination. But he told of having to run for his life after an audience watching "Birth of a Nation" left the college town's only theater.[27]

Tillman dominated the 1895 state constitutional convention that effectively disfranchised blacks and extended the white electorate. Presiding over it was another Edgefield governor, John Gary Evans, a nephew of the unmarried Martin W. Gary. Evans received strong support from Edgefield state Rep. John William Thurmond, who seven years later would become Strom's father.

Evans won the election as a handsome, thirty-one-year-old bachelor. On a trip to Connecticut, he attended Sunday worship services at an Episcopal Church, where a message scribbled on a card was passed to him. It said, "Sir, you are sitting in my pew." It was signed by David Plume, a wealthy manufacturer, who stated the amount of his annual dues.

Evans sent back a reply: "You are paying too damn much," and signed it "John Gary Evans, Governor of South Carolina." After the morning services, Plume introduced himself and invited Evans home for dinner. There he met and fell in love with his host's daughter, Emily Mansfield Plume, who became Mrs. John Gary Evans, but after his term as governor ended.[28]

The fighting spirit of Edgefield men never dulled. At the rear of the Oakley Park Redshirt Shrine, a well marks where 108 of them gathered to go fight in the Spanish-American War. Twenty-eight of them returned. Inside the house, dominating a wall in an upstairs room is a large wooden seal from the city of Havana, where John Gary Evans served as provisional mayor.

In 1941, two years before his death, Evans gave Oakley Park, which he had inherited, to the United Daughters of the Confederacy. They restored it as a museum and shrine not far from Strom Thurmond's boyhood home. Little is said about the realities of the 1876 Redshirt campaign of terror and fraud.

In December 1881, roughly 5,000 Edgefield County blacks migrated to Arkansas. This organized response by a fifth of the county's African-American population to political and economic repression after Reconstruction remains the largest mass exodus in South Carolina history.

Government land in Arkansas was available at a price of eight acres for a dollar. There were no fence laws to prevent free range for livestock, and farm laborers received cash wages. The people who migrated to Arkansas, says the historian Orville Vernon Burton, "left Edgefield County not out of despair, but out of a faith that somewhere in America they could find a home where they could realize the hopes of equality and prosperity they had conceived during Reconstruction."[29]

Not until a century later did Edgefield blacks regain a full role in local politics, only after the federal courts finally restored the Reconstruction amendments to their original intent. Despite accusations of corruption, historical evidence indicates that local black Reconstruction leaders had been neither inept nor corrupt. Men like Paris Simkins and Lawrence Cain, who served as legislators, created schools and sought economic as well as political rights for blacks, and helped them build their own churches as religious and social institutions.[30]

The fierce intensity with which white Edgefield struck to end Reconstruction and regain power suggests the degree to which they felt loss of control of their destiny during black political dominance. Historian Joel Williamson, himself a native of the South Carolina Upcountry, argues that whites such as those in Edgefield were suffering from a "rising confusion of identity."[31]

As the cohesiveness of their society crumbled, they tended to turn their loyalties toward the family. Religion also became more important. Another response to the South's fragmentation during Reconstruction, Williamson contends, was an intensely personal politics. Thurmond would absorb all these elements into his life as an Edgefield man.

Historian James G. Banks, who in 1970 at Kent State University wrote a dissertation on Thurmond, sees him shaped by Edgefield's history and culture and describes him at his core as "an exceedingly simple man, fiercely individualistic, combative, paternalistic, a citizen soldier who merges the intensity of the evangelical gospel preacher with the fundamentalist values of a simpler time."[32]

South Carolinian W. J. Cash, in his 1941 classic, *The Mind of the South*, described the region as a "tree with many age rings, with its limbs and trunk bent and twisted by all the winds of the years, but with its tap root in the Old South."[33] More than a half century later, his words provided a poetic depiction of Strom Thurmond.

✛ ✛ ✛

1. James G. Banks interview with Strom Thurmond, July 1978, Southern Oral History Project, University of North Carolina at Chapel Hill, p. 8.
2. Orville Vernon Burton, *In My Father's House Are Many Mansions*, Chapel Hill: University of North Carolina Press, 1985, p. 336, (footnote ii).
3. Eleanor Mims Hanson, *The Edgefield Advertiser and Its Editors* (Edgefield, S. C., 1980) p. 2.
4. Modjeska Simkins to Jack Bass, circa 1973.
5. W. W. Ball, *The State that Forgot: South Carolina's Surrender to Democracy* (Indianapolis: Bobbs-Merrill, 1932), p. 22.
6. Bass interview with W. W. Mims, March 11, 1998.
7. Mims letter to Jack Bass, July 17, 1971; *The Edgefield Advertiser*, Oct. 14, 1970 and Aug. 4, 1971.
8. Bass interview with Derrick, op. cit.
9. David Bonderman letters to Jack Bass, April 23, 1998, April 29, 1998; W. W. Mims letter to Jack Bass, May 7, 1998; Bass interview with Mims, March 11, 1998.
10. Bass interview with Joseph Anderson, Columbia, S. C., June 24, 1997.
11. Bass interview with Bettis Rainsford, Edgefield, S. C., March 12, 1998.
12. Mims interviews with Jack Bass, March 11, 1998 and Marilyn Thompson, circa 1981.
13. Marilyn Thompson interview with W. W. Mims, circa 1981.
14. Banks oral history, op.cit., p. 26.
15. Orville Vernon Burton, *In My Father's House*, p. 139.
16. Ibid., p. 140.
17. Ibid.; Carol K. Rothrock Bleser, ed. *The Hammonds of Redcliffe* (New York: Oxford University Press, 1981), pp. 11-12; Drew Faust, *James Henry Hammond and the Old South: A Design for Mastery* (Baton Rouge: Louisiana State University Press, 1982), pp. 86-88, 314-17.
18. Burton, Ibid., p. 292.
19. Burton, Ibid., pp. 297-301.
20. Burton, Ibid., pp. 93-95.
21. Benjamin Ryan Tillman, *Struggle of 1876: How South Carolina Was Delivered from Carpetbag and Negro Rule*, 1909. Also *The Edgefield Advertiser*, February 12, 1936.

22. Burton, op. cit., p. 290.
23. Francis Butler Simkins and Robert H. Woody, *South Carolina During Reconstruction* (Chapel Hill, North Carolina, 1932), p. 564.
24. David Bruck, "Strom Thurmond's Roots," *The New Republic*, March 3, 1982, p. 16.
25. Simkins and Woody, op. cit., pp. 185-87.
26. Burton, op. cit., p. 227.
27. Mays at dinner in his honor given by Dorn in 1979, attended by Bass.
28. Bass telephone interview with Carlanna Hendrick, biographer of John Gary Evans, July 26, 1998.
29. Burton, op. cit., p. 238.
30. Burton, op. cit., pp. 199, 276.
31. Joel Williamson, *The Crucible of Race: Black-White Relations in the American South Since Emancipation* (Oxford University Press, 1984), pp. 80-81.
32. James G. Banks, unpublished "preface," p. 4, copy in possession of the authors.
33. W. J. Cash, *The Mind of the South* (New York: Vintage Books 1941), p. x.

Clemson College cadet Strom Thurmond, circa 1921-22.

CHAPTER THREE

+

Good Genes

When Strom Thurmond was six years old, his father hoisted him into a horse-drawn buggy on a Sunday afternoon and set off for the home of Sen. "Pitchfork Ben" Tillman, six miles down the road. The boy had never met the one-eyed former governor who got his nickname by promising when he went to Washington to stick a pitchfork in President Grover Cleveland's "old fat ribs." Strom sensed even then that he was about to encounter an uncommon man.

J. William "Will" Thurmond, by then Tillman's personal lawyer and campaign manager, had tried to prepare the youngster to expect the unexpected. Tillman was known for his outrageous temper and profane language, and the patch he wore over a sightless eye could be unsettling to children. Strom's father told him that when they pulled into the Tillman farm he should jump down and offer a handshake.

When they arrived, Tillman was waiting, and Strom jumped down and said, "I want to shake your hand." As Thurmond would later recall this vivid moment, he stood there holding Tillman's hand until the old senator barked at him, "You said you wanted to shake. Why the hell don't you shake!"

Strom hesitated for only a moment and, as he later told it, "I shook and I shook, and I've been shaking ever since."[1]

From the time he climbed out of the buggy at Tillman's place, Strom learned from his father and taught himself to court the average citizen of feisty Edgefield. Will Thurmond already was an established political leader when his wife gave birth on December 5, 1902, to the son who would carry out his own thwarted political ambitions. They named him James Strom Thurmond, after his maternal grandfather, but never called him by his first name.

Will Thurmond grew up on a farm in the Colliers community in western Edgefield County, between Stephens Creek and the Savannah River. His father, George Washington Thurmond, owned a few slaves and farmed cotton and corn. When Will was born in 1862, George Thurmond was off fighting in his third war — he already had battled Cherokee Indians and Mexicans and had lived with a first wife in Galveston, Texas, before meeting and marrying Mary Jane Felter in New Orleans and carrying her to Edgefield. (The Thurmond family came to the Edgefield District from Virginia's Albemarle County in 1784.) When the Civil War ended, family lore has it that Corporal George Thurmond, one of only two men left alive in his infantry company, was present in tattered uniform with Robert E. Lee for his surrender at Appomattox, then walked home penniless and maimed — he'd lost an arm — from Virginia. He stopped long enough in Columbia to see the devastation. When General William T. Sherman left South Carolina's capital city, half of it had burned to the ground. As memory faded, some locals there would refer to it as the city's first urban renewal program.

Strom remembered hearing that his grandfather was a tough outdoorsman who "could drink liquor and work out in the open" and had all his teeth when he died in 1904 at eighty-four.[2]

Will Thurmond rode by horse to a country academy to get his schooling, studying extra at night with his mother. He saved enough money to spend a semester at South Carolina College in Columbia, a breeding ground for state political leaders. He returned to Edgefield, worked as a teacher, and spent nights studying law at the office of John Sheppard, an Edgefield attorney who served a few months as governor. When the self-taught Thurmond wrote his bar examination, the state Supreme Court cited it as the best of the year. Strom Thurmond called his father "the ablest lawyer I ever knew."[3]

Located on a Cherokee trail that ran from present day Asheville, N. C., to nearby Augusta, the Edgefield village of 2,500 still reflected a frontier culture during Strom's youth. "The whole atmosphere you grew up under was that you had to fight to get ahead, and whatever's necessary to do, you did," he recalled.[4] Strom and his two brothers, growing up after the turn of the century, were accustomed to seeing men take target practice in the town square, shooting bottles off of store railings.

"They were mean people — but of good honest character," younger brother Allen George Thurmond once described Edgefield's citizenry. "They were good about helping each other, but they would also shoot you. They would fight for what they believed in."[5]

Once Will Thurmond became a lawyer, politics was an irresistible lure. He offered for the job of town attorney and won the votes of all three councilmen. Building on his contacts, he then was elected in 1894 to the state House of Representatives. As a legislator, he nominated Tillman for the U. S. Senate and worked ardently to elect him to the seat held by aging Edgefield Confederate hero M. C. Butler.

Edgefield had divided into what were called the Tillmanites and the anti-Tillmanites, and Tillman's enemies also became Will Thurmond's enemies. But he ran in 1896 for solicitor, the judicial circuit prosecutor, and easily defeated the incumbent.

He also served informally as Tillman's man back home, soothing riled tempers and obediently stepping on toes on the senator's behalf. Men with scores to settle looked on Tillman's Edgefield operative as a target. Thurmond's enemies referred to him derisively as "Pussyfoot Bill." As one of his contemporaries described it, the title recognized Thurmond's ability to "slip around quietly to arrange things. He'd move around the way a cat slips up on a rat."[6]

On a March morning in 1897, a confirmed Tillman hater by the name of Willie Harris came to town apparently looking for a fight. Folks had seen him reeling from whiskey, loitering outside the courthouse talking tough with his drinking buddies. One witness heard him say, "I've got a good knife and a Colt's pistol in my pocket."[7]

When Will Thurmond routinely left the courthouse and headed toward the small white cottage that housed his law office, Harris planted himself in his path and began taunting him. As a witness later described it during a coroner's inquest, Harris asked Thurmond, "Weren't you elected by the Tillmanites? Didn't Bennie send word to elect you?" Harris persisted, walking beside the lawyer and bellowing so loudly he could be heard across the square, finally calling him a "low, dirty scoundrel." His honor assailed, Thurmond then pulled a pistol and shot Harris, hitting him between the nipples on his chest, and killing him instantly. Even before Harris's body was carted away, Thurmond pleaded self-defense.[8]

The Thurmond family version is that Will Thurmond shot only after going inside his law office and being threatened. Newspaper accounts portray Thurmond pulling his pistol outside his law office and firing in plain view of a handful of spectators.

Despite Edgefield's traditional hypersensitivity to matters of honor, South Carolina had long outlawed dueling, and Thurmond's behavior as a sworn officer of the court initially shocked many. *The Edgefield Advertiser* branded the killing "one of the most deplorable homicides in recent years. Both of the men were young and well-liked and the cause of the difficulty was so trifling as to make the results all the more pitiable."[9]

The outraged Harris family pushed for prosecution. Thurmond felt sure he would be cleared, but recognized the case's political implications. In early April, with the trial scheduled for August, he announced in a statement to the *Advertiser* that he would not prosecute cases until his own name was clear and that he would pay for an interim prosecutor. "While I sorely regret said unfortunate occurrence," he wrote, "I feel perfectly justified before God and man in what I did, and do not believe that I will be blamed in the least when the facts are known." To defend himself, he hired a Tillman family law firm.[10]

At his trial for murder on August 2, the courthouse was packed. The trial started promptly at 9:30. Seated behind the defendant was Eleanor Gertrude Strom, the young woman who had recently become his fiancee. A delegation of distinguished citizens from as far away as Columbia attended as character witnesses. They included Gov. Sheppard, his legal mentor. One followed another to testify that J. William Thurmond was a noble man who would not have pulled the trigger without first fearing for his life.

The white male jurors listened politely to all the testimony, retired late in the day to deliberate, and returned thirty-five minutes later to clear his name, which the *Advertiser* noted was "according to general expectation."[11]

Will Thurmond's marriage in 1899 to Gertie Strom helped further restore his reputation. Her father, James Harrison Strom, was a country doctor and state legislator who owned thousands of acres of land in upper Edgefield County. He sent her to Augusta to order a custom-designed trousseau.

The marriage linked together two important families that politically dominated the county, the Stroms the upper half, the Thurmonds the lower. As a child, Strom Thurmond found the political union fascinating and once asked his father if he married Gertie because she came from such a prominent clan. "He said he married her because he loved her," Thurmond recalled years later. "There was a big connection there — the Thurmonds and the Stroms both. They practically covered the county in influence in one way or another."[12]

Will Thurmond launched a race for Congress in 1902, Strom's birth year, campaigning for a month from the stump in the district's seven agricultural counties. The last black officials in South Carolina were voted out of office that year, with none to reappear as legislators until 1970. Race, however, wasn't an issue in the Third District congressional campaign.

Edgefield residents considered Thurmond a strong candidate when he entered the race to join Senator Tillman in Washington. The *Advertiser* endorsed him as a "just and reliable" man who "considers duty more sacred than holding a public office" and "would work for the poor man." Letters to the editor praised him.[13]

The 1902 stump meetings were unusually civil, without the traditional name-calling and fist fights. Thurmond's two opponents were both distinguished legislators. Except for blacks who could swear under oath that they had voted for Wade Hampton in 1876 and had voted Democratic in all subsequent elections, only white men voted in the Democratic primary that would elect the next congressman. Thurmond called for free trade, trust-busting, rural mail delivery, and federal aid to local governments, reflecting the Progressive spirit of the period.

No one mentioned the Willie Harris episode and it didn't seem to hurt Thurmond in Edgefield County, which he carried. But he lost badly elsewhere, finishing last in a field of three.

Years later, he told his children his version of the Willie Harris episode and said, "Never kill anybody. It will hurt you all your life." Will Thurmond never again sought elective office. Instead he channeled his political energies into working on Tillman's behalf as a local troubleshooter while developing a lucrative law practice.[14]

His legal skill and finely tuned political instincts paid dividends in the courtroom as he established a reputation as the man to see for anyone facing legal trouble. He had an uncanny ability to pick a sympathetic jury and taught Strom that helping others could help himself.

When an Edgefield man died, the town's citizens would soon see Thurmond's wagon loaded with food or supplies roll down the street to the widow's home. In lean times he gave away crops from his fields and offered his name as collateral on loans. Children thought of him as a Santa Claus, handing out candy as he walked home every afternoon.

When Strom was four, his father moved the family to a four-acre tract about three miles from town. One of the grandest homes in Edgefield graced the property. A two-story with wide wrap-around porches and tall windows that looked out on pecan and peach trees, it was a country gentleman's home with heart pine floors and fireplaces in every room. Thurmond paid $5,000 for the new home place, a considerable sum at the time.

He owned another fifty acres or so in nearby tracts of farm and pasture land. He wanted to be closer to the land, to instill an appreciation for it in his children, and to have them learn the virtues of farm work. "He wanted us to see how hard it was to make a living on a farm," Strom said.[15] During their school years, the boys would rise early to turn the cows out to pasture, with homework and farm chores filling their afternoons.

Strom became the milker. His sisters often gathered round to taunt him, and he would turn an udder in their direction and squirt, sending them away shrieking. But he was also the first to call the children together for a ball game or swimming lesson, and his sisters regarded him as a substitute father whenever Will Thurmond was traveling.

Even as a child, Strom displayed an obsession for cleanliness and order. He liked to organize the family storeroom, stacking canned goods by size. He would get in a bad mood if he couldn't brush his teeth after eating. Even in the U. S. Senate, he kept a toothbrush in his suit pocket.

At harvest time, the Thurmond children helped pull river bottom yellow corn and picked cotton, working beside black farm laborers. Brother Allen George remembered that their paternalistic father taught them to respect the black workers — "darkies" as he called them — and tend to them in times of need. Sister Mary recalled, "If they needed food or clothes, he'd send them down to Reel's store and tell them to get whatever they needed."[16]

Will Thurmond owned another thousand or so acres in the county, worked by sharecroppers. Thurmond furnished fertilizer and cottonseed, a mule and plow, credit to purchase necessities, and shelter. The sharecropper's family provided the labor. Sharecropping had evolved throughout the rural South as an economic system after the Civil War, when the freedmen refused to work in labor gangs as they had as slaves. The system provided them a degree of autonomy, but little opportunity for economic independence.

Strom would often ride in the buggy with his father on trips to visit and talk with the sharecroppers. "My father would talk to me going out there and back. I found it very interesting to be with him."[17]

Strom accompanied his father by train to the state Capitol in Columbia, where portraits of Tillman and John C. Calhoun, the champion of nullification, decorated the walls. He peered over the brass rails of the General Assembly to watch the heated legislative debates. He watched his father's every move, the way he offered the same strong handshake to a Negro laborer that he gave a white landowner. His father sometimes sat as a special judge on the state Supreme Court, and he introduced Strom to all the justices.

At home he watched his father work his magic in the courtroom and saw his fearlessness there, once telling a hostile witness, "If you want to fight, let's fight," and offering to settle the dispute outside the courtroom. In his Senate office, Strom Thurmond prominently displayed an enlarged photograph of his father. He told a visitor, "He was my idol. I tried to imitate him as much as I could."[18]

Already aware of Strom's interest in politics, Will Thurmond took him in 1912 to a stump meeting in Edgefield that featured gubernatorial candidates Cole Blease, a rousing race-baiter, and Ira Jones, an able but staid chief justice of the state Supreme Court. The event left an indelible impression on the boy.

Thurmond would recall, "They put up a platform for them to speak on and brought a big pitcher of water. Jones, he made a good talk, a literary talk. But he just didn't stir the people. Well, Cole Blease was a fiery kind of fellow and a great orator. You could see people who were not really the thinking people who were carried away by his speech. I could see then the influence that he was going to have over the state for being such a good speaker.

"After hearing him speak, I knew that I was going to run for governor. And I was going to learn to speak, and I would never let a man do me like Blease did Jones that day."[19]

His mother, Gertrude, was a pious woman known for delivering wonderful prayers. She laid down the law for her children about church attendance. Strom was often charged with hitching the horses to the carriage for the Sunday morning ride into town to the First Baptist Church.

When he was eleven, Strom expressed his desire to be baptized, which for Southern Baptists meant full immersion in water, usually in the church baptismal pool. Gertrude was proud. Strom said years later that she shaped his life in religious and spiritual matters as profoundly as his father shaped his political instincts.

At the time of Strom's childhood profession of faith, many Southern Baptists tended to treat man's relationship with God as a direct and highly individual experience, not unlike that of Jews. Thurmond took his religious beliefs seriously throughout his life, but prayer for him tended to be a private matter. Years later, in the Senate, he became a regular member of organized weekly prayer breakfasts. His key aide Harry Dent said Thurmond "never missed it. He kept it on his calendar as a highest priority." He surprised fellow senators when he gave a thoughtful, moving message about Abraham Lincoln. Dent did some special research on that one, entitled "The Long Road to Faith."[20]

Dent said religion fit into Thurmond's "overall framework of virtues. He lived by his perspective of right and wrong."

Back in Edgefield, Tillman had looked for ways to reward his friend. He saw a chance twelve years after Will Thurmond lost his bid for Congress. After Woodrow Wilson — who had spent part of his boyhood in Columbia as a Presbyterian minister's son — regained the White House in 1912 for the Democrats, Tillman recommended Thurmond for U. S. Attorney in South Carolina when the post became vacant.

The White House found him unsuitable because of the Willie Harris slaying. Tillman dug in his heels. Over stiff opposition he split the state into two federal judicial districts. The western district was designed for Thurmond. When Wilson balked again, Tillman exploded. He wrote the Attorney General that Thurmond had to "crawl around on his belly and be kicked around" before he killed Harris.

The nomination went through and Thurmond became U. S. Attorney for half of the state, with headquarters in Greenville. He considered moving the family to a large farm near Greenville, six hours away by car at fifteen miles per hour. But by then the family had grown to six children—John William, Strom, Gertrude, Allen George, and the twin girls Mary and Martha. Their father decided to rear his children in Edgefield, though he would be gone much of the time.

Although the Thurmonds were landed gentry and respected citizens, their rural origins set them apart from the old families of Edgefield who considered themselves the community's sophisticated social elite. They coalesced around the Episcopal Church, a smaller brick structure on a hill overlooking First Baptist.

But the Thurmonds led a prosperous life. Mary remembered her father taking the girls on trips to New York and Niagara Falls. The family always had a black domestic staff of three — a live-in cook, houseboy, and gardener, with substitute help when needed.

A typical meal included garden vegetables, meat cured in the family's smokehouse, and hot bread made of whole wheat grown on the farm. There were almost always visitors. Will usually walked home from town with a companion for the evening meal, which was followed by listening to recordings of John Philip Sousa's marches (Will's favorites) or to Gertrude's spirited Bible readings. Many guests stayed overnight, and Strom learned early that doing so enabled them to strengthen their relationship with his family.

Will Thurmond became an adviser not just to Tillman, but to political up-and-comers like the young James F. Byrnes, an ambitious court stenographer from Aiken. He sometimes dropped by the Thurmond family home and spent the night. Eventually, he found his way to Washington as congressman, U. S. senator, U. S. Supreme Court justice, and Secretary of State—before returning home as governor.

"Our house was like a hotel," Strom recalled. One country cousin lived there for months so he could go to better schools in Edgefield, moving on to become a physician. Grandmother Mary Thurmond lived there for years, tutoring the older children in grammar and becoming an important force in the household. She died of pneumonia when Strom was eleven, her body laid out in the parlor.[21]

More than any of the children, Strom found the physical demands of farm work challenging. When a neighbor went into the Army during World War I, Strom and his older brother bought the unharvested crop, hoping to make a sizable profit. William quickly backed out, and Strom bought his interest, then worked long hours in the field. But it was a drought year, with a skimpy return. A frugal teenager, Strom worked Saturdays at a store in town, and saved $600 before going to college.

But he also had a streak of mischief. With his father out of town, he was caught more than once sneaking up the back stairs late at night, and a lingering family story tells of Strom hiding out on the roof to avoid his mother's whipping, only to be fetched down by a servant.

He boxed and played football in high school, rode horses bareback, and drove a motorcycle at high speeds on country roads with his hands off the handlebars. He developed a life-long (and life-lengthening) zealous devotion to physical fitness. But his consuming interest was girls. He was a good dancer and played the field.

When he finished tenth grade, Strom had the option of continuing to the newly added eleventh grade and getting a diploma or going off to college. He enrolled at Clemson, where many of his Edgefield friends were going. Then an all-male military school as well as the state agricultural college, the Clemson campus is nestled in the rolling hills of the state's upcountry.

The campus is located on part of John C. Calhoun's estate, given to the school by his son-in-law, Thomas Clemson. From their spartan barracks, cadets could look out at Calhoun's graceful white-columned plantation home, Fort Hill, and hear the softly chiming clock from the tower of Tillman Hall, the center of university life.

Strom enrolled in the fall of 1919, not yet seventeen. The rigid routine suited him. Up by 6:30 to Reveille, the daily routine consisted of calesthenics ("taking exercise" is what Strom called it), class work, mandatory chapel, study hall, and military drills before Taps at 10:30 p.m. College rules barred mustaches, long hair, cigarettes, drinking and card playing, and leaving the barracks without permission or behaving irreverently during chapel were grounds for dismissal.

College administrators routinely tolerated physical hazing of freshmen and, with war veterans returning to school in 1919, Strom's freshman year was rougher than usual. "I've had many a broom handle broke over my rear end," he recalled with a laugh.[22]

Clemson nurtured the transformation of a shy but determined boy into a confident, disciplined, and driven young man stamped with the mark of potential success. He learned to speak, practicing for hours to correct an adolescent stammer. Although never a spellbinding orator, Thurmond developed great skill in honing a political message to its core and expressing it with conviction in clear, concise and simple language.

At Clemson, he became president of the Calhoun Literary Society, where he debated and learned parliamentary procedure. No professor influenced him more than Daniel Wistar Daniel, a polished orator of national reputation who taught English, brought in nationally renowned speakers, and laced his classroom lectures with wit and country wisdom. At Thurmond's 1947 inauguration as governor, he had Daniel share the podium and introduce him for his inaugural address.

He enjoyed the biweekly dances, earning a reputation in the college yearbook as a "ladies' man of the first order." What he wrote years later to a friend's son about to enter Clemson, however, reflected Strom's sense of purpose there: "A great many boys will flit away their time at college, in the pool room, loafing and fooling around. You will be at college only four years. Make every minute count. During the time you are not in classes, I suggest you be on the athletic field or in the gymnasium taking exercise, in the library reading or conversing with ambitious and enterprising men with whom you will form a deep friendship."

At Clemson, the competitive edge that would last a lifetime found an outlet as a distance runner. Strom earned points on the track and cross-country teams, but was no star athlete. He distinguished himself, however, by displaying an awesome will power, gutsy determination, and an unwillingness to admit defeat.

At the end of the fall cross-country season in 1922, his senior year, Strom and four teammates decided to find out if they could run the twenty miles from Clemson to Anderson. The hilly dirt road became paved for only the final two miles. Strom wore new canvas tennis shoes that were too large. By the time he and his teammates reached the paved road, his feet were blistered and his toenails had rubbed off.

"But if I stopped I wouldn't have accomplished what I wanted to, so I kept on," he remembered more than half a century later. "Every time you put your foot down it'd feel like you were driving a nail right in your leg."[23] He went the distance.

A few weeks after attending Strom's graduation from Clemson, his father typed the following letter of "ADVICE" from J. Wm. Thurmond to his son J. S. Thurmond:

Remember your God.
Take good care of your body and tax your nervous system as little as possible.
Obey the laws of the land.
Be strictly honest.
Associate only with the best people, morally and intellectually.
Think three times before you act once and if you are in doubt, don't act at all.
Be prompt on your job to the minute.
Read at every spare chance and think over and try to remember what you have read.
Do not forget that "skill and integrity" are the keys to success.
Affectionately.
It was signed, "Dad."

More than seventy years later, Strom was still signing copies of the document for special friends and associates. And he was still doing calisthenics every morning. Not as many push-ups or sit-ups, but still twisting, bending, and stretching, then riding a stationary bicycle, and still swimming a half mile once or twice a week. He was still starting the morning with a glass of prune juice and watching his diet, eating lots of fruit and vegetables and avoiding caffeine. In addition, he said, "I have good genes."[24]

1. Thompson interview with Strom Thurmond, December 22, 1980.
2. Banks, oral history interview, op. cit., p. 7.
3. Ibid., p. 7.
4. Ibid.
5. Thompson interview with Allen George Thurmond, circa 1981.
6. Thompson interview with C. Granville Wyche, July 18, 1981.
7. *The Edgefield Advertiser*, account of coroner's inquest, March 25, 1897.
8. Ibid.
9. Ibid.
10. *The Edgefield Advertiser*, April 7, 1897.
11. *The Edgefield Adversiter*, August 11, 1897.
12. Thompson interview with Strom Thurmond.
13. *The Edgefield Advertiser* accounts of 1902 campaign.
14. Thompson interview with Allen George Thurmond, op. cit.
15. Banks oral history, op. cit., p. 1.
16. Thompson interview with Allen George Thurmond, op. cit.
17. Banks oral history, op. cit., p. 2.
18. Thompson interview with Thurmond, op. cit.
19. Ibid.
20. Alberta Lachicotte, *Rebel Senator* (New York: Devin-Adair Company, 1966), p. 128. Harry Dent telephone interview, March 27, 1998.
21. Thompson interview with Thurmond, op. cit.
22. Banks oral history. P. 17.
23. Ibid., pp. 29-30.
24. *The Atlanta Journal and Constitution*, April 23, 1995, p. N4.

CHAPTER FOUR

✢

The Political Launch

Before his college graduation, Strom considered a military career, but decided to take a reserve commission "and be available if war ever came." He believed he could make more money and show more initiative in civilian life. "And if I worked hard I could rise faster," he would explain.[1]

The *Advertiser* noted Strom's "credible record" at Clemson and said he left Edgefield on June 28, 1923, for a job with the AA Fertilizer Co. in Carteret, N. J. It lasted two months.

He returned home and accepted a teaching job that combined teaching agriculture and coaching all sports in McCormick, a sleepy county seat twenty-six miles northwest of Edgefield. Strom hit it like a buzz saw. A rare male teacher in the eleven-grade, two-story, red brick school for white children, he dressed smartly, stood ramrod straight after marching into his classroom, and lectured with enthusiasm on the intricacies of pig farming and peach tree pruning. He developed his best students into a special livestock judging team. He piled them into his automobile, raced down country roads, and lectured from behind the wheel not just about chickens and livestock, but values like sportsmanship and temperance.

In a letter to the weekly *McCormick Messenger*, he offered "to teach any white adults who have had poor opportunities for an education the fundamental principles, even the alphabet itself . . . at any time, day or night, when not engaged in my duties at the high school."

He wrote monthly columns for the *Messenger* on such subjects as the pleasure and satisfaction of growing fruit (with detailed instructions on choosing varieties for planting), the importance of good seed in growing vegetables, and the proper spray schedule for peaches, plums, and cherries.[2]

He wrote an article defending football as an activity that promotes a good physique, teaches boys to be "aggressive and persistent" — lessons essential to achievement, and provides training for "quick thinking" and "alertness of action."[3] His McCormick team lost 19-6 to heavier, more experienced Greenwood, a much larger town, which the previous year had won 66-0. Everyone soon noticed him.

When he took his outclassed boys and girls basketball teams to play against the bigger high school in Edgefield, Strom gave his charges a special treat — a sampling of high society in the larger town. After tea at the Dixie Highway Hotel, they went to a lavish dinner at Gertrude Thurmond's table, followed by a party at Miss Addie Sue McGlendon's where, as recorded in the *Advertiser*, "progressive conversation and dancing were enjoyed until a late hour."[4]

Strom could live at home in Edgefield and depend on meals from his mother. But he did nothing to undermine the "ladies man" reputation he had earned at Clemson. He had no intention of getting married any time soon. A half century later he explained, "I wouldn't be tied down, because I felt sooner or later I'd end up in statewide politics. So I could make more contacts — if I'd had a wife it'd hold you back. Have to come home every night, or you'd have to be in by a certain time, or take your wife out. I felt that being unfettered that I could make my own schedule and wouldn't inconvenience anybody."[5]

After two years, Edgefield lured him home to teach, with the *Advertiser* predicting he would be "a valuable factor in this county, just as he has been in McCormick." When Edgefield lost its county farm agent, an important figure in the rural county, Strom took up the slack. He wrote long informational columns about poisoning boll weevils, controlling corn smut, and preserving eggs. When a surplus of chickens developed, he arranged to ship fryers by train "somewhere up north" and saw that farmers got paid in cash. "An indefatigable worker and efficient painstaking teacher," the *Advertiser* called him.

He left Edgefield for a year in 1925, the *Advertiser* reported, heading for Florida to seek his fortune in a real estate boom that soon went bust. Then he returned to teach at Ridge Spring, a hamlet nestled along the road to Columbia.

Back in Edgefield after a year, he became president of the Baptist Young People's Union. As an organizer, he traveled the county, visiting all rural churches, accruing political capital as he met and charmed people who would remember him as voters.

He coached the football team. Editor Mims remembered Strom crouching as he moved along the sideline, following his team with unforgettable intensity.

Thurmond helped develop Summerland, a six-week summer camp for bright farm boys, teaching academic courses and the latest agricultural advancements. He went to the Lions Club and to churches, getting them to raise funds for $12 scholarships — and expanding his contacts. Over four years, enrollment grew from 14 to 200. Thurmond publicized the program with articles in nearby county newspapers and a Sunday feature in the *Augusta Herald*.

The camp became a launching pad for his political career. He became a hit with his students, firmly established himself with the rural population, and gained an appointment to the Edgefield School Board. "I made a lot of friends working with those boys," he later recalled. "I wrestled with them and I played with them and ran with them. . . . But I was interested in young people, and it turned out to be very helpful politically."[6]

One year at Summerland, he told almost 200 boys that he would call each of them by name, "and if I don't you can send me through the belt line." A former student vividly remembered Strom calling off the names one by one, row behind row, without a miss. Afterwards, a teacher told him "that Strom Thurmond could run for governor with that kind of talent."[7]

He early courted the press, inviting editors not only to visit Summerland to write stories, but to speak to the boys. He often dropped by the *Advertiser*, sometimes taking gifts that got a mention in the paper's society columns, such as, "The finest peaches of the season that we have seen were presented to us by Strom Thurmond, having been plucked from his orchard."

In 1928 he announced he would challenge the incumbent county superintendent of education, W. W. Fuller. Although Fuller's wife was a cousin of the Thurmonds and the *Advertiser* reported he had won the respect of teachers by "paying them promptly in cash," Strom knew as a school board member that Fuller's poor fiscal management kept the county in debt and that he provided little leadership.

Strom had ideas and ambition. He wanted a health course to

teach all students that "if you don't have a healthy body you can't do anything." From his experience as a youth who had saved $600 by the tenth grade (equivalent to more than $15,000 in 1998 dollars), he believed in fiscal responsibility.

But his ambition went far beyond improving the schools in Edgefield County. Larger goals had begun to crystallize. "Back then, you couldn't just get out and run for governor," he said a half century later. "You had to work your way and develop a reputation. You had to prove yourself."

He believed the superintendent's job could help him establish a progressive record on the first rung of a ladder to higher office. It also would give him time to study law after hours in his father's office and at home. "I kind of hated to run against old man Fuller," Thurmond remembered, "but he'd been there a long time; all he did was hunt."[8]

Strom said his father's only advice was "if you want it, go after it," but that he stayed out of the race. Strom had developed his own contacts and organized an army of volunteers who fanned out across the county, handing out flyers and giving word-of-mouth praise — and being Will Thurmond's boy didn't hurt him.

He delivered his first political stump speech from a platform at the Colliers community, a long-awaited rite that must have conjured up all his boyhood images of fiery Coleman Blease and Ben Tillman. He began by quoting Thomas Jefferson, "I believe in education of the masses, not the classes," then vowed to serve as "an inspiration" to the hundreds of pupils who would come under his supervision. He went house to house, knocking on doors and shaking hands as he solicited support. He won 1,312-802, a landslide sixty-two percent victory in the Democratic primary, the only election that mattered and one in which only whites voted.

The general election ballot listed only the Democratic nominees for state and local office. Although some local Baptist leaders urged voters to abstain in the presidential election in opposition to New York Gov. Al Smith, an urban, Catholic "wet" who wanted to repeal prohibition, open support for Herbert Hoover was all but unthinkable because he was a Republican. Among South Carolinians who voted, Al Smith got ninety-two percent.

The majority black population in Edgefield remained political objects rather than participants in an era in which white supremacy reigned without challenge, implemented by Tillman and sanctioned by the U. S. Supreme Court. Edgefield whites accepted segregation as the way things were and presumably would remain, like the sun rising in the morning and setting in the evening.

The school system Thurmond took over in the summer of 1929, at twenty-six the state's youngest county superintendent, was typical of rural public education in a state that ranked at or near the bottom in every measurable standard of education. Black pupils, many of them in dilapidated one-room schoolhouses, outnumbered whites by two to one. Edgefield County spent $5.35 per year for each black child's education and $63 for each white child. School terms for whites were almost twice as long. White male teachers earned a respectable $1,530 a year and white women $826. The typical black teacher earned less than $300. Only white children received bus transportation to school. (At the end of Thurmond's term in 1932, there would remain forty-two one-room schools in Edgefield County for blacks, compared with eight for whites.) These numbers buried in the state superintendent of education's annual report reflected the norm — and went unnoticed.

"I was trying to prove myself as a superintendent," Thurmond said later. "I always felt if you did a good job, then you would be appreciated and it would help you for the next position you occupied." He got the school board to raise taxes and pay off debt, equalized taxes and expenditures among the local school districts in the county, and pared expenses to produce a surplus.

He also launched an innovative program in which the state health officer and local dentists went into the schools to examine children and treat defects. Although Thurmond's recollection years later was that all children — black and white — participated, a faded clipping from *The State* reported, "Examination of 1,500 white school children of Edgefield County began Tuesday under direction of Dr. Ben Wyman, state director of county health work, assisted by a staff of seven county health officers, six nurses and two inspectors in addition to local physicians."

But Thurmond did talk about health care for all children in 1932 to Modjeska Simkins. She first met him when she represented the South Carolina Tuberculosis Association, in charge of their "Negro program." She traveled the state, trying to get health education into the black schools.

She had found most white school officials insensitive, often rude, and seldom more than condescending. But in Edgefield, she found Thurmond courteous and sincerely interested in her pleas. He told her of his plans to bring doctors and dentists to rural schoolchildren whose parents couldn't afford preventive medicine.

When they finished talking, he walked Mrs. Simkins to her car. She drove away impressed by the vigorous young man whose work was gaining the attention of the state Department of Education in Columbia. Heading back to the capital, she thought that leadership of the state could be looking "up and out" with men like Thurmond exerting influence.[9]

Two years earlier, he had launched a countywide "Write Your Name" campaign against adult illiteracy. The program began in January 1930 and took aim at the almost thirty percent of the county's black population — 3,289 persons — that the 1920 census had revealed could neither read nor write.

Thurmond urged blacks to come out to "Moonlight Schools," for which he hired sixty-nine black teachers to work overtime for a dollar a night — at a time when a proficient adult cotton-picker might earn no more than that in a day of harvesting the white lint. They taught three nights a week in schools and churches during nine-week sessions designed to reduce to as few as possible the number of people who would sign an "X" for the 1930 census. Separate classes were set up for the county's 140 illiterate whites.

Within a month, the *Advertiser* reported that more than one fourth of the illiterates were being taught to read and write their names "through the commendable efforts of Mr. Thurmond." A black teacher wrote, "Our county superintendent is leaving no stone unturned in helping us to eradicate illiteracy in our group. He has been instrumental in helping to obtain efficient teaching faculties and is urging every colored teacher to support the work."

By the end of the campaign, 798 black adults had learned to write their names, 648 had learned basic reading, and all who attended had received, at Thurmond's insistence, lessons in hygiene and "good principles of living." Black illiteracy in the county dropped by more than one fourth, from twenty-nine percent to twenty-one percent in the 1930 census. A young black principal years later told his children he could get what he needed from Thurmond.[10]

Strom had moved the superintendent's office next door to his father's law office, and he secluded himself there at the end of each day, studying law. The future chairman of the Senate Judiciary Committee followed the LaSalle University Extension Course, a course prescribed by the state Supreme Court, and *Thurmond's Key Cases*, a respected reference book compiled by his father. He studied three years, his father tutoring him. "It was just like having a full-time law teacher," Thurmond remembered. "He saved me hours of looking stuff up because he could answer it right there."[11] Strom also had learned much from sitting in at trials, watching his father try cases.

In 1929, however, the elder Thurmond suffered the first of a series of debilitating heart seizures that would lead to his death five years later. He called on Strom for help, even before he had taken the bar exam.

The first time involved a hearing before the state Supreme Court, and J. William got the court's permission to allow Strom to argue the case for his client. Strom won that case and two others in the trial courts before passing the three-day bar exam in 1930. He bragged that he tied for the highest grade with J. Robert Martin, a Harvard Law graduate from Greenville who later achieved a reputation for fair-minded toughness as a jurist. Martin ultimately issued many of the state's major desegregation orders on his way to becoming chief judge for the United States District Court of South Carolina.

Thurmond studied law in his father's office with a friend from McCormick, J. Fred Buzhardt. They were close and later practiced law together, in Edgefield and McCormick. Buzhardt recalled Strom had "more girl friends than you could shake a stick at," big-busted women who would come to the office and sometimes wait hours for him to finish his work and take them out.[12] His son, Fred, Jr., a committed conservative ideologue with a first-rate mind, later worked many years for Thurmond. He helped draft major speeches and ultimately became a lead attorney for President Richard Nixon in the final days before he resigned.

After Strom and Buzhardt passed the bar exam, Thurmond practiced law with his father while completing his term as county superintendent of education. After Strom won an acquittal for a murder defendant in one of his first cases, the *Advertiser* characterized his jury argument as "very eloquent and effective."

In 1932, Edgefield County's state senator, a friend of J. William's, announced he wasn't seeking reelection.[i] Strom, twenty-nine, paid his $15 filing fee. Although much younger than the typical senator, who usually had served first in the House, he seemed headed for a free ride. He had proven himself progressive, yet tight with the purse strings.

---

i. Until the Supreme Court's "one man, one vote" reapportionment decisions ruled it unconstitutional, South Carolina functioned under a "little federal" system. The 46-member Senate provided for one senator from each county. A 124-member House of Representatives was based on population, but with at least one member from each county — a system that assured rural domination.

State senator also was a powerful local office. Until "home rule" legislation passed in the 1970s, the senator chaired the county legislative delegation. It controlled county government, filling many local offices and writing the county budget, or supply bill. The legislature passed it as local legislation.

As the filing deadline approached, opposition came from an unexpected source, Benjamin Ryan Tillman, Jr., Pitchfork Ben's son. The younger Tillman, however, resembled his father only in name. He had a reputation as a heavy drinker and had outraged most of Edgefield in a bitter divorce case in which the state Supreme Court had to settle custody of his children. He had grown up mostly in Washington, while his father was senator.

Thurmond, running as a "Progressive Democrat," pledged to reduce spending and cut legislative salaries, but called for more state support for public education. He already had been selected as a delegate to the Democratic national convention, which gave him de facto support from the party organization. He trounced Tillman in the August primary, 2,350 to 538.

A week later, Strom went to Chicago and joined in nominating New York Gov. Franklin D. Roosevelt for president. Roosevelt had spent time at Warm Springs, Georgia, for therapy after being stricken with polio. He would ride around, stopping for long talks with farmers. He developed empathy for the South, its people, and its problems. Only Grover Cleveland and Woodrow Wilson had served as Democratic presidents since the Civil War, and an enthusiastic Thurmond returned home to campaign.

"I think our whole delegation was impressed with Roosevelt," Thurmond remembered. "He had a grasp of what needed to be done for the farmers, and at that time farming was the main industry in South Carolina. I was impressed with FDR because he was a man of action and I felt he would get things done."[13]

Thurmond organized a Saturday afternoon Democratic rally in which hundreds of school children paraded and an overflow crowd filled the courthouse. One speaker, J. E. Stanfield of Aiken, called Edgefield "the cradle of liberty" in South Carolina and referred to the role "that Edgefield leaders had played in ridding the state of Republican tyranny in 1876."[14]

Roosevelt won South Carolina with ninety-eight percent of the vote.

Meanwhile, with brash self-confidence, the twenty-nine-year-old Thurmond prepared a set of proposals to present to the legislature, but a serious case of influenza that lingered for ten days kept him in Edgefield on opening day in January. In his letter of resignation that day as county superintendent of education, he appealed to the school children to have ambition for an education and try to prepare themselves for service and a useful calling.

While confined, he sent a letter published in *The State* outlining a six-point legislative program. It included a fifty percent cut in legislative salaries to $200, reorganization of state government to reduce costs, and slashing appropriations — "for our people are simply not able to pay high taxes." He proposed school consolidation as a means of reducing expenses, but said that state government must function and the schools must operate.[15]

In Columbia, the western wall of the granite State House still bears ten brass stars to mark where it was struck by small cannon balls fired from across the Congaree River by General William Tecumseh Sherman's artillery, which pounded the city where the initial Ordinance of Secession (written by an Edgefield lawyer) was signed after Abraham Lincoln's election in 1860.

When Thurmond arrived to take his seat in the Senate, the seventy-five other freshman lawmakers had quietly settled in. Many of the newcomers, mostly country lawyers and prosperous farmers elected by their neighbors to keep a careful eye on state spending and to see that the "right people" ran things at home, had begun to discover eager lobbyists with access to good bootleg whiskey and easy women. Others joined all-night songfests in local cafes or simply enjoyed the lavish display of food at evening receptions. Except for the delegation from Charleston County, with its wide-open port city, the newcomers explored an atmosphere that for them passed as hedonism.

South Carolina's skepticism about executive authority in state government lingered from its colonial past, when the governor was appointed by the king of England. Charleston editor W. W. Ball observed of the state's politicians: "Nothing is so much abhorred . . . as an idea. And if the idea happens to be new they faint."

Thurmond's arrival in Columbia coincided with the beginning of a shift in state political power to Barnwell, a county-seat town fifty-seven miles southeast of Edgefield. Barnwell Sen. Edgar A. Brown and Rep. Solomon Blatt both had razor-sharp minds, and they practiced what Brown preached when he would explain to Senate newcomers who came under his tutelage,

"There's no education in the second kick of a mule."

A lean, bespectacled, stalwart Democrat and close friend and political ally of James F. Byrnes, Brown already had made a race for the U.S. Senate in 1926. As chairman of the Senate Finance Committee for more than four decades, he would hold the tightest grasp of anyone on the state's purse strings. He earned the sobriquet of the "Bishop from Barnwell" from a habitual promise to "give prayerful consideration" to entreaties for support of legislation he questioned.

Across the lobby, Brown's new colleague Sol Blatt was the son of a Jewish immigrant who saved enough to open a store in the Barnwell County village of Blackville and send his boy to the University of South Carolina and its law school. Blatt was beginning his climb to Speaker of the House. He would hold that position for thirty-three years, setting a record unmatched by anyone in any legislature in the United States. At a political barbecue the previous year, his hosts realized they had failed to provide chicken for their Jewish candidate, serving nothing but pork. "That's all right," Blatt told them, "We'll just call it goose."

Over the years, Thurmond's career would intersect with both men, who would become known collectively as the Barnwell Ring, a term Brown would define many years later as "two old men who sometimes agree and sometimes don't." One observer said they spent the state's money like it was their own, dominating like-minded rural colleagues. They generally resisted change, but were open to persuasion.

Thurmond had visited the legislature several years earlier, hawking *Thurmond's Key Cases* for five dollars a copy. One senator remembered that he "wouldn't take no for an answer. You had to pay him five dollars just to get rid of him."

Some of his new colleagues eyed him warily from the beginning, and Strom confirmed their skepticism about him by introducing his bill to cut legislative pay in half and to prohibit extra pay for an extended session. His efforts failed, raising hackles among those forced to vote against it, but it got Thurmond some good press. He also joined four other senators as part of Gov. Ira Blackwood's official party to attend Roosevelt's inauguration. And later in the year he returned a $260 voucher to the state Comptroller, with a note that he had voted against extra pay and refused to accept it.

On two matters affecting race, Thurmond introduced an

unsuccessful bill to allow hiring of only white people to work in the capitol, and he voted to exempt Ku Klux Klan property from state taxation. No similar legislation showed up again during his legislative career.

A supporter of Roosevelt's New Deal, Thurmond sought to shift the tax burden to the wealthy, proposing to end state property taxes and offset the loss with taxes on income and intangibles (stocks and bonds). The legislation didn't pass, but it added to an overall reputation he developed as a serious liberal. Speaking out for a bill to outlaw the practice of locking employees inside mills as a means of keeping them on the job, Thurmond called himself a "friend to capital but more a friend of labor."

Thurmond became a major supporter of Gov. Olin D. Johnston's proposal for a state-owned and developed electric power project. The project would dam the Santee River and divert its flow to the Cooper River, create two major inland lakes for recreation, and generate low cost electricity, much of it to be sold to rural electrification cooperatives. The project would get federal funds and create thousands of jobs.

Johnston was a hulking and determined former textile worker who managed his way to college, played tackle on the football team at the University of South Carolina, and worked his way through law school there. He remained forever loyal to his roots. Unlike Gov. Eugene Talmadge in Georgia, who in the 1934 textile strike, called out the National Guard to suppress the strikers, Johnston supported the workers. The largest walkout in American history, it ended in South Carolina only after five workers in Honea Path were shot to death by armed guards working for the textile mill, whose superintendent was mayor of the town.

Roy Powell, a gubernatorial aide during Thurmond's early Senate years, said, "Strom always impressed me as an effective senator. He tended to his chores. He looked after his county. He never forgot a friend."

Even when he was selected to represent the Senate as its representative in a challenge of the House to a mule race at the state fairgrounds, Thurmond took it seriously. "I know mules, so I picked a long-legged one whose ears laid back," he explained years later.[16] He shipped in the speedy mule from Aiken, a horse-racing center. His genial House counterpart, Frank Hampton, saw the contest as a joke to promote bonhomie and showed up at the starting line with an underfed, overworked ice wagon mule.

"When they said 'go,'" Hampton remembered, "Strom's gone. I can still see that fellow taking off on that mule. Strom took it all so serious."[17]

Strom pursued the opposite sex with equal diligence, developing a "shady reputation" among the ladies of Columbia's Junior League, one former senator remembered, because of his flirtation with a woman who ran a snack stand in the State House. "He was a little heavy-handed and redneck with the women," the former colleague recalled. "He might have fit right in with the morals of today, but back then he was considered a Casanova."

Powell, who sometimes double-dated with Thurmond, remembered him as "persistent" with women; Powell so admired Strom's "eye for beauty" that he got the governor to appoint Thurmond a judge in the Tomato Queen beauty contest.[18]

Marshall Williams, later state senator for many years from Orangeburg, double-dated with Thurmond. "I always had to drive," Williams said, "because Strom needed both hands in the back seat."[19]

But Strom headed for Edgefield each week when the Senate adjourned, picking up his load in the law practice with his father, whose health continued to deteriorate. He was too weak to attend son Allen George's graduation from medical school in 1934. A year later he sent Strom to accept an honorary degree for him from the University of South Carolina at the 1935 spring commencement.

His life slipped away a few weeks later on a Sunday afternoon. By sunset, the *Advertiser* would report, the Thurmond home was besieged by a "stream of sorrowing people from all walks of life who came to pay their respects." The newspaper devoted half the front page to his obituary and funeral coverage.

Editor Mims remembered the funeral as a show of J. William Thurmond's statewide political reputation and the growing influence of Strom. "When Mr. Thurmond died, Strom Thurmond sent wires to all the dignitaries and prominent people everywhere in South Carolina," Mims said, "and as I recall, the street was literally lined with these nice black cars, these status symbols, with, I think, in one or two cases, chauffeurs."[20]

The county commissioners ordered that a portrait of Will Thurmond hang in the courthouse to serve as "an inspiration to present and future generations." The portrait is one of a heavyset, robust man with piercing eyes. Strom would always consider him "the smartest man I ever knew."[21]

Strom assumed more of the workload of a prosperous law firm that, with his growing influence in the legislature, attracted handsome retainers from such state-regulated corporate clients as Southern Railway and Security Bank. Forty years later such payments to a lawyer-legislator would raise questions of ethics, but not in the 1930s.

In Columbia Thurmond won appointment to the Senate Education Committee and became known among teachers as a champion of public schools. He introduced bills to expand the school term from six months to eight, to increase teacher pay by ten percent, and to provide a system for renting textbooks at a modest fee. He pushed for compulsory school attendance. Finally, he became concerned about Communists infiltrating South Carolina's schools and pushed for a law requiring teachers to take a loyalty oath before being hired.

His loyalty oath bill apparently was linked to his becoming state councillor in 1935 of the Junior Order of United American Mechanics, essentially an American nativist organization opposed to immigration. The Junior Order's motto was "Put none but Americans on Guard." Their creed was "One language, One school, One country, One flag."

In this role, Strom traveled around the state making speeches. He mentioned the "disturbance and discord growing out of the Communistic propaganda among the ignorant and unthinking people." He blamed growing crime on "illegally entered foreign born and those that have no other reason to be in this country than to accumulate a competence and go back to their native lands."[22]

In insular Edgefield, Thurmond had known no immigrants. Had he even known Sol Blatt better, he would have discovered a World War I doughboy who deeply loved his country for the freedom and opportunity it gave an immigrant's family.

As chairman of the Senate Public Works Committee, Thurmond pushed hard to fund a new classroom at Winthrop College, the school for women that Tillman had created. Thurmond served on the Winthrop board of trustees, who named the new building for him, a tribute the young legislator enjoyed.

After reelection without opposition in 1936, Thurmond returned to Columbia in 1937 amid talk of his becoming a candidate for lieutenant governor in 1938. But fate intervened on a sweltering August day in Newberry, forty miles northwest of Columbia, where alumni of Lutheran-affiliated Newberry College gathered for a reunion. State trial judge Carroll Johnson Ramage, whose four-county judicial circuit included Edgefield County, spoke for the occasion under a blazing sun. Moments after he finished, he dropped dead of a heart attack.

The legislature elects judges in South Carolina, and speculation over a successor began almost immediately. Ramage had been a close friend of Will Thurmond, and Strom served as a pallbearer and delivered a stirring eulogy.

Although he had given little thought to a judgeship before Ramage's death, Thurmond understood that a circuit judge holds court in every county in the state over a six-and-a-half-year period. "I decided I'd better take that and try to do a good job at it," Thurmond remembered, "and then I'd make friends going around traveling as a judge over the state. And that would be a good foundation if I cared to resign and later enter politics for governor or the United States Senate."[23] A lieutenant governor, on the other hand, did little more than preside over the Senate. Despite his earlier vote for a bill prohibiting members from filling offices elected by the legislature, he announced his candidacy almost immediately after Ramage's funeral.

Opposition came from George Bell Timmerman, Sr., an older and established lawyer who had served as solicitor for the circuit and once practiced law with Will Thurmond. They had remained friends. Timmerman served as chairman of the state highway commission, where he strongly supported the politically powerful highway administrator, Ben Sawyer, in a raging battle with Gov. Johnston. Considered one of the state's leading lawyers, Timmerman was the early favorite.

Strom understood that he faced an election involving 169 other voters, and he campaigned relentlessly. "I ran into Strom on Broad Street in Charleston," said Robert Figg, a former legislator who became one of Thurmond's key advisors a few years later. "He said, 'I've been all over the state and talked to everybody in the legislature.' Well, it wasn't too long before I saw him in Charleston again. I wouldn't be surprised if he didn't make three swings across the state that fall and talked to everybody in the House and Senate."

Blatt considered his candidate Timmerman a shoo-in until he saw Thurmond's intensity. "What he used to do was find somebody in the House who lived maybe eight or ten miles out in the country. Strom Thurmond would go right out to his house, probably in the afternoon, and then the fellow would invite him to eat supper or spend the night and he'd do it. He did that in many, many places. And every time he spent the night at a house, he got a vote. George Bell Timmerman handled it differently. He'd approach a fellow in his place of business. He didn't play the political game as it should have been played. But Strom was as good as I've ever seen."[24]

When the General Assembly convened in January 1938, Thurmond politicked until the last moment, then took a seat in the visitors gallery with pencil and paper to tally the vote. His House colleague from Edgefield nominated him, but there was silence when the lieutenant governor asked if there were other nominations. After a buzz of surprise spread about the floor of the chamber, Edgar Brown moved that the nominations be closed and that Thurmond be elected by acclamation.[25] Blatt said later of Timmerman supporters, "We took a count, and he didn't have anything like enough votes to win."[26]

Contemporary political reporters theorized that Gov. Johnston quietly threw his support to Thurmond, who had remained essentially neutral in the bitter highway battle (Johnston eventually called out the National Guard to occupy the state highway department). State House reporters simply missed the story of Thurmond's unflagging and effective pursuit of votes. *The Anderson Independent*, however, correctly called his victory "a political upset of major proportions, which stunned even those who usually feel that they know what is going to happen."[27]

Thus, at thirty-five, Thurmond was elected circuit judge without opposition to become the state's youngest jurist.

1. Banks oral history, op. cit., p. 37.
2. *The McCormick Messenger*, April 3, 1924, Feb.7, 1924, and May 8, 1924.
3. *The McCormick Messenger*, November 28, 1923.
4. *The Edgefield Advertiser*, contemporary accounts, 1924.
5. Banks oral history, op. cit., p. 37.
6. Thompson interview with Thurmond, op. cit.
7. Thompson interview with T. A. Logue, July 24, 1981.
8. Banks oral history, op. cit., p. 40.
9. Thompson interview with Modjeska Simkins, February 26, 1981.

10. Bass interview with Clem McIntosh, whose father was a principal in Edgefield County when Thurmond was county superintendent of education, April 16, 1998.
11. Thompson interview with Thurmond, December 22, 1981.
12. Bass interview with Harry Dent, Columbia, S. C., June 26, 1997.
13. Joseph C. Ellers, *Strom Thurmond: The Public Man*, Sandlapper Publishing Co., 1993, p. 33.
14. *The Edgefield Advertiser*, undated clipping.
15. *The State*, January 12, 1933, Letters to the Editor.
16. *Saturday Evening Post*, October 8, 1955, p. 120.
17. Thompson interview with confidential source.
18. Thompson interview with Roy Powell, circa 1981.
19. Williams, a Democrat, told the story publicly at the investiture of his daughter-in-law as a federal judge, appointed by a Republican president while Thurmond chaired the Senate Judiciary Committee. (confidential source who attended the investigation)
20. Thompson interview with Mims, op. cit.
21. 1979 Thurmond interview with James Banks, copy in possession of the authors.
22. Ellers, op. cit., pp. 38-39.
23. Banks oral history, op. cit., p. 43.
24. Thompson interview with Solomon Blatt, June 1981.
25. Contemporary press accounts in *The State*, *The Anderson Independent*, and *The Yorkville Enquirer*.
26. Thompson interview with Blatt, op. cit.
27. *The Anderson Independent*, January 16, 1938.

CHAPTER FIVE

✢

Judge Thurmond

Strom Thurmond looked back on his years as a judge as "the easiest, nicest job I ever had, just from the standpoint of health — and respect. Everybody respected you."[1]

His record wasn't universally admired. Harry Ashmore, a fellow Clemson graduate who went on to become a Pulitzer Prize-winning newspaper editor in Little Rock, as a reporter in Greenville covered Thurmond as a judge. "Strom was a competent and, in a way, absolutely honest judge," Ashmore recalled, "but he was totally humorless. I couldn't see much signs of compassion. And he didn't seem to me the kind of a person who could dispense justice without kind of an arbitrary, doctrinaire view of whatever the case was. I never detected any signs of race bias in his court, but segregation was absolute in South Carolina in those days. There was no challenge to it."[2]

Historian Joel Williamson grew up in Anderson, S. C., and regularly attended court as a teenager in the 1930s. He found watching trials more entertaining than the movies. "I saw J. Strom preside and thought it was terrible," he recalled six decades later. "He looked arrogant. He looked in a rush. From my point of view, there seemed to be no heart. There was no warmth. There were other judges who impressed me. In my young eye, he was the worst one."[3]

Lawyer Thomas A. Pope, never a political ally of Thurmond, also found his performance on the bench unimpressive. "I thought Strom was the weakest circuit judge we had since Reconstruction," said Pope, who became speaker of the state

House of Representatives during Thurmond's last two years as governor. "I said that to Judge [Eugene] Blease [chief justice of the state Supreme Court], and he said, 'Well how about . . .' and named one other judge, from Orangeburg. That was his only comment. Thurmond didn't know the law very well."[4]

Pope believed Thurmond's lack of formal legal education limited him. The training under his father prepared him to try cases, but gave him little background in broader concepts of legal theory and deprived him of the intellectual stimulation of class discussion. Later, as a U. S. senator, he seemed to have little grounding in constitutional law.

Thurmond would often call attorneys into his chambers to persuade them to quietly work out a settlement. Before issuing important opinions, he would call his friends, particularly Robert Figg (whom Pope called the most brilliant lawyer in the state) for legal advice. Figg remembered being asked by Thurmond, who was holding court in Charleston, to go with him to the YMCA for exercise during a recess. "He shook every hand in the place and said, 'I'm the judge and I'm running the court down here, but I want you to remember me because one day I'm going to be running for governor.'"[5]

As a judge, Thurmond denounced the activities of masked night riders. In the opening court term in Greenville in January 1940, he responded to a letter from a lawyer there urging him to speak out against the Klan (who had been active in the area) when charging the grand jury.[6]

After reading the state statute outlawing masked threats or assaults, Thurmond asserted, "I am not in sympathy with any such doings. Anyone convicted need expect no mercy at my hands." Such incidents, he added, "are in my judgment the most abominable type of lawlessness."[7]

Political opponents later charged that Thurmond set an all-time reversal rate by the state Supreme Court, but he conducted his own research on the issue to refute the charge. Some of the cases in which he was reversed suggested more compassion and sense of justice than his critics perceived.

For example, he ruled in favor of a textile worker in a workmen's compensation case against Judson Mills in Greenville. The man, a weave room worker, collapsed and died after working a full shift in eighty-five degree heat. Thurmond agreed that temperatures were too hot and decided the man's family should collect compensation. The Supreme Court reversed him, saying the decision had been based on "conjecture and speculation." No liability was found against the company.

In another case involving two young men arrested and imprisoned for loitering in a vacant lot in Greenville, Thurmond ruled there was no cause for their detention and arrest. The Supreme Court overturned him, saying there was sufficient cause. Other reversals, however, involved applications of the law to complex financial and other matters.

Without question Thurmond used his time as a judge to lay the foundation for his larger goal. In charging the grand jury on his first visit as a judge in Charleston, he congratulated the state for nominating Charleston Mayor Burnet Maybank for governor. *The News and Courier* also quoted the judge commending the city for its "hospitality, charm and culture." He referred to Maybank as "one of the cleanest, most able and most public-spirited men in South Carolina" and envisioned "a new era of great progress for the state."

The newspaper added as a social note that Thurmond planned to "move from general sessions court to a tennis court for a game with S. Henry Edmonds."[8]

Meanwhile, newspaper notices and stories reported Thurmond speaking to such groups as a church Sunday School, to the Exchange Club in Columbia, the Knights of Pythias in Anderson, and the Lions Club in Charleston. He attacked the national crime rate and blamed it on corrupt politicians, a "breakdown of parental responsibility," and "foreigners."

At a time when Nazi Germany was intensifying violence against Jews there, Thurmond was introduced at a Charleston civic club by a Jewish alderman. But Thurmond repeated his hard-line stance on immigration, saying the United States should not, under any circumstances, let the guard down for a wholesale immigration of foreigners.[9]

He also urged a state system of supervised parole, especially for young offenders. "I had just as soon send them to a college of crime as to the reform school," Thurmond said, "for there they are placed in contact with seasoned criminals and learn the new art of crime."[10]

Thurmond remained active in public affairs. He joined a small delegation from South Carolina and Georgia that went to Washington to urge favorable action on the proposed $21 million Clarks Hill power, navigation, and flood control project that would border the western boundary of Edgefield County. And he remained active in the Junior Order of United American Mechanics, attending a national meeting in Philadelphia.

He resigned as a Winthrop College trustee after criticism from a legislator. He also attended a banquet there for South Carolina newspaper editors, addressed the graduating class of the Winthrop Training School, and established a $1,000 loan fund for home economics students at the college. He attended the ceremony at Winthrop naming the new Home Economics building for him.

When the afternoon newspaper in Anderson published a fortieth anniversary edition, Thurmond wrote a letter to the editor praising it as "one of the finest editions of any newspaper that I have ever read." He praised "your progressive city" and suggested, as the only improvement he would make, "the elimination of noise" from automobile horns.

Although the vast majority of his cases involved petty crimes and minor civil disputes, Thurmond's four death penalty cases revisited him four decades later. As chairman of the Senate Judiciary Committee, he held hearings in 1981 to bring back the death penalty for a number of federal crimes. He cited his experience as a state trial judge who pronounced the death sentence in four cases.

"I am convinced the death penalty is a deterrent to crime," he said. "I had to sentence four people to the electric chair. I did not make the decision; the jury made it. It was my duty to pass sentence, because the jury had found them guilty and did not recommend mercy. But if I had been on the jury, I would have arrived at the same decision in all four of those cases."[11]

The first case, in February 1940, involved a twenty-seven-year-old white textile worker from Pickens County, where Clemson University is located. J. C. Hann killed his ex-girlfriend, slitting her throat with a razor and almost decapitating her.

At his trial he blamed the victim for a case of gonorrhea, which interfered with his plans to marry another woman. He testified that the former girlfriend's taunts about his predicament enraged him. Penicillin, which cures the disease, had not yet been discovered.

Although he begged for mercy on the witness stand, the jury found Hann guilty without recommendation of mercy.[12] Thurmond recalled the case years later as a brutal killing. "It was a terrible crime, and I would have reached the same verdict if I had been on the jury," he said.[13] The Associated Press reported that before Thurmond imposed the automatic death sentence, Hann made no statement when asked by the judge if he had anything to say, then sat down quietly beside his mother. The state Supreme Court rejected his appeal. He was executed on Feb. 7, 1941.

The other three cases involved black men, each of whom was threatened by lynch mobs after their arrests. The first defendant, a Saluda County sharecropper named George Abney, was indicted on a Monday in July 1940 for the murder of his employer's wife. Thurmond that same day appointed Billy Coleman, a lawyer just out of law school, to defend him. The trial was held on Wednesday, and Thurmond sentenced Abney to death on Thursday.

Coleman had known Abney since they were boys. Abney's father had sharecropped on land owned by Coleman's father. Coleman had played and hunted rabbits together with George's older brother; George had been almost like his little brother.

Coleman recalled four decades later that Abney was suffering from an advanced case of syphillis and that his employers, instead of taking him to a physician, took him to a black root doctor who prepared a foul-smelling concoction of "scummy, green, slimy stuff like what you would get off the top of a stagnant pond." The employer's wife brought a bottle of it to Abney's house and, assisted by his wife, tried to hold him down and force him to swallow a dose.

Abney went berserk, grabbed his shotgun off the wall and killed both women. He then walked six miles into Saluda, where the local magistrate noticed "a darky on the street with a shotgun" and arrested him. The man mumbled incoherently. When the bodies were found, he was rushed from the jail to the state penitentiary to avoid a possible lynching.

Coleman recalled that he wanted the jury to understand his wretched client's half-deranged condition, that the actions of the employer's wife were a provocation and she had no business there. "But back in 1940, you couldn't say that," Coleman said. "It would have been dangerous to say anything like that. You're talking about white people and black people. I'd have been run out of town if I'd said that." He expressed remorse for being unable to save Abney's life, but believed that if he had succeeded, a lynching was likely.[14] "I did the best I could, but in those times it just wasn't good enough," he said.[15]

On September 6, 1940, Abney was electrocuted.

Years later, the lawyer said he supports the death penalty, "but if the same thing had happened today, George Abney wouldn't have been electrocuted. And I don't think he should have been electrocuted."[16]

The next case involved a black man in coastal Georgetown, George Thomas, who was accused of raping a young white woman just before Christmas of 1940. Thurmond said that the victim was "a very fine lady who was a clerk at the ten cents store and was walking home after dark and this fellow ran out, pulled her into a vacant lot, and raped her."[17]

After the arrest of Thomas, an angry mob of armed white men gathered at the jail and demanded the sheriff turn over the prisoner. The sheriff stalled for time until a National Guard unit was mobilized and mounted a machine gun on a second-story balcony. By then the mob had grown to 300.

After Thomas was identified as the attacker by the victim, officers took him by back roads to the state penitentiary in Columbia for safekeeping. White vigilantes roamed black neighborhoods for several nights, forcing residents to remain inside their houses, before the National Guard could restore order.

The state Supreme Court scheduled an extra term of court for late January and assigned Thurmond to try the case. An NAACP-retained lawyer reported his own life had been threatened, but prosecutors presented testimony from attorneys and others that Georgetown County would give, as one put it, "as fair a trial" as any man could find in the world. Thurmond turned down the request to move the trial elsewhere.[18] "There's tension in every case you try, no matter where you try it," Thurmond said when asked in 1981 why venue wasn't changed.[19]

Two months before the trial began, Justice Hugo Black of Alabama had written for a unanimous Supreme Court that racial discrimination in jury selection "not only violates our Constitution . . . but is at war with our basic concepts of a democratic society and a representative government."

In Georgetown County, where almost two thirds of the population was black, Thurmond began the jury selection by announcing to the jury panel: "We are about to enter upon the case of the State against George Thomas. George Thomas is a negro, so it will be unnecessary to inquire as to [any kin] relationship to him, since all jurors at this term of court appear to be white." The jurors were also all male, because at that time South Carolina excluded women from jury service.

Thomas maintained he was innocent, testifying that he had come home drunk several hours before the attack, eaten supper and fallen asleep, and stayed home until morning. His wife and son corroborated his story, and seven other witnesses supported his testimony as to his whereabouts during the day of the assault.

The victim, however, identified him as her attacker, and a policeman testified that he found burrs and grass in the front of Thomas's underwear after his arrest. The jury deliberated little more than an hour. It found Thomas guilty of rape, with no recommendation of mercy. Judge Thurmond imposed the automatic death sentence.

When the defendant appealed, contending he had been denied a fair trial because the judge refused to move the case out of Georgetown, Thurmond had to describe local conditions in a report to the state Supreme Court. He made no mention of the lynching attempt or the rioting following Thomas's arrest. He said Thomas had been sent to Columbia "due to the congested condition at the county jail."

The Georgetown Times reported that the courtroom was packed throughout the trial and traffic was barred from passing by the courthouse. A special detachment of thirty-five state policemen stood guard. Gov. Burnet Maybank sent a representative with authority to order out a National Guard contingent on duty a few blocks away.

Thurmond's report said that "only a few people attended court," that the presence of the National Guardsmen had no connection, "directly or indirectly," with the trial, and that nothing out of the ordinary occurred. Based largely on the judge's assessment, the Supreme Court found his refusal to move the case justified. Thomas was electrocuted on February 20, 1942.

The next man Thurmond sentenced to death was seventeen-year-old Sammie Osborne, a sharecropper in majority black Barnwell County, then a backwoods region of blackwater swamps, modest farms, and pine forests. As elsewhere in the state, blacks neither voted nor served on juries.

Osborne sharecropped for a contentious white farmer named

William Walker, who wore a pistol strapped to his side when going into the fields. Young Osborne already had exhibited an independent attitude and a quick temper.

When Walker forced him at gunpoint to work in the fields on Saturday despite Osborne's claim of an injured foot, the teenager responded later that day by placing a crude, cardboard sign with a taunting message on a stick near the house where the fifty-eight-year-old Walker lived alone. "Please come on," the note said. "Bring sixteen at a time down here in the house. Please come on. I like bad man like you to come." The sign had Walker's name printed on it and the word "Hell," printed twice, at the bottom.

Although Osborne would testify he intended the sign to scare Walker and keep him away, the prosecution contended it was a challenge intended to lure the landowner into an ambush. Osborne spent that Saturday evening at the other tenant house on Walker's property, occupied by an eighteen-year-old friend. Osborne slept with his friend's loaded shotgun next to the bed.

Walker found him there the next morning. Osborne told police that Walker, armed with a pistol and stick, entered the house and started beating him while he was still in bed. Osborne said he grabbed the shotgun and shot the older man, whose body was found with the pistol and stick beside it.

After the shooting, Osborne walked barefooted to his father's house, six miles away. His father drove him fifty miles to the state penitentiary in Columbia. A posse already was out looking for him.

When he returned a month later to stand trial, Sol Blatt and Edgar Brown had agreed at the request of Walker's relatives to serve as prosecutors. Osborne stuck to his story throughout — that he killed Walker in self-defense — in interviews at the penitentiary, with the prosecutors, and at the trial.

As in Georgetown, Thurmond denied a motion for change of venue after a heated hearing before an overflow crowd. The prosecution relied on Osborne's taunting note to show that the killing had been a premeditated ambush, not self-defense. There was a problem in that the note challenged Walker to come to Osborne's house, not his friend's. But there was no question that an impudent young black man had killed the white man on whose land he lived.[20] Thurmond remembered Osborne as a "very vitriolic, stubborn and hard young man . . . who was looking to challenge somebody."[21]

The jury found him guilty, made no recommendation of mercy, and Thurmond sentenced him to die. The state Supreme Court, however, ruled on appeal that Thurmond had incorrectly explained the law of self-defense to the jury. At a new trial in the same courthouse before a different judge, another all-white jury took fifteen minutes to find Osborne guilty again, and he was again sentenced to death.

By the time of his electrocution, two years after Walker's death, twenty-year-old Osborne spoke as the electrodes were placed on his head. "I'm ready to go," he said, "because I know that I am not guilty."

Almost forty years later, eighty-six-year-old Sol Blatt told David Bruck, a lawyer in South Carolina specializing in death penalty cases who wrote a lengthy article on Thurmond for The Washington Post, "The Osborne case always did worry me. It still worries me."

Despite Thurmond's strong belief that the death penalty deters crime, the murder rate for South Carolina in the 1940s was two to four times that of the rest of the country, even though the state executed people at a far greater rate. During his four years as governor in the late 1940s, a total of twenty-one men were electrocuted, all of them black.[22] Thurmond later insisted, "I didn't know what color they were. I never did ask what color."[23]

Of the four Thurmond sentenced to death, Bruck wrote that not one could have been executed under the revised South Carolina law adopted after a 1973 Supreme Court ruling that the death penalty statutes failed to include rational guidelines for deciding which crimes or criminals did or did not merit the death penalty, thereby violating the constitutional ban on cruel and unusual punishment.[24]

As judge, however, Thurmond's most heroic moment came when he was called upon leaving church on a November Sunday in 1941 to intervene in an Edgefield County shoot-out that left two men dead, another dying, and a fourth wounded by gunfire.

1. Banks oral history, op. cit., p. 43.
2. Bass interview with Harry Ashmore, June 7, 1997, Athens, GA.
3. Telephone interview with Joel Williamson, February 14, 1998.

4. Bass telephone interview with Thomas A. Pope, May 15, 1998.
5. Figg interview with Marilyn Thompson, June 9, 1981.
6. Stephen Nettles letter to J. Strom Thurmond, January 3, 1940, pointing out that Judge G. Duncan Bellinger had spoken out against the Klan recently in Spartanburg and suggesting that Thurmond do the same. (Strom Thurmond papers, Clemson University Special Collections.)
7. *The News and Courier*, Charleston, S. C., (Associated Press story), January 9, 1940.
8. *The News and Courier*, September 16, 1938.
9. *The News and Courier*, December 8, 1938.
10. *The Anderson Daily Mail*, February 22, 1939.
11. David Bruck, "Outlook" section, *The Washington Post*, April 26, 1981. This article was the longest ever to run in the Outlook section of the newspaper.
12. Ibid.
13. Thompson interview with Strom Thurmond, August 8, 1981.
14. Bruck, op. cit.
15. Thompson invterview with Billy Coleman, June 2, 1981. Copy in possession of author.
16. Bruck, op. cit.
17. Thompson interview with Thurmond, op. cit.
18. Bruck, op. cit.
19. Thompson interview with Thurmond, op. cit.
20. Bruck, op. cit.
21. Thompson interview with Thurmond, op. cit.
22. Bruck, op. cit.
23. Thompson interview with Thurmond, op. cit.
24. Bruck, op. cit.

CHAPTER SIX

✤

Sue Logue

Of all the women with whom Strom Thurmond was ever romantically linked, none was more deadly than Sue Logue. The trial judge believed the murder that sent her to the electric chair was "the most cold-blooded . . . in the history of the state."[1] It also generated enduring lore, legend, and myth about Thurmond.

The dispute that escalated into violence began with an argument over a calf kicked to death by a mule and ended with nine people dead. In the Edgefield County crossroads community known as Meeting Street, the relationship between the neighboring Logues and Timmermans resembled the fabled Hatfields and McCoys. The lingering quarrel between slightly built, forty-three-year-old Davis W. Timmerman and his thick-necked, barrel-chested, forty-nine-year-old neighbor, J. Wallace Logue, over compensation for Logue's calf turned into a raucous and violent confrontation at Timmerman's Store on September 30, 1940. With witnesses present, it ended when Logue grabbed an ax from a rack and swung at Timmerman. He stepped aside, grabbed a revolver from a drawer beneath his cash register, and put a single bullet through Logue's head.

Immediately after Wallace Logue's death, his widow, Sue Stidham Logue, and his unmarried brother, George Logue, began plotting revenge. Sue lived with her mother-in-law and George in a farmhouse about a mile from Timmerman's store. Joe Frank Logue, thirty-three, a city policeman in Spartanburg, attended his uncle Wallace's funeral on October 1, 1940, then visited his uncle George and aunt Sue. He was loyal to them because they had helped care for him after his father's death. Sue said that night, "I will kill Davis Timmerman or see that he is killed."

Before Timmerman went on trial for murder, Joe Frank made several more visits to his Edgefield County relatives, a two-hour drive from Spartanburg. Each time, Sue and George Logue repeated their vow that they would kill Timmerman or have him killed. Their resolve only intensified after a jury acquitted Timmerman in March 1941 on a plea of self-defense. "Well, they told lots of lies today," Joe Frank heard Sue Logue say, "but it won't do them any good."

They first took their plan to Fred Dorn, a devoted sharecropper. A few weeks later, a black hired hand of Timmerman's was killed by a single rifle shot. The killer was never identified, but suspicion centered on the Logues and Fred Dorn.[2]

In July, the whole Edgefield Logue clan drove to Spartanburg to visit Joe Frank and his school teacher wife. On that trip, Sue took Joe Frank aside:

"Joe, I want you to get a man to kill Davis Timmerman. You can do it, and you have got to help us get the man."

"I don't know whether I can or not, and I don't want to have anything to do with it."

"You've got to help us."

"I don't know."

They talked for twenty minutes, and Sue pleaded, "We haven't had any luck in getting somebody to kill Davis Timmerman. We've raised you, fed you, and taken care of you and all your brothers and your sister, and sent them off to school. You've got to help us. Get somebody to help us. We will pay the man five hundred dollars."

Joe Frank said he told her killing was wrong and wouldn't bring Wallace back. But she said, "Davis Timmerman has told lots of lies on me, and I'm going to get rid of him one way or the other. Fred Dorn never could get close enough to him to kill him; every time he went down there in front of the house in those woods he would get up and go in the store, or a car would come along, or something, and you have just got to help us."

Later, Joe Frank testified she became threatening, warning him if he didn't help them, "Something will happen to your mother and your wife." He believed the threats were real because he knew "what they would do, what they had done."[3]

Days after Sue's offer to pay, Joe Frank approached Clarence Bagwell, a less than leading citizen of Spartanburg, on the street. Joe Frank asked him, "Clarence, some parties want you to bump a fellow off; will you do it for them? I'll tell you more about it later."

Bagwell responded, "All right, I'll let you know."

About a week later they saw each other again, and Bagwell asked how much was in it for him.

"They'll pay five hundred dollars," Joe Frank said.

"I'll kill everybody in Spartanburg County for five hundred dollars," Clarence responded, "as broke as I am."

Joe Frank explained the details — Timmerman killing his uncle, the trial and acquittal, the widow and brother wanting Timmerman killed. He described the section of Edgefield County where Timmerman lived.

"I'm ready to go at any time," Bagwell told him.

Joe Frank next saw Sue and George on August 2, while on vacation visiting his mother in Edgefield County. As soon as Joe Frank walked into their house, George asked, "Have you found the man?"

Joe Frank said, "Yes, I think I have."

Sue asked, "How much will he do it for?"

"For the five hundred dollars," Joe Frank replied.

Joe Frank saw Sue and George every day that week and heard them talk about having Davis Timmerman killed. They wanted it done immediately.

After Joe Frank returned to his job, George came to see him again in Spartanburg.

"The man hasn't backed down on you?" he asked. "We've been waiting on you. When will he be ready?"

"Right away," Joe Frank said.

A few days later, Joe Frank and Bagwell drove to Edgefield County. Joe Frank showed him where his Aunt Sue and Uncle George lived, explaining that they were the ones who wanted him to kill Davis Timmerman. He then drove Bagwell past Timmerman's Store and his house, then headed up the Greenwood Highway to Spartanburg.

On September 15, a Monday, George again showed up in Spartanburg and approached Joe Frank on the street.

"We want it done this week; we want him killed. Sue is in Albany, Georgia. I want it done late in the afternoon, Wednesday or Thursday of this week."

"All right, all right."

"When are you coming down for the money? We'll have the money ready for you. Tell the man not to worry; we'll have the money ready for him."

The next day Joe Frank bought a pistol at a pawn shop. He saw Bagwell and told him everything was set and ready. On Wednesday afternoon, they met at 2:30 p.m. at Spartan Billiard Parlor on North Church Street. Bagwell said he would get a taxi and meet Joe Frank on the outskirts of Spartanburg on the Woodruff highway.

Joe Frank borrowed a black Ford two-door sedan from Pierce Motor Company in Spartanburg and picked up Bagwell a mile outside the city limits. Driving toward Edgefield, they each took swigs from Bagwell's bottle of Canadian Club whiskey.

As they approached Timmerman's Store to scope out the situation, Joe Frank stopped the car, moved to the back seat, and lay down on the floor. Bagwell continued to the store, got out and asked how far it was to Edgefield. Joe Frank heard Mrs. Timmerman reply, "eleven miles." She noticed that the man in the gray suit, with light brown hair and blue eyes, headed instead toward Saluda.

Waiting for the sun to lower, when Mrs. Timmerman would be inside the house cooking supper, they stopped in Saluda for cold soft drinks, then headed back toward Timmerman's Store. Pulling off onto a side road, they parked for thirty to forty-five minutes, drinking again from the bottle of whiskey.

As the sun set, Joe Frank lay on the back floor under a raincoat, and Bagwell drove back to Timmerman's Store. He left the motor running and walked inside.

Timmerman was standing behind the counter when Bagwell walked in and asked for a Coca-Cola. He opened the bottle, but didn't drink any. Then he asked for some cigarettes.

Bagwell steadied his pistol on the counter as Timmerman reached up to get a pack. Bagwell didn't want to shoot him in the back and said, "Turn around." As Timmerman turned, Bagwell told him, "I come here to get you."

Joe Frank heard five shots fired in rapid succession, after which Bagwell got back in the car and drove toward Saluda. Joe Frank climbed into the front passenger seat. In the scramble, they barely avoided a wreck with a horse-drawn wagon, then continued toward Spartanburg, arriving around 9:30 p.m.

Bagwell took the pistol with him as he went on his way. Joe Frank returned the borrowed car and went home to his wife. The next day he returned to duty as a policeman.

Two nights later, Bagwell became anxious about getting paid, telling Joe Frank, "I want you to go down and get my money from your uncle and aunt." They agreed to meet Monday morning at a sandwich shop, and Bagwell warned, "Don't bring any cops.

"On Sunday Joe Frank went back to Edgefield with his wife and brother. When the visitors arrived, George took Joe Frank aside. "The man did a damn good job," he said. Back of the barn, George handed over five hundred dollars in five, ten, and twenty dollar bills, saying, "That's the best money I've ever paid in my life." Sue joined them on the front porch. With calm satisfaction, she said, "Well, Joe, the man did a good job." Off and on during the day, George and Sue cautioned Joe Frank not to discuss the killing and especially not to tell his wife.

The next morning, Joe Frank picked up Bagwell at the Montgomery Sandwich Shop and handed him the money. They drove north, crossed the North Carolina line, and rode around Lake Lanier. At the edge of the lake, they used a hammer to batter the pistol into pieces that they threw into the water.

Joe Frank drove back to Spartanburg and went on duty. On Saturday afternoon, George approached him on North Church Street to warn, "They're raising the devil down there. They've turned it over to the F.B.I. Tell the man he had better go to Chicago and get away from around here." A reward had been offered.

But Bagwell remained in Spartanburg and presumably drank good whiskey for awhile. After a fight, his girlfriend went to the sheriff's office and told Chief Detective O. L. Brady that Bagwell had killed someone. She didn't remember where, but it was a place with a "field" in it. It could have been Fairfield or Chesterfield or Edgefield. A quick check narrowed it down.[4]

After Bagwell's arrest, Mrs. Timerman identified him and he confessed, implicating Joe Frank Logue. A city policeman confirmed he substituted for Joe Frank the day Timmerman was murdered. The sheriff's office located a witness who saw Joe Frank and Bagwell together on the Asheville Highway after the murder.

Joe Frank was arrested on Sunday, November 9, and transported to Newberry County, where Bagwell was being held. One of the lawmen present at the jail was a cousin of the Logues. He was Edgefield Sheriff Wad Allen.

At first Joe Frank denied knowledge of the murder, saying, "I know nothing about it and have no statement to make." He claimed he worked on the day that Timmerman was killed.

Sue and George visited him the next day at the jail. He then was transferred to the state penitentiary in Columbia. He decided to to tell the truth after he talked with his attorney, Edgefield state Sen. B. E. Nicholson III — whose father had once practiced law with Strom's father. After getting a pledge from Sheriff Allen to protect his wife and mother, Joe Frank gave and signed a full confession, telling the role of Sue and George.

The next morning, Sheriff Allen went unarmed with his deputy, W. L. Clark, to the Logue house to arrest his cousins. As they were entering the house, George Logue and Fred Dorn, the faithful sharecropper, ambushed them with gunfire. Bullets from Logue's pistol killed the sheriff and wounded Clark, who pulled his gun and wounded Logue in return. Although a blast from Dorn's shotgun sent him reeling, Clark was able to draw his pistol and fatally shoot Dorn. After Clark crawled outside, a passing motorist carried him to Edgefield. Although rushed to a hospital in Augusta, he soon died.

Word spread quickly in Edgefield as church was letting out, and by early afternoon several hundred people had converged around the Logue house. Many were armed — including a few Logue family friends who went inside as reinforcements. The Logues threatened that anyone who came in after them would be killed.

There are several versions of what happened next. One is that Judge Thurmond heard the news as he was leaving services at First Baptist Church, got in his car, and headed for the scene as he realized there was no other law enforcement in the county left to take charge.[5]

Charles Simons, later a law partner and confidante of Strom Thurmond before becoming a U. S. District Judge, was present at the scene. Then in his mid-twenties, he knew Deputy Clark as a fellow townsman from Johnston. Simons saw Thurmond walk onto the porch and heard someone inside yelling out, "Don't come in, Strom, or we'll have to kill you."

Thurmond removed his suit jacket, unbuttoned his vest, and turned his pants pockets inside out to demonstrate he was unarmed. Then he entered. He talked Sue into surrendering and escorted her out of the house. More than fifty-five years later, Simons said, "Now that takes guts!"[6]

Contemporary accounts pay tribute to Thurmond as a hero determined to prevent further bloodshed, saying that after going alone to the house and demonstrating on the porch that he was unarmed, he asked to speak to George and Sue Logue. A voice said that George had left the house and Sue was not feeling well. Thurmond insisted on speaking to her and finally was told to come to the back door. There he found himself facing a shotgun held by a Logue family friend. After talking his way inside, where he learned that George was gone and Dorn's body had been removed, he persuaded Sue to surrender. He escorted her safely through the hostile crowd outside.[7] Hortense Woodson would write that "Judge Thurmond was accorded widespread commendation for his courageous act."

Although these accounts allude to Thurmond knowing the Logues, the stories still whispered in Edgefield tell of Strom's long affair with Sue, who campaigned for him when he ran for county superintendent of education and whom he allowed to teach in the county schools despite unwritten rules generally excluding married women from teaching positions. Her reputation for sexual prowess was such that men told stories of her reputed vaginal muscular dexterity. The lore includes a tale of her and Strom found *flagrante delicto* in the superintendent's office.

Three weeks after Strom escorted Sue out of the farm house, the Japanese bombed Pearl Harbor. Judge Thurmond responded by sending a telegram the next day to President Roosevelt volunteering for active duty. Although a new state law would allow a leave of absence, as a judge he was exempt from military duty.

His political enemies later contended that he volunteered at least partly to get away from the sensational atmosphere of the Logue case, which was written up in April 1942 for *Official Detective Stories*. He had resigned from the Army Reserve in 1937, and his correspondence shows he expected to go on active duty soon after after war was declared. Whatever the timing with the Logue case, however, for Thurmond to volunteer immediately was consistent with his record as a man of action imbued with the tradition of Edgefield. He held a core belief that a people must be willing to defend freedom. His subsequent volunteering for the most dangerous type of combat duty clearly demonstrated his desire to be part of the fight.

By the time Thurmond got orders on April 8 to report to active duty as an Army captain, Clarence Bagwell, Sue Logue, and George Logue all had been convicted in Lexington County for the murder of Davis Timmerman, without recommendation of mercy. Joe Frank Logue testified as a key state witness.[8]

The state Supreme Court turned down their appeal, and all

three died in the electric chair on January 15, 1943. Sue Logue was the first woman ever electrocuted in South Carolina.

Randall Johnson, a black man who supervised "colored help" at the State House and often served as a driver and messenger, drove Sue from the women's penitentiary to the death house at the main penitentiary in Columbia. In the back seat with her, he said many years later, was Thurmond, then an Army officer on active duty. They were "a-huggin' and a-kissin' the whole way," said Johnson,[9] whom Thurmond later as governor considered a trusted driver.

Joe Frank Logue was tried separately soon after the electrocutions. An Edgefield County jury found him guilty, without recommendation of mercy. The Supreme Court denied his appeal. On the date of his scheduled electrocution, he had his head shaved, but an hour before time was to run out, Gov. Johnston commuted his sentence to life imprisonment.

Joe Frank worked for years as a trusty for the State Law Enforcement Division (SLED), training the bloodhounds and "running" them, achieving a lasting reputation for catching many runaway criminals and escaped convicts. He worked part of the time for O. L. Brady, the former chief of detectives who had arrested Clarence Bagwell (as governor in the late 1940s, Strom Thurmond appointed Brady chief of the state constabulary, the forerunner of SLED). Joe Frank's wife visited him on weekends at his cottage near the dog kennel, and he conducted Sunday morning religious services at a penal institution. He eventually received a parole, but briefly continued to work for SLED until a severe auto accident. Returning to his wife's home at Cross Anchor in Spartanburg County, he preached at several churches and sold automobiles and Bibles.[10]

In whispered "graveyard" talk — the kind of stories not to be told to outsiders — the word around SLED was that Joe Frank said his aunt Sue was the only person ever seduced on the way to the electric chair.[11]

1. Judge G. Duncan Bellinger, *State v. Joe Frank Logue,* order denying a new trial, October 25, 1943, p. 129, 104 S. C. 1H.
2. Alberta Lachicotte, *Rebel Senator,* Devin-Adair Company (New York, 1966), p. 6. Joseph Ellers, *Strom Thurmond,* supra, p. 65.

3. Joe Frank Logue transcript, pp. 50-51.

4. Jack Bass interview with a retired officer of the South Carolina State Law Enforcement Division (SLED), who had worked with Joe Frank Logue when he trained the bloodhounds for SLED after his sentence for electrocution was commuted.

5. Lachicotte, op. cit., p. 7.

6. Bass interview with Charles Simons, August 13, 1997.

7. Cohodas, op. cit., pp. 73-74.

8. The story of what happened not otherwise cited, including dialogue, is recreated from trial transcript, *State v. Joe Frank Logue*, 204 S. C. 171; *State v. Bagwell et al*, No. 15461, Supreme Court of South Carolina, November 9, 1942; and *State v. Logue*, No. 15613, Supreme Court of South Carolina, January 19, 1944.

9. Bass interview with Randal Johnson, Columbia, S. C., at home of Modjeska Simkins, circa 1980.

10. Bass telephone interviews with retired SLED agents, April 29, 1998.

11. Bass interview with confidential source, December, 1997.

Lt. Col. Thurmond receives the Bronze Star.

CHAPTER SEVEN

✛

D-Day

Three weeks after his rapid promotion from major, Lt. Col. James S. Thurmond climbed into glider No. 34 of the 82nd Airborne Division late in the afternoon of June 6, 1944. The initial wave of American infantry forces had waded ashore on the beaches of Normandy twelve hours earlier that day under withering fire from German defenders, and Thurmond was one of three officers from his civil affairs unit who volunteered to go in behind German lines on D-Day.

At 6:52 p.m. (1852 military time), tow planes moved the glider contingent out from Greenham's Common, an airfield near Newbury. It took more than an hour for the 150 or so motorless aircraft, each towed by a C-47, to form as a column in the air over England. They crossed the English Channel, passing the coastline of France above Utah Beach at 2100 (9 p.m.). They approached the point where the planes would break the tow lines and return to base, the motorless chaft gliding on with five paratroopers and a land vehicle ready to strike behind the German lines.

Minutes later the column came under anti-aircraft fire. The pilot of the lead plane delayed cutting his glider loose. Ground fire intensified, and the gliders were released over enemy territory deeper than planned.

Glider No. 34 headed for an apple orchard near St. Mere-Eglise, seeking cover at dusk from the leafy trees. The flimsy craft bounced from one apple tree to another, falling apart as it came to a halt.

Thurmond suffered cuts on both hands and another jagged

wound on a severely bruised left knee, yet he and the four paratroopers were able to walk out of the wreckage. He helped them release their jeep, then joined Maj. Bernard P. Deutsch, another civil affairs volunteer, whose glider had come down nearby. The men immediately came under enemy small-arms and mortar fire.

Deutsch and his crew set up a protected area for the wounded and injured. Thurmond borrowed a vehicle and surveyed other nearby gliders, assisting injured troops in getting to the assembly point. Thurmond and the men from his glider then set out to locate a 4th Infantry Division command post to effect a rendezvous point with American ground troops.

He soon radioed Deutsch that a tentative rendezvous had been established at a crossroads near Blosville. With directions from friendly civilians, they proceeded under less intense enemy fire, carrying the wounded in vehicles taken from the gliders. They remained surrounded by German forces, with small-arms fire continuing from all directions and shells falling in the vicinity as foxholes were dug in ditches and under hedges and trees. Patrols were set up to defend the position throughout the night.

Thurmond received medical treatment at an aid station, and a doctor suggested that he rest. The Edgefield man said he didn't want to rest, telling the medics just to put antiseptic on the wounds and bandage them.

The next morning they realized the enemy still surrounded them. At one point when Thurmond was walking beside him, an 82nd Airborne flight surgeon's head was blown off by a German shell. After establishing radio contact with Division Headquarters, which also was surrounded, Thurmond's detachment moved from one place to another throughout the day, constantly under fire and seeking the protection of ditches, hedges, and foxholes.

They moved into six different positions. At about 7 p.m. it was determined the detachment, loaded into six vehicles, could be saved only by somehow getting through to division headquarters. From there, an infantry patrol was dispatched to lead the detachment by secondary roads. Three times within a quarter of a mile, intense machine-gun fire from both sides of the road forced the column to stop. The men took cover in the ditches and returned fire.

Whenever enemy fire lessened or stopped, the column dashed on, reaching division headquarters shortly after 9 p.m. Although the enemy remained on all sides and snipers were abundant, friendly troops surrounded the division headquarters. The next morning, after the 82nd Airborne took control of the town of Cretteville, Thurmond and another officer entered the town, conferred with the mayor, and saw to the feeding and care of refugees. They held a ceremony to raise France's tricolor flag.

The remainder of Thurmond's civil affairs unit landed in France the next day. Their job was to assist in establishing local government to organize the region behind the Allied forces and to maintain law and order, but not to set up a military government in France.

On June 26, Thurmond and another officer slipped into the port city of Cherbourg to make arrangements for their civil affairs unit to move in. While riding in a jeep with a driver, they came upon and captured four German paratroopers.[1] Guarding them with their own pistols, Thurmond had two of the prisoners lay across the hood and the other two on the back seat.[2]

In a letter a couple of months later to a South Carolina friend, who released it to the Greenwood *Index-Journal*, Thurmond wrote there were "so many narrow escapes that it is a miracle to me that any of us who landed by glider are still alive."[3]

On November 28, 1944, he was awarded the Bronze Star "for heroic achievement in action" June 6-14. A two-column photo of Thurmond, wearing an infantryman's metal helmet and standing at attention while receiving the award, ran a month later on the front page of *The State*.[4]

Years later, when asked why he volunteered for such a dangerous assignment, he said, "I gave up my judgeship position temporarily to come into the war and fight, not just sit behind a desk."[5] Until D-Day, he had been chair-borne rather than air-borne, once getting a bit of notice for defending a private trying to recover $310 worth of seized furniture.[6]

Thurmond saw little additional direct combat action in Europe, but his unit accompanied combat troops, and he participated in the Battle of the Bulge. "It was rough," he remembered. "That's the coldest I have ever been in my life." On one occasion as he was walking down a street, he decide to cross to the other side. Moments later, a bomb fell where he had been walking.[7]

In April 1945, near the war's end in Europe, Thurmond's unit had crossed France and Belgium and entered Germany. He was near Liepzig when the first American troops entered the nearby Buchenwald concentration camp. Thurmond arrived shortly thereafter, totally unprepared for and astounded by what he witnessed.

More than a half-century later, he recalled, "Men were stacked up like cordwood, ten or twelve feet high. You couldn't tell whether they were living or dead. We thought nearly all were dead, but we found some still alive. So we had the medics come in and examine them, and some were found living and they received treatment. And some were saved. Most of them died.

"I found the Germans were killing these people in three different ways. One was to starve them to death. The only food they received was a bowl of thin pea soup once a day. They gradually starved them. And most of the people I saw, hundreds of them stacked up like cordwood, were killed that way.

"Another way that some of them were killed, agents of the Germans in charge suggested to them that they go down and cross the fence, that they might get out. And when they did, they'd shoot them and kill them.

"The third was a booth like a telephone booth, and they would have those people walk in the front of the booth. And there was a door in the rear of the booth where a big S.S. guard had a mallet. And when they came and sat down in that booth, they'd crush their head. I saw the mallet that was used and saw the blood splattered all over it.

"I had never seen such inhuman acts in my life. I couldn't dream of men treating men in such a manner. It was awful. And I was told that the wife of the commander there was fond of tattooing, and if anyone had tattooing on them, they'd take the tattooing off and enough skin with it, and she would make lamp shades out of it. I did not see those, but everything I saw was distressing. And when I look back upon it, I cannot realize now how cruel anyone could be in treating other people."

Although Thurmond had heard of death camps where people were gassed and had heard of the Buchenwald camp, he wasn't aware of what went on there. "I didn't dream of such terrible circumstances taking place," he said.

When asked the effect his first-hand experience with the Jewish Holocaust had on his political outlook and philosophy, he said, "It's very difficult to say what effect it has on anybody, but it's an experience you would never forget."[8]

Thurmond served a month in the Philippines as the war against Japan was winding down, but the chest full of medals he received came from his role in Europe. They included the Purple Heart, French Croix de Guerre, Belgian Order of the Crown, five battle stars, and a dozen other decorations in addition to the Bronze Star.

He also had been reelected in absentia by the South Carolina legislature to another term as judge.

Thurmond demonstrated on the battlefield the characteristics that would mark his political career. A man of bold action rather than reflection, he made swift and decisive tactical moves based on instinct and intuition. He never looked back, and he fought to win.

He later told a story of Secretary of State James F. Byrnes meeting Gen. George Patton in Europe and commending him on his legendary record of leading Allied forces there. When Byrnes said he must have done a fine job of planning, Patton replied, "No, I didn't plan it. [Omar] Bradley planned it. I executed it."

Byrnes said that Patton added, "I couldn't have planned it. I don't have that kind of brain. Bradley couldn't have executed it, either."

Thurmond admired Gen. Bradley, but he called Gen. Patton "probably the best we had because he was so aggressive."[9]

When he was discharged on October 19, 1945, at Fort Bragg, N. C., Thurmond seemed to have in mind the message his friend Bob Figg sent in a letter after reading about Strom's glider landing. Figg wrote, "You better get back to South Carolina and run for governor when the war is over!"[10] Thurmond got a ride from Ft. Bragg to South Carolina with Jules Brunson, later a physician in Camden, who remembered, "He told me then that he was going to run for governor, and we stopped at two or three places along the way for him to shake hands."[11]

A month later in Abbeville, Thurmond held his first term of court. Before leaving, he attended a local rally honoring veterans and ate barbecue.

1. Primary account from Civil Affairs Section II, *Civil Affairs Takes the Field*, Military Series, Box 4, "Civil Affairs 1943-1944, Special Collections, Clemson University Libraries, Clemson, S. C. Augmented by James Banks 1979 interview with Strom Thurmond, copy in possession of author, pp. 17-21.
2. Undated 1945 article from *The State*, interview with Lt. Col. Thurmond just before his release from active duty, after end of war.
3. Letter from Thurmond to J. F. Ouzts, printed in *Index-Journal*, September 14, 1944.

4. *The State*, December 28, 1944, p. 1.
5. Banks 1979 interview, p. 17.
6. *The Edgefield Advertiser*, June 17, 1942.
7. Banks 1979 interview with Thurmond, p. 19.
8. Dale Rosengarten and Ron J. Menchaca interview with Strom Thurmond, for Jewish Heritage Project, Charleston, S. C., October 11, 1996.
9. Banks 1979 interview, p. 21.
10. Thompson interview with Robert Figg, June 9, 1981.
11. Thompson interview with Jules Brunson, July 16, 1981.

CHAPTER EIGHT

✛

The Liberal Governor

Outwardly, the South Carolina Strom Thurmond returned to after the war looked the same. Segregation remained in place, but beneath the surface a developing nucleus of black leadership was emerging. It would use the federal courts to unlock the doors of political participation closed a half century earlier. The evolving politics of race would become a central element of Thurmond's career for the remainder of the century, but not immediately.

Politically, Sol Blatt and Edgar Brown had consolidated their power, with Blatt entrenched as Speaker of the House and Brown as powerful chairman of the Senate Finance Committee. This Barnwell Ring, as they came to be known, dominated the legislature. Brown and Blatt took care of Barnwell County, the state, and themselves. They also served respectively as trustees of Clemson and the University of South Carolina, where as patrons they were first among equals.

Barnwell County still had a second representative, Winchester Smith, and Blatt got him named chairman of the House Ways and Means Committee, from which the state appropriations bill starts its journey to determine who got what. Smith's brother, a tombstone rear admiral whose qualifications for the job seemed reflected by his campus nickname of "Snuffy," thereby became president of the University of South Carolina.

On a cold January evening in 1946, Blatt was celebrating at home with family and a handful of close friends to welcome Sol Jr. back from the war. As the dishes were cleared amid the sounds of laughter and reminiscing, Mr. Speaker rose to escort his guests to the living room. A knock on the door interrupted the conversation.

With the invited guests all present, an annoyed Blatt walked to the door wondering who might be calling. He opened it and there stood a smiling Strom Thurmond. "We invited him in, asked him to sit with us and have some of the food there or have some dessert," Blatt would recall. "He declined and sat there for a moment or two in the presence of all those people and said that he was going to run for governor and wanted my support. I told him how sorry I was, but I could not support him. And that made him mad, and then he told me, 'I'm going to Edgefield. I'm going home.' Well, I thought he'd gone and that was the end of it."

As Blatt strolled to his law office the next morning, the county sheriff alerted him that Thurmond was still in town and had gone to call on Edgar Brown. "Well, Sen. Brown told him the same thing. He wouldn't support him," Blatt remembered. "So he exploded and condemned us very severely and made the statement that he didn't want our votes. And I remember I made the statement, 'Who ever heard of a man coming to a home and visiting with people whose votes he didn't want?'"[1]

Blatt and Brown already had pledged their support to Gov. Ransome Williams, an uninspiring man elevated from lieutenant governor to fill an unexpired term. Olin Johnston, like Burnet Maybank before him, had left the governor's office at mid-term to run successfully for the Senate, Johnston defeating six-term octogenarian Ellison D. "Cotton Ed" Smith.

Thurmond also called newspaperman Harry Ashmore, then the new editorial page editor of *The Charlotte News*. Ashmore had covered the South Carolina legislature before the war, and Thurmond asked him to take a leave of absence and manage his campaign. "I politely said I didn't think I was ready to abandon the career I had started," Ashmore recalled. "I didn't say what I really thought, that he would really have been a bad choice for governor because of his sort of rigid, doctrinaire approach to any question that came up. And I thought politicians had to do some trading."[2]

Thurmond announced his candidacy on May 15, calling for "a progressive outlook, a progressive program and a progressive leadership." He proposed expanding and modernizing public schools and colleges, with better-paid teachers. He linked educational opportunity to economic expansion. He advocated better pay for working people and expanded programs "of public health, public welfare, and assistance to the aged, the blind, and our dependent children." Thurmond had returned from the war with his New Deal liberalism intact.

He entered an eleven-man race, a returning war hero with a solid record of public service. At the opening stump meeting on June 11 at Winnsboro, Thurmond heard another candidate charge that the state was being run by a "ring." Detecting the scent of its emotional appeal, Strom dropped in a line that South Carolina government "is under domination of a small ring of cunning, conniving men," and that's what the newspapers quoted.

By the time the corps of candidates reached Barnwell on June 25, Thurmond already was attacking the "Barnwell ring," declaring on June 19 at Conway he "would gladly accept the challenge of opposition from that crowd," and adding, "it will be interesting to see whom they lavish their money on in this race."

Six days later at Barnwell, Winchester Smith gave fifty dollars to gubernatorial candidate Roger Scott, a rural populist with a gift for barnyard invective whom a reporter once described as looking "like a man who stuck his finger in a light socket." Scott, who would precede Thurmond as speaker, was told to raise hell with the Barnwell ring, to take the edge off of Thurmond. When Smith congratulated him afterwards, Scott offered to do an even better job at the next stop in Allendale.[3]

Brown presided and had asked the crowd to give each speaker "a good hand, regardless of what he might say." Thurmond got booed, as expected, when he attacked "the ring and its henchmen" for blocking "reforms the people want." Thurmond continued to dominate media coverage, emerging as the courageous crusader against the "Barnwell ring." He then lured Blatt and Brown into a response.

Fellow candidate Marcus Stone, a lumberman from Florence who attempted to defend the Barnwell leaders, accepted a challenge from Thurmond to debate the "ring" issue. Stone then withdrew at the request of Blatt and Brown, but released letters from them asserting with pointed detail that Thurmond had sought their support before formally entering the race.

Thurmond called the letters "a lot of baloney," denied he had sought their support, and said they didn't want a debate "because they are scared of what I'll say." The voters would have to decide who to believe, a war hero and former judge or two men known only as powerful politicians.

Thurmond led the first primary — including ninety-two percent of the vote in Edgefield County, where he had campaigned as though making his first race for county superintendent. In the runoff, he attacked his opponent, Florence physician James McLeod, for being insufficiently supportive of President Roosevelt at the 1944 Democratic national convention. Thurmond won the runoff with almost fifty-six percent of the vote, 139,821 to 106,749, to become the first Edgefield governor since Pitchfork Ben Tillman.

The one outspokenly white supremacist candidate, state Sen. John Long of Union, received only six percent of the vote in the first primary. Thurmond made one bare mention of race, saying, "I will never sign a bill to mix the races." A brief Associated Press item on the first primary took note that "ten negroes voted in Spartanburg," despite Democratic Party rules limiting balloting to whites, and a smaller number attempting to vote in Columbia had been turned down. The story added that "South Carolina, alone of the southern states, bars negroes altogether from voting."[4]

In a profile of the governor-elect, the Associated Press reported, "His energy and determination amazes his associates. His campaign this summer was so arduous . . . he had to exchange drivers each week—so fast was the pace and hard did he strive to become governor."

When a distant relative of Thurmond's was asked during the campaign what job he would get, he replied, "If Strom's elected governor, I wouldn't work for the state of South Carolina for anything on earth. He would work me to death. He believes in working all the time, and he can't understand how other people don't have the same idea."[5]

A national A.P. story added that Thurmond "makes up with earnestness what he lacks in finesse. He is not a finished public speaker and appeared ill at easy in many of his campaign appearances."[6]

Three months after the runoff primary and during the week of his 44th birthday, Thurmond attended the Southern Governors Conference as a guest and promptly set off a lively discussion. When Thurmond asked the group to endorse American foreign policy as directed by Secretary of State Byrnes, the resolutions committee found it "not proper for its consideration."

In January with a raw wind blowing, Thurmond took his oath of office at a swearing-in ceremony in front of the State House, using the Bible he carried with him throughout World War II and standing beside his mother. A half-century later, his inaugural address stands out as a progressive and realistic assessment of the state's needs, a 15,000-word document of reform that set the direction of

South Carolina government for much of the next four decades.

Thurmond read a condensed version. Like many of his best speeches, it reflected the fine craftsmanship, thoughtful knowledge of government, and first-rate mind of its draftsman, Robert Figg. Later named dean of the University of South Carolina Law School after arguing before the U. S. Supreme Court the state's losing case for maintaining segregated schools, Figg advised a succession of governors.

After declaring, "We are on the threshold of a new era," the liberal new governor called for ending the poll tax and developing a system of permanent voter registration. He advocated a state minimum wage (one of his few proposals never adopted), stronger child labor laws, and "working conditions which make for health, decency and the welfare of our workers," including temperature controls and cafeterias in textile mills.

He proposed an eight-point educational program that included free textbooks and expanded vocational education. He advocated "federal aid for education, with the proviso that states maintain control of the schools."

In calling for "more attention given to Negro education," Thurmond asserted, "The low standing of South Carolina, educationally, is due primarily to the high rate of illiteracy and lack of education among our Negroes. If we provide better educational facilities for them, not only will much be accomplished in human values, but we shall raise our per capita income as well as the educational standing of the state."

He called for reorganizing and consolidating the state's unwieldy system of overlapping state agencies. He proposed a commission of top lawyers to revise the outdated state constitution and submit changes as constitutional amendments on which the public would vote. He advocated a system of county governments and urged enforcing the existing state constitutional ban on dual office-holding.[i]

He called for industrial development, protection of natural resources from polluters, control by laymen of the State Board of Health, free treatment for sufferers of venereal diseases, and mandatory premarital blood tests.

He called for $5 million in increased liquor license fees and taxes and proposed a ban on all liquor advertising. He added that

---

i. Thurmond won the fight to end dual office-holding. One way it worked in practice was that Blatt gave up his seat on the U.S.C. Board of Trustees, but not his voice. He was replaced by Sol Blatt, Jr. Clemson got a system in which the legislature named part of the board, which then elected a group of "life trustees," one of whom happened to be Edgar Brown.

if the legislature had a better plan, "I will sign it."

Blatt stepped aside as Speaker, and Thurmond ignored tradition — actively supporting Bruce Littlejohn of Spartanburg in a spirited campaign against Tom Pope of Newberry. Littlejohn won.

Less than a month after taking office, Thurmond got a call from the city editor of the *The Greenville Piedmont*, telling him that a black man accused of murdering a white taxi driver had been taken from jail by a mob of white men and killed. There had been no lynching in the state for fourteen years, and Thurmond's call for vigorous prosecution resulted in state and local police working with F.B.I. agents.

Willie Earle had been arrested after the fatal stabbing and robbery of Greenville taxi driver Thomas W. Brown. A deputy sheriff followed clearly outlined shoe tracks from the abandoned taxi to the dying Brown, then on to the home of Earle's mother in the Pickens County town of Liberty, twelve miles from Greenville.

The deputy discovered a recently washed Scout's knife with blood stains in Earle's pocket, blood stains on a freshly washed jacket. The twenty-four-year-old Willie Earle "fit . . . perfectly" the description of the assailant Brown gave during a brief period of consciousness before dying at a hospital. Earle's mother said her son had come home drunk and told her that he had come by bus.

After Earle's arrest on a Sunday night, eight taxis and another automobile assembled at about 4:30 a.m. on a bridge near Greenville, then took off for the Pickens County jail. More than thirty men woke the jailer, one of them pointing a shotgun at him, and demanded he turn over the Negro.

The concerted police-F.B.I. investigation resulted in the arrest of thirty-one men, twenty-six of whom made confessions, some naming the individuals who slashed and tortured Willie Earle and then shot him to death with a shotgun as he lay on the ground.

One confessor told of arriving at the scene after Earle had been driven down a country road, apparently placed on the ground, "and I could hear licks like they were pounding on him with the butt end of a gun. I also heard the Negro say, 'Lord, you done killed me.' Then I saw Herd aim the single-shot shotgun toward the ground in the direction of where I judged the Negro was lying, and pull the trigger." The confessor added that prior to the shot he heard another man say, "Don't beat that nigger with that gun and get blood on it."

In addition to Greenville Solicitor Robert Ashmore (editor Harry Ashmore's cousin and later a congressman) Thurmond brought in Solicitor Sam Watt of Spartanburg, a prosecutor who had convicted 471 of 473 persons brought to trial the previous year. "We in South Carolina want the world to know we will tolerate no mob violence," the governor said.[7]

Thurmond got many letters of support. James McBride Dabbs, South Carolina's poet-philosopher who would serve as president of the biracial Southern Regional Council, wrote, "We who look to the future are proud to follow your leadership."[8]

With thirty-one white defendants, it was the biggest lynching trial in the nation's history. Presiding was state Circuit Judge J. Robert Martin, at thirty-eight already known for his no-nonsense toughness.

None of the defendants testified before the all-white male jury composed of textile workers, a farmer, a mechanic, a salesman, and a divinity student. In charging the jury, Judge Martin told them "not to allow any so-called racial issues to enter" into their deliberations. He had already dismissed charges against several defendants. After seven hours of deliberation, the jury acquitted the remaining twenty-eight.

Martin turned his back to the jurors and dismissed them without thanks. Then he slammed his Panama hat on his head and stormed out of the courtroom.

The Atlanta Journal termed the outcome "a ghastly farce," but acknowledged that mob murders of blacks the previous year in Georgia's Walton County "were never brought to even the semblance of a court trial."[9]

The New York Times said in an editorial that the outcome "hurts the United States" as the story is told abroad. The editorial pointed out that Thurmond and other officials "did their utmost to bring Earle's slayers to justice" and that they received support from local press and ministers "and a strong body of public opinion throughout South Carolina."

The editorial concluded, "There has been a victory for law, even though Willie Earle's slayers will not be punished for what they did. A precedent has been set. Members of lynching mobs may now know that they do not bask in universal approval, even in their own disgraced communities, and they may begin to fear that some day, on sufficient evidence and with sufficient courage, a Southern lynching case jury will convict."[10]

In response to a letter, Thurmond asserted, "I think great good was accomplished by having the accused arrested and tried even though the jury acquitted them. I believe that position will assist in the future in preventing lynchings."[11] No lynchings subsequently occurred in South Carolina.

Roughly half of Thurmond's ambitious program passed the legislature, but insiders were giving far more attention to a pair of federal lawsuits, one aimed at desegregating the University of South Carolina law school and the other to end the all-white Democratic primary.

In the 1944 Texas case of *Smith v. Allwright*, decided while Thurmond was preparing for D-Day, the U. S. Supreme Court ruled the white primary unconstitutional. South Carolina responded by repealing all its election laws, a legal ruse to convert the Democratic primary into a "voluntary association" over which the state ostensibly had no control.

Meanwhile, the scattered few local chapters of the National Association for the Advancement of Colored People in the state had organized a statewide conference of branches. The NAACP developed strong leadership and would emerge as the state's dominant civil rights organization. The national organization sent in its first-rate legal team, headed by Thurgood Marshall.

He found a sympathetic federal judge in eighth-generation Charlestonian J. Waties Waring. A former white supremacist who changed his mind,[ii] he began following the Supreme Court's new direction with gusto.

On July 12, 1947, he issued rulings in both the law school and the voting rights cases. Plans had already been made to open a law school in September at all-black South Carolina State College, and Waring accepted the state's argument. Although four law professors were hired by September, plaintiff John Wrighten refused to enroll until the following year, when a law school building and library were provided.

In the voting case brought by George Elmore, a Columbia taxi driver/businessman turned away from the polls in 1946, Marshall argued that the repeal of state primary laws made "no difference"

ii. Waring's social equals in Charleston blamed his conversion on civil rights to his marrying a liberal Yankee after divorcing his first wife. His biographer, Tinsley Yarbrough, attributes Judge Waring's developing sense of racial injustice as flowing from his experience in the Isaac Woodward case. Woodward, a World War II veteran returning to his wife in Winnsboro in February 1946 after his discharge as an Army sergeant, was arrested in Batesburg after exchanging harsh words with a bus driver in a dispute arising from Woodward's need to use a restroom. He was knocked unconscious with a billy club, then punched in the eyes, leaving him permanently blinded. After charges brought by U. S. Attorney General Tom Clark, Waring presided over the trial of the police chief who administered the beating. An all-white jury deliberated only 30 minutes before finding him innocent. The Woodward case played a key role in President Truman's decision to appoint his President's Committee on Civil Rights. (See Kari Frederickson, "'The Slowest State' and 'Most Backward Community': Racial Violence in South Carolina and Federal Civil-Rights Legislation, 1946-1948," South Carolina Historical Magazine," April 1997, p. 184.)

because the Democratic Party was still "exercising a governmental function." Waring agreed, naming other Deep South states that allowed blacks to vote in primaries.

"I cannot see where the skies will fall if South Carolina is put in the same class with these and other states," he declared. "It is time for South Carolina to rejoin the Union. . . . all citizens of this State and Country are entitled to cast a free and untrammeled ballot in our elections."

Thurmond, in Salt Lake City to deliver a National Governors Conference speech on military preparedness, avoided comment on the voting rights case. He met the next month, however, with a group of blacks — including state NAACP leader James M. Hinton and political activist John McCray, editor of *The Lighthouse and Informer* in Columbia — to talk about improving conditions at the John G. Richards Industrial Training School for Negro Boys, an institution for juvenile offenders. Thurmond said afterwards their proposals had merit.

In September he outraged realtors in the state by declaring, in a speech officially welcoming delegates to a regional convention, his support for rent controls and denouncing "profiteering real estate owners" who withdrew rental units and sold them "ridiculously and exorbitantly overpriced." The president of the National Association of Real Estate Boards retorted that Thurmond's speech sounded like a release from "the international office of the Communist party." Thurmond replied, "I said what I meant. I meant what I said."[12]

October 1947 would become a time of transition for Thurmond, politically and personally. He participated in a panel discussion on October 2, 1947, in Louisville, Kentucky. and delivered a short radio speech entitled "Let's Look at '48." What he said reflected a philosophical peak from which he would rapidly descend. He asserted that the "ineptitude of the Republican leadership in the present Congress" provided a timely warning to the American people "not to trust their economic future to the tender mercies of the Republican Party."

Thurmond concluded by declaring, "We who believe in a liberal political philosophy, in the importance of human rights as well as property rights, in the preservation and strengthening of the economic and social gains brought about by the efforts of the Democratic Party . . . will vote for the election of Harry Truman and the restoration of Congress to the control of the Democratic Party, and I believe we will win."[13]

Later in the month, the President's Committee on Civil Rights issued a report, "To Secure These Rights." It chronicled the nation's tragic history of civil rights. It called for federal laws against lynching, against discrimination in employment and voting, and legislation to end the poll tax. It called for strengthening the civil rights division in the Justice Department to enforce such legislation. Politically, it proposed undoing the Compromise of 1876, which had tacitly agreed to the states having control of issues involving race. Several months would pass before President Truman responded. In reaction, Strom Thurmond would make a backward somersault with a reverse twist.

But matters of the heart would take immediate priority.

1. Thompson interview with Solomon Blatt, June 1981.
2. Ashmore interview, op. cit.
3. Bass interview with John C. West, Hilton Head Island, January 2, 1998.
4. *The News and Courier*, July 24, 1946, p. 1. Associated Press, Columbia dateline, August 13, 1946.
5. *The State*, September 8, 1946.
6. *The Sun*, Baltimore, Maryland, December 8, 1946.
7. *The New York Herald Tribune*, April 20, 1947, p. 1. Article by reporter Earl Mazo, who had grown up in South Carolina.
8. James McBride Dabbs letter to Strom Thurmond, February 22, 1947, Strom Thurmond gubernatorial papers, Clemson University Special Collections.
9. *The Atlanta Journal*, May 23, 1947.
10. *The New York Times*, May 23, 1947.
11. Cohodas, op. cit., p. 112.
12. *The Anderson Independent*, September 16, 1947.
13. "Let's Look at '48," address by J. Strom Thurmond at panel discussion over radio station WHAS, Memorial Auditorium, Louisville, Kentucky, October 2, 1947. Special Collections, Robert Muldrow Cooper Library, Clemson University.

CHAPTER NINE

✟

Jean Crouch

Strom first met Jean Crouch in the fall of 1941 when her father, Horace, took her high school class to observe a session of Judge Thurmond presiding at the Barnwell County courthouse. Her father, a cog in Barnwell's Democratic political organization as elected county superintendent of education and a native of Edgefield County, called his daughter up to meet the judge. Strom told Jean she had "pretty eyes," and she never forgot it. She was fifteen.

A blue-eyed tomboy and captain of the Williston-Elko girls basketball team, she was class valedictorian and winner of the Solomon Blatt Medal for Expression before heading off to college at Winthrop. Strom next saw her there briefly in the spring of 1946, when he came to a college function.

That fall, as governor-elect, he visited Horace Crouch at his home in the village of Elko to talk about state educational problems. Spotting a portrait of a strikingly attractive young woman with dark, silken hair and deep-set eyes, he casually asked who it was. "That's my daughter, Jean, whom you met some years back at court in Barnwell," Crouch said. "She's a senior at Winthrop."

Thurmond learned she was studying commerce (a major designed to train young women in secretarial skills, as careers or for teaching them to high school students) and wondered if she might like to work in the governor's office. He was told she would be visiting Columbia for an education meeting. "Maybe you can talk with her then," her father said.

Thurmond made it a point to address the coordinating council of the South Carolina Education Association. Jean, Winthrop's senior class president, was among a group of college students on the program. She planned to teach the next year in Sumter, forty-five miles east of Columbia.

She was asked that day to consider working awhile for the new governor. She soon received a "Glad-to-have-seen-you" postcard sent from the Southern Governors Conference in Miami, which Thurmond as governor-elect attended as a guest.

Thurmond, his boyhood political ambition achieved despite a confirmed reputation as a skirt-chaser, realized a wife would now be a political asset. At forty-four, he felt it time to start a family. The only issue was finding the right woman. As a soldier he had sat awake at night, pondering whether marriage would enhance his aspiration to be governor. He sensed something special about this girl with the pretty eyes. That she was less than half his age bothered him not at all.

His moment of glory, inauguration as governor on the State House steps on January 21, was coming up when Strom cooked up a scheme to lure Jean there to witness it. He called Henry Sims, president of Winthrop. As Thurmond related it, "I told President Sims to send a group of seniors down here if he wanted to, and we would take care of them at the inauguration. And I said, 'You might send the president of the senior class and some representatives.' He didn't know that I kind of had my eye on the president of the senior class."[1]

Thurmond said it would be "a nice experience" for the young women, and Sims conveniently agreed it was "a fine idea." A month after that trip, another carload of Winthrop girls drove down from the campus in Rock Hill to attend an event in Columbia and visit the governor's office, Jean Crouch again among them. Governor Thurmond learned from an aide that she was there and invited her to have lunch at the mansion with his sister, Gertrude — whom he had installed as official hostess — and himself.

Jean hastily accepted, before any of the other girls could blurt that she had already eaten lunch. After forcing herself to eat a raw oyster cocktail — she despised oysters — she then ate a full-course meal while silently praying for digestive peace. When the other girls teased her on the return trip to Winthrop, Jean smiled blandly and said nothing.

In March, Thurmond invited her to the American Legion horse races in Columbia, specifying, "Bring along a friend, a girl friend." Strom used the occasion to appoint Jean Crouch to serve as the host Miss South Carolina for Charleston's annual Azalea Festival in April. The governor was there to crown the Queen of the Azalea Festival. He planted the usual kiss on the queen, and kissed Miss South Carolina for good measure. She beamed — and made a mental note about governors crowning beauty queens. He saw her several times on official trips to Winthrop, a college now getting more attention than usual from a governor.

With his interest quickened, the governor explained to Jean that a position in the governor's office automatically limited personnel to purely official relationships, and he offered to place her in a state agency job. Jean retorted, "What are you hunting, a secretary or a playmate?"

He told her, "Come on down. We'll expect you."

She thought it over and announced acceptance of a secretarial vacancy on his staff. Thurmond accepted it as indifference toward him. She later explained to him, "I knew if you saw me every day you couldn't forget me."

She reported to work on July 1, two weeks before her twenty-first birthday. She soon was asked to join Wilma Smith as the second secretary in an entourage to accompany Thurmond to the National Governors Conference in Salt Lake City.

After Jean had sat in her room typing a speech while the governor and a bachelor aide escorted the attractive daughters of Gov. Earl Warren of California to a rodeo, she teased him the next day about his date. Thurmond sensed her irritation — and that she was interested in him after all. That night they sat and talked for two hours. It marked a turning point in the relationship.

Wilma Smith, who had adored Strom Thurmond since he taught her seventh-grade class at Ridge Spring, remembered that the conference had planned "all these things for the ladies to do while the men were in meetings. But Jean did not go to a single thing for the ladies. She just stuck with Strom."[2]

The office staff no doubt noticed that the governor soon decided it was dangerous for Jean to walk the three blocks from the State House to the apartment she shared with two former classmates. He frequently arranged his schedule to be free to offer her a ride to her door. Finally, she told him that her "boy friends" found the competition a bit stiff, that if he really liked her, that was one thing, otherwise no more rides home.

Taken aback, Strom mumbled something about their both knowing soon what they should do. On September 9 Jean confirmed in a letter to her parents her and Strom's informal but definite under-standing that they would marry. She wrote that they would be dri-ving to Elko Saturday night:

I suppose you all know we're really serious now. We've thought and thought about it. We know what we want. He'll always be so good and kind to me, so we're going to do what will make us happy for always. Please don't think for a minute that I'm swept off my feet 'cause I know what I'm getting into. He's Governor now, but that will last only three years. Marriage will last a lifetime. . . . He doesn't know I've written you all this—he just said let's go down Saturday and talk to my folks. . . . Please think hard and realize that I'd always regret not marrying him 'cause he'll always love me to death just as I do him.

On Saturday, Strom made his proposal formal by calling Jean in after lunch so he could dictate a letter for her to type. Written to "My Darling Jean," and with a touch of his dry humor, it began:

You have proved to be a most efficient and capable secretary, and the high caliber of your work has impressed me very much. It is with a deep sense of regret that I will have to inform you that your services will be discontinued as of the last day of this month.

. . . you can serve humanity best, perform duties that will be more worthwhile to the State, and most especially make the Governor happier, in the new duties which I desire you to undertake.

. . . I must confess I love you dearly and want you for my own. I didn't realize that a girl could attach herself so to a man and could 'twine herself around his heartstrings as you have done. It seems to have been no special effort heretofore to fight off love, but in your case, I have made a complete failure in the attempt and frankly admit that your charms have won me — heart and soul. . . .

Anticipating an early reply and hope that it shall be forthcom-ing as quickly as possible as upon your answer will depend my future happiness.

Again assuring you of my deep love and expressing the hope that the time is not too distant when we can be joined as one and live happily forever.

Jean closed her shorthand pad and left, soon returning with the letter neatly typed for signature. The governor read it and looked fondly but firmly. "I didn't say 'twine herself,'" he said with feigned seriousness. "I said 'entwine herself.' Please fix that.'"[3]

With no change of expression, Jean departed. She let the governor cool his heels until the end of the day, then handed him the corrected letter. And her typed acceptance: "My dearest Strom, Yes! My love always, Jean."

Strom, the fearless hero at Normandy, fidgeted nervously that night as Horace and Inez Crouch listened with masterly evasion. The age difference bothered them, and Mrs. Crouch suggested that they wait awhile and get to know each other better, but Strom insisted they knew each other well enough. Finally, he said, "Well, as long as you haven't voiced any objections, I'll conclude that at least you don't object."[4]

Before formal announcement of their engagement, *The State* ran a three-column front-page photo of the pair seated together in the governor's box at Carolina Stadium for a football game. A headline over the photo stated, "The Governor Takes a Pretty Girl to the Game."[5]

The press quickly fell in love with Jean. "This striking young lady is a tall brunette with laughing blue eyes and an infectious smile that gives her an unaffected charm," the A. P. wrote in a typical dispatch. "South Carolinians will find their new First Lady, though youthful, poised and intelligent as well as pretty and talented."[6]

After a November wedding in the governor's mansion and a two-week honeymoon in Miami and Havana, they returned to view unhappily the coverage given by *Life* magazine. Its three-page spread included a full-page shot taken the day before the ceremony of Thurmond clad in tennis shorts standing on his head. In the background leaning on a bicycle was a smiling and shapely Jean, dressed in shorts and a sweater.

The caption read, "VIRILE GOVERNOR demonstrates his prowess in the mansion yard day before wedding. He asked the photographer to feel his muscles and observed, 'Why, I can stand on my head,' and promptly proved it. Then the Governor noticed his fiancee's sweater and commented, 'If I could look that good in a sweater, maybe I'd put one on!'" The entire state clucked over "Strom standing on his head," and the photo would come back to haunt him politically.

Thurmond meanwhile issued a public invitation for the entire state of South Carolina to come to meet their new First Lady at a Sunday afternoon reception at the mansion. Between 5,000 and 10,000 people showed up, some driving several hours, to wait in a line that sometimes extended for five blocks. Most were visiting the governor's mansion for the first time. Jean, clad in her flowing ivory wedding gown beside Strom, greeted them at the door.

Jean would charm South Carolinians skeptical about the age difference. She quickly learned protocol and management skills for running the social operation at the governor's mansion. She filled an inner void, making Thurmond more whole. She bought new clothes that made him look more dignified. She put an end to his crowning beauty queens.

Together, they rode horseback, swam, and played tennis. She intuitively assessed the strengths and weaknesses of his staff, served as a sounding board, and gave sound political advice. She displayed poise, mature judgment, and a gracious charm — the rare kind of woman who seems to radiate an inner beauty and strength.

On New Year's Eve, Strom in a gesture of love conveyed to Jean two tracts of real estate worth $20,000, the equivalent of almost two years of a governor's salary, "in order that you may have some income of your own." It included two filling stations rented to Gulf Oil and two dwelling houses. In a letter, he expressed hope "that you can keep it rented on a satisfactory basis."[7]

Early in 1948, Strom invited the twenty-four-year-old rookie Columbia bureau chief for United Press to the mansion for lunch. Gene Patterson, who would succeed the fabled Ralph McGill as editor of *The Atlanta Constitution*, vividly remembered Jean making him feel welcome. "She kept up a playful whispered commentary to me about Strom, who looked more like her father than her husband," Patterson remembered half a century later.

"'Have you noticed he wears the same color tie every day?' she asked. I had not. The tie was a plain one, without figures, in a shade between red and maroon. 'It goes with whatever suit he decides to wear,' Jean said, 'so he sees no need to complicate the matter.'

"Later she giggled as the governor started squeezing lemon on his fish filet. 'He loves lemon, but watch his face,' she whispered. Sure enough, Strom licked the lemon slice and the astringency of the thing caused his face to draw up and pucker into a comical grimace. 'He looks just like a big old baby when his face does that,' Jean laughed."[8]

✢ ✢ ✢

1. Thompson interview with Thurmond, op cit.
2. Thompson interview with Wilma Smith, circa 1980.
3. *Saturday Evening Post*, October 5, 1955, p. 121.
4. Most of the material in this chapter not otherwise credited comes from: Alberta Lachicotte, *Rebel Senator*, pp. 10-29.
5. *The State*, October 12, 1947, p. 1.
6. Associated Press, October 16, 1947.
7. Strom Thurmond/Jean letters, Special Collections, Clemson University.
8. Eugene Patterson letter to the author, February 14, 1998.

TIME

THE WEEKLY NEWSMAGAZINE

THE DIXIECRATS' J. STROM THURMOND
Is the issue black and white?

Strom thunders Dixie's message, 1948.

CHAPTER TEN

+

Dixiecrat

For decades, a favorite item on the breakfast menu at Cogburn's Grill in Columbia was the Dixiecrat — link sausage wrapped with a slice of plain white bread. A *Charlotte News* headline writer coined the term for the States Rights Democratic Party, Strom Thurmond's presidential vehicle in 1948.

The campaign transformed Thurmond's image from progressive governor of South Carolina to reactionary national champion of white supremacy. Thurmond forever denied that he had run a racist campaign.

"When I ran for president as a States Righter," he explained in 1980, "some people considered that a racist fight. But it wasn't that. They misconstrued the whole thing. It was a battle of federal power versus state power. That was my fight. That was the way I viewed it."[1]

Here's what he said in a nationwide radio hook-up on the eve of his defeat by Harry Truman: "Don't forget that the so-called civil rights program would bring about the end of segregation in the South, forcing mixing of the races in our hotels, in our restaurants, in our schools, in our swimming pools, and in all public places. This change in our customs is not desired by either the white or the colored race.

"To bring all this about, the federal government would set up a super-police force with power to rove throughout the states and keep our people in constant fear of being sent to a federal jail unless we accepted the decrees turned out by a bunch of anti-Southern bureaucrats in Washington."[2] The rhetoric during the campaign had been even stronger. It would take three decades for Thurmond's image to begin to recover.

Southern progressives lost a champion they could have used. Thurmond had never before exploited racial politics. Until 1948 the term "States Rights" barely existed in his political vocabulary. His leadership in prosecuting the white mob that murdered Willie Earle, his ultimately successful effort to repeal a state poll tax, and his concern about improving educational and economic opportunities for blacks provided a foundation for leading his state and region into an era of new racial relationships. Had he continued in that direction, a man of his political skill, determination, and energy might well have pulled it off.

Instead, he helped generate forces that over the next half century moved his state, his region, and his country in a different direction. The role of defending white supremacy was one he chose. One interpretation is that he reacted viscerally to his internalized Edgefield County heritage, hearing again the echoing hooves of the Redshirts. Another is that for his all his talk of constitutional principles and "States Rights," Thurmond acts on the basis of politics. Here, principle and expediency may simply have melded.

A governor could not then succeed himself in South Carolina (Olin Johnston was elected twice, but not in succession), and any political future for Thurmond meant a seat in the U.S. Senate. Johnston and Burnet Maybank both had run successfully for the Senate at mid-term as governor, Johnston defeating decrepit "Cotton Ed" Smith and Maybank taking the seat vacated when President Roosevelt appointed James F. Byrnes to the Supreme Court.[i]

Despite press speculation that he might run in 1948 against Maybank, Thurmond had pledged during his gubernatorial campaign to serve a full term, and his eye clearly was on Johnston, who would be up for reelection in 1950. As a champion of organized labor, Olin D. would be a target for fiscal conservatives. Johnston as governor called the special legislative session in 1944 that repealed the primary election laws to keep blacks from participating in the Democratic primary. His championing of white supremacy helped win him a Senate seat that year.

---

i. Byrnes subsequently resigned from the court to become director of the Office of War Mobilization in the White House under Roosevelt. Roosevelt rejected him as running mate in 1944, at least in part because of opposition from organized labor. President Truman appointed Byrnes secretary of state, then fired him. He returned home to South Carolina in 1950 as the state's honored elder statesman and was elected governor. He deftly demonstrated his bitterness toward the national Democrats by inviting and introducing Republican presidential nominee Dwight Eisenhower at a huge State House rally in 1952, then supported Thurmond's write-in bid for the Senate in 1954.

Although Thurmond was eyeing the Senate, he also was responding to events. In his words, "I did not run for president just to get in line for the Senate. I ran for president because I felt very deeply that Truman would not represent what I felt was the best type of government for this country. I ran to give people a choice."[3] He would add that he defended segregation as law and custom, and "it was the thinking of the people I represented."[4]

After Judge Waring struck down the white primary in the summer of 1947, U. S. District Judge George Bell Timmerman, Sr., Thurmond's old opponent and then the father of Thurmond's lieutenant governor, issued a stay order. But a three-judge panel of the Fourth Circuit Court of Appeals in Richmond unanimously upheld Waring. On December 30, 1947, Chief Judge John J. Parker wrote for the court, "No election machinery can be upheld if its purpose or effect is to deny the Negro, on account of his race or color, an effective voice in the government of his country or the state or the community where he lives."[5]

In the ensuing months, Thurmond supported the state Democratic Party efforts to somehow discourage blacks from voting — the next stratagem was a loyalty oath that required voters to pledge fealty to white supremacy. Eugene Patterson reported it all for United Press. Much to the surprise of Associated Press veteran Alderman Duncan, Patterson's dispatches included quotes from the NAACP's James M. Hinton and activist editor John McCray, leaders of the virtually all-black Progressive Democrats.

Duncan, a tall South Carolinian with big blue eyes and an affinity for Panama hats, walked up the three flights of a downtown building to Patterson's U.P. office. Winded, he put one foot on the window sill, pushed back his hat, and stared for a moment at his youthful rival. He said he'd noticed Patterson was quoting Negroes and was curious as to why.

Patterson told him he'd been taught to cover both sides of any story and guessed he would go right on, no matter what A.P. did. Duncan took his foot down, stood erect, and looked at Patterson with genuine puzzlement. Finally, he said, "Gene, do you think niggers should vote?"

"Yes, Dunc," Patterson said, "I guess I do." Duncan shook his head and walked out. To Patterson he looked thunderstruck.[6]

This political context existed in South Carolina when President Truman finally responded to the 1947 report of the President's Committee on Civil Rights, "To Secure These Rights." Thurmond was like a man wading into a wide, sloping channel separating two islands. As the water rose above his neck, he finally started swimming. Once on the other side, he never returned.

On January 7, 1948, Truman promised in his annual address to Congress to present a comprehensive civil rights program. Two months earlier, presidential advisor Clark Clifford had presented him a strategic political memo, "The Politics of 1948." He predicted Truman would face two opponents, former Vice President Henry Wallace as a liberal third-party challenger and New York Gov. Thomas E. Dewey as the Republican nominee. The outcome would be decided, Clifford wrote, by the urban black vote in four states — California, Illinois, New York, and Ohio.

To cut the loss of liberals to Wallace and to rally black voters, Clifford recommended a civil rights package to Truman. He dismissed as "inconceivable" any possibility of a Southern revolt, explaining, "As always, the South can be considered safely Democratic. And in forming national policy can be safely ignored."[7] Later, after Thurmond raised the Dixiecrat banner and the president issued an executive order to desegregate the military services, Clifford wrote in a shrewd subsequent memo to Truman, "The Negro votes in the crucial states will more than cancel out any votes the President may lose in the South."[8]

A week after Truman's State of the Union address, Thurmond outlined his progressive second-year program to the General Assembly of South Carolina. He made only a brief reference to Truman's remarks.

Two weeks later, however, 48 of the 170 Democrats in the one-party legislature denounced the national Democratic Party's advocacy of "ideas flagrantly repugnant to the South." In a letter to state Democratic Chairman William P. "Bill" Baskin, they suggested it was time to "reconsider our position in the national party."[9]

Truman delivered his civil rights program to Congress on February 2. He proposed eliminating the poll tax, making lynching a federal offense, ending segregation in interstate commerce, and creating a statutory Fair Employment Practices Commission (FEPC). "The protection of civil rights is the duty of every government which derives its powers from the consent of the people," the president said.[10]

Thurmond's initial response was guarded. Congressman Bryan Dorn demanded that Southern governors "march on Washington," but Thurmond wired support for "holding the line as far as . . . possible" in resisting all efforts "to invalidate the practices, customs and institutions which we in South Carolina cherish."

In contrast, Sen. Richard Russell of Georgia compared the president's ordering the F.B.I. to work with the Civil Rights Division of the Justice Department to the "Gestapo" of Nazi Germany.

At a special session of the Southern Governors Conference the next week in Wakulla Springs, Florida, the strongest castigation of Truman came from Govs. Ben Laney of Arkansas and Fielding Wright of Mississippi. Wright had already declared to the people of his state that "vital principles and eternal truths transcend party lines" and that drastic action might be necessary to protect "our institutions and our way of life."[11]

Thurmond's rhetoric intensified. "The people of the states represented by the members of this conference have been shocked by the spectacle of the political parties of this country engaging in competitive bidding for the votes of small pressure groups by attacking the traditions, customs and institutions of the section in which we live," Thurmond asserted in a conference speech. "They talk about breaking down the laws which knowledge and experience of many years have proven to be essential to the protection of the racial integrity and purity of the white and Negro races alike. . . . Their sudden removal would jeopardize the peace and good order which prevail where the two races live side by side in large numbers."[12]

Thurmond proposed challenging Truman through the electoral college, the system by which each state is allotted electoral votes equal to its representation in Congress, and a presidential candidate must win a majority to get elected.

Thurmond also authored a resolution to reconvene in forty days, during which a special committee would recommend "joint and common action." It demanded that Truman's proposals not be included in the party platform. Thurmond was named chairman.

But many others thought the issue should be fought within the Democratic Party. For example, Georgia Gov. M. E. Thompson called Truman's program "unnecessary," but declared that "for the South to bolt the Democratic Party would be even more unwise."[13]

Elsewhere, the heat was rising. On February 12 in Jackson, Mississippi, some 4,000 political leaders from all eighty-two counties in the state unfurled the Confederate battle flag, sang Dixie, and sent rebel yells echoing as they adopted a resolution charging that Truman's program "intrudes into the sacred rights of the state." The resolution called for the South to withhold, if necessary, its electoral votes in the presidential election. Mississippi's newly elected senator, John Stennis, cautiously urged that the fight be kept within the Democratic Party, but in that frenzied atmosphere, he was politely ignored.

The same day the Mississippians were whooping it up, the House of Representatives in South Carolina's General Assembly unanimously adopted a resolution condemning Truman's civil rights proposals as "un-American."

A week later, on February 19, Thurmond's executive assistant in the governor's office, William Lowndes Daniel, encouraged him in a memo to consider "the opportunity" of becoming the South's leader in the segregation fight. "Please do not discount your own ability during this wrangle," wrote Daniel, who at thirty-seven had served as an Army colonel. "I shall be glad to help put you to the front at the opportune moment, if it presents itself. Others will join in a big way. I know that you will be hesitant in considering that you can play on the varsity on such a team, but I can assure you that after all my observations you can. President Truman would not be in the White House today except for having taken advantage of a similar situation when it occurred. If we watch developments carefully, the opportunity may present itself to work wonders with you, also. The difference in these two cases would be that wonders were worked with Truman, who in my opinion just does not have it — you do have it — All you need is the opportunity." [14]

The same day Daniel's memo crossed Thurmond's desk, Olin Johnston got into the fray with a carefully orchestrated snub of the president that became widely publicized. Gladys Johnston, the senator's wife, was a vice-chairman of the annual Jefferson-Jackson Day Dinner in Washington at which President Truman was slated as featured speaker.

A few days beforehand, she called Democratic National Committeeman J. Howard McGrath, senator from Rhode Island, to ask for assurance that none of Johnston's associates would be seated next to an African-American. When McGrath gave no such guarantee, the South Carolina party, which included the Thurmonds, refused to attend. Their table was located near the speaker's platform because of Mrs. Johnston's expected role. Olin Johnston hired a former heavyweight boxer to attend the dinner and see that the highly visible table remained empty.

News stories about Johnston's boycott prompted a flood of

congratulations from constituents, including a proud letter claiming that "applications for Ku Klux Klan membership are booming and there's a healthy increase in the manufacture of Red Shirts in South Carolina."[15]

On February 23, Thurmond and his committee of governors confronted Chairman McGrath, asking him — in writing — such leading questions as whether he would deny that the proposed federal laws dealing with the separation of races "would be unconstitutional invasions of the field of government belonging to the states under the Bill of Rights in the Constitution of the United States?"

They left empty-handed. *The New York Times* reported in a front-page story that McGrath "would not yield on a single point as they fired question after question at him." A week after the meeting with McGrath, Thurmond told his state Democratic Executive Committee, "The president has gone too far," adding, "as far as I am concerned, I am through with him."

On March 13, Thurmond's committee report called Truman's proposal a "betrayal . . . because so many of the proposals are openly and deliberately directed against our traditions, customs and institutions."

In addition to his political instincts, Thurmond began responding from an inner core that had absorbed through osmosis the ethos of the historic crucible of Edgefield, of honor and fighting spirit in defending the white South against those who aroused the region's deep feelings of grievance.

At a March 16 rally, he cited a passage from the "To Secure These Rights" report and bitterly complained, "*They* have the idealism and prestige; we in the South are the wayward." With the echoes of Preston Brooks, Martin Witherspoon Gary, and John C. Calhoun seemingly rising from the ground, Thurmond declared, "No fight was ever won by staying out of it. Our cause is right and just. We shall honor ourselves by pressing it to the end."

A day later, Thurmond asserted that the civil rights report had "gathered dust" until revived because of political considerations. Thurmond's rhetoric intensified. He called Truman's civil rights proposal to Congress "the most astounding president's message in American history" and declared, "We may as well have a showdown once and for all."[16]

He was now openly calling for Southerners to stand together and throw the presidential election into the House. The Constitution provides that if no candidate has a majority of the electoral vote, the House will select from the three top candidates, with each state having a single vote.

Although most other Southern political leaders, including those in Washington, chimed in with attacks on Truman's proposals, few were joining Thurmond's call for revolt. Congressional leaders feared risking the privileges and power of seniority and loss of patronage at home that would come with Democratic defeat. They understood that acts have consequences.

And, unlike Thurmond and the other governors in the provinces, the Southerners in Washington knew Harry Truman personally and believed that his political needs suggested his commitment on civil rights was limited. Congressman Frank W. Boykin of Alabama quoted the president as saying, "Frank, I don't believe in this civil rights program any more than you do, but we've got to have it to win."[17]

On April 19, the U. S. Supreme Court announced its decision not to hear a challenge to the Fourth Circuit's affirmation of Judge Waring's ruling. The Democratic primary in South Carolina would be open to black voters. Thurmond waited two days before commenting, finally saying he was "shocked" by the refusal to hear the case and proclaiming that "every American has lost part of his fundamental rights." *The State*, in an editorial headlined "No Cause for Shock," accepted the decision as a "matter of course" and suggested that Thurmond only spoke out because he "felt called upon to." The afternoon *Columbia Record* asked whether blacks had "won anything by the Supreme Court decision to which they were not entitled."[18]

Thurmond chose to feed the fears of panicky South Carolinians who saw their social order crumbling. He blamed it all on Harry Truman. Thurmond told an audience, "I took Truman's picture off the wall of my office when he stabbed the South in the back. Let's fight this battle to the end."[19]

On April 22, the Mississippi Democratic Executive Committee agreed to nominate Thurmond for president at the national convention, declaring him "a man of vision and courage who thinks and acts and feels like we do."[20] In Columbia, Thurmond said, "I was surprised."

But he accepted an invitation to give the keynote address at a southwide May 10 meeting in Jackson. The day before, a Sunday, Gov. Wright had made a 7:30 a.m. radio address specifically aimed at black Mississippians. Even in the bizarre politics of that state, it had a touch of the surreal. Wright told black Mississippians "to place your trust in the innate, uncoerced sense of justice of the white people with whom you live." Then he warned, "If any of you have become so deluded as to want to enter our hotels and cafes, enjoy social equality with the whites, then kindness and true sympathy requires me to advise you to make your home in some state other than Mississippi."

Thurmond brought Figg with him to draft a fiery message, and Jean accompanied her husband as Wright's guests in the governor's mansion. Roughly 1,500 delegates showed up from throughout the South, and another 2,000 spectators — almost all of them Mississippians — sat in at the city auditorium. Except for Wright, Ben Laney of Arkansas was the only other governor who attended.

The New York Times correspondent, John Popham, wrote that Thurmond "has been mentioned as a likely Presidential candidate on a States Rights ticket." His story reported some Southern states were barely represented and quoted Georgia Democratic state chairman James S. Peters as saying that "the Democratic party is like religion and nobody is going to desert the party." The *Times* quoted Thurmond as asserting that the South was "tired of being a doormat for Presidential candidates," and that it had now been "betrayed in the house of our fathers."[21]

Thurmond went much farther, however. He aroused all the elements of Southern grievance, from discriminatory freight rates to not getting credit for having "cared and provided for the Negroes in our midst." He prophetically added, "Whenever a great section of this country is regarded as so politically impotent that one major party insults it because it is 'in the bag' and the other party scorns it because there is no chance for victory, then the time has arrived for corrective and concerted action. When this campaign is over, leaders in both political parties will realize that we no longer intend to be a doormat on which presidential candidates may wipe their political shoes every time they want to appeal to a minority in doubtful states. . . .

"We of the South are a proud people. We come from a stock that has never buckled even in the face of defeat or rule by federal bayonet. We meet here today with no apology. We want no one to be mistaken or misled. We are going to fight as long as we breathe, for the rights of our states and our people under the American constitution and come what may, we are going to preserve our civilization in the South."

One by one, he blasted the particulars of Truman's civil rights package. Why did the nation need anti-poll tax laws, he asked, when states like South Carolina were working to abolish them? Why did the country need an anti-lynching law when the crime had practically been eliminated? The proposals to eliminate job discrimination were not only unconstitutional but the beginnings of a frightening police state that would produce more "duress and apprehension" than the mind of man could conceive.

For him personally, Thurmond said, "the Rubicon is crossed, I care not whether I ever hold another public office. . . . As the Governor of a sovereign state, I do not intend that the right of my people shall be sacrificed on the block of blind party loyalty."[22]

And he made his meaning of "States Rights" absolutely clear. "On the question of social intermingling of the races our people draw the line," he declared, his voice rising and his right hand chopping in a gesture of defiance, "And all the laws of Washington and all the bayonets of the army cannot force the Negro into our homes, our schools, our churches, and our places of recreation and amusement." He would repeat this language as the central theme of his core political message later in the year. He went on, "No decent and self-respecting Negro would ask for a law to force people to accept him where he is not wanted."

William Winter, a first-term Mississippi legislator still in law school who would become a leading force for progressive politics in his state, a half-century later vividly remembered that day:

"I had the feeling that a lot of people must have had in 1861, that we were becoming swept up in a political hysteria that was just throwing caution to the winds as to what the ultimate result might be.

"It was Mississippi and South Carolina again, as in 1860 when they were the first two to take the lead in secession. Again they were the first two to take the lead in seceding from the Democratic Party. I was troubled that this was going to run us into a dead end, that we were getting ready to forfeit our influence in the Democratic Party and in the Congress by what appeared to be a very iffy course. I saw it as a move toward isolating ourselves politically."[23]

An argument can be made, however, that the Democratic "solid South" indeed did have its roots in the states rights argument, that in exchange for Democratic loyalty the region would be left alone in determining race relations. For the South, it meant a system of white supremacy. But in a changing world emerging from a world war against totalitarian regimes and in which fragile nonwhite democracies were emerging, the historic moment had come when the American people confronted their racial dilemma.

As Thurmond made clear, the heart of the matter involved race — his defense of white supremacy. He used the term, "States Rights," in no other context. The argument is based on the one-sentence Tenth Amendment of the Constitution: "The powers not delegated to the United States by the Constitution, nor prohibited by it to the States, are reserved to the States respectively, or to the people."

Under the American governmental system of federalism, the States retain the police power — laws regulating the general security, health, safety, morals, and welfare except where legally prohibited.

After the Civil War determined that the United States is an indestructible union, the Fourteenth Amendment of the Constitution was ratified. It granted citizenship to black Americans and declared that no state could deprive a citizen of "equal protection" or "due process" of the law. Article Six of the Constitution states plainly that federal law is supreme.

The late nineteenth-century Supreme Court gutted the Fourteenth Amendment of its framers' intention. Instead of protecting the former slaves and their descendants, it became an instrument to protect corporate economic interests.

But beginning in the late 1930s, the Supreme Court began restoring the Fourteenth Amendment to its intended meaning. Thurmond may well have viewed this legal trend as a "battle of federal power versus state power," but his words at the time make clear that his primary concern was the power to maintain racial segregation and white supremacy. In his constitutional argument, Thurmond was fighting the tides of history.

Although Thurmond apparently internalized a genuine belief that he was acting in defense of constitutional principle, he ignored that the Supreme Court is the final arbiter for interpreting the Constitution. Yet, Thurmond's dogged stubbornness in politicizing the issue ultimately would make a difference. Over time Thurmond, the former judge, intuitively grasped that if the Supreme

Court interprets the Constitution, then who the justices are matters.

As the 1948 campaign developed, Gene Patterson recognized Thurmond's evident popularity in South Carolina. He remembered, "His wholehearted embrace of racial segregation pleased the bourbons and the boobs alike, of course. But he did not strike one as being exceptionally bright, and the country-cured accent of his uninspired speechmaking paled in comparison to gentlemanly Burnet Maybank with his clipped Low Country combination of Gullah and Tidewater brogue and shambling Olin Johnston with the Piedmont millhand bawl.

"So I asked Wayne Freeman [later editor] of *The Greenville News* to tell me the secret of Strom's charm over the masses." One of the most knowledgeable political reporters around, Freeman rented an office in one of the two rooms of Patterson's United Press bureau. "It's very simple," Freeman told him. "Strom may not be all that smart. But he's a rarity in South Carolina politics. He's honest. He won't steal."[24][ii]

On May 19 South Carolina Democrats held one of their most infamous state conventions. Thurmond kept a low profile, but his forces controlled the event. They instructed delegates to the national convention to vote for him on the first ballot as a favorite son candidate and to reject Truman or any candidate who supported the president's civil rights program.

To discourage blacks from voting, the convention adopted an oath requiring primary voters to swear that they "understand, believe in and will support the principles of the Democratic Party of South Carolina," to support racial segregation in religious, social, and educational activities, and to oppose and work against the FEPC. Ten days later, three of the state's most prominent lawyers, who had handled the challenge to Judge Waring's decision, publicly disclaimed having any role in the new Democratic Party oath. *The Columbia Record* disdainfully asserted that "only a member of the Nazi party in Germany could take the oath and mean it."[25] The oath energized white moderates as well as blacks, who filed a lawsuit.

On May 26, South Carolina's Progressive Democrats

---

ii. When Gov. Thurmond vetoed an appropriations bill in 1947 that included a $4,500 annual salary increase for the governor, the legislature overrode the veto. Although funds were appropriated, Thurmond refused to accept the pay increase for all of his term.

responded with their own convention, whose roughly 250 delegates from twenty-six of the state's forty-six counties included two whites. Keynote speaker Arthur Clement of Charleston assailed Thurmond as one whose training and culture had "evaporated like the morning dew" and who had transformed himself into "another wailing rabble-rouser." The group agreed to send a full twenty-eight-member delegation to the Democratic National Convention in Philadelphia in July.

Political turmoil continued in the state throughout June. A grassroots group of racially moderate white activists organized as the Citizen Democratic Party. When party chairman Baskin refused their request to reconvene the state convention to reconsider the controversial oath, this group decided to send its own challenge delegation to Philadelphia, including two black college presidents.

In Philadelphia, a week after Republicans nominated New York Gov. Thomas E. Dewey for president and California Gov. Earl Warren for vice president, Thurmond found little support for a southwide revolt. On Sunday night, July 11, a caucus that attracted less than a third of the 600 Southern delegates heard him berate the president, saying, "We have been betrayed, and the guilty shall not go unpunished." *The New York Times* reported the next morning that the Southern revolt against Truman's nomination had collapsed.

Southern opponents failed to come up with an alternate candidate (Thurmond had joined an unsuccessful effort to draft Dwight Eisenhower). The caucus adopted two resolutions threatening nothing worse than a floor fight over the party platform.

At the convention, the state's Progressive Democrats and Citizen Democrats made separate appeals to the Credentials Committee. The black group sought eight of the state's twenty delegate seats to reflect their forty percent proportion of the state's population.

David Baker, a young lawyer from Columbia, argued two points for the Citizen Democrats. First, the regular Democratic delegation was unlawful because blacks were excluded from participating at the state convention. Second, the oath "has disfranchised all the thinking and intelligent people of South Carolina."

Thurmond spoke, maintaining that the regular delegates "constitute the regular Democratic Party of South Carolina." He threatened a walkout if the Progressive Democrats got their proportional representation. After Thurmond's testy refusal to answer directly whether precinct meetings were open to participation by blacks, McCray explained his group hadn't filed protests when excluded from the meetings because they couldn't get in.

Although the committee recommended a new rule be adopted to meet future situations "such as have been developed in the South Carolina case," Olin Johnston seconded the motion to seat the official South Carolina delegation, and it passed, 24-3.

Meanwhile, the platform committee adopted a compromise civil rights plank, ambiguously urging that "Congress should exert its full constitutional powers to protect these rights." On the convention floor, several southerners argued for specific "states rights" language. They contended the party was repudiating its historic position, but former Gov. Maurice Tobin of Massachusetts pointed out that no states rights plank had appeared for twenty years in the Democratic National Convention platform, not since 1928.

Hubert H. Humphrey, the dynamic thirty-seven-year-old mayor of Minneapolis, followed. He spoke out for a minority report drafted by the liberal Americans for Democratic Action that would "support our President in guaranteeing these basic and fundamental American principles: The right of full and equal political participation, the right to equal opportunity of employment, the right of security of persons, and the right of equal treatment in the service and defense of our Nation."

Humphrey's speech reflected one of those electric moments, with applause interrupting him eight times. "To those who say that this civil rights program is an infringement on States Rights," Humphrey said in making his first impression on a national audience, "I say this, that the time has arrived in America for the Democratic Party to get out of the shadows of States Rights and to walk forthrightly into the bright sunshine of human rights."

By a vote of 654½ to 582½, the convention adopted his position. In the tumult that followed, half the Alabama delegation walked out (one who remained was state Rep. George C. Wallace), followed by the entire Mississippi delegation. Had the South Carolina delegation been inclined to leave, they knew the Progressive Democrats were ready to take their places.

Thurmond still had a bit role to play, seconding the nomination of Georgia's Richard Russell, a patrician who at fifty was the established leader of the Southern bloc in the Senate and now agreed to stand as a protest candidate. Thurmond earlier had released his delegates to Laney, but the Arkansas governor found little support and backed out.

After an introduction as "one of the outstanding heroes of the last war," Thurmond was unbending. "We do not wish to take from any American his constitutional rights," he said, "but we do not intend that our constitutional rights shall be sacrificed for the selfish and the sordid purpose of gaining minority votes in doubtful States."[26]

Thurmond returned home from Philadelphia on Friday, with plans to head to Camp Stewart, Georgia, to inspect a South Carolina National Guard unit the next morning. The Mississippi delegation and others had gathered in Birmingham, reconvening the group that had met in May, and Govs. Wright and Laney called Thurmond, urging him to attend. He decided to go.

After stopping at Camp Stewart, he flew on to Birmingham. Laney and former Gov. Frank Dixon of Alabama already had turned down offers to become the group's presidential nominee. Thurmond had hardly arrived at the boisterous gathering of 7,000 Confederate flag-waving, Dixie-singing enthusiasts than he was offered the nomination. He had an hour to decide.

Thurmond recalled, "I knew that accepting the nomination would have future political repercussions, but I had little time to make up my mind, and I thought somebody ought to do something, so I finally decided to take the plunge."[27]

One can only speculate if the future political repercussions involved alienating himself from the Democratic Party nationally or raising his profile for greater stature at home as a prelude to the 1950 senate race. Thurmond presumably weighed both.

By the time he came to the podium, earlier speakers had warmed up the audience with a statement of principles endorsing "racial integrity" in specific detail, and keynoter Frank Dixon got caught up in the mood, denouncing civil rights as a program "to reduce us to the status of a mongrel, inferior race."[28] Thurmond never stooped to that level of racist language. But he drew a roar of approval even before he began speaking, and he didn't disappoint his audience. He used notes on pieces of paper, stuffing each page into his pocket as he finished.

Thurmond biographer Nadine Cohodas tells of showing film clips from Movietone News footage to two top Thurmond aides forty years later, young men accustomed to his version of standing on constitutional principle and not running a racist campaign.

They watched the footage of an energized Thurmond gripping the podium with both hands and exclaiming, "I want to tell you that the progress of the Negro race has not been due to these so-called [and here he spit out the word as if he had bitten into a rotten apple] e-MAN-ci-PATERS—but to the kindness of the good Southern people." Then, renewing the main theme from the May speech in Jackson, he jabbed his right index finger at the crowd to emphasize each point and declared, "I want to tell you, ladies and gentlemen, that there's not enough troops in the Army to force the Southern people to break down segregation and admit the Negro race into our theaters, into our swimming pools, into our homes, and into our churches." The crowd loved it.

The Thurmond aides were stunned. One shook his head in silence. The other remembered chills running down his spine and said, "I couldn't believe I was working for the same man."[29]

At the time of his speech, Modjeska Simkins read his characterization of blacks and was outraged. "I said, 'I'm gonna fight Thurmond from the mountain to the sea. He will not get away with these things he is saying about my people.'"[30]

The Baltimore Afro-American, then one of the nation's largest black newspapers, launched its own crusade against Thurmond, charging in early August that his "race-baiting" had prompted cross burnings at two black schools in South Carolina. Later that month, the newspaper printed stories and photographs about miscegenation in the Thurmond clan, interviewing blacks who claimed kinship with the governor. Mrs. Eva Thurmond Smith said, "I remember well when Gov. Thurmond used to visit my grandfather, and they used to sit and eat and talk for hours. I remember asking my grandfather why did that white man always visit our home. My grandfather told me they were brothers."[31]

White-owned newspapers ignored the charges, but they circulated widely among South Carolina blacks, who also heard stories in their community of Thurmond having a "daughter" at all-black South Carolina State College.

The leaders at Birmingham sought not to create a third party, but to take over the Democratic state party organizations and make the Dixiecrat candidates the nominees of the Democratic Party. They defined the national Democratic Party as simply a federation of independent state parties. They succeeded in four states: Alabama, Louisiana (where Gov. Earl Long called a special session of the legislature to get Truman's name on the ballot, even if not as the official Democratic candidate), and South Carolina. Georgia didn't go along, even though newly elected Gov. Herman Talmadge was Thurmond's cousin. (Talmadge's mother spent her early years in Edgefield County, her father a much older half-brother of Thurmond's father.)

Jean didn't make the trip to Birmingham, unaware that anything significant was happening there. When she finally got together alone with Strom after he flew back to South Carolina late that night, she asked, "What about the political repercussions? You're really sticking your neck out."[32]

Finally, she said, "I'm sure everything will turn out all right in the end." Having just turned twenty-two, her first political campaign would be as wife of a presidential candidate.

Time magazine would soon come out with a cover story on Thurmond that mentioned one of those attending the Birmingham convention was Gerald L. K. Smith, a notorious racist and anti-Semite. Robert Lipshutz, then a lawyer in his late twenties who later became White House counsel for President Jimmy Carter, went to Birmingham to scout around for the Anti-Defamation League's regional office in Atlanta, which wanted to find out if there was any anti-Semitism in the Dixiecrat movement. Lipshutz learned that Smith was in a motel room, confirmed it, and passed the information to *Time*'s Atlanta bureau chief.[33] Thurmond rejected Smith's support. He said, "We do not invite and we do not need the support of Gerald L. K. Smith or any other rabble-rousers who use race prejudice and class hatred to inflame the emotions of the people."[34] Despite his own rhetoric, Thurmond clearly was seeking respectability.

And some respected mainstream northern newspapers believed his past record gave the Dixiecrats a leader who deserved to be heard. *The Christian Science Monitor* noted his war record, youthful vigor, and political ability. "His nomination gives people everywhere pause," the *Monitor* said. "Many of those whom he earnestly referred to as 'the good people of the South' will think before writing off a man of Gov. Thurmond's stature."[35] *The Washington Evening Star* wrote that "Thurmond's record as a progressive advocate for a better deal for the Negro of the South entitles him to a respectful hearing."[36]

Back home, however, *The State* warned that the South's problems weren't "going to be solved by fiery speeches. . . . This is no time for hotheadedness."[37]

Looking back years later, adviser Figg expressed disappointment about Thurmond's decision to make the presidential run. "He hadn't reached the halfway point in his administration of South Carolina government," Figg said, "and for this side issue to come along . . . Strom just jumped overboard down there."[38]

The Dixiecrat protest went beyond race. It built on cracks and fissures already developing in the Democratic structure in the South. It was fueled by conservative critics of the New Deal's expansion of Washington power and by new issues, such as ownership of tidelands oil. During the 1930s, the federal government claimed it owned the mineral rights in submerged coastal areas. The states most affected — Texas, Louisiana, Mississippi, Florida, and California — protested. The oil companies supported the states, mainly because their tax rate was much lower than the 37.5 percent federal royalty.

Congress passed legislation in 1946 that affirmed state ownership, and Truman vetoed the bill. The Supreme Court ruled in favor of the federal claim in 1947 (and would do so again in 1950. Truman vetoed another bill in 1952.) Columnist Stewart Alsop wrote that Texas oil interests, specifically naming H. R. Cullen, were supporting Thurmond's candidacy. Alsop wrote that Cullen's private plane transported Thurmond around Texas. The Dixiecrats denied the link to the oil interests.

With Fielding Wright as his running mate, Thurmond campaigned with the vigor of a man who expected to win. In the end he carried the four states in which he was on the ballot as the official candidate of the Democratic Party. He received more than a million votes and got 38 electoral votes from these four states, plus a 39th from an elector in Tennessee.

In one of the major upsets in American political history, Harry Truman won — and Clark Clifford was vindicated. Political analysts later concluded that a switch of some 21,000 votes in Ohio and Illinois from Truman to Dewey would have shifted enough electoral votes that Truman would have failed to get a majority.

Thurmond would always say — and seem to believe — that under such circumstances he could have been elected. He contended that the Democrats wouldn't have voted for Dewey and the Republicans wouldn't have voted for Truman. Had no candidate received a majority of the electoral vote, the House of Representatives would have determined the winner. The Constitution provides that each state would have a single vote.

After the 1948 elections, Democrats had a majority in twenty-five of the forty-eight House delegations (Alaska and Hawaii weren't yet states) — including the four that Thurmond carried. Republicans held a majority in only twenty. Three states — Montana, Idaho, and Connecticut — had split delegations.

The first round of voting might have given Thurmond 4 votes for the states he won, with 21½ for Dewey. Truman, with 22½, would need only two more states for a majority. In Louisiana, where Thurmond received only a plurality, the House delegation would have no reason to stick with him. In Alabama, whose governor and both senators were national party loyalists, the House delegation would have everything to gain and nothing to lose by backing Truman. Truman would have won.

The important political reality isn't what might have happened in 1948, but what did happen. Thurmond's campaign both foreshadowed the coming politics of massive resistance and broke loose the psychological moorings that tied the Deep South to the Democratic Party. It would never again be "like religion."

Donald Fowler, the South Carolina political scientist who became Democratic national chairman under Bill Clinton, likened it to someone losing one's virginity. It became easier the second time.[39]

From never voting more than five percent Republican, South Carolina went almost fifty percent for Dwight Eisenhower in 1952. As Thurmond said, the South was no longer in the bag. Future presidential candidates of both political parties did campaign in the South. Social and demographic forces would drive political change, but the Dixiecrat campaign unlocked the floodgates.

At home, Judge Waring had tossed out the Democratic oath as "absurd," after a hearing at which Bill Baskin was unable to explain its purpose. Freshman Congressman Dorn had called for Waring's impeachment as a prelude to Dorn's brash challenge of Burnet Maybank in the August Democratic primary. Even with three other opponents, Maybank won a majority in the first primary. Although Maybank had criticized Waring's earlier ruling, he left it at that. Waring had alienated whites — one, whose beach cottage next to his was struck by lightning, put up a sign that read, "Dear God, he lives next door." But Waring had become a hero to blacks in South Carolina. An estimated 35,000 of them voted, and they went solidly for Maybank — enough to give him his majority. Astute though he was, Thurmond failed until much later to grasp the full significance of this new patch of blackness in the electorate.

1. Thompson interview with Thurmond, December 22, 1980.
2. November 1, 1948, address over ABC. Original in Thurmond gubernatorial papers, Clemson University.
3. Banks 1979 interview, op. cit., pp. 29-30.
4. Cohodas, op. cit., p. 137.
5. *The State*, Associated Press story, December 31, 1947, p. 1.
6. Patterson letter to Bass, op. cit. Gene Patterson followed Ralph McGill as editor of *The Atlanta Constitution* and later became managing editor of *The Washington Post* and editor of the *St. Petersburg Times*.
7. Clark Clifford memorandum for the President, November 19, 1947, quoted in Cohodas, op. cit., p. 129.
8. Clark Clifford Memorandum for the President, August 17, 1948, quoted in Numan V. Bartley, *The New South*, Louisiana State University Press, 1995, p. 78.
9. *The State*, January 30, 1948, p. 1. Quoted in Cohodas, op. cit.
10. *The New York Times*, February 3, 1948, p. 1.
11. Fielding Wright inaugural address, January 19, 1948, Jackson, Mississippi, quoted in Cohodas, op. cit., p. 126.
12. Strom Thurmond speeches, quoted in Cohoda, op. cit., p. 132.
13. *The Atlanta Journal*, February 8, 1948.
14. W. L. Daniel memo to Strom Thurmond, February 19, 1948, in gubernatorial papers, Clemson University.
15. Cohodas, op. cit, p. 135.
16. *The Charleston Evening Post*, Associated Press story, March 18, 1948, p. 1.
17. Bartley, op. cit., p. 78.
18. Cohoda, op. cit., pp. 128-143.
19. *The Greenville News*, April 6, 1948.
20. *The Greenville News*, Associated Press story, April 23, 1948, p. 1.
21. *The New York Times*, May 11, 1948, P-1.
22. Strom Thurmond Historical Records, Clemson University, Special Collections.

23. Bass telephone interview with William Winter, May 5, 1998.
24. Patterson letter, op. cit.
25. *The Greenville News*, May 26, 1948; *The Columbia Record*, May 28, 1948.
26. Proceedings of 1948 Democratic National Convention, Records of the Democratic National Committee, Harry S. Truman Library, Independence, Missouri.
27. Lachicotte, op. cit., p. 43.
28. Quoted in Bartley, op. cit.
29. Cohodas, op. cit., p. 177.
30. Thompson interview with Modjeska Simkins, 1980.
31. *The Baltimore Afro-American*, August 24, 1948.
32. Lachicotte, p. 45.
33. Bass telephone interview with Robert Lipshutz, May 26, 1998.
34. United Press story, *The New York Times*, July 19, 1948.
35. *The Christian Science Monitor*, July 19, 1948.
36. *The Washington Evening Star*, July 21, 1948.
37. *The State*, August 2, 1948.
38. Thompson interview with Figg, June 9, 1981.
39. Thompson interview with Donald L. Fowler, 1981.

Strom and Jean in controversial *Life* magazine photo.

CHAPTER ELEVEN

✢

Campaign
of the Century

When Ernest F. "Fritz" Hollings faced reelection in 1998, he had served thirty-two years in the Senate, longer than any other junior senator in U.S. history. Strom Thurmond kept him in that status by setting two records, the oldest person ever to serve in the Senate and the longest service of any senator.

Although Hollings and Thurmond carefully kept out of each other's political races and worked cooperatively on projects for South Carolina, their voting records, life styles, and personalities could hardly be more different. A handsome, polished Citadel man whose thick Charleston accent combines with a razor-sharp mind, deep intellectual curiosity, and a wit sometimes too quick, Hollings in many ways represents the opposite side of the coin from Thurmond. One South Carolinian who knows both men well — and likes them — once said that "what vanity is to Strom, arrogance is to Fritz."

They share in common one deeply etched experience. Each ran for the Senate at the end of his term as governor — Thurmond in 1950 and Hollings in 1962. And each lost to Olin D. Johnston.

In his own words, Johnston was "of humble origin. I was born the son of a tenant farmer and spent some ten years of my early life working in the cotton textile mills of my home state. . . . I know how to toil with my hands. I am proud of my heritage. It is noble and honorable. I believe in the dignity of hard, honest toil."[1]

Like Huey Long of Louisiana, Johnston was "for the man farthest down" and delivered for him, but he lacked both Huey's overweening ambition and his vindictiveness. Five years older and far more introspective than Thurmond, Johnston set aside a daily period of reflection, up to an hour, when his Senate staff knew to leave him undisturbed.

As a cotton mill worker, he persuaded the president of Wofford College to admit him without an accredited high school diploma. Rejected by the Marine Corps in 1917 because of flat feet and color blindness, Johnston managed to get into the Army. He served more than a year in France, returned to Wofford, got his degree, then worked his way through the University of South Carolina law school. By the time Thurmond took him on in 1950, Johnston had served three House terms in the legislature and run six statewide campaigns, wearing baggy suits and colorful ties. He lost once for governor (by 960 votes) and twice for senator (to Cotton Ed Smith in 1938 and Burnet Maybank in 1941) and won twice for governor and once for senator.

Richard W. Riley, President Clinton's Secretary of Education and the first person to serve two consecutive terms as South Carolina's governor (1979-87), worked a year for Olin Johnston after finishing law school. Strom Thurmond already was in the Senate and still a Democrat.

A few months into the job, two prominent men from Riley's hometown of Greenville, brothers who ran an architectural firm, came by to see the senator. Young Riley walked into Johnston's office to let him know. Olin thanked him but asked that he show in instead Mr. Jones, a shift foreman from a Greenville textile mill there with his wife.

After some time, Riley went back in to remind Johnston of the brothers still waiting outside. Olin nodded, then said he was taking Mr. and Mrs. Jones to the Senate dining room for lunch. He left the architects waiting.

When the trio returned from lunch, Olin brought the Joneses back into his office for a few minutes before bidding them goodbye, then called in his new staffer. "Dick," he explained, "Mr. Jones is my precinct manager at the Parker Mill precinct, and he's been one of my good supporters for many years." Then chairman of the Senate Post Office and Civil Service Committee, Johnston indicated he was now ready to see the two Greenville brothers.

"You can tell those two Republican sons-of-bitches to come on in," he drawled in a voice that rumbled like a slow-moving freight train. "They want to see me about getting that contract to design the new post office we're going to build in Greenville."

Herman Talmadge considered Johnston "the dumbest senator I knew," but Bryan Dorn, who perhaps knew him better, said, "Olin was dumb like a fox."[2]

Roy Powell, one of Johnston's closest aides and later a Columbia municipal judge, recalled that Johnston supported Thurmond in the 1946 race for governor. "He came to Sen. Johnston, I remember it was in the old Wade Hampton Hotel. He talked to Sen. Johnston, Mrs. Johnston and Bill Johnston, the senator's brother — all of us — and he promised the group that if it would support him for governor that he would never run against Sen. Johnston. Of course, we all agreed, and the senator, he went touring around the Piedmont and Chester and all around, and Strom Thurmond was elected. But no sooner had he become governor than he began campaigning for the U.S. Senate."[3]

In South Carolina's one-party Democratic structure, Thurmond and Johnston represented separate factions that went back to the Civil War, rooted from seeds planted by the rivalry of the state's revered soldiers M. C. Butler (reputedly the youngest general in the Confederate Army) and Martin Witherspoon Gary, the head of the Red Shirt campaign. Both were Edgefield men.

"It is rumored that Butler received a promotion to major general over Martin Gary," explained Bryan Dorn, a student of the state's politics. "They kind of patched things up in the campaign of 1876, when they won the state from radical rule, but the feud and jealousy and rivalry continued to simmer underneath and blossomed into Gen. Gary's hatred of the aristocrats. Gary was the patron saint of Ben Tillman (it was Tillman who displaced Butler in the Senate in the 1890s). You'll never understand South Carolina politics until you go back to that. Since then, there's always been factions in South Carolina politics. They never had a two-party state, but they've always had two parties within the Democratic Party.

"If you study real carefully, you'll find that Jimmy Byrnes kind of gradually inherited the Tillman faction, although it had become sophisticated when Byrnes came along. The other faction was more radical really than Tillman. That was Cole L. Blease. This is the only state, you know, in American history where you had the terms Bleasism and Tillmanism, completely personalized political organizations. Olin Johnston, then, I would say kind of inherited or fell heir to the Blease element, which was the cotton mill boys, the lint heads and their champion, Coley Blease. They would die for him.

"Then on into the 1950s, I see Thurmond carrying the banner of the Jimmy Byrnes faction and Olin Johnston the Blease crowd. Again, Thurmond generally getting some of the Byrnes support, which had kind of graduated to the aristocracy, to the textile magnates, the newspapers. So that campaign in 1950, that was the last real line-up of those old factions which existed and, really, go back to Martin W. Gary and M. C. Butler."[4]

In 1950, Byrnes returned home to run for governor. Immediately the front-runner, at seventy-one he initially indicated he would forego the grueling forty-six-county tour. Byrnes then reversed his position and said he would participate. As a shrewd politician, he understood that no matter how revered he might be, South Carolinians expected their candidates to campaign vigorously. Failure to do so might raise questions about his physical vitality for the job.

But a campaign aide also advised that prominent people insisting that he attend the county-by-county meetings "seem to be pro-Thurmond folks who believe it would be to his advantage and Johnston's detriment for you to make the circuit."[5]

In pre-television 1950, the forty-six county-by-county Democratic stump meetings exposed the candidates directly to the voters. Part carnival, part revival, and part theater, the stump meetings linked politics and popular culture. People ate, drank, and frolicked. They not only heard candidates express their positions on the issues, but saw them react to an opponent's jabs, think on their feet, and respond forcefully or with unease to hecklers. Voters could still expect to shake a candidate's hand, look him in the eye, and get an intuitive feel for his character. That kind of retail politics has largely disappeared from the American landscape except for the New Hampshire presidential primary, which remains so important for these reasons.

The 1950 Senate race resembled a rolling heavyweight bare-knuckles boxing match — with Strom and Olin slugging away with words, and once barely avoiding fists. From the beginning, Thurmond attacked Johnston as a "Trumanite" in Washington who wanted to be an anti-Truman Democrat when in South Carolina. He called it a choice between "candidates who are following the President and those who are willing to stand up and be counted in opposition to his un-American, Communistic and anti-Southern programs."[6]

At the first stump meeting on May 23 in Lexington, Thurmond

attacked Johnston for being pro-Truman and soft on segregation. He would soon add that as governor, Johnston ran a corrupt "pardon racket" in return for political favors and future support. Johnston initially ignored Thurmond's charges, saying he was running a "Christian" campaign.

That changed in the final weeks, when voters pay more attention and Thurmond had run out of political ammunition. Johnston switched to a slugging counter-attack. He always understood that he would have to prove to his white working class base that he wasn't vulnerable to Thurmond on segregation. Simultaneously, he would depend on newly enfranchised blacks accepting his harsh racial stand as a political necessity and responding to his overall progressive record. With Thurmond's hated Dixiecrat image, black leaders understood. "It was a matter of choosing between a rattler and a moccasin," explained the Rev. I. DeQuincey Newman, who would emerge as the state's top NAACP official and then become the first black state senator since Reconstruction.[7]

After the Dixiecrat campaign, Gov. Thurmond spoke in 1949 to almost 150 blacks in Sumter. John McCray wrote afterwards that the governor "missed an excellent chance to win the race's confidence" by denouncing as "agitators" those who urged blacks to fight for their rights. Thurmond paid tribute to Davis Lee, a New Jersey editor whose writings Thurmond quoted in his Dixiecrat campaign as "one of America's great Negro leaders."

McCray wrote that blacks generally repudiated Lee's writings as "treason," adding, "Mr. Thurmond, in his own way, spoke from his heart. He believed in what he was saying as firmly as Negroes disbelieved in what he said."[8] Years would pass before Thurmond learned to listen to blacks rather than lecture to them.

Although Johnston sought to distance himself from Truman, belittling him as "the little man in the White House," he argued that the Democratic Party represented a broad coalition in which Southerners had always protected their interests. In a slap at Thurmond, he contended that a third party meant political isolation. He recognized that the Republican Party, which in 1950 still retained a large black base in the South as the party of Lincoln, remained too stigmatized to become a viable option for most whites.

Johnston did not actually vote in the 1948 election because a driving rain kept him from getting to the polls before closing time. But at 11 p.m. that night — a time when the president himself believed he had lost the election — Johnston announced that he would have voted for Truman. That set him apart from the state's other politicians.

Although a first-term senator, Johnston already had become chairman of the Post Office and Civil Service Committee, which gave him influence among colleagues at a time when the postal service was an important source of patronage. He emphasized the power of seniority and what it meant, often citing nearby federal projects he had helped get funded. With Maybank chairman of the Banking and Currency Committee, Johnston boasted that for the first time in more than a century both South Carolina senators chaired major committees. A sweeping Republican victory in 1946, followed by a huge loss in 1948, had restored Democratic control of a Senate with large numbers of freshmen from the North and the West.

Johnston had voted to sustain Truman's veto of the anti-labor Taft-Hartley bill. When attacked for that vote, he used it to demonstrate that he had influence with the president that helped get increased cotton and peanut acreage allotments for farmers. When Thurmond charged he was a tool of the C.I.O., Johnston simply replied he was for the working man.

Thurmond failed to ride in on his 1948 momentum in large part because race remained the central issue in 1950, but this time two segregationists were running instead of one. Johnston portrayed himself as a team player on the twenty-two-member Southern bloc led by men like Richard Russell of Georgia and Harry Byrd of Virginia. They used the filibuster and delaying tactics to defeat the Fair Employment Practices Commission (F.E.P.C) bill that spring. Johnston's office churned out press releases depicting him as a central player in the fight, and on the stump he called the bill's defeat "a personal victory."

Thurmond liked to relate the fanciful story of Johnston rushing back to Washington after the 1948 election to meet Truman's victorious return from Missouri: "He elbowed his way through the crowd, almost knocked down several admirals and generals and pushed Cabinet officers aside. They had to make a special seat in the parade because they didn't know he was going to be there."[9] Thurmond also charged Johnston with violating an oath to support the party when he declined to endorse the States Rights Democratic ticket in 1948.

At every stop on the county-by-county tour, attacks such as these would get applause, often begun with vigorous clapping by

Jean and her driver, a Presbyterian College student named Harry Dent. (His loyalty so impressed the Thurmonds that he later became Thurmond's Senate administrative assistant.)

Dent had chosen the small liberal arts college in Clinton over the University of South Carolina, preferring to be a big fish in a small pond. Because of special circumstances, he became student newspaper editor his freshman year and soon thereafter doubled as the school's public relations director. He met Gov. Thurmond in 1950, when the college president invited him for a campus political emphasis week. Dent got an invitation the next day for lunch at the governor's mansion.

Dent remembered "being scared to death. I was just a boy from St. Matthews and grew up in the back of a house where we didn't have any etiquette and all that kind of stuff." He took a seat as servants were setting the table. Someone explained they were prisoners, this one a murderer and that one a murderer.

Dent was still worried about etiquette when the governor came in and sat down. Thurmond cleaned his plate in minutes, talking as he chewed. "We got right into it," Dent remembered. "He ain't got no etiquette, so I felt much relieved. I said, 'Man, I can handle this.'" Thurmond wanted him to drive him and Jean across the state. "I said, 'yes, sir, I'll do that.'"

Strom and Jean usually rode in different cars, with Dent driving her. Strom would go early to the courthouse, and Jean and Harry would hit Main Street, distributing brochures. A couple of years older than Harry, Jean and he forged a platonic bond of trust, almost like brother and sister.

Jean had demonstrated during the 1948 campaign that she would support fully her husband's political life. She proved adept at campaigning, accepted its strains, and she and Strom drew closer.

In 1949, they wrote regularly when he was traveling without her, Jean addressing him as "My darling husband" or "Hey Sugar!" and frequently signing her letters, "Sugie." Often she went to stay with her family in Elko. When he was on a trip to New York recruiting new industry, she ended a chatty three-page letter, "I do miss you so very, very much and love you more every day that passes. Behave yourself and be sweet."

While on Army Reserve duty at Fort Bragg in North Carolina, he seemed frustrated, writing, "I do love you so much. Sometimes I may not express to you my deep love, but it is simply that I am rolling over in my mind the hundreds of important matters and responsibilities of State and otherwise."

Later, on another industry-hunting trip, Strom wrote to "My Darling Wifey" of making good contacts with DuPont in Wilmington, Delaware about locating a plant in South Carolina. He concluded, "Honey, I miss you so much. I love you more and more each day. Be sweet and know I am thinking about you all the time."[10]

As the 1950 Senate campaign moved forward, Thurmond added a final link between Johnston and Truman. Thurmond compared the senator to two well-known Southern liberals in the Senate who had just been defeated in Democratic primaries in their states, Frank Porter Graham of North Carolina and Claude Pepper of Florida.

One Thurmond campaign ad showed a cartoon figure, labeled "Southern Voter," who already had scratched lines through Graham and Pepper's names on a blackboard and had started a line through Johnston's name. The caption said, "Attention Harry Truman: Two Down — One to Go!"[11]

Unlike Graham and Pepper, both F.E.P.C. supporters, Johnston's record on segregation wasn't soft. He understood the lesson of their defeat and displayed photographs of Southern senators with whom he was aligned to defeat the F.E.P.C. bill.

Johnston then slammed Thurmond for being "in the same boat" as Frank Graham, who had appointed a black youth to West Point. Thurmond had appointed a black physician in Charleston, Dr. T. C. McFall, to the state medical advisory board based on a recommendation by the state medical association. McFall became the first black appointed in the twentieth century to a state board or commission in South Carolina. Johnston charged that Thurmond, like Graham, "broke down segregation" and that Thurmond, like Graham, "is going to be defeated."[12]

Johnston made his switch from dignified restraint to emotional attack on June 22 at Marion. "Any man that says I am for the mixing of the races in an unmitigated liar . . . a low down contemptible liar. . . I'm getting tired of this," he shouted. "Someday there might be a break in the situation and some of you know about Olin Johnston and how I will rave when I cut loose."[13]

A day later, Johnston held up a copy of the notorious *Life* magazine photo of Thurmond and commented, "You know you get addled when you stand on your head."[14]

Then he returned to McFall's appointment. State law had specified that the governor's appointments to a state hospital advisory council under the federal Hill-Burton Act should be based upon the recommendations of the state medical association. The appointment of McFall in the summer of 1949 generally received praise if noticed at all; *The News and Courier* headlined an editorial, "Excellent Appointment."[15]

Johnston blasted Thurmond for ending segregation by placing a black man on an official board to sit with white men and women. The senator called Thurmond both a hypocrite for accepting McFall for appointment while posing as a hard-line states rights segregationist and an opportunist for doing so to court the new black voters. On June 26 at Newberry, the campaign hit its tempestuous peak. Johnston waved a copy of *The Lighthouse and Informer*, which had boldly displayed McFall's appointment while most of the white press ignored it. Thurmond repeated a charge that Johnston had done nothing to protest the Truman administration's executive order desegregating the armed forces, that he was "silent as a tomb." Then he taunted, "If that's not so, Senator, stand up and deny it."

Johnston, sitting in the front row of the courthouse audience, stood up and yelled, "I want to tell you, you are a liar, for twenty-two of us. . . ."

As bedlam erupted, Strom looked at Olin and said, "I'll see you outside afterwards." An Edgefield man felt his honor assailed.

And afterwards, Dent recalled, "Strom Thurmond went out front. He was standing there ready." Johnston came out and reached out as if to shake hands. Thurmond grabbed his hand and pulled him around. Before blows were struck, but just barely, a Johnston aide and Dent, backed up by other supporters, moved in to separate them.

Walking away, Johnston was quoted as telling his supporters, "After the campaign I'll fix him up. I was a heavyweight boxer in the Army and I'll knock hell out of him with one blow."[16]

To the delight of his core supporters, Johnston next ridiculed Thurmond for a letter he sent to William Hastie, the black former dean of Howard University Law School who Truman had appointed governor of the Virgin Islands. The letter — which Thurmond sent to all governors after he attended his first national governors con-ference — invited Hastie to visit South Carolina and stay overnight in the Governor's Mansion. Hastie sent a letter expressing regret he was unable to accept. Johnston gleefully displayed both letters, while Thurmond lamely brushed it off as a clerical mistake.[17]

In the final days, Thurmond defended his appointment of McFall, saying he had followed the law and had no choice. Johnston poured it on. He contended that Thurmond should have asked for another recommendation until a white doctor's name was sent for-ward. Johnston's campaign ran full-page newspaper ads with blar-ing headlines: THURMOND APPOINTS NEGRO. Subheads read: "Wade Hampton's Era of Segregation Ends in South Carolina as Thurmond replaces White Doctor with Charleston Negro in Bold Bid to Capture Negro Vote of State! First Negro appointed to State Position Since Days of Carpetbaggers and Scalawags."

Four days before the primary, in Charleston, Johnston declared before an audience of 4,000 at the city's baseball park, "Had I been Governor Thurmond, I would never have appointed the nig-ger physician of Charleston, Dr. T. C. McFall, to displace your beloved white physician of this community . . ." When the 400 or so blacks protested loudly enough to drown out the rest of the sen-tence, Johnston thundered, "Make those niggers keep quiet!"[18]

One observer called the senator's crude racist assault on Thurmond's appointment of McFall as "a moral low point in Olin D. Johnston's political career . . . yet it cannot be denied that the black physician's appointment proved to be a devastatingly effec-tive weapon in the senator's quest for a second term."[19]

There's no record of Thurmond ever using the "n" word or other blatantly racist language. But the contrast between him and Johnston in the 1950 campaign reflects that there have always been two types of racism in the South. One is the "democratic" racism based on South Carolina Upcountryman John C. Calhoun's theory that black inferiority provided the basis for a white equality based on skin color. In its rawest form, poor whites gained a measure of status based on skin color, and blacks were looked upon virtually as subhuman. Johnston's core support came from Upcountry working class whites imbued with Calhoun's racial theories. Until the 1964 Civil Rights Act outlawed racial discrimination in employment, the South Carolina textile industry hired only whites for production jobs.

Thurmond reflected more the "aristocratic" racism that pre-dominated in the Lowcountry plantation region. It combined a paternalistic attitude with a belief in racial superiority based on blacks having an innate childlike capacity. The aristocrats looked down on poor whites, too, which Thurmond avoided.

The appointment of the highly regarded Dr. McFall could have opened the door earlier as a first step toward new racial relationships. Thurmond never defended the appointment, however, on grounds of qualifications or that it was the right thing to do. He continued to say he had no choice until citing it many years later as an example of his progressive views on race.

Johnston and Thurmond also vigorously debated federal aid to education. Thurmond, who had supported such aid in his inaugural speech as governor, changed his mind. He told the South Carolina Education Association, the professional organization for thousands of public school teachers, that federal aid would lead to federal control and become a weapon to force school desegregation. Johnston supported a federal aid bill in 1950 that explicitly granted state control over spending, but Thurmond maintained that desegregation would be demanded in the future.

Johnston said, "I am not for the races mixing because God did not mix them himself." He supported the pending education bill because it would allow South Carolina to raise salaries for its badly underpaid teachers, with no large tax increases.

On June 5, 1950, the Supreme Court issued three opinions that weakened the constitutional basis for segregation.[i] Johnston put Thurmond on the defensive by arguing that the court decisions meant facilities would have to be truly equal and that federal funds would be needed because of a projected shortfall in state tax revenue. "We don't like them," Johnston said of the decisions, "but you have to abide by the Supreme Court."[20]

When Thurmond argued that federal money would weaken segregation, Johnston countered that the state's colleges and universities received federal aid, but remained segregated. "I have three children and I want them to go to school with white children," Johnston said near the end of the campaign, emphasizing his commitment to segregation while pointedly contrasting himself with the childless Thurmond.

Throughout the campaign Johnston consistently had good timing. The Supreme Court decisions diverted attention away from Thurmond's attack on Johnston's gubernatorial pardon and parole

---

i. In *Sweatt v. Painter*, the court ruled that a separate black law school in Texas was unequal to that of the University of Texas because of the latter's superior faculty, resources, and reputation. *McLaurin v. Oklahoma* outlawed that state's practice of segregating black graduate students in the library, cafeteria, and classrooms. And *Henderson v. United States* desegregated dining cars on trains that crossed state lines.

record. Thurmond won a legislative battle to take that power away from the governor and place it in a state board. Early in the campaign, he charged that Johnston as governor had conducted "an unconstitutional, unbridled and unbelievable pardon and parole spree." Thurmond said Johnston had released 3,221 criminals from prison, including murderers and rapists. "It was easier to get out of the penitentiary," he put it, "than it was to get in it."[21] Thurmond hammered at the issue for a month before Johnston responded.

He quoted from a letter from Secretary of State O. Frank Thornton that state records showed Johnston as governor pardoned, paroled, or commuted the sentences of 671 persons, compared to 714 by Gov. John G. Richards from 1927 to 1931 and 1,091 by Gov. Ibra C. Blackwood from 1931 to 1935. Johnston denounced Thurmond's charges as "false and malicious" and countercharged that some he released had been named honorary "colonels" by Thurmond. The governor refused to make public the list of the hundreds of people he had given certificates designating them with the honorary title.

Then, on June 24, barely two weeks before the July 10 Democratic primary, North Korean communists invaded South Korea. Thurmond initially criticized Truman for not taking a firmer stand earlier against the Communists, but Johnston immediately supported Truman and the United Nations for committing to fight. As usual in a foreign policy crisis, the commander-in-chief's popularity rose, at least initially, and the opening weeks of the Korean conflict undercut Thurmond's assault on the "Trumanite" Johnston.

After winning more than seventy percent of the South Carolina vote in his Dixiecrat campaign, Thurmond was perceived less than two years later as the clear favorite at the start of his campaign against Johnston. William D. "Bill" Workman, Jr., then *The News and Courier's* Columbia correspondent and considered the state's top political reporter, privately was predicting a 57-43 landslide for Thurmond on the eve of a primary climaxing one of the most bitter campaigns in the state's history. His newspaper editorially opposed virtually everything (except segregation) that Johnston stood for and vigorously attacked him almost daily. Shortly before the election it exulted that "J. Strom Thurmond's majority . . . will be overwhelming."[22] Johnston stunned the political establishment, decisively winning with 186,180 votes (fifty-four percent) to Thurmond's 158,904 (forty-six percent).[23]

With Olin Johnston winning by less than 28,000 votes, *The*

News and Courier concluded that blacks "apparently supplied the margin . . . of victory." In Columbia's Ward 9, an almost all-black precinct, Johnston received more than ninety-five percent of the vote, beating Thurmond 1,249-72. Of the half million registered voters in the state in 1950, an estimated 73,000 were black. If the percentage of turnout was the same as in 1948, roughly 50,000 voted.[24]

To the extent Thurmond ran in 1948 to set up his 1950 Senate campaign, it misfired. Johnston proved capable of neutralizing Thurmond's appeal as a segregationist. His defense of the national Democratic Party and its economic policies won him support from newly enfranchised black voters who wanted to defeat the Dixiecrat candidate. As Modjeska Simkins put it, "Strom villified Negroes in 1948 . . . and we swore vengence."[25]

In the end, Thurmond failed to penetrate Johnston's base of support. The Dixiecrat campaign, whatever its long-term consequences for expediting the breakup of the "solid South," cost Thurmond the support of black voters and the progressive elements that helped elect him governor.

Looking back almost three decades later, Thurmond thought he made a mistake in attacking Johnston's record rather than running on his own. "I think I had a good record as governor, a progressive record, and had done so much for the people I think I'd have been elected," he said of the 1950 race.[26]

Charles Simons, who Thurmond was about to join in an Aiken law practice, was his county campaign manager there and carried every precinct, including the textile town of Graniteville. He believed Thurmond's opposing federal aid to education was decisive, that he lost support of teachers and their supporters.[27]

When the returns came in on election night, young Harry Dent felt devastated, but Thurmond took it all in stride. He noticed the young man's distress and told him, "Harry, never look up a dead horse's rear end."

1. Typed manuscript, April 10, 1947, of a speech for delivery to a Democratic audience in Atlanta, Olin D. Johnston Papers, South Caroliniana Library, University of South Carolina, quoted in "Defending the Faith: The 1950 U.S. Senate Race in South Carolina," Masters Thesis by Luther Brady Faggart, University of South Carolina, 1992.

2. Talmadge to Bass, June 2, 1998; Dorn to Bass, October 1974.
3. Thompson interview with Roy Powell, July 1981.
4. Thompson interview with W. J. Bryan Dorn, September 13, 1981.
5. James Lever letter to Byrnes, April 15, 1950, Byrnes papers. Quoted in Faggart, op. cit., p. 25.
6. Cohodas, op. cit., p. 201.
7. Thompson interview with Newman. [circa 1981]
8. John McCray, "The Need for Changing," *The Lighthouse and Informer*, April 19, 1949.
9. *The State*, June 21, 1950, p. 1B.
10. Jean Thurmond to Strom Thurmond, August 9, 1949; Strom Thurmond to Jean Thurmond, August 15, 1949 and August 27, 1949; Special Collections, Clemson University.
11. Thurmond advertisement, [circa 1950], Johnston Papers, cited in Faggart, op. cit., p. 51.
12. *The State*, July 5, 1950, 1, and June 30, 1950, 5B.
13. *The State*, June 23, 1950, 1; *Rock Hill Evening Herald*, June 23, 1950, p. 2.
14. *The State*, June 24, 1950, 1.
15. *The News and Courier*, June 28, 1950, 4.
16. Dent interview, op. cit. *The News and Courier*, June 27, 1950, 1. Faggart, op. cit., p. 163. Cohodas, op. cit., p. 211.
17. Faggart, op. cit., 114-115.
18. *The News and Courier*, July 7, 1950.
19. Faggart, op. cit., p. 107.
20. *The State*, June 10, 1950, p. 3.
21. *The State*, June 9, 1950. p. 1.
22. Workman to Greenville newspaperman Judson Chapman, July 9, 1950, and *The News and Courier*, June 23, 1950, cited in Faggart, op. cit., p. 5.
23. Official election returns reported in *The State*, July 19, 1950, p. 1.
24. See Faggart, p. 252, note. He cites Steven F. Lawson, *Black Ballots: Voting Rights in the South, 1944-1969* (New York: Columbia Univesity Press, 1976), 54, 134. According to Lawson, 35,000 blacks voted in the 1948 Democratic primary in South Carolina, a year after an estimated 50,000 were registered.
25. Robert Sherrill, *Gothic Politics in the Deep South*, op. cit., p. 242.

26. Banks 1979 interview with Strom Thurmond, p. 28-29.
27. Bass interview with Charles Simons, Aiken, S.C., August 13, 1997.

Strom, his mother, and Gov. Jimmy Byrnes.

CHAPTER TWELVE

✝

Opportunity Knocks

Agentrified community with streets named for all of the state's other counties, the planned town of Aiken presents a sophisticated appearance that differs from the typical South Carolina county seat. Race horses are trained there, and the town exhibits a certain pretentious charm. With an interstate highway running nearby and a four-year campus of the state university, it is far more cosmopolitan than Edgefield to the north, its mother county more than a century ago.

Strom and Jean Thurmond settled in easily in 1951, enjoying some of their happiest years. Strom thrived in the practice of law with Charles Simons and Dorcey Lybrand, smart lawyers and shrewd, well-connected political activists. Thurmond organized Palmetto Federal Savings and Loan, got it chartered, and became its president.

As governor he had been briefed on the federal government's plan to choose Aiken and bordering Barnwell County to locate the massive Savannah River Site to manufacture raw materials for nuclear weapons. He and his law partners prospered. Whole towns were displaced. The law firm quickly demonstrated that it could negotiate more money for farmers and others whose land was being condemned.

The firm took the cases on contingency, keeping a third of the difference between what the government originally offered and what was finally paid. With their reputation established, the lawyers got rich.

Strom often took time off in the middle of the day for tennis or swimming or horseback riding with Jean. As the state's former first couple, their social life was full. Strom began experimenting for the first time with implanting plugs of hair into his balding scalp. They wanted children, but learned that Jean could not conceive. They talked about adopting.[1]

Strom enjoyed trial work, achieving a lasting mark for his defense of Mrs. Margie Kennedy. She had shot her husband three times in front and three more times in the back.

Although she lived across the Savannah River in Augusta, Georgia, where the shooting took place, she was a native of Edgefield. She called Strom Thurmond to represent her. He focused on the case with the same intensity he gave a political campaign.

He painted a picture to the jury of a frail woman whose 220-pound husband, a politically prominent former fire chief in Augusta, beat her and refused to give her any money. (The prosecution presented evidence that he gave her no money because she would spend it on whiskey.)

The husband had taught her to shoot a .22 caliber pistol, and she grabbed it while he was chasing her from room to room. She shot him three times. When he wheeled around, perhaps to head for a doctor, she fired three more times. Each bullet hit him in the back between the shoulders.

He lingered for a week before dying. Although Thurmond argued that Mrs. Kennedy was mentally deranged by terror and maltreatment, he turned the jury after getting a friendly coroner to testify that the husband already suffered from kidney trouble, uremia, and diabetes. It wasn't those puny little .22 bullets that killed this great big man, Thurmond argued after the coroner agreed that they were only "secondary causes" of his death.

In that era in the South, where respectable white women were placed on a pedestal, they relinquished control for protection. If a woman who killed her husband wasn't certifiably crazy, there was a community presumption that she gave up his protection because for some reason he "deserved" killing. The sticky point was always the law of murder. A creative lawyer's job was to figure out a way for a jury to rationalize an acquittal and leave with a clear conscience. In Margie Kennedy's case, Thurmond performed the job masterfully. The jury acquitted, and the Augusta newspapers displayed photographs of the grateful Mrs. Kennedy embracing her lawyer, with Thurmond resolutely looking away from her.[2]

By the summer of 1954, Thurmond's political ambitions surfaced a bit. He invited Bryan Dorn, always a champion of veterans interests, to his Aiken home for an American Legion meeting. Dorn had regained his seat in 1950, two years after his ill-fated challenge to Sen. Maybank. Now Maybank was unopposed in a reelection bid.

Thurmond asked Dorn to step into a back room. "When we got back there," Dorn recalled, "he said, 'You realize that some day both of these seats for the United States Senate will be coming open. Now Bryan, Maybank's seat is yours. You ran for it before. But Johnston's seat is mine.'

"We shook hands on it. We weren't making a deal, but we shook hands on it as though that is the way it would be. It was clear he wanted to eliminate me as a challenger for Senator Johnston's seat."[3]

On September 1, having won the Democratic primary without opposition there and facing none in the general election, Maybank died unexpectedly in his sleep while vacationing at his summer mountain cottage in Flat Rock, N.C., apparently of a heart attack. He was fifty-five. How to select his successor touched off a political firestorm.

The legal deadline for the Democratic Party of South Carolina to certify its nominees was three days away. Every political figure of note went to Maybank's funeral two days later in Charleston. As the funeral procession left St. Michael's Episcopal Church for the cemetery, a black limousine pulled away and headed at high speed toward Columbia. It was carrying Edgar Brown.

1. Bass interview with Charles Simons, op. cit.; Thompson interview with Strom Thurmond, December 22, 1981.
2. *Saturday Evening Post*, "Dixiecrat in Washington," by Ashley Halsey, Jr., October 8, 1955, p. 32-33; *The Augusta Chronicle*, October 18, 1951, p. 1.
3. Thompson interview with Bryan Dorn, September 13, 1981; William Jennings Bryan Dorn and Scott Derks, *Dorn: Of the People* (Columbia and Orangeburg: Bruccoli Clark Layman and Sandlapper Publishing, 1988), pp. 157-159.

SAMPLE COPY

POSTAL PATRON
LOCAL

The Edgefield Advertiser

Oldest Newspaper In South Carolina

ESTABLISHED FEBRUARY 11, 1836   THE EDGEFIELD (S. C.) ADVERTISER — WEDNESDAY, OCTOBER 27, 1954   VOLUME 115 - NUMBER 37

WRITE IN
STROM THURMOND

HERE'S HOW TO DO IT!

SAMPLE OF OFFICIAL BALLOT

OFFICE	DEMOCRAT ⃝	REPUBLICAN ⃝	
Governor	☒ George Bell Timmerman, Jr.		
Lieutenant Governor	☒ Ernest F. Hollings		
Secretary of State	☒ O. Frank Thornton		
Attorney General	☒ T. C. Callison		
State Treasurer	☒ Jeff B. Bates		
Comptroller General	☒ E. C. Rhodes		
State Superintendent of Education	☒ Jesse T. Anderson		
Adjutant General	☒ James C. Dozier		
Commissioner of Agriculture	☒ J. Roy Jones		
United States Senator	☐ Edgar A. Brown		*Strom Thurmond*
Representative in Congress District 3	☒ Wm. Jennings Bryan Dorn	☐ C. M. Smith	

INSTRUCTIONS—To vote a straight party ticket, make a cross (X) in the circle (O) under the name of your party. Nothing further need or should be done. To vote a mixed ticket, or in other words for candidates of different parties, omit making a cross (X) mark in the party circle at the top and make a cross (X) mark in the voting square ☐ opposite the name of each candidate on the ballot for whom you wish to vote. If you wish to vote for a candidate not on any ticket, write or place the name of such candidate on your ticket opposite the name of the office. Before leaving the booth, fold the ballot so that initials of the manager may be seen on outside.

THE ABOVE IS THE WAY YOUR BALLOT WILL LOOK WHEN YOU VOTE FOR THURMOND

REMEMBER 4 THINGS

1. Do not touch the circle under the words "Democrat" or "Republican" at the top of the ballot.

2. Place a cross in front of all names in the column headed "Democrat" except Edgar A. Brown.

3. Write in the name of Strom Thurmond (or have the manager do it for you in your presence) in the last column on the right opposite United States Senator as shown above.

4. It is not necessary to strike out any name on the ballot.

Front page of *The Edgefield Advertiser* when it was supporting Strom.

CHAPTER
THIRTEEN

+

The Write-In Candidate

Edgar Brown's was not the only car that left Charleston and headed for Columbia after Maybank's funeral. Other members of the state Democratic Executive Committee also sped away that Friday. At 6 p.m. the deadline would expire for the Democratic Party to certify its nominee for the Senate. The procedure was spelled out in a statewide statute that, ironically, Thurmond had helped draft when he was a state senator.

But it was all so unseemly. Fewer than fifty politicians met in the club room of the Jefferson Hotel with legal authority to name a United States senator for a full term. A vote to circumvent the law and hold a primary failed by a vote of 28-18. The executive committee then voted 31-18 to nominate Edgar Brown, handing him a Senate seat that voters had twice before denied him, in 1924 and 1938. The sixty-six-year-old Brown had served on the state executive committee since 1914 and for many years had served as Democratic National Committeeman. In South Carolina he was "Mr. Democrat."

His state Senate buddy, Rembert Dennis of Berkeley County, made the motion to nominate Brown. "I, too, as many of you, favor a primary to get a candidate," Dennis said, but added, "In this emergency we do not have time for a primary under our election laws."

The press in the state, led by *News and Courier* editor Thomas R. Waring — an admring nephew of the by-then infamous Judge Waring — would light a fire of protest. Gov. James F. Byrnes would fan it into a consuming blaze.

Although publicly calling for a primary, Byrnes had let the

state executive committee know through a friend that he was interested in the nomination and would submit to a draft.[1] As governor, however, Byrnes in 1952 had actively supported Republican Dwight Eisenhower for president, and party loyalists on the Democratic Executive Committee weren't about to lose face by naming an apostate. This meant they wouldn't have considered Thurmond either because he also had endorsed Eisenhower.

Other loyal Democrats were waiting in the wings. Thirty-eight-year-old Bryan Dorn drove home to Greenwood after Maybank's funeral believing he had a commitment from friends on the executive committee to put his name in nomination. He expected to get overwhelmed by Brown, but the move would position him to make a write-in challenge against Brown based on principle.

"I would have announced as a write-in immediately, had my name been put up before the executive committee," Dorn explained a quarter-century later, after he had served twenty-six years in Congress and twice run unsuccessfully for governor (In the 1960s, he was among the first elected officials in South Carolina to speak out as a moderate on racial issues). "The race would have been between Dorn and Brown. As the former runner-up for that seat in the Senate, I would have really charged fraud, chicanery, unfairness and everything. It just automatically would have been a race between Dorn and Brown, and I would have won. There's no question about that.

"But when I came back here, I was bitterly, sorely disappointed because my name had not been put before the executive committee at all. Well, I made some statements in the news media that they were wrong, that they should have considered other candidates, and I was the runner-up, all this kind of stuff. But then I came back home.

"A friend of Donald Russell (then president of the University of South Carolina and a protege of Jimmy Byrnes and later governor, senator, and federal judge) came and sat right over here, and he had a statement written, typed up, announcing Donald Russell as the write-in candidate for the U. S. Senate. And if I would tell them that I would not run as a write-in, he would go get on the phone and call Don Russell and he would announce that night for the U. S. Senate on a write-in. Well, I didn't do it. I just didn't tell them, because I knew that I was the logical one to run. I had made that race [in 1948] and spent all that money — all this kind of doings. I just wasn't prepared to do that that night.

"Of course, I had to hesitate because I was a nominee of the Democrats for this seat in the Congress. I could not ignore that. This did pose a dilemma. I didn't want to lose both of them.

"I went to church and I told my wife, Millie, to buy me some radio time, and I would announce. I was naive enough to believe that Thurmond would follow his own suggested program and support me as a write-in candidate. Also, I hesitated because I didn't know if I could get the money I needed to get on radio and TV to run an effective campaign. Millie had researched the cost of radio and determined that we would need $15,000 just to make a 15-minute announcement on a statewide hook-up.

"I think the fellow at the station that Mrs. Dorn was working through called the other side. They concluded that I definitely was going to run. And so, Thurmond announced Tuesday following all this. I was at a VFW meeting in Darlington. They thought that I was going to announce that night. So they told me when I got there that Thurmond had announced as a write-in. He just beat me to it.

"I still considered it for a couple of days. I didn't want to be buffaloed and halfway cheated out of it. So I considered it for a while and finally abandoned the idea and announced that I would not run. Jimmy Byrnes and others called me to say if both Thurmond and I ran, Brown would get elected.

"Thurmond was pretty slick, you know. He had nothing to lose in that campaign. His stock was low. He was out. He was miserable down there in Aiken. He wasn't in politics, first time in his life. And so, he jumped in there."[2]

Gov. Byrnes clearly understood that the public would see the executive committee's action as a power grab by Brown, from whom he had become alienated. Although Byrnes had served as best man in Brown's wedding many years earlier and Brown had long supported him, Brown refused to follow him in the Eisenhower campaign. Brown, never known for tact, worsened matters when he referred to Byrnes in conversation with friends as "a little sawed-off S.O.B." after the two had quarreled over some trustee matter involving Clemson. For Byrnes, a write-in candidate who could defeat Brown meant a measure of revenge.

Likable William F. "Buddy" Prioleau, who had been a top aide to Thurmond as governor, had joined Byrnes a few hours after Maybank's funeral. "I went over to Maybank's house that night," Prioleau remembered, "and it was just flooded with flowers, and after we got through taking care of all the U.S. senators and people and taking them all back to the airport, we started figuring out what to do with all these flowers. We flooded all the hospitals, and I really wanted to get away from the house anyway, so I said, 'I'm gonna take two or three of these big baskets over to Mrs. Byrnes.'

"They were at their beach home, over at the Isle of Palms, and I called to make sure it was convenient, and the governor said, 'Come on over here. I want to talk to you.' So I went over there, and the phone was just ringing and ringing and ringing. And it was people calling, and they were all upset because the executive committee already had had the meeting and announced the nominee and closed the nominations.

"I guess I was in a terrible plight because I was extremely fond of Edgar Brown, always had been. I knew that he was making a terrible mistake. I'm not gonna say I knew he would get beat.

"I'm not sure that without all those phone calls that Byrnes would have taken the active part that he took. But they just poured in. Byrnes and Maybank were so close, and he still was so shook up over the unexpected death and all. As the various ones kept calling, he told them, 'I swore that I would never get into another campaign, but I'm gonna get into this one.'

"He wanted a candidate, and he wanted one right away. There was a lot of speculation about Donald Russell. Russell didn't want to do it. Russell was president of the university, and he was concerned about the fact that if he got into it and was defeated what it would do to the university's appropriation and that sort of thing."

Byrnes then asked Prioleau, "Do you think Strom would do it?"

"At the drop of a hat. He's sitting there in Aiken waiting on you to call him."

"You talked to him?"

"No, but I know him like a book."

"Well, call him and see if he can come up tomorrow."

Prioleau remembered, "I knew how bad he'd been wanting to get in the U. S. Senate. He was making more money than he'd ever made in his life, but Strom is basically a political being. He was destined to get back into public life one way or the other."[3]

Alex McCullough, a top aide to Byrnes at the time, had remained in Columbia during the funeral to take care of matters in the governor's office. He stayed in touch with Byrnes. "I told him we were getting a lot of telegrams and calls saying, 'Get somebody to run against Edgar Brown. Don't let him do this.' Mr. Byrnes really would have liked Donald Russell to run and urged him to step forward. So I said, 'How about showing these messages to Mr. Russell?' And Byrnes said, 'Well, don't tell him I said to do it,' and he hadn't, really.

"So I called Russell and I said, 'I've got a lot of messages here that I'd like you to see. People are really upset about this nomination of Brown.' I volunteered to take them over to the university [about two or three blocks away], and he said, 'No, I'll come by there.' He and Mrs. Russell came by and I showed these things to him, and I said, 'Gee, if anybody thought that the public was upset, you could sure see it from what we had.' It wasn't just stacks of them, but it was enough.

"And he read these and looked at me and said, 'Yeah, well how do you keep this alive until the general election?' He didn't really have the insides for going into battle like Thurmond did. He really just didn't have the kind of political courage it took."[4] Russell thanked McCullough and added, "Tell Mr. Justice that I appreciate him thinking about me, but tell him I didn't see Donald Russell's name on any of those letters."[5]

Charles Simons remembers Thurmond "getting a multitude of calls" from people asking him to run. Thurmond emphasizes that Byrnes asked Russell to run, not him. "He did not call me and suggest that I run. I called him and told him I was going to run. I had waited several days and was rather hopeful that some other candidate would announce, but I felt it was essential that someone enter the race and not delay longer."[6]

Thurmond recalled twenty years later, "I called Donald Russell and told him that I was going to run, and he said, 'Well, since you are going to run, I won't consider it any further.' I called Bryan Dorn and told him that I decided to run, and he said, "Well, if you are going to run, I won't run.' I am not too sure though that either one of them would have run because they had plenty of time before I announced. "I don't think that anybody could have been elected on a Republican ticket at that time. I wasn't too anxious to run myself on a write-in basis because when I look back over it now, I don't see how in the world I got elected. It was a hard decision for me to make, but I made up my mind after giving time to Russell and Dorn and the rest of them who had been mentioned. And once I made the decision I then was going to run regardless of who ran, and I called them and told them.

"Governor Byrnes did announce support for me and he based it mainly on the fact that people were denied the right to vote."[7]

Thurmond recalled that Tom Waring "probably did" urge him to run, but that no other newspaper editors in the state contacted him directly. He thanked Waring afterward "for the masterful job" he and his newspaper did in connection with the election.[8]

The News and Courier set the tone and provided the leadership for the state's press. The morning after the Democratic Executive Committee nominated Brown, an editorial in the newspaper acknowledged his ability, but asserted, "His mandate comes not from the people but from the politicians." Thurmond had said just before the meeting that if the people of South Carolina were denied the opportunity to choose their senator, they "would strongly resent any other procedure, and they would resent it rightfully."

When he announced his write-in candidacy on September 7, he hedged by offering Brown an opportunity of resigning and running in a primary. Otherwise, Thurmond said, "This is a fight for principle. It is a fight for government by the people instead of government by a small group of committeemen."

In the campaign that followed, fourteen of the state's sixteen dailies — all but the two in Anderson — supported Thurmond's write-in efforts, as did seventy-three of the state's eighty-six weeklies.

On the day after he announced, *The News and Courier* headlined an editorial, "Thurmond is the man." It said:

Once before, when Southerners hunted for a way out of voting for a deal they resented, Strom Thurmond came forward. That was in 1948. He was the states rights candidate for president. He didn't have a chance of election, but he ran anyway, as a matter of principle. Again a principle is at stake. It is bigger than personalities, though we do not hesitate to endorse Mr. Thurmond on his own merits.[9]

Thurmond campaigned with his usual vigor, Jean beside him all the way. Dolly Hamby, one of three female partners in a well-connected and respected Columbia public relations firm known in the trade as "the girls," was a tennis player who had played mixed doubles with Strom from his days as a judge. When she saw he was considering the race, she called him and offered to help.

Strom told her he had no money or campaign headquarters. She talked the manager of the Columbia Hotel into providing a private room for Strom and Jean and the whole mezzanine as a campaign headquarters.

"One of his greatest assets was Jean," Hamby said. "She

laughed at his foibles and called him 'Pappy.' Jean would say, 'Pappy, you remember so-and-so.' She always remembered names. At one point in October, Strom all but lost his voice. It was a bare whisper. At a speech before several thousand people at Valley Park, he said, 'Jean, you have to talk.' She made a great speech.

"We'd leave his hotel room at 3 a.m. in the morning to finish taping commercials. And he'd say, 'Come on for a walk with us. Jean and I are going for a walk.' And he'd raise Cain with you if you smoked. I've never seen anyone who could campaign like Strom. He never stopped.

"We did all his ads, all his TV spots. He couldn't read the teleprompter. He was too vain to wear glasses."[10]

The state's three largest newspapers, *The News and Courier*, *The State*, and *The Greenville News*, all had followed Byrnes in his support for Eisenhower in 1952. With their movement toward the Republican Party, Brown gave them an opportunity to attack on the basis of principle, and they took it.

Had Brown been less greedy for power and shrewd enough to accept the nomination with a pledge to resign after two years, he might well have pulled it off. Years later, he lamented his poor judgment. "I think that if I had made that statement that night — that this is an emergency, the nomination has come to me in a dramatic way, but it's not the way to elect a senator for six years to serve all the people — I'll accept it, but I promise you that I'll resign before the next primary in 1956 — if I'd done that I don't think that they would have ever come out against me."[11]

To make matters worse he kept getting help from Washington that always backfired. For example, the chairman of the Democratic National Committee, Stephen Mitchell of Illinois, implied in an endorsement that South Carolinians lacked sufficient literacy to allow a write-in campaign to succeed.

In addition to the crusading support of the state's press, the relentless backing of Byrnes for Thurmond proved at least as important. Byrnes possessed far more political sophistication than anyone else in South Carolina.

Prioleau said that Byrnes "had the best public relations sense that I have every seen in anybody. He was an old newspaper man himself — he published the Aiken paper down there. He really was an international figure, and the state was pretty much inclined to say, 'Well, gosh, if that's what Jimmy Byrnes thinks, that's good enough for me.'

"He literally called hundreds and hundreds of people who

were real entrenched Byrnes people around the state. His whole theory was, 'Forget the personalities. What we've got to do is run an educational campaign. Nobody had ever had to write in. Everybody's got to be tipped off on how to do it.'"

Byrnes wasn't reluctant to call a friendly editor and suggest an idea for an editorial. *The News and Courier* launched a campaign of running front-page directions on how to cast a write-in vote. Near the end of the campaign, the directions included a replica of the ballot with an arrow pointing to the line on which to write in — depicted with a handwritten "Strom Thurmond."

Prioleau continued, "Byrnes was the one who had thousands and thousands of pencils printed up with Thurmond's name on it in big letters so they could spell it right. He was the old pro. He looked into the possibility of 'Suppose they spell it incorrectly, but it's clearly visible?' He got rulings in advance on all this sort of thing that nobody else would have thought about.

"We ran out of money. Well, there wasn't anybody who could raise money like Byrnes. He could pick up the phone and call three people and have $50,000 in thirty minutes. He was in it deep."

John West, a newly elected state senator from Kershaw County, accepted Brown's request to serve as campaign manager. West recalled that after each Saturday afternoon University of South Carolina home football game that fall, Brown had a reception at his Wade Hampton Hotel headquarters, directly across the street from the governor's office in the State House.

The first one in September drew a comfortably large crowd of county and municipal political leaders. The attendance got progressively smaller with each succeeding game. West and Brown could see the lights on in the governor's office every night, and they learned Byrnes stayed on the telephone for hours exuding his persuasive charm on local political leaders.[i]

About three weeks before the election, Thurmond went into a brainstorming session with Byrnes and Hamby and her associates. "We figured we needed something to get us over the hump," Hamby remembered. "Strom said, 'I could agree to resign after two

---

i. Almost two decades later, when West was governor, he persuaded Brown to allow legislation to pass — Brown still retained his power as chairman of the Senate Finance Committee and had been blocking it — to erect a statue of Byrnes on the northeastern corner of the State House grounds. West then arranged for Brown to visit Byrnes, who was retired and living in Columbia's Heathwood section. The two men hadn't spoken since 1954, but they sipped bourbon and relaxed and told stories. Mrs. Byrnes joined them. Brown returned from the visit in a genial mood. He told West, "I always did love Maude." (Bass interview with John West, January 2, 1998)

years.'" Byrnes agreed it was a splendid idea, and they planned to make an announcement a few days later, but it got out sooner.

Charles Wickenberg, one of the state's top journalists, saw Thurmond leave the meeting and asked, "What's new?" Strom said, "Well, I'm going to resign after two years." Wick had a scoop.

In the history of the United States, no write-in candidate had ever been elected to either house of Congress, and none has since. But on November 2, South Carolina voters took their pencils to the polls, and 143,444 of them wrote in the name of "Strom Thurmond" or "Strum Thormond" or something equally close — enough to defeat Edgar Brown by 60,000 votes.

1. Robert Sherrill, *Gothic Politics in the Deep South* (New York: Ballantine Books, 1969), p. 248.
2. William Jennings Bryan Dorn and Scott Derks, *Dorn: Of the People: A Political Way of Life.* (Orangeburg, S. C.: Bruccoli Clark Layman/Sandlapper Publishing) 1988, pp. 155-158; Thompson interview with Bryan Dorn, September 13, 1981.
3. Thompson interview with William J. Prioleau, 1982.
4. Thompson interview with Alex McCullough, February 8, 1982.
5. Bass telephone interview with Charles Wickenberg, March 5, 1998.
6. Thurmond to Thomas R. Waring, December 20, 1954, Waring correspondence files, The South Carolina Historical Society, Charleston, S.C.
7. Bass interview with Strom Thurmond, February 1, 1974, Bass-DeVries collection, Folio A166, Southern Historical Collection, The University of North Carolina at Chapel Hill.
8. Thurmond letter of December 30 to Waring, op. cit.
9. *The News and Courier*, September 8, 1954, p. 4.
10. Bass telephone interview with Dolly Hamby, March 5, 1998.
11. William D. Workman, Jr., *The Bishop From Barnwell: The Political Life and Times of Edgar Brown*, (Columbia: The R. L. Bryan Company, 1963), p. 256.

New Senator Strom Thurmond and wife Jean arrive in Washington.

CHAPTER
FOURTEEN

✦

Rambunctious Democrat

Fifty-two-year-old Strom Thurmond arrived in Washington with a strategic swing vote that made Senate Majority Leader Lyndon Baines Johnson court him. LBJ's propensity for control and Strom's for independent action only intensified their philosophical differences, but for now Thurmond had a vote that Johnson needed.

He also had a jump on seniority, thanks to Gov. Byrnes and the early resignation of interim Senator Charles Daniel, a politically active Greenville construction magnate. Vice President Richard Nixon swore Thurmond in on December 24, a few weeks before eight other Senate freshmen took office in January 1955. He got good committee assignments on government operations, interstate and foreign commerce, and public works.

The new Senate, presided over by Nixon, consisted of forty-eight Democrats, forty-seven Republicans, and Independent Wayne Morse of Oregon. Strom's shaky party allegiance was crucial to every Democratic committee chairman as well as Lyndon Johnson.

Johnson's top operative, South Carolinian Bobby Baker, had served as the national Democratic Party's emissary to Edgar Brown and delivered cash to his campaign. After managing Thurmond's write-in campaign, Alex McCullough went to Washington as his administrative assistant. McCullough remembered, "Johnson and Bobby Baker immediately began courting Thurmond because they weren't at all certain whether he was going to vote with the Democrats to organize the Senate or not. The senator learned to take these things at face value — about how happy they were to see him and so on."

Thurmond quickly demonstrated his independence. "Pretty quickly after the Senate was organized," McCullough said, "Lyndon Johnson seldom gave Thurmond any attention except to send a threat that he was never going to get on that Armed Services Committee if he kept on voting the way he was, something like that."[1] Johnson, the Texas senator whose domineering personality became the stuff of legend, quickly realized that Thurmond would not be influenced by intimidation.

Political writer Robert Sherrill described his first visit to Thurmond's office, when the senator was having one of his weekly staff meetings. "They are a combination pep talk, lecture on Politics 301, and sermon," Sherrill reported. "He was telling the youngsters on his staff about how the Constitution does not allow the federal government to monkey with religion. He ended by saying 'There's just so much power, and you've got to decide where it will be put: in the states or up here.' It was, I discovered, a perfect key to his view of the world . . . of metaphysical absolutes — where love and hate and jealousy and power and truth are not limitless, but bounded; where qualities and impulses can be weighed by the pound. It is a world of pure blood. It is a world of one Eden, one Hell, one Heaven, one Right, one Wrong, one Strom."[2] All of Washington would soon discover it.

From the beginning, Strom hovered over his staff. He advised them to avoid coffee and fatty foods, encouraged perfection, and organized weekend staff bicycle rides through Rock Creek park. Strom and Jean would lead the way, with panting staffers trailing them. "The secret of strength and health is proper eating, proper exercise and reasonable sleep," he told a reporter soon after his arrival — and continued telling them more than forty years later.

Young Harry Dent had returned from two years as an Army lieutenant and dropped out of the University of South Carolina law school in mid-semester when offered a reporting job in Washington in the fall of 1953 for Sims News Service. A one-person operation, it provided newspapers back home with coverage of South Carolina news from Washington. With Jean's prompting, Strom quickly hired Dent as his press secretary.

Lyndon Johnson would work over Thurmond's aides in the Senate cloakroom when he had a problem with Strom. They often discussed these sticky issues with Jean, and many times Thurmond would come in the next morning saying he had reflected on a matter and changed his mind. "She had more influence over him than any of us had," Dent said. But Jean also protected her husband when his aides pushed for something they wanted to do. "He'd go home and come back the next morning, and it's dead," Dent said. "It was Jean."[3]

But Thurmond was no ordinary freshman senator. "He wasn't regarded lightly," said McCullough. "Anybody that's in politics who sees somebody get elected on a write-in vote to the United State Senate — they knew there was a reason."[4]

Meanwhile, Thurmond's quirkiness attracted amused attention. He ordered pounds of South Carolina yellow grits for his personal use in the Senate dining room. Olin Johnston received a truckload of watermelons from a South Carolina farmer and sent out a photograph of himself and staff. When Olin saw the print in a newspaper back home he found a smiling Strom had squeezed in among the crowd. Johnston steamed about the extent Strom sought publicity.

Thurmond and Johnston soon reached a truce, their staffs working together on home state projects. But there was never any warmth between the two senators.

Contrary to custom, Johnston and his wife made no effort to introduce the state's new junior senator and his wife to the social circuit. The youngest Senate wife except for Jacqueline Kennedy, at twenty-eight Jean attracted the attention of Patricia Nixon, the vice president's wife. She personally took Jean under her wing. After two statewide campaigns and one national, Jean was politically seasoned. She adapted quickly to Washington's ways.

When a group of South Carolina newspaper editors came up for a convention, she and Strom had a reception for them at their apartment. Neither Jean nor Strom drank, and she debated whether to serve alcohol, knowing that many of the newspapermen might have expected it. But she offered the same nonalcoholic punch that she had in the governor's mansion in Columbia.

As a brigadier general in the Army Reserve, Thurmond went with other Congressmen and staffers on an overseas trip for their active duty assignment, Dent joining him. At the Turkish national military academy, Thurmond reviewed the cadet corps, rejoined the others at a social gathering, and toasted the bravery and fighting record of the Turks.

He raised to his lips a glass of what he thought was apple juice, gulped half of it, then choked. The word hadn't been passed, and Thurmond spit his mouthful of Scotch whiskey back into the glass. As the concerned Turkish hosts fretted and the Congressional party snickered, Thurmond innocently explained, "Er-ah, I thought this was apple juice."[5]

Thurmond's reputation as a maverick preceded him, and he lived up to it. In a system built on the art of compromise and in a chamber with unwritten rules about teamwork and cooperation, his stubbornness or "bullheadedness," as former Sen. J. William Fulbright of Arkansas described it, promptly set him apart as a lonely outsider. "He was a rebel on the Democratic side, and he was always breaking up the china closet," said Dent, who functioned as the senator's alter ego. He became administrative assistant after McCullough returned to South Carolina in 1957 to work as a bank executive.

McCullough's interest was in the process of governing, not politics. Dent believed that McCullough, a stern Calvinist, wanted things done his way and tried to tell Thurmond what to do. Alex just couldn't get along with the senator," Dent said.

McCullough remembered, "The thing that bothered me most was that every decision was a political decision. There were a lot of things that I didn't think he should do at all, and he'd done some of them as governor, such as writing letters to people with whom he had absolutely no relationship, no acquaintance with them, to express sympathy on a death in the family. And there were a lot of people in the state who resented it. A lot of people thought it was great. I simply thought it was inappropriate, at a time like that." He added, "I remember once Jean Thurmond said, 'Well, Alex, let him be a politician until after the next primary, then let him be a statesman.'"[6]

Strom believed he owed little allegiance to the Democratic Party — he got elected without its help. But Jean worked to mend those party ties. The legislative process interested her, and she regularly attended Senate sessions and developed a folksy relationship with LBJ, who on many days spotted her in the Senate gallery and waved.[7]

After succeeding McCullough, Dent finally confronted Thurmond about the political gall of sending what the staff called "c and c's" — congratulations and condolences — to strangers. The image remained forever vivid to Dent.

"There was a death that day in the paper of a little five-year-old boy outside Aiken whose father was bailing hay, and the little boy got caught up in the hay bailer," Dent says. "He got crushed to death. I saw the condolence come across the desk, and I said, 'Watch this.'"

Dent marched in, confronted Thurmond, told him it was "terrible" to write a sympathy letter to people he didn't know, that it was transparently political. Dent added, "I'm just trying to keep you from hurting yourself." He tore up the letter, threw it into the trash can, and proudly walked out. He said the staff agreed with him. "I said, 'We took care of that. There'll be no more of it.'"

A few weeks later in Aiken Dent and the local manager went out to breakfast. "There were two old guys that came walking in. And one of them turned to my companion and said, 'Ain't you Senator Thurmond's friend?' He said, 'I run Senator Thurmond's office down here. I want you to meet Mr. Dent. He's the man who runs everything in the Washington office.'

"The man said, 'Well, let me tell you something. My family will never forget Strom Thurmond as long we live.' Tears welled up in his eyes. He said, 'A couple of weeks ago I was out there in my field and I was bailing hay with my little boy. He got caught in that bailer and smashed to death.

"'You know, I got a letter from Senator Thurmond and you know, Mr. Dent, I figured he didn't write that letter. I figure you wrote that letter, but I'll tell you this, Mr. Dent. Me and my family and everybody I know will vote for him as long as we live.'"

Dent said, "It blew me away. I went back to Washington and told the staff. I said, 'The senator knows what he's doing.' I didn't try to give any more advice about bad politics. He was a master."[8]

Dent was not alone. Fred Buzhardt, Jr., was to Dent "the greatest friend I ever had." Buzhardt's father and Strom had practiced law together after studying under J. William's tutelage. "Old man Fred and Strom were like brothers," Dent said. "Young Fred was like a son to Strom Thurmond because of that relationship. Fred was brilliant, first honor graduate in law school, a graduate of West Point."[9] He wrote many of Thurmond's speeches and position papers and advised him on committee work.

Terrill Glenn, a law school classmate who at thirty-one became U. S. attorney in South Carolina in the Kennedy administration, remembered young Fred as "absolutely brilliant, but way out on the right."[10] For this reason, Jean had reservations about his advice to Strom. Buzhardt ultimately served as Richard Nixon's final lawyer before the president resigned after the House voted for impeachment. He died soon afterwards of a heart attack.

Thurmond organized his staff like a military outfit. If anyone drifted in after 9 a.m., their name went on a late list, which the senator reviewed. One staffer said, "If you were repeatedly late, you got talked to, and nobody was late after that." He demanded a twenty-four-hour turnaround for constituent letters and decreed that a telephone should not ring more than twice.

Constituent service was always a priority. (By 1989, his office had worked on 523,340 requests. He had posed for 10,600 pictures with school groups and office visitors — it hasn't slowed down since.)[11] Graduating high school seniors in South Carolina got letters of congratulations. The "c and c's" occasionally got absurd. One young couple once got a letter from Thurmond congratulating them on the birth of their first child, and the infant received one congratulating him for having such fine parents. Washington staffers would get tested after special training to sign his signature on photographs and routine correspondence.[12]

Thurmond arrived between 8 and 9 a.m., sometimes after a prayer breakfast. He began each day in the office by checking an obituary list compiled by staffs from his state offices — Aiken, Charleston, Columbia, Florence, and Greenville-Spartanburg. He personally called several of the families, then underlined in red everyone whose family he wanted to get a condolence letter. All of his correspondence included the phrase, "If there's anything I can do to be of help. . . ."

Thurmond learned from his father not to punish his enemies, but to convert — or at least neutralize — them. If a former political enemy needed a favor, Strom delivered. For example, a few years after the 1954 write-in campaign, Edgar Brown called Dent about a matter. "He wouldn't dare call the senator," Dent said. "He thought the senator wouldn't have anything to do with him. I said, 'Hell, let me put you on the phone with the Senator.' I put him on the phone with the Senator, and he said, 'What do you want?' And he got it done just like that. That's good politics."[13]

At the end of Thurmond's first year in Washington, he was getting pressure from men of influence at home not to resign, as he had pledged in the 1954 write-in campaign, but to stay in office and do his job. He and McCullough visited Gov. George Bell Timmerman, Jr., the lieutenant governor under both Thurmond and Byrnes. Thurmond wanted to know if he did resign, would the governor reappoint him? "I won't do that," Timmerman said, then pointedly reminded them of Thurmond's pledge to allow the people to elect their senator.[14] It was Timmerman's father, of course, whom Thurmond had defeated in the hard-fought race for circuit judge almost twenty years earlier. The Timmermans had long memories.

On March 4, 1956, Thurmond submitted a resignation letter to Timmerman, effective April 4, the day before the Democratic primary filing deadline. Thurmond said he would be a candidate but wanted to give sufficient notice to others. No one stepped forward. He moved back to Aiken and rejoined his old law firm for seven months. Interim Sen. Thomas Wofford of Greenville, a close associate of Timmerman's, kept the seat warm until after the election, with Dent remaining on board. "The senator gave his word, and he kept it," Dent said, "And people remembered."

Simmering in the background during Thurmond's first year in Washington was the Supreme Court landmark decision on May 17, 1954, *Brown v. Board of Education*, which ruled that state-mandated, racially segregated public schools violated the Fourteenth Amendment of the Constitution.

White Southerners initially responded calmly, but disquiet grew quickly in those areas where the population was majority black, such as Southside Virginia. Sen. Harry Byrd, Sr., whose "Byrd Machine" ruled the state with a paternalistic iron hand, began pushing the idea of "massive resistance."

A few months after Thurmond arrived in Washington, the Supreme Court in May 1955 issued its implementation order in the case known as *Brown II*. The Supreme Court said school desegregation should proceed "with all deliberate speed" and directed the lower federal courts to implement the process. Moderate white political leaders in the South felt relieved. The road seemed open for delay and evasion with friendly local judges.

In the spirit and atmosphere of "massive resistance," however, the young editor of *The Richmond News-Leader*, James Jackson Kilpatrick, soon unearthed the doctrine of "interposition," the theory that a state could "interpose" its sovereignty and invalidate a federal law. He argued for "principled" defiance. Upon close examination it amounted to little more than John C. Calhoun's nullification theory, an issue that the Civil War had clearly resolved. Under the Constitution's supremacy clause, federal law is "the supreme law of the land" in cases of conflict with state law. "Interposition" amounted to legal nonsense.

But for two months, Kilpatrick hammered away at the doctrine of interposition in editorials widely reprinted across the South, helping create a climate of resistance. Posturing state legislatures throughout the region passed interposition resolutions, creating false hopes among fearful whites and encouraging defiance.[i] Alabama Gov. James "Kissin' Jim" Folsom, compared the legislature's action there to a hound dog baying at the moon, but as blacks in the South began to ask for and then demand the same rights as other Americans, white fears mounted. Folsom's political standing rolled downhill.

The 1954 decision consolidated four cases, one involving the overwhelmingly black Summerton school district in South Carolina's Clarendon County. With the school cases looming and South Carolina defending its "separate but equal" doctrine, Gov. Byrnes in 1951 won legislative approval for a three percent sales tax, with revenue earmarked for public education. Byrnes declared, "We should do it because it's right. For me, that is sufficient reason. If any person wants an additional reason, I say it is wise."[15] Millions of dollars initially went to upgrade buildings and facilities at clearly unequal black schools. The state also quietly repealed its mandate for a public school system.

In its May 1954 decision, Eisenhower appointee Chief Justice Earl Warren wrote for a unanimous Supreme Court: "Today, education is perhaps the most important function of state and local governments. . . . it is a principal instrument in awakening the child to cultural values, in preparing him for later professional training and in helping him to adjust normally to his environment. In these days, it is doubtful that any child may reasonably be expected to succeed in life if he is denied the opportunity of an education. Such an opportunity, where the state has undertaken to provide it, is a right which must be made available to all on equal terms."

He concluded "that in the field of public education the doctrine of 'separate but equal' has no place. Separate educational facilities are inherently unequal."

---

i. At a seminar at Emory University in the spring of 1998, Kilpatrick responded to a question about his role in popularizing the concept of interposition. He said that at the time there was talk of "blood running in the streets" and that he believed then it would be helpful to elevate the public dialogue. He acknowledged, however, that in terms of constitutional validity, he had been wrong.

For three years Senate Majority Leader Lyndon Johnson and House Speaker Sam Rayburn, both Texans, had achieved an armistice on civil rights among Congressional Democrats by appealing to both sides for restraint. Early in 1956, a critical election year, Thurmond led the effort to shatter that armistice. Knowing he would resign and amid some speculation that Timmerman might challenge him, Thurmond began trying to unify Southern senators to make a declaration against the 1954 *Brown* decision. Most were wary, but Virginia's Byrd worked with Thurmond to get a meeting.

Because of the *Brown* opinion's references to contemporary psychology and a footnote referring to Swedish sociologist Gunnar Myrdal's *An American Dilemma*, which focused on the conflict between the "American Creed" and the prejudiced place of African-Americans, Thurmond maintained that *Brown* was based on psychology and sociology rather than law and therefore invalid. As the Supreme Court indicated in *Brown*, however, *Plessy* itself clearly reflected the prevailing "scientific" theories of its day about race. As a lawyer and former judge, Thurmond surely knew that a unanimous Supreme Court opinion clearly is law, whether or not one agrees with it. He also surely knew that attacking the Court would be good politics at home.

In his first draft, mimeographed on February 6, 1956, Thurmond condemned the *Brown* decision as a "clear violation of the Constitution by the Court." He commended states that had approved resolutions of "interposition" and their intention to use "every lawful means at their disposal."

Many of his Southern colleagues resisted a meeting. With its lock on committee chairmanships and the weapons of filibuster and cloture (Senate rules then required a two-thirds vote to shut off a filibuster — extended debate — instead of the current three-fifths), the South's Democratic team had the capacity to block legislation or force compromise. They effectively exercised Calhoun's complex theory of the concurrent majority. Most of the Southern senators, understanding both constitutional law and the depth of white fears about the decision, sought to promote calm.

Thurmond and Byrd let the others know they might issue the manifesto themselves, with as many as would sign without a meeting. With that, Sen. Walter George of Georgia, the senior Southerner in the Senate, called a meeting on February 8. Sen. George himself faced potential strong opposition that year from former Gov. Herman Talmadge. (In the end, George withdrew and Talmadge was elected in a campaign in which he began to court black voters.)

On the morning of the meeting, newspapers carried stories of a crisis in Tuscaloosa, Alabama, where mob violence was forcing Autherine Lucy off the University of Alabama campus. She had just enrolled as the first black student. (Seven years would pass before the color line was finally broken there — a day history would remember as Gov. George Wallace's "stand in the schoolhouse door.")

At the meeting of the Southern senators, Thurmond introduced his second draft, which continued to endorse interposition. This draft escalated the rhetoric by condemning "the illegal and unconstitutional decision of the Court." George appointed Richard Russell to chair a committee that also included John Stennis of Mississippi and Sam Ervin of North Carolina to study and revise Thurmond's draft.

By the fourth draft — this one written with Thurmond and Fulbright, a former university president who had little use for Thurmond — the word "interposition" was gone. Although toned down by Fulbright, the document still condemned the "illegal . . . seizure of power by the nine men composing the Court." It commended "the motives of those states which have declared the intention to resist this invasion of their sovereignty by the Court by every lawful means."[16]

A final draft, with Sen. Price Daniel of Texas taking Ervin's position on the committee, was presented to the Senate on March 12. Nineteen of the twenty-two Southern senators signed what became known as the Southern Manifesto. They were joined by eighty-one House members. As Majority Leader, Lyndon Johnson wasn't asked to sign it, and the two Tennessee senators, Estes Kefauver and Albert Gore, Sr., refused.

The final document declared that the Supreme Court, "with no legal basis for their action, undertook to exercise their naked judicial power and substituted their personal and political ideas for the established law of the land." It deplored the court's "clear abuse of judicial powers" and commended "the motives of those states which have declared their intention to resist integration by any lawful means." The fact that Fulbright signed the manifesto and Lyndon Johnson did not was later given as an explanation why Johnson was acceptable to John F. Kennedy as a running mate in 1960 but Fulbright was unacceptable as his secretary of state.

Gore called the manifesto "a dangerous, deceptive propaganda move which encouraged Southerners to defy the government and to disobey its laws, particularly orders of the federal court."[17]

After George introduced the manifesto, officially the "Declaration of Constitutional Principles," Thurmond called it "a historic event" in remarks to the Senate. He denounced "outside agitators" who employed "professional racist lawyers" to end segregation in public schools and disrupt "the harmony which has existed for generations between the white and the Negro races."

He declared, "The propagandists have tried to convince the world that the States and the people should bow meekly to the decree of the Supreme Court. I say it would be the submission of cowardice if we failed to use every lawful means to protect the rights of the people."

He asserted that "the white people of the South are the greatest minority in this Nation. They deserve consideration and understanding instead of the persecution of twisted propaganda."

In response, Oregon's Morse said, "you would think today Calhoun was walking and speaking on the floor of the Senate." Thurmond no doubt took that as a compliment.[ii]

Morse acknowledged the desegregation decision created problems for the South, but declared, "I think it is a correct decision, a sound decision, and a decision that was long overdue." He said the Supreme Court "has at long last declared that all Americans are equal, and that the flame of justice in America must burn as brightly in the homes of the blacks as in the homes of the whites."

If Southerners really wanted "to put themselves above the Supreme Court and above the Constitution," Morse challenged, "let them propose a constitutional amendment that will deny to the colored people of the country equality of rights under the Constitution and see how far they will get with the American people."[18]

The Southern Manifesto meant the overwhelming majority of the South's political leadership was urging defiance. Adlai Stevenson, counting on support of Southern moderates in seeking renomination as the Democratic presidential candidate, dispatched Harry Ashmore, a key Southern adviser, to Washington. Ashmore,

ii. More than a century earlier, Harriet Martineau (in *Retrospect of Western Travel*) had characterized Calhoun as ". . . the cast iron man, who looks as if he had never been born and never could be extinguished; . . . he is wrought like a piece of machinery, set going vehemently by a weight and stops while you answer; he either passes by what you say, or twists it into suitability with what is in his head." James G. Banks, a leading academic scholar of Thurmond, used this quote to characterize him in a paper on "A Study in Continuity" that was presented at The Citadel Conference on the New South.

by now executive editor of *The Arkansas Gazette* in Little Rock, had questioned Thurmond on a radio program there during the Dixiecrat campaign. He recalled trying "to get him to talk about something other than segregation, and I didn't succeed at all."[19] Ashmore met in Washington with Olin Johnston, who told him, "It's no use trying to talk to Strom. He *believes* that shit."[20]

In Alabama, Judge Richard Rives of the Fifth Circuit Court of Appeals, which soon would become the legal battleground over civil rights, walked down the hall of the federal courthouse in Montgomery for a quiet visit with his friend, Sen. Lister Hill. He explained that changed political realities had forced him and fellow moderate John Sparkman, Stevenson's 1952 running mate, to go along.

After listening intently, Rives said in his usual soft drawl, "Well, Lister, I think I understand it now. You fellas have just risen above principle."[21]

Throughout the South, the Citizens Council movement had begun to spread and grow from its 1954 birthplace in the Mississippi Delta. These "responsible people" vowed to act together to stop any move toward desegregation. They eschewed violence, opting instead for economic intimidation against uppity blacks who might seek to vote or enroll their children in white schools. The Montgomery bus boycott that began in January 1955 and the emergence there of the young black clergyman, Martin Luther King, Jr., accelerated the growth and spread of the Citizens Councils into a grassroots movement providing southwide links of massive resistance. From east Texas to Virginia, they stretched across the region, concentrating in rural counties with heavy black population. Strom Thurmond became one of their heroes.

A few months after issuance of the Southern Manifesto, two North Carolina Democratic congressmen who didn't sign it were defeated. In Arkansas, Gov. Orville Faubus, running for reelection to a two-year term, was attacked as being "soft" on integration by a segregationist opponent who got forty-two percent of the vote.

In 1957, with segregationists lining up to oppose him and the entire Arkansas congressional delegation on record to resist integration "by any lawful means," Faubus called out the National Guard to block nine black children from enrolling at Central High School in Little Rock. He contended he did so because he feared rioting, but no mob materialized. In the end, President Eisenhower mobilized federal troops to enforce the court's order. They

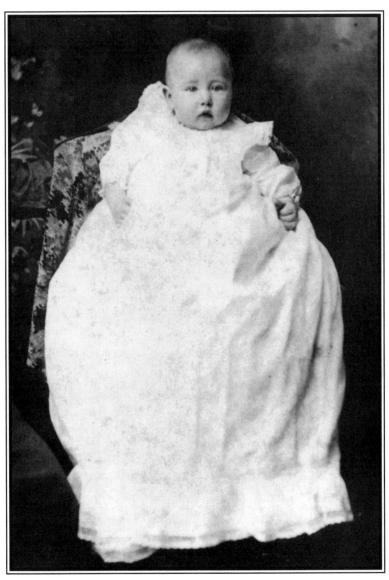

Baby Strom

School teacher

Sen. Strom admires portrait of Judge Strom Thurmond.

Gov. Strom and beauty queen

Strom and Jean on honeymoon

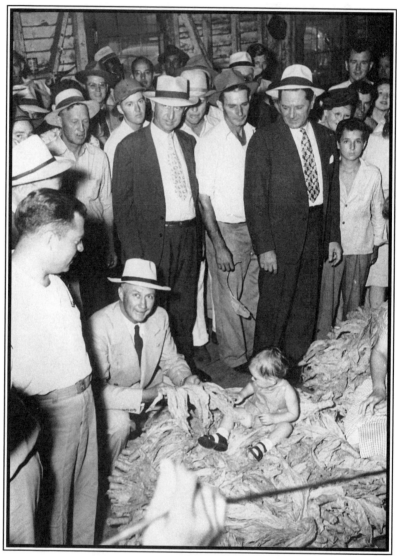

Gov. Thurmond opens tobacco market.

Sen. Burnet Maybank and Gov. Thurmond

The Barnwell Ring: Edgar Brown (l) and Sol Blatt

Thurmond becomes a Republican for the 1964 presidential campaign.

Miss South Carolina 1966, Nancy Moore

Strom shows Nancy his Washington office.

Festive days for the senator and family

Third in line for presidency

With Ronald Reagan at the White House

(l-r) Sen. Thurmond, Coretta Scott King, and Armstrong Williams

(l-r) Strom Thurmond, Armstrong Williams, and Duke Short
at Inauguration Party.

The Grand Ol' Man — with homefolks at Johnston, S.C., 1997

remained until the end of the 1957-58 school year.

Faubus later blamed federal authorities and the Eisenhower administration for putting him on the spot in a politically explosive situation. He asserted, "They could sit back and issue a court order that was going to cause literally hell and destroy many people, economically and politically. And they would just sit back and fold their hands and let somebody else reap the storm. Well, hell, it was their storm. A bunch of goddamn cowards for not coming in in the beginning and saying, 'This is a federal court order. We're going to have federal authorities here to see to it that it's obeyed and enforced.' Then I wouldn't have been involved."[22]

Ashmore, whose editorial page condemned Faubus for reckless irresponsibility, received a Pulitzer Prize for editorial leadership in the crisis. But Faubus won sixty-nine percent of the vote in the June 1958 Democratic primary, carrying all seventy-five counties. His 1956 segregationist opponent, after being wiped out in 1958, complained ruefully, "He used my nickel and hit the jackpot."[23] Faubus's display of defiance led to four more terms as governor, but the state's image suffered from news coverage of the turmoil. After emotions subsided, he died with a tarnished reputation.

Although Harry Byrd, Sr., continued to advocate a "last ditch stand" against integration, Virginia's commitment to "massive resistance" crumbled when white moderates organized in opposition after public schools in several communities were closed in 1958 to resist integration.[24]

Interposition finally played out in 1962 when Mississippi Gov. Ross Barnett claimed it gave him authority to defy federal court orders and block James Meredith from breaking the color line at the University of Mississippi. Meredith enrolled, but only after a riot that left two people dead and scores of federal marshals injured. Barnett's hero status didn't last long. In 1967 he ran fourth in attempting a comeback in the Democratic primary for governor.

But Thurmond had set his course. He would take his 1956 respite in Aiken, then return to Washington to resume his role as a symbol of Southern resistance to change. Although Thurmond would forever deny he had ever engaged in racism, his rhetoric of states rights always remained attached to the preservation of segregation. He avoided overt race-baiting, but for more than a quarter of a century, beginning with the Dixiecrat campaign, he championed with gusto the cause of white supremacy.

He also condemned the Supreme Court, calling for the

impeachment of Supreme Court justices who had ruled that defendants accused of subversive activities involving Communism were entitled to see F.B.I. and other files. He called the court a "great menace to this country," but denied his opinion was influenced by the 1954 school integration ruling.[25]

He received letters of approval from Stanley F. Morse of Charleston, president of the ultraconservative Grass Roots League, Inc., and W. J. Simmons of Jackson, Mississippi, executive director for the Citizens Councils. Simmons sent a copy of his letter to Morse. Thurmond corresponded extensively for well over a decade with Morse, once getting him royal treatment from the American counsel general when Morse visited Seville, Spain.[26]

To Stanley Morse, the "Communist negro [sic] drive was started in the United States in 1920" and spread forward until many clergymen, educators, scientists, and others had become "duped . . . to aid the Communist conspiracy." Morse's "Research Department" reported that "the Commies are making sure that [Martin Luther] King operates according to their plans."[27]

The record isn't clear whether Thurmond took Morse seriously or merely was humoring a friendly supporter, but in response to one letter from Morse on "documented proofs" connecting the Communist Party USA with "the Civil Rights Drive," Thurmond replied, "The material which you furnished has been invaluable in exposing the true nature of the Negro demonstrations." Morse's proof included a report that young Americans at a World Youth Festival in Helsinki, Finland, had sung such "un-American" songs as "We Shall Overcome" and "We Ain't Going to Study War No More."[28] Whatever Morse told Thurmond over a decade about Communist influence in the civil rights movement got reinforced from F. B. I. Director J. Edgar Hoover's well-documented vendetta against Martin Luther King, Jr.[29]

The 1957 filibuster was pure Strom Thurmond. It came after Sen. Russell orchestrated a successful eight-day filibuster in early July, in which Thurmond participated, that watered down the Civil Rights Bill. In exchange for allowing a bill to pass — the first civil rights legislation since 1875 — Russell got two concessions in hard bargaining with Lyndon Johnson. One involved removal of Title III, the main enforcement mechanism, which would have authorized the Justice Department to initiate school desegregation suits and to seek court injunctions against other forms of discrimination. With its primary enforcement mechanism gone, what remained were sections creating a fact-finding Civil Rights Commission and a new Civil Rights Division in the Justice Department that would begin the process of gaining for Southern blacks the right to vote.

The second concession involved amending the bill to require jury trials in contempt of court cases. Civil rights advocates opposed the jury-trial provision, arguing that Southern juries — with their record of refusing to convict whites who had brutally killed blacks — would never convict a white official charged with keeping blacks from voting.

After several weeks of debate, a compromise amendment allowed a jury trial in contempt cases involving a fine of more than $300 or imprisonment of more than ninety days. As the nation became more aware of issues involving voting discrimination and other forms of discrimination, Southerners in Congress found themselves losing allies.

Thurmond still wanted to fight, but at a caucus in Russell's office on August 24, agreement was reached that there would be no organized filibuster. Each individual could protest as he saw fit, and Southerners would vote as a bloc against the bill.

Three days later, Gov. Timmerman said citizens should "demand that their representatives stand up for what is right — or step aside and let there be elected men with political courage who will."[30] Thurmond sensed a potential opponent in Timmerman. The next afternoon, Wednesday, August 28, Thurmond again called on Russell, who declined to call a caucus meeting unless a majority of the South's senators requested it. Russell believed the South had gotten the best deal available, that a bargain had been struck, and that you played by the rules — written or unwritten. Thurmond was given a 9 p.m. speaking slot, in the belief that even if he droned on past midnight, he would get little attention. Thurmond apparently already had made up his mind to stage a one-man filibuster, taking steam baths for several days to dehydrate his body so it would absorb liquids without his having to leave the Senate chamber for the bathroom — and lose his right to continue speaking.

Thurmond let his staff know he planned to talk at length and took another long steam bath on the final afternoon. Thurmond planned to focus on the jury-trial issue — a provision that also bothered some of the most liberal members of Congress.

Jean expressed misgivings when the staff told her the plan, but brought Strom dinner and stayed for the duration.

Thurmond began speaking at 8:54 p.m. He did not finish until 9:12 p.m. the next night, twenty-four hours and eighteen minutes later. He drew laughter from his colleagues by concluding, "I expect to vote against the bill." He spoke almost two hours longer than the record set three years earlier by Wayne Morse. Thurmond's record still stands.

Sen. Barry Goldwater of Arizona briefly spelled Thurmond at one point, reading a report on military manpower policy, an act that helped develop a strong bond between the two men. Sen. Paul Douglas of Illinois, a former Marine and liberal Democrat who strongly believed in any person's right to a jury trial, sufficiently admired Thurmond's determination and stamina that after fourteen hours, he brought a full pitcher of orange juice — Thurmond's favorite beverage. Thurmond downed it all during the day, his dehydrated body absorbing the liquid like a sponge. Dent had arranged to have a bucket in the cloak room if the senator needed to relieve himself, keeping one foot inside the Senate chamber. Thurmond needed no relief.

Thurmond had hoped that news about his one-man stand would generate pressure on other Southerners to join him, but Russell held them in line. Minutes after Thurmond sat down, his distant relative Talmadge accused him of "grandstanding."[31] The next day, Russell coldly commented, "If I had undertaken a filibuster for personal aggrandizement, I would have forever reproached myself for being guilty of a form of treason against the South."[32]

The Senate approved the final bill 60-15.

Although Thurmond offended his Southern colleagues, they came to respect him. Talmadge would look back on him as "strong-willed and independent, resolute and dedicated. He was the ablest politician in the body. He never let a chance pass to cultivate a voter."[33]

Despite Talmadge's reputation as a committed segregationist, by 1958 he had turned the corner on race. After Ernest Vandiver won election as governor as a segregationist candidate that year, he accepted Talmadge's invitation to visit him at his home near Lovejoy, a half-hour southwest of Atlanta. Vandiver walked in to find Talmadge with a group of Atlanta's top black political leaders. Vandiver abandoned his segregationist stance.[34]

But Thurmond had set a course he continued to follow for another sixteen years. In 1963, as President Kennedy proposed to end discrimination in public accommodations after viewing the police dogs and fire hoses used against civil rights demonstrators in Birmingham, Thurmond called it "dictatorship over American business . . . to appease the Negro vote bloc."

When Congress passed the Civil Rights Act in 1964, Thurmond said, "This is a tragic day for America, when Negro agitators, spurred on by communist enticements to promote racial strife, can cause the United States Senate to be steamrolled into passing the worst, most unreasonable and unconstitutional legislation that has ever been considered by the Congress."

Thurmond said in 1965 that passage of the Voting Rights Act "shows that [Martin Luther] King [Jr.] must always have an agitation objective lest he end up in the street one day without a drum to beat or a headline to make."

When the Voting Rights Act came up for renewal in 1974, Thurmond called it "unfortunate that the Congress ever enacted such an unconstitutional piece of legislation."[35]

Was Olin Johnston right, that Thurmond simply believed it? Was he simply too obtuse to recognize that blacks in the South wanted the same rights under law that white citizens had? Was it all a charade, the same political exploitation of race that made Alabama's George Wallace a champion of segregation until the political calculus changed and it no longer paid off? Or did Thurmond simply have to experience new relationships himself, to absorb through osmosis that conditions had changed? Or was it all of the above? The answer to those questions should emerge as the rest of the story is told.

1. Thompson interview with McCullough, op. cit.
2. Robert Sherrill, *Gothic Politics in the Deep South* (New York: Ballantine Books, 1969), p. 256.
3. Bass interview with Dent, op. cit.
4. Thompson interview with McCullough, op. cit.
5. Lachicotte, *Rebel Senator*, op. cit., p. 126.

6. Thompson interview with McCullough, op. cit.
7. Ibid., p. 120.
8. Bass, Thompson interviews with Dent, op. cit.
9. Bass interview with Dent, op. cit.
10. Glenn to Bass, circa 1973.
11. *The State*, Nov. 25, 1989, p. 3-B, quoting former Administrative Assistant Dennis Shedd.
12. Bass telephone interviews with Ellie Beardsley and Missy Britt Barkdoll, March 1998.
13. Bass interview with Dent, op. cit.
14. Bass telephone interview with Charles Wickenberg, Timmerman's executive assistant, who witnessed the meeting, May 31, 1998.
15. Jack Bass, *Porgy Comes Home* (Columbia, S. C., R. L. Bryan Co., 1970), p.32.
16. Early drafts of "Origin of the Southern Manifesto", Special Collections, Cooper Library, Clemson University, Clemson, S. C.
17. Merle Miller, *Lyndon, An Oral Biography* (New York: Putnam, 1980), p. 187.
18. Special Collections, Robert Muldrow Cooper Library, Clemson University, four drafts of the Southern Manifesto and undated, unsigned two-page document, "Origin of the Southern Manifesto;" *The Congressional Record*, 84th Congress, 2nd Session, Vol. 102, Pt. 4, pp. 4515-16, 4461-62.
19. Bass interview with Ashmore, op. cit.
20. Dan T. Carter, *The Politics of Rage: George Wallace, the Origins of the New Conservatism, and the Transformation of American Politics* (New York: Simon & Schuster, 1995), p. 86.
21. Jack Bass, *Unlikely Heroes* (New York; Simon & Schuster, 1981), p. 65.
22. Jack Bass and Walter DeVries, *The Transformation of Southern Politics* (Athens: University of Georgia Press reissue, 1995), quoting Jim Johnson, p. 92.
23. Ibid.
24. *The Transformation of Southern Politics*, op. cit., p. 92.
25. Ibid., p. 347.
26. *The New York Times*, July 8, 1957, p. 15.

27. Stanley Morse letter to Strom Thurmond, July 16, 1957; W. J. Simmons letter to Strom Thurmond, July 22, 1957; Morse letter to Thurmond, March 31, 1964; Stanley Fletcher Morse papers, South Caroliniana Library, University of South Carolina, Columbia, S. C.
28. Grass Roots League, Inc. Research Bulletin No. 2, October 1, 1954, "Truth About Supreme Court's Segregation Ruling;" Grass Roots League Fact-Finding memo "C," January 1961, and memo "F," August 1962. Stanley F. Morse papers, op. cit.
29. Stanley Morse letter to Strom Thurmond, August 3, 1963; Thurmond letter to Morse, August 19, 1963.
30. See Taylor Branch, *Parting the Waters* (New York: Simon & Schuster, 1989), p. 403; *Pillars of Fire* (New York: Simon & Schuster, 1998), pp, 27-28, 526-31; David Garrow, *The FBI and Martin Luther King, Jr.* (New York: W. W. Norton, 1991), pp. 54-59, 78-85.
31. *The Charlotte Observer*, Hoke May column, September 1, 1957.
32. Quoted in Roscoe Drummond column, September 10, 1957, *New York Herald Tribune*.
33. *The Atlanta Constitution*, August 31, 1957, p. 1.
34. Bass interview with Herman Talmadge, Lovejoy, Georgia, June 2, 1998.
35. Vandiver to Bass, November 1997.
36. Cohodas, op. cit., p. 435.

A beautiful life together lasted only twelve years.

CHAPTER FIFTEEN

✛

Tragedy Strikes

Jean's magnetic personality helped prevent Strom's political relationships from deteriorating. She attended Senate sessions regularly, read periodicals, kept her husband informed, and remained socially engaged. She made friends with the elevator operators and the capitol police. She escorted visiting South Carolinians around the capital, giving guided tours.

Gov. Timmerman once sent a quartet of legislators to Washington to represent South Carolina on some matter. They included John West, the young state senator who had managed Edgar Brown's campaign, and Robert "Bob" McNair, a young representative from Allendale and a protege of Speaker Blatt. (Little more than a decade later, West followed McNair as a progressive governor.)

Jean ran into them at the Capitol and insisted on taking them out to dinner. Strom was off to an Army Reserve meeting, and she told them, "There's nobody I'd rather see and be with than this group." Everyone except Jean was drinking.

When she asked West why he wouldn't support her husband, he replied, "I'd vote for you for anything! I'd even vote for your husband!"

She laughed and said, "You've been drinking." West shrugged and said, "If I say it, I mean it. I'd even put it in writing."

She reached in her purse and pulled out a notebook. West wrote that he would vote for Strom Thurmond and signed it. The others all signed it, too. Months later West attended a rally for Thurmond in Kershaw County. Jean saw him, smiled, reached inside her blouse, and pulled out the piece of paper.[1] She seemed to have no enemies.

As summer approached in 1959, Jean began to tire easily. Driving one day, she ran into the back of a truck. It was at slow speed and there were no injuries. Then one day in early August, at home at their Foggy Bottom apartment, she collapsed. When Strom came home, she was barely able to get to the door and let him in. Another seizure followed three days later.

Her physician brother, Dr. Robert Crouch, practiced in the Maryland suburbs. She went to the National Institutes of Health. After extensive tests, she underwent surgery on September 17 for removal of a nonmalignant brain tumor. She confided to friends that she worried the operation would leave her damaged and a burden to her busy husband.

Her condition worsened that fall and she returned, partially paralyzed, to her mother's home in Elko. Strom considered resigning from the Senate, telling Jean he would do so if she wanted him to and it would in any way help. "You mean everything to me," he wrote, "and I shall follow the course that is best for you."

She returned to N.I.H., but her condition continued to worsen. She told family and close friends, "I've had everything a girl could want. I've experienced more in thirty-three years than most people experience in a lifetime twice as long as mine."

She returned with Strom to South Carolina for Thanksgiving. Although her condition deteriorated, for Christmas they went to the home of Strom's sister, Martha Bishop, in Greenwood. But her physician husband had to take Jean to his office for special treatment.

Nine days later, as her condition grew increasingly critical, doctors recommended on Sunday, January 3, that she return immediately to N.I.H. She underwent surgery on Tuesday to remove pressure on the brain, with both her physician brother and Strom's brother Allen George, also a doctor, observing. The surgeon found a "rapidly progressing malignant tumor."

Her condition was hopeless. Strom Thurmond had been unable to believe his beautiful young wife was dying. He kept vigil through the night, and she died at 8:35 a.m. on January 6, 1960. When told the morning after the surgery that she was dead, he told doctors, "But this can't be. You can't mean that."[2]

Strom called his close friend and former law partner, Charles Simons, to meet him the next morning at the train station in Augusta, where he would be accompanying Jean's body. "It was a cold, dreary, foggy morning," Simons remembered, "just the setting for something like that. Strom got out and was crying like a baby. He was crazy about Jean." Back in Washington, after Lyndon Johnson announced her death, Olin Johnston paid tribute in the Senate to "this sweet and beautiful woman."

At Strom's home in Aiken, his brothers and sisters gathered and discussed whether to bury Jean in Edgefield or Aiken. Strom asked Simons to go to Edgefield to the family plot. It was raining. At Willowbrook Cemetery, Simons remembered, "It was so wet, water would cover your shoes. I couldn't see Jean being buried in a watery grave." He returned to Aiken. "They called me in and really put me on the spot. They said, 'Charlie, where do you think we should bury Jean — in Edgefield or Aiken?' I said, 'Well, Jean loved Aiken and Aiken loved Jean. I think she ought to be buried here.'"[3]

She was buried on a plot of high ground at Bethany Cemetery. Lyndon Johnson led a delegation of senators who came down from Washington for the funeral. Harry Dent, who viewed LBJ's presence there cynically, was standing next to Thurmond when Johnson came through the line to express sympathy. The grief-stricken Thurmond told him, "I hope you're the next president of the United States," then broke down and cried. Dent saw it as LBJ's temporary breakthrough in a relationship with Thurmond marked by antagonism.[4]

For years the engraved tablet over Jean's tomb was mounted vertically on a stone obelisk. Later it was placed flat on the ground, her parents buried beside her.

The full inscription reads:

JEAN CROUCH THURMOND
JULY 14, 1926-JANUARY 6, 1960
BORN ELKO, S.C., DIED WASHINGTON, D.C.
WIFE
JAMES STROM THURMOND
DAUGHTER OF
HORACE J. AND
INEZ BREAZEALE CROUCH
HONOR GRADUATE WINTHROP COLLEGE
AND PRESIDENT SENIOR CLASS 1947
FIRST LADY OF SOUTH CAROLINA 1947-51
FIRST AIKEN COUNTY
WOMAN OF THE YEAR 1953
INCLUDED IN VOLUME I
WHO'S WHO OF AMERICAN WOMEN, 1958

ONE OF THE MOST BEAUTIFUL CHARMING
AND ADMIRED LADIES IN SOUTH CAROLINA
AND THE NATION
AS THE WIFE OF A LAWYER, GOVERNOR-
PRESIDENTIAL CANDIDATE-UNITED STATES SENATOR
HER LIFE WAS AN INSPIRATION TO HIM
AND TO ALL WHO KNEW HER
SHE FILLED AN EXALTED PLACE IN
CIVIL AND GOVERNMENTAL LIFE
BOTH STATE AND NATION, WITH DIGNITY
AND GRACE
GENTLE, LOVING, HELPFUL AND FRIENDLY
SHE WAS A GRACIOUS EXAMPLE OF
WOMANHOOD AT ITS FINEST
HER UNSELFISH LOVE AND SERVICE TO
OTHERS EXEMPLIFIED THE BEST IN
CHRISTIAN FAITH

1. Bass interview with John West, January 2, 1998.
2. Lachicotte, *Rebel Senator*, pp. 140-156.
3. Bass interview with Charles Simons, August 13, 1997.
4. Harry Dent, *The Prodigal South Returns to Power* (New York: John Wiley & Sons, 1978.) p. 61.

CHAPTER
SIXTEEN

✛

The Republican Road

The last thing Jean Thurmond told her husband from her deathbed, Strom told Dent soon afterwards, was, "Never let Fred get you alone with his advice because Fred is a cause man. He loves you, you know, but he's a cause man. But Harry is your man. His cause is your cause. You can get Harry alone and talk to him, but make sure that Harry is there when Fred is filling you in on anything." Dent was a supreme and practical political strategist. Buzhardt was driven by ideology. They and Thurmond and forces of history would converge in 1964 to accelerate the development of a two-party South.

But in the years immediately after Jean's death, Thurmond buried his grief in his work. He would stay in his Senate office until midnight, rearranging files, eating his evening meal in the Senate dining room or at a hotel on the walk back to his lonely apartment. He soon moved into a smaller unit with fewer memories.[1]

In 1960, Thurmond won reelection with ninety percent of the vote against token opposition from R. Beverly Herbert, a genteel octogenarian lawyer in Columbia who argued that Thurmond had failed to make the right case for the South. Herbert's case was that the rest of the country didn't understand what "we have done for the Negro race."[2]

Although as promised, he had supported Lyndon Johnson's 1960 bid for the presidential nomination, Thurmond backed away from the Democratic ticket of John F. Kennedy and Johnson as too liberal on civil rights. Thurmond didn't openly endorse Republican

Richard Nixon, who lost South Carolina by fewer than 10,000 votes, but much later acknowledged voting for him.

When Fritz Hollings, then governor, challenged Thurmond on his position during the campaign, Thurmond pointedly replied, "I hope Senator Kennedy's pledge at his news conferences to push for enactment of all points in the 'civil rights' plank in January will serve to alleviate the Governor's lack of understanding about my refusal to be in the bag in this election."[3] Thurmond called the civil rights plank "the most extreme, unconstitutional and antisouthern civil rights planks ever conceived by any major political party."

His rhetoric grew more strident and his sense of humor seemed to disappear. Thurmond continued to link the civil rights movement with Communism. Early in 1962, after Ku Klux Klan members and other thugs in Alabama attacked "Freedom Riders" testing a Supreme Court ruling outlawing segregation in interstate transportation facilities, Thurmond called the civil rights activists "Red pawns and publicity seekers."[4]

He saw Communism's influence everywhere. When the Supreme Court in 1962 ruled unconstitutional a government-written, nondenominational, and mandatory school prayer, Thurmond denounced the court for favoring "Communist interests." He said, "It seems the court is helping attain the objectives of Karl Marx 'to dethrone God and destroy capitalism.'"[5]

After his assignment to the Senate Armed Services Committee and promotion to major general in the Army Reserve, he became an increasingly biting Cold War critic of foreign policy and military preparedness. He soon denounced the "no-win" policy of the Kennedy administration and launched an attack on "muzzling" of the military — terms he coined.

On the latter issue, Thurmond engaged Senate Foreign Relations Chairman Fulbright in embattled debate that reflected deep philosophical differences. Knight Newspapers' Washington Bureau Chief Robert S. Boyd summarized statements made by both men. Their views:

FULBRIGHT:

The principal threat is
External — the armed might of
Russian and Chinese imperialism.

Military men who equate
domestic welfare legislation
with communism are out of step
with their commander-in-chief.

Military men should stay out
of politics. They're not the
people to teach the public
about communism.

We're in for a long struggle
on many fronts and cannot hope
for quick, dramatic solutions.

THURMOND:

The principal threat is
internal — Communist subversion
and creeping socialism here at home.

Much of the Administration's
domestic program is socialism,
and socialism is communism.

Military men understand the
Red menace better than the
White House or the State Department.

The Administration's foreign
policy adds up to "softness"
and "appeasement" of communism.[6]

Thurmond's relentless one-man crusade against "muzzling" of military leaders speaking out on the dangers of Communism led to a Senate Armed Services subcommittee investigation. Thurmond's enemies accused him of McCarthyism, referring to Wisconsin Sen. Joe McCarthy's discredited, name-calling Communist witch-hunt of the 1950s.

Once hearings began, an F.B.I. agent warned Dent, "Protect your man. Don't let him call anybody a Communist." After Thurmond received inside information from the F.B.I. that an early witness had known Communist affiliations, Dent and Buzhardt briefed the senator until well past midnight, repeatedly warning him not to use the word.

Thurmond appeared unmoved and Dent was worried. "Once that brain locks into place," he recalled, "you can't move it." Sticking his finger over his heart, he continued, "What's in here," then pointed to his mouth, "comes out here."

When hearings began, before an overflow crowd in the Senate caucus room, Dent sat next to Thurmond, stationing his foot within easy kicking distance of the senator's shin. Whenever he sensed Thurmond on the verge of using the banned word, Dent kicked sharply. "I kicked the senator's shin until it was bleeding," he said, "but we got him through it without calling anyone a communist."[7]

After hearing sixty-seven witnesses during thirty-six days of testimony, the subcommittee issued a 90,000-word majority report concluding it was "convinced that a system for prior review and clearance of military speeches is altogether proper and desirable." Thurmond felt vindicated, however, because the committee report added, "The record of the hearings reflects that the actual operation of the present system has left much to be desired." Although emphasizing the importance of America speaking with one voice, the White House acknowledged there had been inconsistencies and the State Department began requiring its reviewers to explain why changes were made. Thurmond, who submitted a 160-page independent report drafted by Buzhardt, won grudging respect for his doggedness.

Unlike South Carolina's major newspapers, which rarely criticized Thurmond editorially, *The Charlotte Observer* across the border in North Carolina, which circulated in both states, challenged him unreluctantly.

In December 1962, after the *Observer* criticized Thurmond's lack of a factual basis for attacking a "secret" Kennedy administration plan to turn over America's nuclear weapons to the United Nations, Thurmond responded. His source, he proclaimed, was a booklet published by the State Department proposing "general and complete disarmament in a peaceful world." After printing Thurmond's rebuttal, the newspaper pointed out that his earlier allegation of a "secret" plan, rather than a published booklet proposing phased disarmament that was available to the public for fifteen cents, had suggested a subversive plot.[8]

Meanwhile, South Carolina faced its first break of the color line, and it would come at Clemson, Thurmond's alma mater. Four months after the riot at Ole Miss and the same month that George Wallace proclaimed "I say segregation now — segregation tomorrow — and segregation forever" at his inauguration as governor, architectural student Harvey Gantt of Charleston was scheduled to enroll at Clemson University as a transfer from Iowa State.

State Rep. A. W. "Red" Bethea, who ran unsuccessfully for governor in 1962 by promising "to close it so tight you can't get a crowbar in it" if a black were ordered into a state-supported college in South Carolina, vigorously opposed changing the name of Clemson College to Clemson University. He changed his mind when a fellow legislator told him, "Red, if we change it to Clemson University, it'll mean there will never have been a black student enrolled in Clemson College."[9]

Bethea had received only seven percent of the vote in the race for governor. Donald Russell won while giving lip service to segregation by asserting that South Carolina needed the best legal mind to protect it. He received sixty-two percent of the vote against Bethea and Lt. Gov. Burnet Maybank, Jr. One of the state's top historians had written that the central theme of South Carolina history, certainly since the Civil War, had been the quest for stability.[10]

As state leaders sought to accept the inevitable without turmoil, Thurmond was no help. "I am opposed to Gantt's admission to Clemson," Thurmond said on December 30, 1962. "The admission of students is a responsibility for the trustees and any other action in connection therewith would have to be taken by the executive or the legislative branch of the State government."[11]

In contrast, Gov. Hollings stood solidly for obedience to law. Early in January, in his final speech to the legislature, Hollings declared, "As we meet, South Carolina is running out of courts. If and when every legal remedy has been exhausted, this General Assembly must make clear South Carolina's choice, a government of laws rather than a government of men. As determined as we are, we of today must realize the lesson of one hundred years ago, and move on for the good of South Carolina and our United States. This should be done with dignity. It must be done with law and order."[12]

When the Fourth Circuit Court of Appeals then ordered Gantt's admission, Thurmond said it "substituted fiction for fact, and expedience for law." After Chief Justice Warren refused to issue a last-minute stay of the order by the Fourth Circuit Court of Appeals, the *News and Courier* on January 23 approvingly quoted Thurmond's reference to the "mockery of judicial procedure" in the case.[13]

The Charleston newspaper was sure that black activists were seeking "total mingling of the races" and not token integration. "In recognizing racial differences," the editorial stated, "civilized people are only exercising selectivity which nature itself long ago installed without reference to modern sociological theories."[i]

A few days before Gantt enrolled at Clemson, Russell set the tone by inviting "all the people of South Carolina" to a barbecue at the Governor's Mansion to celebrate his inaugural. More than 8,000 attended, ranging from black maids clad in house dresses and society matrons in furs to NAACP officials and white business leaders.

Attorney General Robert Kennedy called Russell a few days before Gantt's admission on January 28 to inquire whether trouble was anticipated and to offer federal help. Russell assured him the state would handle the situation and that the administration "would not be embarrassed."[14]

The State Law Enforcement Division (SLED) had heavily infiltrated the Ku Klux Klan in South Carolina. When an informant reported plans for a carload of Klansmen in a Lowcountry County to drive to Clemson for disruptive purposes, SLED Chief J. P. "Pete" Strom (Thurmond's distant cousin) had them arrested and jailed for a day.[15] Gantt quietly enrolled in an event the *Saturday Evening Post* reported as "Integration with Dignity."

Gantt, who remained in the South, served as mayor of Charlotte, and lost two close races for the U. S. Senate to Jesse Helms, said at Clemson, "If you can't appeal to the morals of a South Carolinian, you can always appeal to his manners."

The other side of that genteel coin, however, was an assessment once made by Fritz Hollings that the typical South Carolinian "gets up in the morning, salutes the flag, recites the Pledge of Allegiance, and spends the rest of the day fighting."[16]

The outcomes of the 1962 elections in South Carolina reflected a new political dynamic in the state. Donald Russell's overwhelming defeat of Lt. Gov. Burnet Maybank, Jr., in the Democratic primary indicated a potentially strong opponent for Thurmond four years later. Olin Johnston handily defeated Gov.

---

i. The biting editorial opposition to integration by The News and Courier soon came to a quiet end after editor Thomas R. Waring, selected as a board member of the Southern Education Reporting Service to assure conservative representation, was assigned a dinner seat next to a black college president one evening in Nashville. (The Ford Foundation funded SERS to provide objective reporting of information on the progress of school desegregation in the South.) The planner for the event, President Henry Hill of Peabody College, made the seating assignment deliberately. Waring later told him of being initially quite uncomfortable, as he had never been seated before at a meal next to a black person, but that as the evening progressed he found his dinner companion erudite and charming, and he enjoyed the evening.

Hollings in the Democratic Senate primary, but political journalist Bill Workman challenged Johnston as a Republican in the fall and received forty-three percent of the vote.

Grocery chain heir J. Drake Edens of Columbia, Workman's campaign manager, began providing skilled leadership in building a statewide Republican political organization. Growing up, Edens "heard my daddy cuss the Democrats from about 1935 on." Edens went to his first Republican precinct meeting in 1960. The next year he helped draft young local business executive Charles Boineau to run in a special election. He won, becoming the first Republican to sit in the state legislature in the twentieth century.

An economic conservative and racial moderate, Edens became Republican state chairman. He took a manual produced, ironically, by the AFL-CIO Committee on Political Education and made it his guide for building the first genuine political party organization the state had seen. "I went into towns that I never knew existed. . . . I think the toughest county I ever hit was Chester. I tried to set up a county organization and went back to some of the people who had worked for Workman. I remember one night we called an organizational meeting, and I think three people showed up. We had a party rule that required at least six people organize a precinct, and you had to have at least three organized precincts in the county. I probably made a dozen trips to Chester County and finally put an organization together."[17]

Elsewhere in the South, an unknown college professor in Texas named John Tower ran as a Republican and won a special election in 1961 to fill the Senate seat vacated by Lyndon Johnson. A year later in Alabama, veteran Democrat Lister Hill barely survived a Republican challenge to his Senate seat.

Clearly, the political winds were shifting. For Strom Thurmond, the Republican Party not only offered a more congenial philosophical home, but it was building a political organization with muscle in South Carolina.

Meanwhile, Arizona Sen. Barry Goldwater took aim at making the conservative wing dominant in the Grand Old Party (GOP), and he had in mind a Southern strategy, first outlined in a 1961 speech in Atlanta. "We're not going to get the Negro vote as a bloc in 1964 and 1968, so we ought to go hunting where the ducks are," he declared at a southwide gathering of Republicans. Goldwater then spelled it out, saying that school integration was "the responsibility of the states. I would not like to see my party assume it is the role of the federal government to enforce integration in the schools."[18]

In 1961 Thurmond and Goldwater had identical voting records on every major issue before the Senate. A year later, they appeared together as speakers at a Madison Square Garden rally sponsored by Young Americans for Freedom. Goldwater proclaimed conservatism "the wave of the future."

As Goldwater began developing his successful campaign for the 1964 Republican presidential nomination, Thurmond continued to be a voice of protest in the Democratic Party. He drew loud applause at home in January 1963 from a Jaycee (Junior Chamber of Commerce) group in Rock Hill, sounding like Rhett Butler by declaring, "I don't give a damn" how the Kennedy administration viewed his party loyalty.[19] For Thurmond, whose use of profanity is as rare as his consumption of alcohol, it was strong language.

That summer, Thurmond questioned Attorney General Robert Kennedy at length about the public accommodations section of the president's proposed civil rights bill. Thurmond asked how many black men from Charlotte would have to attempt to have their hair cut at a barber shop in Fort Mill, across the state line in South Carolina, for it to be covered under the bill. Thurmond was making an arcane point that Kennedy couldn't answer with precision because the public accommodations section was based on the expansive interstate commerce clause of the Constitution. The bill was crafted that way by constitutional scholar Archibald Cox because the Supreme Court in 1883, in the *Civil Rights Cases*, had struck a federal public accommodations law based on the Fourteenth Amendment.[ii]

After extensive questioning, an exasperated Thurmond handed Kennedy an elementary booklet about the Constitution, illustrated with cartoons. "It's written in such a way, such an interesting way, that almost anyone can understand it," Thurmond said. He was serious.

Kennedy replied with cool irony, "Thank you, Senator, for your kindness and your courtesy." An amused fellow senator, who apparently viewed the little book as genuinely reflecting

---

ii. Five years later, however, the most tragic civil rights conflict in South Carolina occurred over the confusion created by the issue Thurmond focused on, whether a bowling alley in Orangeburg was covered by the 1964 Civil Rights Act because the facility contained a snack bar serving food that traveled in interstate commerce. A federal court ultimately ruled the bowling alley was covered, but only after a confrontation that ended with three black students killed and twenty-seven others wounded by highway patrol gunfire on the campus of South Carolina State College. The 1968 event, which became known as the "Orangeburg Massacre," received little national coverage when it happened.

Thurmond's simplistic understanding of the Constitution, told a reporter, "Bobby didn't know whether to laugh or to cry."[20]

Thurmond's bitter opposition to Kennedy's civil rights bill during the July 1963 hearings drew a rebuke from committee chairman John O. Pastore. The Rhode Island senator chastised Thurmond for "browbeating" Atlanta Mayor Ivan Allen, who endorsed the public accommodations bill.

A furious Thurmond denied asking any "loaded" questions and said he resented Pastore's accusations.

Pastore testily replied that Thurmond had asked a question that went something like, "Mr. Mayor, since the enactment of this bill would close many businesses in small towns throughout the South, don't you think that would mean a taking of property by the federal government without due process of the law?"

When Thurmond angrily denied asking such a question, Pastore asked the committee stenographer to read it back.

Thurmond interrupted, shouting, "Well, all right, suppose I did ask the question. I reserve the right to cross-examine these witnesses any way I see fit."

Pastore bristled in response, shouting, "What do you mean, 'cross-examine?' This is not a courtroom. These are distinguished people whose presence before this committee is a service."

"I'm only trying to get at the truth," Thurmond asserted.

"Your truth is not my truth," Pastore replied.

At that, the crowd attending the hearing broke into laughter and applause.

Thurmond then accused Pastore of failing to maintain decorum and said he should have stopped the laughter.

"How can I stop it when it's already happened?" Pastore asked. "I didn't know they were going to laugh."

With that the crowd laughed again.

Thurmond accused Pastore of impropriety for condoning outbursts from an audience "full of leftwingers and sympathizers for this bill."

"Mr. Thurmond," Pastore now roared, "I've been around here a long time, and that question you asked was a loaded question." He then banged his gavel and told the crowd it would have to control itself.[21]

As Thurmond grew more shrill, he attracted the admiration of fringe groups. The anti-communist John Birch Society hung his portrait in a place of honor at its Belmont, Massachusetts, national headquarters. Its founder, candy manufacturer Robert Welch, had written that Dwight Eisenhower was "a conscious agent" of the Communist Party. In Savannah, Georgia, at the end of August 1963, a Ku Klux Klan unit expressed support for Thurmond as the 1964 Democratic presidential candidate.[22]

Although Thurmond's zealotry on civil rights issues seemed to dominate his activities, he was an early and persistent advocate within the Armed Services Committee for developing an anti-missile defense system. His persistence from 1961 onward led to the initial appropriations for research and development of an advanced system that would emerge as the costly and controversial "Star Wars" program of the Reagan administration. Its advocates would contend that this initiative helped end the Cold War and bring down communism in Soviet bloc countries. History will have to judge whether communism collapsed because of such external pressure or the system's internal failure to hold the allegiance of the Russian people and other ethnic groups that made up the Soviet bloc.

Although Thurmond joined in the national grieving after President Kennedy's assassination on November 22, 1963, he may well have shared the views of Mississippi's James O. Eastland, who sat for ten years in front of John Kennedy. "He didn't know how to put proposals through Congress," Eastland said later of Kennedy as president. "We had him blocked." On that tragic November 22, Eastland was driving through Virginia's Shenandoah Valley on his way to Mississippi when he noticed a flag at half-staff in a small town, and the same thing a little farther down the road. He switched on his radio, heard the news, turned his car around to head back to Washington, and said to his wife, "Good God, Lyndon's president. He's gonna pass a lot of this damn fool stuff."[23]

Thurmond's initial response for the record, however, was to express "gratitude to the late President for his foresight and vision in selecting as the man to succeed him in office, in the event of such a tragedy, one of the most experienced and capable leaders I have ever known." The next spring Thurmond got Johnson to nominate Charles Simons as a federal district judge in South Carolina, an objective that the Kennedy administration had thwarted for three years.

But the first of that "fool stuff" Eastland foresaw was the 1964 Civil Rights Act. On its final vote, Goldwater led five other Republicans in joining twenty-one Southern Democrats in opposition. This landmark legislation would have major impact in transforming the American South.

It outlawed discrimination in public accommodations and employment and created an enforcement mechanism that would lead to meaningful school desegregation. As an afterthought that proved important, it outlawed discrimination based on gender as well as race. It also established a Community Relations Service.

One of Thurmond's fabled legends is the tale of his wrestling with liberal Sen. Ralph Yarborough of Texas outside a committee room. Thurmond was attempting to prevent a quorum from confirming former Florida Gov. Leroy Collins as director of the new Community Relations Service.

Thurmond reacted personally in December 1963 to a speech that Collins made in Columbia, S.C., denouncing bigotry. Then director of the National Association of Broadcasters, Collins told the Columbia Chamber of Commerce, "How long are the majority of Southerners going to allow themselves to be caricatured before the nation by these Claghorns? . . . It is time the decent people of the South told the bloodyshirt-wavers to climb down off the buckboards of bigotry."

Thurmond issued a statement — written in Buzhardt's style — saying, "For one who professes to abhor the emotion of hate, Mr. Collins proves himself singularly adept at verbally purveying this most violent emotion."

At Collins's confirmation the next summer, for three hours Thurmond engaged in his customary line of questioning. He asked Collins about past statements of his about race that now were embarrassing. Collins explained, ". . . later events bring a modification of one's thinking."

On the last day of hearings, determined to prevent a quorum, Thurmond stationed himself outside the committee room door, trying to talk others out of entering. A couple of senators simply walked down the hall and slipped in through a back door.

But Sen. Ralph Yarborough of Texas came down the hallway, shook Strom's hand, and playfully tugged him toward the committee room. It was the mule race all over again. Strom took it as a challenge. Both men were sixty-one, belonged to the same Army Reserve unit, and as youths had wrestled. But the heavier and less fit Yarborough said he learned later that Thurmond had judo training in the Army. Strom went for Yarborough's knees. Yarborough knew a fight could lead to a formal censure. With an election coming up, he wanted to avoid that, and said he slid down on the floor with his back to the wall. The Thurmond version is that he threw Yarborough to the floor and pinned him there, saying, "Tell me to release you, Ralph, and I will."

Yarborough said he told Thurmond, "This is ridiculous. If they get a picture of us here, they'll defeat both of us." The Texan continued, "But he wanted me to holler 'quits, I've got enough.' I said, 'Not on your life.'"

Finally, committee chairman Warren Magnuson of Washington learned what was taking place, came out, and roared, "Stop that! Get off the floor!" Both men were standing when photographers showed up.

At the urging of his press aide, Yarborough rushed over to Thurmond's office, grabbed his hand and raised it up, and declared, "Strom, you're the champ." Yarborough said several senators chastised him for not knowing better than to mess with Thurmond. "I wouldn't say they regarded him as crazy," Yarborough said, "they regarded him as kind of a wild man."[24]

Thurmond's aides chastised him, but South Carolina constituents called to congratulate him on "showing that liberal." The Thurmond staffers claimed that Texans flooded Yarborough's office with boxes of Wheaties.

For Thurmond, the wrestling match on July 9, 1964, symbolized his last fight within the Democratic Party. He didn't attend the Democratic national convention. With Dent and Buzhardt pushing him, he reached a difficult decision, but it was one he was headed toward on his own.

After Goldwater received the Republican nomination in mid-July, he began his campaign's self-destruction with his acceptance speech. Goldwater declared that "extremism in the defense of liberty is no vice, and moderation in the pursuit of justice is no virtue." To many Americans that line cast an image of him as an immoderate extremist whose itchy finger they chose not to trust with a Cold War nuclear trigger.

But his vote against the Civil Rights bill, his commitment to a strong military, his ardent anti-communism, his belief in decentralized government and a market economy, and his "strict" interpretation of the Constitution all resonated with Thurmond. The South Carolina senator had been speaking out about political realignment since 1961.

"After I got up here," Thurmond later reminisced, "I soon

found that the Republican Party was more in line with my thinking and the philosophy of the people of South Carolina than the Democratic Party at the national level."[25]

With their finely calibrated political sense, Dent and Thurmond intuitively knew it was time to move boldly. Their tactical plan was flawless. Dent's objective was to build a two-party political system in the South, and Buzhardt fully agreed. They also believed it was in Thurmond's interest, that he could be vulnerable in a Democratic primary. Dent and Buzhardt pushed Thurmond to switch to the Republican Party, but Dent said, "If Jean had lived there wouldn't have been a switching."[26] Jean was comfortable as a Democrat and recognized that Strom wasn't without philosophically compatible colleagues among his fellow Southerners in the Senate.

Thurmond and Dent flew to South Carolina and met with key supporters and opinion leaders, letting them in on the idea of switching parties and listening to their response. They first visited Walter Brown in Spartanburg, a top assistant to Jimmy Byrnes in Washington and now a television station owner on whose behalf Thurmond had intervened with the Federal Communications Commission. Dent made the pitch for switching parties and endorsing Goldwater. He remembers, "Walter just went livid. 'You're crazy, Strom. This young boy isn't even dry behind the ears.' He assured Thurmond there was no way he could get reelected in South Carolina as a Republican."

They next drove to Greenville to see newspaper publisher Roger Peace. Walter Brown had already called him. "He lacerated me," Dent said. "He said, 'Strom, that boy is going to destroy you.'"

The next stop was Columbia, where Bill Workman had moved in as editorial page editor for *The State*. Publisher Ambrose Hampton, a direct descendant of the Redeemer governor Wade Hampton III, listened intently. Dent remembered, "Ambrose sat there and listened and said, 'That would be one of the most refreshing things I've ever heard of.' That's all he said. He didn't say yes or no. He just made that comment."

Then they drove across town to see Byrnes. Strom went to the bathroom, and Byrnes said, "Harry, what are you and Strom up to?" Dent recalls, "He had already gotten a call from up there in Spartanburg. He didn't tell me that, but I knew he had.

"I said, 'We're talking about switching parties.' He said, 'Maude, Maude. Bring me another drink. Strom Thurmond is about to commit political suicide.' And then the senator came out from the bathroom. We sat down and Jimmy Byrnes said, 'Now, what you need to do is be an Independent.'"

After returning to Washington, Dent thought Thurmond had been talked out of switching. Buzhardt had written a statement lambasting the Democratic Party with a broad-based frontal assault. It was ready to go. "I went back and talked to the senator," Dent said, "and talked to the senator some more. And I saw him come back to life. Once he made his decision, there was no changing it."

Thurmond got an appointment with Goldwater on Saturday, September 12. Dent accompanied him, but this time Thurmond did the talking. Dent recalled that he wasted no time, telling Goldwater, "I have three choices open to me. I can keep quiet, I can come out for you but remain a Democrat, or I can come out for you and go all the way to the Republican Party. I'll do what will help you most."

Goldwater, of course, said that going all the way and switching parties would help the most.

"Well, that's along the line I've been thinking," Thurmond said. He showed his statement to Goldwater for his approval. "Don't change one word," Goldwater told him.[iii]

The candid Arizonan then commented he intended to present his views and candidacy forthrightly to the American people. "If they don't want me, I'll just go back to Arizona and operate my ham radio," he said.

Thurmond and Dent recognized immediately that Goldwater felt he had little chance of success. But Thurmond asked him to call Drake Edens to alert Republican officials in South Carolina. Thurmond said he would make his announcement there on Wednesday, September 16, so he could be on hand the next day for Goldwater's rally in Greenville.

Dent telephoned Dolly Hamby, who had handled press relations for Thurmond's write-in campaign, and asked that she arrange television time for a ten-state hookup.

Thurmond then flew to South Carolina on Monday for the funeral of industrialist Charles Daniel. Dent was worried. He knew that all the big boys of South Carolina politics would attend

---

iii. Dent's memory of the meeting was far more vivid than Goldwater's, who in a 1982 letter told Marilyn Thompson he didn't remember any direct conversations with Thurmond "relative to his decision to become a Republican." But Goldwater said Thurmond "gave me tremendous support and . . . was the major single factor in making it possible for me to have carried the south." He added, "I think that Strom's becoming a Republican was the major factor in the south being able to switch over from a solid Democratic block to a place where Republicanism has been growing ever since 1964."

and would gang up on Thurmond. Dent told Buzhardt, "We're going to get shot out of the saddle. These guys are going to stop him." The senator's staff had television film packets to mail across the South, and Dent said to hold them.

The telephone in Thurmond's office rang early Monday afternoon, and it was the senator calling Dent to ask if the press material had been mailed out. Dent said "no" and explained, "Senator, I knew those guys would get you and talk you out of it." Thurmond said, "Yes, they talked to me. Put those things in the mail."[27]

In retrospect, Thurmond's action looks more shrewd than courageous. It was bold, but not as risky as his aides make out. Bryan Dorn saw it as "a smart maneuver. If you gonna do it, that's about the only way I know that you can do it and get by with it. You call everybody and say, 'What do you think about it? You know my principles are so and so and so.' Every one of them say, 'Well, it takes a lot of courage to do that. If it was up to me I wouldn't do it.' But when he does it, you see, he's got all of them sewed up. Every one of them. They're in on the act. That's just a tactic, and it's a good tactic.

"In time, if not right then, it would have been very difficult for Senator Thurmond to win a primary with a liberal Democrat and the black vote and all that against him, with a Republican sitting off in right field, you know, already nominated. So he was smart along that line. He is a master politician."[28]

He was shrewd enough to cast his decision not in the context of joining his main group of supporters, which would appear opportunistic, but by castigating the Democrats as an evil group who no longer represented "the people." In addressing "My Fellow South Carolinians" that Wednesday night, Thurmond said:

The Democratic Party has abandoned the people. . . . It has repudiated the Constitution of the United States. It is leading the evolution of our nation to a socialistic dictatorship.

The Democratic Party has forsaken the people to become the party of minority groups, power-hungry union leaders, political bosses, and big businessmen looking for government contracts and favors. . . .

The Democratic Party has invaded the private lives of the people by using the powers of government for coercion and intimidation of individuals.

The Democratic Party has rammed through Congress unconstitutional, impractical, unworkable, and oppressive legislation which invades inalienable personal and property rights of the individual. . .

The Democratic Party has succored and assisted our Communist enemies through trade and aid at the expense of the American people.

The Democratic Party has established and pursued for our government a no-win foreign policy of weakness, indecision, accommodation, and appeasement.

The Democratic Party, as custodian of government, faltered at the Bay of Pigs and in the Cuba crisis of 1962 — at the very moment when victory was at hand — and thereby forfeited Cuba to Soviet domination, subjected our nation to the perils of an armed enemy camp ninety miles from our shores, and opened the doors of the hemisphere to Communist subversion.

The Democratic Party, as custodian of government, has sent our youth into combat in Viet Nam, refusing to call it war, and demanding of our youth the risk of their lives without providing either adequate equipment or a goal of victory. . . .

The Democratic Party has demonstrated a callous disregard for sound fiscal policies and practices.

The Democratic Party, while hiding behind the deceitful gimmick of a darkened White House, has increased deficit spending and squandered, at home and abroad, billions of hard-earned dollars taken from the American people.

The Democratic Party has utterly disregarded the disastrous effects of the resulting inflation on people with fixed incomes, such as retirees, pensioners, Social Security beneficiaries, and those who have their savings invested in insurance. . . .

The Democratic Party has endangered the security of the nation by negative decisions of military preparedness, preoccupation with bilateral and unilateral steps toward disarmament, and by use of the military services domestically as instruments of social reform. . . .

The Democratic Party has encouraged, supported, and protected the Supreme Court in a reign of judicial tyranny, and in the Court's effort to wipe out local self-government, effect law enforcement, internal security, the rights of the people and the states, and even the structure of the State governments. . . .

The party of our fathers is dead. Those who took its name are engaged in another reconstruction, this time not only of the South, but of the entire nation. If the American people permit the Democratic Party to return to power, freedom as we have known it in this country is doomed, and individuals will be destined to *lives of regulation, control, coercion, intimidation, and sub-servience to a power elite who shall rule from Washington. . . .*

The man who has gained the Republican nomination for President against all the odds and opinion polls . . . has demonstrated his fidelity to freedom, independence, and the Constitution by his actions and his votes in the United States Senate. I personally know him to be able and responsible. He is an honest man of courage and conviction, who trusts the American people to hold the reins of government and rule themselves. . . .

I do know we have a fighting chance under Barry Goldwater's leadership and that we are welcomed to his banner. I know also that the course for the Democratic Party has been set toward socialism and arbitrary rule. I know further that the Democratic Party's line of succession is Hubert Humphrey and Robert Kennedy. . . .

For me there is no alternative. The future of freedom and constitutional government is at stake, and this requires that I do everything in my power to help Barry Goldwater return our nation to constitutional government through his election to the Presidency. . . .

I have chosen this course because I cannot consider any risks in a cause which I am convinced is right.

For added drama, a tag line of "Strom Thurmond (D., S.C.)" flashed across the screen, changing two thirds of the way through the speech to "(R., S. C.)."

When introducing Thurmond the next day at the upstate rally for Goldwater, Drake Edens read this epitaph on the tomb of Strom's grandfather, George Washington Thurmond: "He did not tread on the rights of others and he did not permit others to tread on his." The crowd of 25,000 cheered wildly.

In the fall campaign, Thurmond thundered across the South, drawing large audiences and making more than a dozen appearances with Goldwater. The state's Democratic establishment fought him in South Carolina, but Goldwater came to Columbia for a televised indoor rally on October 31. He won fifty-nine percent of the vote in South Carolina, the first Republican presidential candidate to carry the state since Rutherford Hayes' contested victory in 1876.

Elsewhere, Goldwater won only his native Arizona, Georgia, and the three other deep South states Thurmond had carried as a Dixiecrat—Alabama, Louisiana, and Mississippi. Lyndon Johnson, won the other forty-four states and received sixty percent of the popular vote, a landslide victory.

1. Bass interview with Harry Dent.
2. *The Charlotte Observer*, Associated Press story, May 22, 1960.
3. *The Columbia Record*, September 2, 1960.
4. Associated Press, May 27, 1961.
5. United Press International, July 4, 1962.
6. *The Charlotte Observer*, August 21, 1961.
7. Thompson interview *with* Dent, December 13, 1982.
8. *The Charlotte Observer*, December 12, 1961.
9. Former state Rep. David Taylor to Bass, 1973.
10. George Rogers, *The Encyclopedia of Southern History*, Louisiana State University Press.
11. *The News and Courier*, December 31, 1962.
12. Jack Bass, *Porgy Comes Home*, p. 7.
13. *The News and Courier*, Dec. 31, 1962, p. 1; Jan. 23, 1963, p. 8A; *The State*, Jan. 9, 1963, p. 1. *The Charlotte Observer*, Jan. 22, 1963, p. 1-B.
14. Nadine Cohodas, op. cit., p. 335.
15. Pete Strom to Bass, 1970.
16. Hollings to Bass, 1968.
17. Jack Bass and Walter DeVries, *The Transformation of Southern Politics*, University of Georgia Press edition, 1995., pp. 23-24.
18. Ibid., p. 27.
19. *The Charlotte Observer*, Jan. 26, 1963.
20. Lachicotte, *Rebel Senator*, p. 220.
21. *The Charlotte Observer*, July 27, 1963, file clipping.
22. United Press International, August 25, 1963.
23. Jack Bass, *Unlikely Heroes*, University of Alabama Press edition, 1990, p. 146.
24. Thompson interview with Ralph Yarborough,1982.
25. Bass-DeVries interview with Strom Thurmond, February 1, 1974, op. cit.
26. Bass interview with Dent, June 26, 1997.
27. Bass and Thompson interviews with Dent. Lachicotte, *Rebel Senator*, pp. 229-235.
28. Thompson interview with Dent.

CHAPTER
SEVENTEEN

+

Abe Fortas

It is difficult to conceive of a contemporary native Southerner more unlike Strom Thurmond than Abe Fortas. He grew up in Memphis, the home of the Blues, a son of lower middle class, immigrant Jewish parents. Fine music became as important to him as fitness was to Thurmond.

Born in 1910, eight years after Thurmond, Fortas went to college on scholarships and excelled at Yale Law School when Strom was reading law under his father's tutelage. His Yale faculty mentor was future Supreme Court Justice William O. Douglas. Yale was the center of the developing concept known as legal realism that emphasized the importance of facts and treated law as an instrument of social policy.

Major law firms hired no Jews in those days. Fortas spent his early years after law school shuttling back and forth between New Haven and Washington, as a junior law school faculty member at Yale and as one of the bright, creative, young men who helped shape Franklin Roosevelt's meritocratic New Deal. He befriended a hard-driving and equally smart and ambitious young Texas congressman named Lyndon Baines Johnson. Fortas helped him get a rural electrification project for his constituents. The two men shared a liberal political philosophy that believed in an active government with "a concern for people." They became trusted friends.

After World War II, Fortas and his former Yale professor Thurmond Arnold formed a law firm. They soon added a third name, New Deal colleague Paul Porter, who had served as Federal Communications Commission chairman and ambassador to

Greece. With their inside knowledge of regulatory law, they quickly attracted corporate clients and hard-working, bright young associates. Money poured in. But they also believed strongly in civil liberties and were among the few lawyers who became heavily involved — usually charging only expenses — in assisting noncommunist victims of loyalty programs that relied on anonymous informants who frequently were malicious.

After President Kennedy's assassination, Fortas was one of the first people President Lyndon Johnson called. He helped draft the new president's first speech to Congress, emphasizing action, liberal programs, and unity. It urged Congress to adopt Kennedy's civil rights bill and his tax reduction plan. As one aide put it, Lyndon Johnson wanted to "out-Roosevelt Roosevelt,"[1] and Fortas, a valued friend, became a key adviser and confidant. He turned down an offer to become attorney general, but met regularly with the president, recommended people for key positions, and helped shape policy.

In 1965, Johnson coaxed Justice Arthur Goldberg to leave the Supreme Court and become United Nations ambassador, filling the court vacancy by appointing the fifty-five-year-old Fortas. He accepted reluctantly — in part because he made many times more money practicing law and spent accordingly. Johnson announced Fortas's appointment the same day he announced a dramatic 50,000-troop escalation of the Vietnam war. Fortas breezed through his confirmation hearings, and he praised Judiciary Chairman James Eastland of Mississippi for his "fairness and friendliness."

Despite the Constitution's separation of powers among the legislative, executive, and judicial branches of government, former Justice Felix Frankfurter had offered advice while on the bench to President Franklin Roosevelt. But Arthur Goldberg warned Fortas that times had changed and so had views of propriety. Goldberg told him, "Abe, while Felix did it, according to present reactions, people do not like a Supreme Court justice being too close to a president."[2]

Lyndon Johnson wanted advice from Fortas, however, who continued to give it freely. Although he avoided talking about the Court's business, he attended White House meetings, helped shape policy, and continued to recommend people for appointment. Fortas's dual role reflected an arrogance born of loyalty to L.B.J. and a recklessness that as a prudent lawyer he no doubt would have advised against for anyone else.

After President Johnson's further escalation of the war in Vietnam — a policy Fortas encouraged — led to public disenchantment, Johnson stunned the nation on the evening of March 31, 1968, by announcing he would not seek reelection.

In a June 13 letter to the president, Chief Justice Earl Warren wrote that he intended to resign "effective at your pleasure." Johnson, by now a lame duck who seemed not to realize how much his power had dwindled, decided to name Fortas chief justice and Court of Appeals Judge Homer Thornberry, a former Texas congressman and L.B.J. crony, to Fortas's seat. Johnson thought Fortas had the best legal mind he knew, and their philosophical values coincided. The president replied on June 27 to Warren, "With your agreement I will accept your decision to retire effective at such time as a successor is qualified."[3] Had Johnson chosen a solid moderate Republican instead of Thornberry, as some advisers urged, his slick deal with Warren might have worked. And if Warren had simply resigned, creating an actual vacancy, little basis for organized opposition would have existed.

By June, however, Thurmond had cemented a commitment to support Richard Nixon for the Republican presidential nomination. The two men had met, and Nixon promised to appoint "strict constructionists" to the Supreme Court. Although Nixon supported *Brown v. Board of Education*, he expressed "understanding" of the problems involved in desegregation. Thurmond also liked his views on defense and support for strengthening state and local government. Most importantly, he believed Nixon could win.

Thurmond's views about the Supreme Court had been laid out in *The Faith We Have Not Kept*, a thin paperback volume set for publication in July 1968. It was essentially a condensed compilation from his speeches over the years. One scholar who read the book called it "a study in anti-intellectualism" in which the Constitution becomes holy writ and Thurmond its fundamentalist, secular theologian.[4] Thurmond seemed to blame all of society's ills — "crime in the streets, a free rein for communism, riots, agitation, collectivism and the breakdown of moral codes" — on the "Supreme Court's assault on the Constitution."

In his view, the "conspicuous" moment when it all began was 1954 and *Brown v. Board of Education*. The problem, Thurmond argued, was that the Constitution now could be interpreted as having "whatever meaning could be derived from the words—as long as the meaning fit the political philosophy of five Supreme Court justices." His argument's first problem was that a unanimous Supreme Court decided *Brown*. Its more basic problem is that the Constitution has always meant what a majority of the Supreme Court decided, and the legal realists acknowledged it.

The original interpretation of the Fourteenth Amendment, in the 1873 *Slaughterhouse* cases, was itself a 5-4 decision that narrowly limited the protected "privileges and immunities of citizens of the United States." It was a complex case brought by white butchers in New Orleans to protest that city's granting a monopoly that threatened their livelihood. The Supreme Court's majority limited the Fourteenth Amendment's protection to "the slave race," but gave enforcement power over civil rights, "the rights of person and of Property," to the states, which by then in most of the South had reverted to control by white Southerners. In other words, the Fourteenth Amendment meant little. The four dissenters said it had become "a vain and idle enactment, which accomplished nothing."[5]

A week later, as further evidence of how the justices respond to prevailing contemporary attitudes, the Supreme Court ruled 8-1 that the state of Illinois had the right to refuse Myra Bradwell the right to practice law because she was a woman. Little more than a decade later, in *Santa Clara County v. Southern Pacific Railroad*, a Supreme Court composed of nine white men with backgrounds in corporate law unanimously decided that what the Fourteenth Amendment really protected was the economic rights of corporations.[6]

Despite Thurmond's argument to the contrary, what *Brown v. Board of Education* did was restore to the Fourteenth Amendment the meaning intended by its framers — to grant blacks as a class full rights of citizenship equal to that of other Americans. Thurmond acknowledged that the framers designed the amendment to overcome the 1857 *Dred Scott* case.

The "War Between the States" he wrote, happened because the "social revolutionaries refused to stop at the constitutional barrier" the Supreme Court cited in *Dred Scott*.[7] He gives no further explanation of the case. Chief Justice Roger Taney declared not only that even free blacks weren't citizens and therefore lacked standing to sue in federal court, but that they were "altogether unfit to associate with the white race" and "had no rights which the white man was bound to respect."

The slave, Dred Scott, thus could not have a federal court

decide the validity of his claim of freedom for having lived in a free state before his master moved to the slave state of Missouri. The case, officially reported as *Scott v. Sanford*, also ruled the Missouri Compromise of 1820 unconstitutional, thus opening up all the territories for slavery.[8]

Justice Benjamin R. Curtis, one of two dissenters, pointed out that free blacks had voted in some states, including North Carolina, at the time the Constitution was adopted. He factually repudiated almost all of Taney's major points.

In reaction to the *Dred Scott* case, Abraham Lincoln and other "social revolutionaries" organized the Republican Party — and won the presidential election in 1860. In historian Thurmond's version, their doing so apparently is what brought on the Civil War. They presumably got at least help from Thurmond's fellow Edgefield townsman, Francis H. Wardlaw, who drafted South Carolina's Ordinance of Secession. (Wardlaw Academy, the private school in Edgefield organized after the public schools there were desegregated, is named for him.)

Whatever Thurmond's shortcomings as a historian, his political instincts were now sharper than Lyndon Johnson's. When the president announced his Fortas-Thornberry package on June 27, freshman Republican Sen. Robert Griffin of Michigan immediately issued a statement that any Supreme Court vacancy should not be filled by "a lame duck" president. Seventeen Republican senators signed his petition.

Thurmond spoke out the next day. He called Fortas unacceptable for three reasons. First was "his long reputation as a fixer and his involvement with many questionable figures." Next came his alignment with "the radical wing of the Court." And finally, Thurmond denounced Fortas's support of decisions that "extended the power of the federal government and invaded the rights of the states, turned criminals loose on technicalities," and gave aid to communists. Thurmond then attacked the issue that most seemed to bother his fellow Republicans, charging "collusion between President Johnson and Chief Justice Warren to prevent the next president from appointing the next chief justice." For Thurmond, the Warren Court was the enemy, and he saw as clearly as Lyndon Johnson did that Abe Fortas would continue its liberal course.

Five days later, Thurmond demonstrated he was warming up to fight, and this time he knew he had allies who could be mobilized. "Those who have wailed about the damage the Supreme

Court has done the country now have a chance to let the people speak through their new president regarding the court leadership for possibly the next twenty years," he asserted. Republican majority leader Everett Dirksen was supporting Fortas, but soon realized his followers were slipping away.

Johnson had coaxed support of his nominees from Richard Russell, who could bring a cadre of conservative Southerners with him. But that fell apart after an *Atlanta Constitution* editorial questioned the fitness of a Savannah segregationist whom Russell was promoting for a federal judgeship. Attorney General Ramsey Clark infuriated Russell by delaying the administration's support until he could investigate. Before Johnson could overrule Clark and pacify Russell, the Georgia senator withdrew his support and joined Griffin's group, bringing his followers.[9]

Using language that Fortas wrote, Sen. Abraham Ribicoff challenged as "a novel and radical idea" the claim by Fortas's opponents that a president should be deprived of his constitutional power to fill vacancies because he would no longer hold office after November.

No sitting Supreme Court justice had ever before submitted to questioning by a congressional committee. Two prior sitting justices, Edward White and Harlan Fiske Stone, had decided it would be inappropriate when nominated as chief justice to testify. They reasoned some senators would ask about past decisions and that answering such questions would violate the Constitution's separation of powers provision.

Fortas, however, believed he could help his controversial nomination because of his experience with Congress and his knowledge of how Washington worked. The White House agreed. Invited to testify, he accepted.

Led by Griffin, senators initially focused on Fortas's advisory role with the president. He downplayed it to the extent that his biographer concluded, "He simply lied."[10] But he said enough to illustrate the relationship was far more than social, including discussions with the president on the Vietnam war and urban riots. He insisted he never advised on issues that might reach the Supreme Court, but even his supporters found his role unbecoming.

When the subject changed to the record of the Warren Court, Thurmond grilled him for two hours with all the subtlety of an attack dog. He focused on criminal cases and voting rights.

Thurmond repeatedly asked (some fifty times) — and Fortas

repeatedly declined to answer—questions about specific cases. Each time, Thurmond concluded, "And you refuse to answer that?" And Fortas answered each time, "Yes."

He maintained his composure, once explaining, "Senator, with the greatest deference and the greatest respect I assure you, my answer must stand. I cannot address myself to the question that you have phrased because I could not possibly address myself to it without discussing theory and principle. And the theory and principle I would discuss would most certainly be involved in situations that we have to face."

An irritated Thurmond said he could not understand, nor would the people, why Fortas could write and lecture about legal issues, but couldn't answer his questions.

"Senator," Fortas replied, "all I can say is that I hope and trust that the American people will realize that I am acting out of a sense of constitutional duty and responsibility."

Thurmond replied, "Well, I am disappointed, even more disappointed in you, Mr. Justice Fortas."

"I am sorry to hear that, Senator."

Thurmond's antagonism to the Court's opinion in criminal cases extended to those decided before Fortas became a justice. Thurmond angrily resurrected *Mallory v. United States*, a 1957 case, in which the Court overturned the conviction of a confessed rapist because his arraignment was delayed to permit police questioning.

Thurmond by now was shouting. "Do you believe in that kind of justice? Does not that decision, *Mallory* — I want that word to ring in your ears. Mallory! . . . Mallory! A man who raped a woman, admitted his guilt and the Supreme Court turned him loose on a technicality free to commit other crimes."

Wasn't this decision, he continued to rant, "calculated to encourage more people to commit rapes and serious crimes? . . . As a justice of the Supreme Court, can you condone this?"

This public scolding of a Supreme Court justice nominated by the president to be chief justice shocked even Fortas. Reporters saw him look expectantly toward Eastland, as if expecting he might call Thurmond to order. Eastland appeared to be reading something and did not look up.

Fortas sat quietly for well over a minute. Then, in a measured voice, he replied, "Senator, because of my respect for you and this body and my respect for the Constitution of the United States and my position as Associate Justice of the Supreme Court of the

United States, I will adhere to the limitations I believe the Constitution places upon me and will not reply to your question as you phrase it."

Thurmond pushed further, "Can you suggest any way that I can phrase it differently so you can answer it?"

"That would be presumptuous. I would not attempt to do so."

Thurmond got headlines, but Fortas sympathizers showed up the next day as he again faced Thurmond. When asked whether he agreed that the Court's decisions "make it terribly difficult to protect society from crime and criminals [and] are among the principal reasons for the turmoil and near-revolutionary conditions which prevail in our country," Fortas responded with a simple "No." His supporters applauded.[11]

Although Thurmond had forced some loss of composure with his first day's assault, biographer Nadine Cohodas found tucked away in his files a "blisteringly candid memo" from James Lucier, an aide who frequently wrote for the John Birch Society's *American Opinion* magazine and later joined the staff of Senator Jesse Helms. He viewed Thurmond's strategy in the Fortas hearing as "a disastrous mistake" because the line of questioning "did not appear to be a sincere attempt to investigate his views; rather, it appeared to be an irrational attempt to delay and harass." The better strategy, Lucier contended, would have been to show Fortas "a radical and a revolutionary dedicated to remaking society."[12]

Thurmond's *The Faith We Have Not Kept* came out in the midst of the hearings, and he quipped that he might send a copy to Fortas. For Thurmond, the confirmation hearings amounted to a political battle aimed at control of the Supreme Court.

He found the ammunition he needed a few days later, after Fortas completed four days of testimony. James Clancy, who represented a group called Citizens for Decent Literature, claimed that Fortas had cast the deciding vote in forty-nine of fifty-two cases in which the material involved was judged not obscene. He charged that the rulings openly invited pornographers to distribute millions of copies "of what historically had been regarded in France as hard-core pornography."

Under prodding from Thurmond, Clancy contended that pornography bred violence, and he brought with him a pornographic film, *0-7*, which Thurmond arranged for the committee and press to view. Thurmond thanked Clancy "for the contribution you have made to these hearings."

Clancy had been particularly upset because the Supreme Court had issued a one-sentence opinion that he said overruled findings by the lower court that the film, because of its obscenity, was not protected by the First Amendment. In fact, the issue of obscenity wasn't in the Supreme Court's opinion, which overruled the lower courts because police lacked a valid search warrant when they confiscated the film.

And the charge of Fortas casting the deciding vote was also invalid because most of the cases Clancy cited were unsigned. In his one signed dissent in obscenity cases, *Ginsberg v. United States*, Fortas had argued that the Constitution allowed states to enact laws protecting children from obscenity. He even proposed that children and juveniles were entitled to protection from panderers who exploited prurient content of material that was not legally obscene. In another case he helped devise a formula that made it easier to convict those who marketed obscene materials.

But Fortas, having agreed to testify but not to discuss the work of the Court, could not explain these details to the committee. Its members were left with the impression that Fortas was a defender of obscenity. The committee postponed making a report on the nominee, allowing a week to think about the justice's approach to obscenity and to view *0-7*. Congress then adjourned for the presidential nominating conventions before issuing its report.

When the hearings resumed in September, Thurmond got word from Sen. Griffin that Fortas had taught a summer law school seminar at American University and that his salary was paid by private contributors rather than university funds. Thurmond called the law school dean and suggested he avoid a subpoena by appearing voluntarily before the committee.

It turned out that Fortas had received $15,000 for conducting a nine-week seminar, funded by wealthy businessmen solicited by Paul Porter, Fortas's former law partner. The amount was more than a third of his Supreme Court salary and far more than anyone else was paid for such teaching. Although Fortas didn't know until the dean's testimony who the donors were and the seminar itself received glowing evaluations, he had exercised bad judgment in allowing Porter to solicit clients for funds. Thurmond maintained the contributors' wide business interests might well become involved in litigation before the court. Although Fortas had routinely disqualified himself from any cases involving former clients, these new facts raised questions.

Thurmond then called the Los Angeles policeman who had been the arresting officer in the 0-7 pornographic film case. He brought two pornographic films and 150 magazines for the committee to review. Thurmond, who issued a newsletter, "Fortas on Filth," showed committee members the films and magazines.

Attorney General Clark called Thurmond's action "outrageous." A *Washington Post* cartoon depicted Thurmond standing in a doorway holding a film and inviting a straitlaced man to come inside: "Psst — Want to see some dirty pictures?"

When the hearings ended, Senator Dirksen told White House staffers, "The movies are what the opposition needed to make their position jell." He added that Thurmond "tastes blood." He and Majority Leader Mike Mansfield agreed that the lecture fee was "hurtful" as a secondary issue.

The committee voted 11-6 to recommend Fortas on September 17. Griffin immediately launched a filibuster, which Thurmond and others joined. On October 2, a day after a cloture vote to cut off debate failed by fourteen votes, Fortas asked that his name be withdrawn.

Thurmond called it "the wisest decision Justice Fortas has made since he has been on the Supreme Court." Thurmond then suggested he "go a step further and resign from the court for the sake of good government."[13][i]

---

i. Less than a month after going on the court, Fortas accepted an offer to consult for the Wolfson Family Foundation, set up by Louis Wolfson, a Jacksonville, Florida, financier whom Fortas had represented as a lawyer. Justice Fortas would be paid $20,000 a year for life, with such payments to continue to Mrs. Fortas if she should survive him. Fortas was aware that Justice Douglas was receiving $10,000 annually as president of the Parvin Foundation, whose head was a casino operator in Las Vegas. Because Wolfson was a former client and Fortas therefore would disqualify himself if any matter involving Wolfson came before the Court, Fortas had reasoned there would be no conflict. But such an arrangement, with Wolfson's foundation paying an amount equal to half of Fortas's salary as a justice, would have raised obvious ethical questions if made public. Fortas accepted an initial $20,000 payment in the summer of 1968. After Wolfson was indicted for financial irregularities, Fortas ended the relationship with the foundation and returned the $20,000 check in December. Therefore, no income taxes were due on the money and, in a technical legal sense, there was no fee paid. The issue escalated, after the election, with a *Life* magazine investigation. The Nixon administration's Department of Justice became involved, with Attorney General John Mitchell leaking information to the *Life* reporter and others, implying publicly that Fortas had continued to advise Wolfson on legal matters. Fortas had not, but Mitchell's leaks and innuendo resulted in a media feeding frenzy. Fortas resigned from the Supreme Court in May 1969, although he had violated no laws. Mitchell would later go to prison for crimes related to the Watergate scandal that led to President Nixon's impeachment by the House and his resignation as president. Fortas's first cousin and confidant Harold Burson believes Fortas would never have resigned had he been chief justice. Fortas's resignation, soon followed by the retirement of Earl Warren, gave Richard Nixon two appointments to the Supreme Court, which began moving away from the direction set by Warren. For Strom Thurmond, it would be the fulfillment of a dream that only got better.

1. George Christian to Bass, 1974.
2. Laura Kalman, *Abe Fortas: A Biography* (New Haven: Yale University Press, 1990), p. 337. Biographical background of Fortas is drawn heavily from this book.
3. Ibid., p. 328.
4. James Banks to author, July 1998.
5. *Slaughter-House* cases, 83 U. S. 36, p. 82.
6. *Santa Clara County v. Southern Pacific Railroad*, 118 U.S. 395.
7. Strom Thurmond, *The Faith We Have Not Kept* (*San* Diego, Viewpoint Books, 1968), p. 15.
8. *Scott v. Sanford*, 60 U. S. 393, 1857.
9. After Johnson left the presidency, he told former *Atlanta Constitution* editor Gene Patterson that the editorial caused Fortas not to be confirmed. Patterson letter to Jack Bass, July 6, 1998.
10. Kalman, *Abe Fortas, A Biography*, p. 37.
11. Ibid., pp. 340-341; Cohodas, *Strom Thurmond*, pp. 393-394.
12. Cohodas, *Strom Thurmond*, pp. 394-395.
13. Kalman, *Abe Fortas*, pp. 350-357, and Cohodas, *Strom Thurmond*, pp. 395-396. *Washington Post* cartoon, September 8, 1968, cited in Cohodas. Footnote reference, Kalman, Chapter 16, and Bass telephone interview with Harold Burson, April 6, 1998.

Kingmaker Strom Thurmond escorts Richard Nixon.

CHAPTER
EIGHTEEN
✣
Nixon's the One

When Congress took its break in August 1968, for the national political conventions, Strom Thurmond headed for Miami
Beach to hold the South for Richard Nixon. With Lyndon Johnson
out, Robert Kennedy killed in May by an assassin, and amid violent street protests over the war in Vietnam, a raucous Democratic
convention in Chicago two weeks later would select Vice President
Hubert Humphrey as its nominee.

Thurmond understood that the civil rights revolution was sur-
passing party loyalty as a political test in the South. He saw Nixon
as the vehicle for shifting the center of the G.O.P. to the right.

Thurmond's kingmaker role in Miami Beach symbolized that
shift. In the fall he slugged it out with Gov. George Wallace,
whose third-party effort threatened to derail Nixon. Only
Thurmond possessed the credibility among Southerners to tell
them a third-party protest was fruitless, and that "a vote for
Wallace is a vote for Humphrey."

"Strom killed us," said Tom Turnipseed, a key figure in the
Wallace campaign who years later acknowledged and repudiated
his own racism. To Turnipseed, Thurmond remained "a racist in
denial. I've been there, and I know."[1]

✚ ✚ ✚

The road to Miami Beach began four years earlier with Thurmond
switching parties and campaigning for Barry Goldwater. Despite
opposition from a few liberal Republican critics, such as Senator

Clifford Case of New Jersey, Thurmond kept his seniority after the switch. He moved from seventh-ranking Democrat on the Armed Services Committee to fourth-ranking Republican.

Important political developments followed in South Carolina. After House Democrats stripped Albert Watson of his two years' seniority for endorsing Goldwater, the congressman followed the pattern set by Preston Brooks more than a century earlier after his censure for caning Charles Sumner. Watson resigned, ran for reelection as a Republican in a special election, portraying himself as a martyr "who would not let my people be punished." He won seventy percent of the vote against a credible Democratic opponent. With Thurmond in the Senate and his protege in the House, South Carolina Republicans now possessed a base from which to exert southwide leadership in party-building.

As keynote speaker at the 1965 state convention, Thurmond argued for the Republican Party in South Carolina to be "selective in offering candidates," rather than challenging Democrats across the board. Party Chairman Drake Edens disagreed, believing that candidate recruitment was the key to party growth and eventually to real two-party competition.

The mid-sixties were a period of political transition. The Voting Rights Act of 1965 increased and energized black voting strength in South Carolina. Simultaneously, it antagonized a majority of whites, and Thurmond reflected their views. He attacked the measure as vindictive in primarily targeting the states that had voted for Goldwater. "Deep down in his heart," Dent said, Thurmond "felt Lyndon Johnson was getting even. He felt that the Act should be for the whole country, and he's never gotten over that."[2] Segregationists seethed when Johnson declared, "We shall overcome" — the anthem of the civil rights movement — in mobilizing Congress in 1965 to pass the Act after a violent confrontation between Alabama lawmen and blacks protesting discrimination in voter registration at Selma.

The Voting Rights Act eliminated literacy tests in states where less than fifty percent of the voting age population voted in the 1964 presidential election; it required the states to get advance clearance from the Justice Department before implementing any changes in laws affecting voting. In South Carolina the number of black elected officials would climb from 11 in 1968 to 116 in 1974.

Democratic politicians in South Carolina suddenly needed black votes to win and were "scared to death" of seeking them.

Don Fowler, then chairman of the state's Young Democrats, became the main emissary to the African-American community. "I think during that period of time I was the only person who had any status in the Democratic Party who did that, and I did one hell of a lot of it," Fowler remembered.

"I went to black churches when no other white soul would go to black churches," he said. "There was a black preacher in Greenville, dead now, who was minister of the McBee Avenue Baptist Church. His name was David Francis, and he invited me to come up and speak to the county-wide meeting on Sunday afternoon.

"And I called two or three legislators up there (one of them was future Gov. Dick Riley and another was future House Speaker Rex Carter), and they said, 'Well, I guess you should go, but for God's sake don't get caught.'

"And I went and made this speech. It was in the basement of this church, and there were 200 blacks. And if I had gotten caught by a reporter, it would have literally been front page news, not that I was that important, but that there would have been a white guy down there who had any sort of ties within the Democratic Party. The thing lasted about three hours. I was not in any sense uncomfortable being in that crowd, except fear of getting caught."[3]

By 1966, Fowler remembered, "Among normal, middle-class white people, it was about as popular to be a Democrat as it was to have bubonic plague. Lyndon Johnson was Satan incarnate. We were right in the wake of the Civil Rights Act of '64 and the Voting Rights Act of '65, and Lyndon Johnson and his Great Society were really cranking up. And, in the common vernacular, he was 'doing all these things for the niggers.' I mean that was just the atmosphere. If anybody asked an office-holder about the Democratic Party, they would say, 'I'm a *South Carolina* Democrat.'"[4]

Before long, Democratic candidates would be happy to speak in black churches — and Republicans would eventually join them there. Southern black churches traditionally have served as centers of community life, extending their spiritual role to congregational concerns about government and democratic ideals.

Harry Dent returned to South Carolina in the fall of 1965, after Edens stepped down as G.O.P. party chairman, and took over planning the 1966 campaign. Dent was equally intent on building the Republican Party, and the G.O.P. fielded a full slate of candidates for state and congressional offices, with Thurmond at the top of the ticket.

221

The initiative for Dent's move came from political activist James B. Edwards, a Charleston dentist who later became governor and President Ronald Reagan's Secretary of Energy. Edwards made a special trip to Washington to see Thurmond, persuading him that the 35-year-old Dent was the man for the job.[5] Dent's loyalty to Thurmond assured that the party would never undermine his political interests.

Thurmond's run of luck continued. After Sen. Johnston died in 1965, Gov. Donald Russell responded to urging from Lyndon Johnson and, in effect, appointed himself to fill the vacancy. Russell, who actively supported LBJ's losing effort in South Carolina in 1964, resigned as governor. Lt. Gov. Robert E. McNair took the oath as governor and immediately appointed Russell to the Senate. This deal outraged Johnston's widow, who thought she or William "Bill" Johnston, Olin's brother, should have been appointed. But for Thurmond it meant that he wouldn't face an opponent of Russell's stature in 1966, and Strom drew attention for being warm and solicitous to Russell in Washington. But the new senator, with "self-appointment" an issue, lost to Hollings in the 1966 Democratic primary.

In the general election, Thurmond received sixty-two percent of the vote. His strength at the top of the ticket almost spilled over enough to topple Hollings in his bid for the remaining two years of Johnston's term. Watson won reelection, but all other Republicans seeking major office lost. The G.O.P. did gain a foothold in the legislature.

A solid black vote, growing after the 1965 Voting Rights Act, provided the margin of victory for Democrats. Dent sought to capitalize on the white backlash, playing footsie with the segregationist independents allied with George Wallace. In one instance, Dent distributed campaign literature showing Gov. McNair shaking hands with a black man. It obviously wasn't intended to help the Democrats. Although Dent later retreated from that kind of racial politics, it reflected the initial thrust of the Republican "Southern strategy."

State Sen. Bradley Morrah of Greenville became the Democratic sacrificial lamb against Thurmond. Unlike the Republican candidates who had an organized political party to provide them support, Morrah received "not a dime" from the state or national party and believed Thurmond was "majestically treated" by the press.[6] Thurmond further undercut him with endorsements from Democratic Senators Russell and Talmadge of Georgia and Stennis of Mississippi, all of whom presumably believed that endorsing him would help them in their own races.

Although well-regarded and an aggressive campaigner, Morrah was little known outside his base. Thurmond refused to debate him. Morrah simultaneously ran for his established seat in the state senate, losing it to Tom Wofford, and never again held elective office. In the years ahead, Thurmond delighted in the experiences of those who ran against him. They invariably suffered political death.

The most meaningful episode in the 1966 campaign occurred by accident. Dent got Richard Nixon, then practicing law in New York, to come to Columbia for a fund-raiser. Dent drove him back to the Columbia Airport at 11 p.m. to meet a corporate jet and return to New York. The plane was an hour late, and the two men sat in Dent's car, talking politics. When Dent probed, Nixon expressed reluctance about running for president in 1968 because of George Wallace. The Alabama governor planned to run, and Nixon saw him siphoning white voters on the race issue who might otherwise opt for Nixon.

Dent's memory of the dialogue in his car with Nixon captures its essence:

"George Wallace is going to run, and he's going to mess me up."

"There's an answer to that."

"What?"

"Strom Thurmond."

"Strom Thurmond? How? What are you talking about?"

"Well, he was the State Rights candidate for president back in 1948, and he's known across the South. He's got a bigger image across the South than George Wallace has."

Dent went on to explain that Thurmond would take Wallace head-on for Nixon and "stiff him."

"You think Strom Thurmond would do that for me?"

"Yeah, I think he'd do that."

In Columbia Nixon had won points with Thurmond by telling a national interviewer, "Strom is no racist. Strom is a man of courage and integrity."[7] Less than two years earlier — the same month he endorsed Goldwater — Thurmond was named the "least effective" member of Congress in two surveys, one by *Pageant* magazine conducted among members of Congress and the other by Washington journalists. A historian called Thurmond's response to Nixon's words "almost pathetically grateful."[8]

Nixon was seeking his own political resurrection. After serving two terms as Dwight Eisenhower's vice president, he narrowly lost the presidency to John F. Kennedy in 1960. Two years later, he ran for governor of California and lost. The national image from that campaign was one of an exhausted and bitter candidate who stalked into the press room after his defeat, lashing out at reporters and blaming them for his defeat. He asserted as his final memorable line, "Well, you won't have Nixon to kick around anymore, because, gentlemen, this is my last press conference. . . ."[9]

During the Goldwater campaign, however, Nixon made 150 speeches for the candidate, whose support he would also have in 1968. Six months after sitting with Dent in his car at Columbia Airport, Nixon sent an emissary to see him. Dent had spoken to Thurmond and reaffirmed the senator would support Nixon. In the spring of 1968, Governors Ronald Reagan of California and Nelson Rockefeller of New York met with Southern Republican Party leaders in New Orleans. Rockefeller was too liberal and got virtually no support, but established relationships by hosting a steak and grits breakfast. Although Reagan did not commit himself to running, his personality and conservatism made hearts throb.

Nixon met with those party leaders in May at Atlanta, and Dent got Thurmond to attend. Nixon responded to questions about court appointments (he promised to appoint "strict constructionists"), busing school children for integration, protecting textiles, law and order, Communism, national defense, and building the party in the South. Thurmond liked the answers and rode in the car with Nixon to the airport and followed up with a public commitment.

As Nixon feared, George Wallace had become the national lightning rod for what became known as the "social issue." He planned a third-party campaign that would tap into a working class, white electorate, angry and frightened by civil rights and anti-war protesters. He developed code words about race, including "welfare chiselers" and "law and order."

Wallace more than matched Thurmond's capacity for the

symbolic gesture and was a better speaker. Articulate and quick on his feet, Wallace first went national in the winter of 1963, on a tour of major national college campuses that began at Harvard. He avoided racist rhetoric, displayed hillbilly humor, and made constitutional arguments about state rights. Students who expected a raging demagogue found him engaging.

Before dropping out of the 1964 presidential campaign after Goldwater sewed up the Republican nomination, Wallace demonstrated a powerful appeal. In Wisconsin, opposed by the state's political, religious, and AFL-CIO leadership and running with almost no money, he stunned the establishment by getting a third of the vote.

Blue-collar workers responded to his message — the same attacks as Thurmond's, but Wallace articulated them better. In Madison, they sang "Dixie" with Polish accents. Wallace attacked the "godless" Supreme Court. He denounced the civil rights bill as a threat to union seniority that "would impose racial quotas," create chaos in the schools, and "make it impossible for a home owner to sell his home to whomever he chose." Wallace didn't camouflage his message with "states rights," but orchestrated the politics of fear like a maestro.

He followed with thirty percent in Indiana and forty-seven percent in Maryland. But Goldwater's vote against the civil rights bill ended the 1964 boomlet for Wallace, who made a furtive, unsuccessful effort to get Goldwater to choose him as a running mate.[10]

More than any experience in Thurmond's past, the 1968 Republican convention provided a political analogy to his glider ride into Normandy. He went to Miami Beach fully committed, and survival depended on quick and instinctive tactical decisions. Thurmond believed that only Nixon could win the election for the Republicans, and a GOP victory would move the country to the right.

When Nixon arrived by plane late Monday afternoon, Thurmond was there to greet him and ready to warn him of serious problems. *The New York Times* that morning ran a story speculating that, if nominated, Nixon would choose one of three men as his running mate — New York's Rockefeller, New York City Mayor John Lindsay, or Illinois Sen. Charles Percy. All represented the party's liberal wing.

Buzhardt, who had left Thurmond's staff to return to McCormick and take over his father's law practice, joined Thurmond and Dent in Miami Beach. Throughout the day, Buzhardt and Dent experienced the developing confusion and panic among Nixon's Southern delegates.[i]

The *New York Times* story "went through like wildfire," Buzhardt said. "When that *Times* story hit, boy, all day Monday it was just pandemonium." Dent added that the slogan of Reagan supporters was, "The double cross is on, the double cross is on."

Delegates from all over the South, and some from outside the region, sought leadership and came to Thurmond. "Up until Monday night, he said, 'I'm standing firm,'" Buzhardt observed. But by late afternoon, when Thurmond left for the airport, Buzhardt continued, "It had gotten to the place where, really, just the senator's 'standing-firm-with-Nixon' wasn't enough."

Meanwhile, California Gov. Reagan dropped his coyness and formally announced his candidacy for the nomination. Reagan and his forces had been active during the summer, courting Southern state delegations and siphoning off support. James Gardner, the ultraconservative and ambitious chairman of the North Carolina delegation, began spreading the word that he was supporting Reagan. He told Dent his intention at the convention hall as they both entered for the Monday night program.

The Thurmond aides had just gotten confirmation for him to meet with Nixon at 2:30 p.m. Tuesday, working it through Brad Hayes, a Nixon campaign staffer and former Aiken County Republican chairman. This schedule meant they would meet before Reagan's scheduled appearance at 3:15 before the South Carolina delegation.

On the convention floor, Dent could feel slippage. Columnist Rowland Evans told him that Ohio Gov. James Rhodes said after Reagan's announcement, "It's a new ball game." An insider told Dent that Rhodes planned to throw Ohio's support to Reagan, with Rhodes to become his running mate.

i. Jack Bass, then the Columbia, S.C. bureau chief for The Charlotte Observer, and Remer Tyson, political editor for The Atlanta Constitution, covered the 1968 Republican convention, Bass as part of the Knight Newspapers team and Tyson for the Atlanta newspapers. The morning after Nixon's nomination, they taped a ninety-minute interview with Dent and Buzhardt, which was interrupted by Nixon's announcement that Maryland Gov. Spiro Agnew would be his running mate. Publisher Ralph McGill considered the transcript of that interview an important historical document and directed that it be printed in full in the Sunday, August 11, issue of The Atlanta Journal and Constitution. It ran more than a page and a half. The account here of Thurmond's role at the convention is heavily drawn from that transcript and from personal observations by Bass at the convention.

The Nixon convention staff had a designated person serving as a listening post in each state delegation. About 9:30 p.m. on the convention floor, Dent got a call from John Mitchell, who became Nixon's campaign manager. Mitchell said that Nixon could meet with Thurmond that night or on Tuesday.

Dent interpreted the call as a desire to meet immediately, an indication of concern. On the taxi ride to the oceanside Plaza Hilton Hotel, Dent said, "I know Fred was shook, and I was shook. Sen. Thurmond doesn't get shook."

Buzhardt said, "There were people coming in to the senator [all day] and saying, 'Strom, you're laying your damn political life on the line. Get your pound of flesh.' We were told this bluntly — bluntly all over. These people just don't know the senator. That wasn't his nature." Dent added, "Strom Thurmond wasn't coming there with his hand out. He wasn't going to ask for anything."

A little after 10 p.m., Mitchell greeted Dent, Buzhardt, and Thurmond, then took them by elevator to the fifteenth floor. They walked up three flights of stairs to Nixon's remote suite. Nixon and Thurmond greeted each other as if it were a casual social visit. Thurmond got his own cup of coffee and took a seat with Nixon on a sofa. The others sat in chairs, joined by Nixon aide H. R. Halderman. The next minutes were crucial.

Nixon and Thurmond were both seasoned political masters. Both were cool. Each knew without saying, and knew that the other knew, if Strom Thurmond delivered the South for Nixon, allowing him to win the nomination, he would owe a huge political debt. And if Nixon didn't get elected, the debt would be void.

The important thing, to Dent and Buzhardt, was that the top man understand Thurmond's commitment and reassure him that the South was important to the campaign. Buzhardt "was personally afraid that Dick Nixon would not understand how far out on a limb Strom Thurmond had gotten without any assurance from him."

They had heard reports that Nixon's basic strategy was to court the urban vote and write off the South. Dent wanted the senator to "look in Nixon's eyes . . . Strom Thurmond needed to be sure in his own mind that Richard Nixon had not written off the South." Buzhardt added that Thurmond "was saying [to delegates], 'I'm standing with him.' But he didn't want to mislead the people who were coming to him and asking him pointed questions."

The Thurmond strategy was to hold the South as solidly as possible for Nixon, allowing him to lock up the nomination early on the first ballot and not be pressured to make deals near the end of the balloting on selecting a running mate. "We knew the vote count," Buzhardt said. "We knew that if we could hold steady this could be done, and there wouldn't have to be any bargaining." (The 356 Southern delegates amounted to more than half the number required for nomination. Nixon would get 264 of them, almost three of every four.)

The strategy centered on Nixon getting a first-ballot victory. The South Carolina delegation had committed itself to unanimously nominating Thurmond, who would then step aside and cast the state's twenty-two votes for Nixon. But to mollify a couple of Reagan holdouts, they agreed to switch solidly to Reagan if there was a second ballot.[11]

Dent and Buzhardt briefed Nixon on the slippage and told him about Jim Gardner's move to Reagan, which Nixon hadn't known. Nixon gave some orders, and Dent was impressed that he listened to advice. Nixon understood his role was that of candidate with conviction, and he played it well. Although he discussed general principles, Dent said, "He was trying to tell us, 'I do plan to run in the South. I do plan to run strongly in the South.'"

"If Mr. Nixon had not satisfied the senator, if he had said, 'Let's face it. George Wallace has got the South, Strom, and I'm going to have to concentrate strictly on running up north in the big cities, or something else. Now you go on and help me hold the line and that'll be fine,' Strom Thurmond would have gone on and would have helped him because he was committed. That's something Ronald Reagan never understood even though he was told."

When the subject of a vice presidential candidate came up, Nixon made it clear he would pick his own running mate and told them, "I'm not going to ram a man down the throat of any section of the country." And that, Dent said, was "all Sen. Thurmond wanted or needed to hear. It settled his own mind."

As the discussion with Nixon continued, Dent explained, "We said, 'Look, we can't carry your message for you. Senator Thurmond, just one man, can't deliver it. Why don't you tell these people directly?' He said, 'I'll be glad to. I'll answer any question that anybody asks.'

"He talked generally about his philosophy that night at the Hilton. We were pleased and we said, 'Tell these delegates yourself.' His fervor, his conviction, looking you right in the eye, and his complete candor impressed us. We said the same thing would impress those delegates." Nixon met twice the next morning with Southern state delegations, six states at a time.

There, Dent emphasized Thurmond's total commitment to Nixon and added that three surveys taken in South Carolina showed him the strongest among all voters of any Republican candidate. Bo Calloway of Georgia introduced Thurmond, who told them, "We have no choice, if we want to win, except to vote for Nixon. We must quit using our hearts and start using our heads." He continued, "I love Reagan, but Nixon's the one."[12]

When Nixon spoke, he began by saying he supported civil rights. As Dent put it, "He said, 'Let me make it straight at the outset, that I am for civil rights and I have supported it and believe in it.'" But Nixon also alluded to the riots that had occurred in northern cities. He said that most of the problems were caused by "extremists of both races" and that a Nixon administration wouldn't act "to satisfy some professional civil-rights group, or something like that."[13] He repeated his position on selecting judges, and he made it clear he would pick a running mate after the nomination, one who would be acceptable to all parts of the country.

With Thurmond "fully satisfied," the message white Southerners received was clear. Nixon would be "evenhanded" on civil rights, meaning measured enforcement, no new legislative initiatives, and opposition to creative judicial remedies for overcoming discrimination and ending segregation. By now fervently committed, Thurmond resumed the battle.

Buzhardt said that Brad Hayes was afraid that Reagan might get wholesale switches among the Southern delegates. "He had seen these people's heart beat for Reagan," Buzhardt said. "Reagan gives this really heartfelt, sincere pitch that only he can do. He's a master at it. He comes through personality-wise. He comes through with his philosophical pitch. Real simple, direct answers.

"Goldwater never had what Reagan's got. Goldwater was never able to reduce his positions to a flat inspirational message. Goldwater just didn't inspire.

"Reagan has all these answers down and if you listen to him three or four times they're the same ones every time — pop-pop-pop — and they're word for word. He's got them down and they're worked out where they sound really off the cuff, but they aren't. They're simple answers.

"Nixon doesn't give this. If anything, he came across as more sincere."

Later that Tuesday, before meeting with the South Carolina delegation, Reagan met privately with Thurmond in the senator's hotel room. Reagan asked Dent to leave, believing that one-on-one he could persuade Thurmond to support him. Asked a few minutes after the meeting what he told the California governor, Thurmond said, "I told him I would support him next time."[ii] (Dent said that Thurmond was unimpressed with Reagan, finding him shallow.)

When slippage for Nixon was reported in the Florida delegation, Thurmond rushed to meet with them at the Doral Country Club, holding a majority for Nixon in a delegation that voted by unit rule. Elsewhere, he worked to shore up weak spots and to recruit uncommitted delegates.

Thurmond's role wasn't unassisted. Although he visited the Mississippi delegation, so did Barry Goldwater. Mississippi Republican Chairman Clarke Reed said that Goldwater (who won eighty-seven percent of the Mississippi vote in 1964) meant more than Thurmond in holding that state's delegates for Nixon over Reagan.[14]

The final crisis came Wednesday night when delegates streaming into the Miami Beach Convention Center saw newsboys hawking a "bulldog" edition of the next morning's *Miami Herald* with a banner headline that Oregon Sen. Mark Hatfield would be the vice presidential nominee: HATFIELD VEEP PICK.

The story sparked pandemonium again among the Southern delegations. If true, it meant to them that Nixon had lied about waiting to make a decision on whom to choose for vice president. Dent raced from delegation to delegation, insisting the story was false. At one point he spotted Don Oberdorfer, who wrote the *Herald* story, as the reporter was walking in front of the Louisiana and Georgia delegations. Dent cornered him and offered a $300 bet that his story was wrong. Oberdorfer saw Dent jumping up and down and heard something about $300 that he didn't understand. "I thought it was a joke," Oberdorfer said. "I wouldn't bet $300 on anything." Dent yelled through a megaphone to the delegates that Oberdorfer wouldn't bet on Hatfield. He played on

ii. The "next time" would come in 1976, after Nixon's resignation and with Gerald Ford in the White House. At the 1976 convention in Kansas City, Thurmond remained in the background, saying little. Many believed that he wanted to support Ford, the sitting president. Reagan had offended many of the most conservative Southern delegates by announcing moderate Republican Sen. Richard Schweicker of Pennsylvania would be his running mate to balance the ticket. And Harry Dent was running Ford's Southern operation. In the close contest between Ford and Reagan, which Ford won, Thurmond quietly cast his ballot for Reagan.

their suspicion of Yankee journalists to calm the delegates. Nixon's floor leader at the convention, Maryland Congressman Rogers Morton, stayed busy that evening scurrying with Thurmond from one Southern delegation to another.[15]

The Hatfield story was one ordered by John Knight, chief executive officer of Knight Newspapers, which owned *The Miami Herald*. Apparently motivated by vanity, Knight wanted his hometown newspaper to have this scoop. The assignment went to Oberdorfer, an experienced political reporter then in the Knight Newspapers Washington bureau. His source was Gerald Ford, then House minority leader.[16]

Although Hatfield would appeal to the moderate wing of the party, he was a Southern Baptist, and his main sponsor was the Rev. Billy Graham, who joined Thurmond and sixteen other influential politicians to discuss the vice presidential pick with Nixon immediately after the nomination.[17] Except for the *Miami Herald* story, Hatfield might have been acceptable to the South.

When Thurmond left the room, however, he handed Nixon a small piece of paper with columns of names. He named five "acceptables" that included Reagan and Congressman George Bush of Texas, two "no objections" that included Maryland Gov. Spiro Agnew, and "unacceptables" that included Hatfield. Thurmond had deposited his veto.

Hatfield might have been selected if John Knight had simply allowed his newspaper to cover the story as it unfolded. That would have meant Hatfield becoming president after Nixon's resignation. Instead, Agnew got the nomination only to resign the vice presidency in disgrace after revelations of accepting bribes during and before he was governor. The ultimate irony is that Nixon then selected Gerald Ford, who had innocently mentioned Hatfield's name to a friendly reporter, to succeed Agnew. And Ford became president.

When Dent went through a receiving line at the end of the convention, Nixon said he wanted him to come to Mission Bay, California, and work for him on the campaign. Dent always felt Haldeman and fellow Californian John Ehrlichman were suspicious of him. They tried to block him from seeing Nixon. Dent called Mitchell, who got him in. Nixon agreed to Dent's running a separate operation in the South, "Thurmond Speaks for Nixon-Agnew." Dent flew weekly to New York, reporting to and coordinating with Mitchell each Friday night. "I'd tell him what we were doing and planned to do," Dent said. "Everything worked perfectly."[18]

Thurmond took his message from Miami Beach, that a vote for Reagan was a vote for Rockefeller (because many of Nixon's supporters outside the South would find Reagan too conservative) and switched it in the general election to a vote for Wallace was a vote for Humphrey because Wallace couldn't win. In late September, "Thurmond Speaks" saturated the South with radio and television commercials of Thurmond delivering that message. As the former Dixiecrat candidate arguing that the third-party strategy didn't work, he provided credibility. Radio was aimed at country music stations. Tom Turnipseed remembered Thurmond's spots as "very effective" and that Wallace's poll numbers began falling almost immediately. Wallace had led in the border states of North Carolina, Tennessee, and Florida, as well as South Carolina — states that Nixon won, with a collective forty-five electoral votes that exceeded his margin of victory. Nixon squeaked by Wallace in North Carolina and Tennessee, where Thurmond's role clearly made the difference, and won more decisively in Florida.

He also had help from a hard-right message delivered by Spiro Agnew. Nixon himself attacked busing and endorsed "freedom of choice" desegregation plans. The Supreme Court, in *Green v. New Kent County*, earlier that year had ruled out such plans unless they actually resulted in desegregation. They never did.

(Don Fowler got tapes of the Thurmond ads promising freedom of choice in the schools if Nixon were elected and would play them back two years later, with a voice-over that said, "Broken Promises.")

Under "freedom of choice," no whites chose to attend black schools, and few blacks were willing to face the intimidation and hostility that usually came in choosing to attend previously all-white schools.

Thurmond carried South Carolina for Nixon, making it the only state in the South to vote Republican in both the 1964 and 1968 presidential elections. Although the other Goldwater states from 1964 and Arkansas went to Wallace, Humphrey carried only Lyndon Johnson's home state of Texas, and the other Southern states all moved into Nixon's column.

Textile magnate Roger Milliken of Spartanburg, presumably the wealthiest person in South Carolina, led the fund-raising operation for "Thurmond Speaks" that paid for most of the radio and

TV spots to run. "Roger could sit around a table with the other big boys," Dent said, "and tell each one what he needed from them." The Nixon administration responded to Milliken's effort with textile import legislation.

Although Thurmond's efforts gave Nixon a plurality that won South Carolina's eight electoral votes, angry Wallace voters retaliated by voting for Democrats in local elections. The G.O.P. lost two thirds of its twenty-five seats in the legislature, including all four state Senate seats in Charleston.

Dent became a top White House political aide and got President Nixon to appoint South Carolina textile executive Fred Dent — a distant relative — as Secretary of Commerce. "We put in at least twenty-five South Carolina people in good jobs in the Nixon administration," Dent said. "Nixon believed in the Southern strategy," which to Dent went far beyond race and included full participation.

Thurmond was set to return to Washington as an effective political insider, but with some political damage at home. Buzhardt became general counsel to the Department of Defense.

At a meeting Dent attended with Nixon and Mitchell just after the election, Thurmond told them of his plans to marry Nancy Moore, a twenty-two-year-old former Miss South Carolina. Both Mitchell and Nixon seemed to smirk, Dent observed. He felt Thurmond was making a huge mistake.

1. Bass interview with Tom Turnipseed, Columbia, S.C., March 10, 1998.
2. Thompson interview with Dent, December 13, 1982.
3. Thompson interview with Donald Fowler, circa 1981.
4. Ibid.
5. Bass interview with Dent.
6. Dent, *The Prodigal South*, p. 77.
7. Dan Carter, *The Politics of Rage*, p. 329.
8. Dan Carter, *The Politics of Rage*, quoting the *Los Angeles Times*, November 4, 1962.
9. Dan Carter, *The Politics of Rage* (New York: Simon & Schuster, 1995), PP. 196-215.
10. Dent, *The Prodigal South Returns to Power*, p. 91.

11. Dan Carter, *The Politics of Rage*, p. 330, citing Lewis Chester, Godfrey Hodgson, and Bruce Page. *An American Melodrama: The Presidential Campaign of 1968* (New York: Viking), p. 445.
12. Dan Carter, *The Politics of Rage*, p. 329, citing *The Miami Herald*, Aug. 7, 1968.
13. Clarke Reed to Bass, circa 1989.
14. Dent, *The Prodigal South*, p. 100. *The Charlotte Observer*, Aug. 8, 1968.
15. Dent, *The Prodigal South*, p. 101, Oberdorfer to Bass during taxi ride at the convention.
16. Ibid., p. 102.
17. Harry Dent, *The Prodigal South*, pp. 105-110; Bass interview with Dent.

CHAPTER NINETEEN

✢

The Beauty Queen

When Sen. Herman Talmadge's son, Bobby, came to Washington in 1968 to spend the summer with his father, he expressed interest in meeting young women. An alert staffer told him to contact a friend of hers in Strom Thurmond's office. "She can introduce you to Miss South Carolina," she told young Talmadge. "She's working there as an intern." Senator Talmadge reminisced, "He came back and said [referring to Thurmond], 'The competition was too stiff.'"[1]

Nancy Moore met Strom in August 1964 at the grape festival in York, and he took her square dancing. The next year, he routinely called to congratulate her on winning the Miss South Carolina title. She worked for a month in Thurmond's office as an intern in 1967. She returned for the full summer of 1968 after graduating from Duke with honors and before entering the University of South Carolina law school that fall.

Lee Bandy, *The State's* Washington correspondent, remembered her coming over many times late in the evening delivering press releases to him in the Senate press gallery. "She came in, and was a very outgoing person," Bandy said. "And she would sit down, chitchat, and flirt. Sometimes with Roger Mudd. I had no way of knowing that she and Strom were dating or seeing each other. All I knew was that she worked for him as an intern. We were all kind of shocked and surprised when they put out a press release announcing their engagement."[2]

When Strom first called her in 1965, he knew almost nothing about her. "It was just a name," he said. "I just called her up and said congratulations." Eighteen-year-old Nancy, nicknamed "Moose," sang and played the piano to win the Miss Aiken and Miss South Carolina titles.

A brownish-blonde with fair complexion and blue eyes, *The State* reported, "The new Miss South Carolina is 5-6, weighs 116 pounds and is 35-22-35 for those who keep score." She already had a string of beauty titles. Her mother said, "Even in the first grade she had that curious look of amazement and wonder she has today."[3]

Strom hadn't met her parents, Mr. and Mrs. Paul R. Moore. Mr. Moore was an engineer who had moved to Aiken about twelve years earlier — a year or so before Thurmond left for Washington — to work for the Savannah River Plant.

When Harry Dent and Fred Buzhardt returned to South Carolina from the 1968 Republican convention, they began to hear insiders talk about Strom courting the young beauty queen. "People were aghast at the idea that Senator Thurmond (then approaching his sixty-sixth birthday) was considering marriage with this girl," Dent said. "They were saying, 'Can't you stop this? The old man is making a fool out of himself.'" In a "sons-to-father talk," they talked him into staying away from her during the campaign and hoped the relationship would go away.

When Thurmond disclosed his marriage plans to Dent after the election, Harry told him it would "ruin you politically, destroy everything you've worked for in your political life. If you do this, just don't plan to run again in 1972. You might as well resign now, like King Edward [who abdicated the throne in England to marry "the woman I love," an American divorcee, and became the Duke of Windsor] and get public sympathy to offset all the public wrath that'll follow."

The story of what happened next became a relished joke among Thurmond intimates, with Dent enjoying his role as the butt of it. Dent and Buzhardt met with Thurmond, stressing their concerns, and he told them to take their case to Nancy. "If you can talk her out of it, it'll be all right with me," he said. "Go ahead."

Dent and Buzhardt met with her four times over a two-week period, lengthy sessions in which Dent "went so far as to tell her that if she married him and they had children, those children would be messed up. I almost abused her."

Finally, she broke down and cried, telling them, "I love him. I love him. I love him." Dent came away convinced that her love was genuine, but says, "I kept telling the Senator, 'Here you are at the apex of your career and you're making a fool out of yourself. You're going all the way back to what you did at the Governor's Mansion by standing on your head."[4]

Thurmond was unconcerned. Years later he said the approach by his two aides to Nancy didn't worry him. "If they could convince her it was the wrong thing to do and she felt it was," he said, "I didn't want her to do it."[5]

Strom confidently proceeded to marry Nancy in Aiken a few days before Christmas, joined by a handful of family and close friends. After a one-week honeymoon on Grand Bahama Island, they held a public reception at the campus home of University of South Carolina President Thomas F. Jones. Cake, nuts, and cider punch were served.

Some 1,500 from all sections of South Carolina — friends, relatives, acquaintances, and strangers — stood in line on a bright, chilly, late December afternoon. (No black people were seen among them.) Many women wore fur jackets. Those attending included Harry Dent.[6]

"The interesting thing about Strom Thurmond," Dent said, "is I don't ever remember in any way the Senator ever rebuking me or Fred. We would always tell him exactly what we thought and it was OK. . . . The marriage turned out to be a big plus. Especially having those kids. And the children turned out great."[7]

Looking back more than a decade after their marriage, Strom said, "Normally, for a man to marry a woman that much younger wouldn't help his career. But I'd been with Nancy enough to know she had her feet on the ground, she was smart, and I just felt she'd make a good wife and mother. So if she felt she was willing to take the chance, well, I was. We both loved each other."[8]

Nancy began learning to cook when she was five, and as a new bride in Washington ran a good kitchen. Her favorite meal as a hostess was a roast beef dinner. She enjoyed exercise almost as much as Strom did. They swam together and played tennis. "He wins repeatedly," she told Jack Bass in her first interview as Mrs. Thurmond. They rode horses together. "He's an expert horseman. I love it, but I'm not very good."

The new bride wore her hair long, bundled on top. She learned early that Thurmond often worked late or brought work home with him.

Nancy quickly became a Washington attraction. At the Women's National Press Club's dinner for Congress the first week in January 1969, the new Republican senator from Kansas, Robert Dole — a former representative who once said he went to the House broke — quipped, "I decided money wasn't everything. I met Mrs. Thurmond last night."[9]

Dole's lawyer wife, Elizabeth, became a friend and role model for Nancy, who over time seemed to chafe at not having some career of her own. She had dropped out of law school a few weeks before her wedding. She came along a generation after Jean Thurmond, for whom being Mrs. Strom Thurmond seemed quite fulfilling.

The Thurmonds' first child, named Nancy Moore after her mother, arrived in 1970. Strom, Jr., followed two years later; then came Julie and finally Paul.

"As it turned out," Dent continued, "all that stuff I said was going to be bad politics — they had those four kids and they'd be walking or running down the street behind the Senator and Nancy, jogging or something. It was great stuff."[10]

Nancy proved to be a solid campaigner, especially in 1978 when she and the children moved to Columbia for the fall campaign and traveled around the state in "Strom Trek," a recreational vehicle. The older children attended fully integrated A. C. Moore Elementary School, and the campaign literature portrayed an active and happy family. Nancy was good at working the crowds.

Although she enjoyed classical music, with Chopin and Beethoven her favorite composers, when a small-town radio station manager offered on the air to play her favorite song, she asked for "Love Me Tender" as sung by Elvis.

Soon after their baby Nancy was born, Strom apologized at a banquet for his wife's tardiness. "She had to feed the baby," he said, "and this baby isn't raised on Carnation milk." The crowd cheered and applauded a few minutes later when the blushing mother seated herself at the head table, smiling dutifully at Strom's awkward humor.[11]

What was new for Strom, however, was that the dour senator developed a sense of humor. Until his marriage to Nancy, Lee Bandy remembered, "You couldn't joke with him about anything because he thought you were serious."

Fatherhood and the marriage also "helped Strom develop certain sensitivities toward other people he might not have had," Bandy said. It spilled over into his legislative record. A specific case involved his support for the use of fetal tissue in research. His daughter Julie has diabetes, and research in the field requires the material. Thurmond's position was attacked by anti-abortion groups. "His voting record has always been a conservative one, but I would have a hard time today calling Strom an ideologue," Bandy said.[12]

Over time, rumors floated that Strom might retire, with Nancy running for the seat. In response to a direct question from Dent, Thurmond replied, "I have no plans." But in 1981 he told a *Washington Post* reporter that Nancy would "make an ideal public servant — senator, governor, whatever."[13]

A top aide said that Nancy "got anything she thought was important, even for him to hire a certain person in the office, to assign a certain person to some responsibility, how to approach certain speeches."[14] Although Nancy influenced Strom, she seldom got involved in major policy issues. "She wasn't Jean Thurmond in any respect," Dent said.

She also never had the staff rapport that Jean had, nor their confidence in her judgment that Jean did. In the early 1980s, Thurmond made a Law Day address at the University of South Carolina law school, perhaps the most important annual event in legal education. The prepared text addressed lofty issues, but Nancy edited it and inserted a number of jokes that drew laughter, but left the Senator's staffers shaking their heads. For example, Thurmond talked about getting up in the middle of the night to do something, "but at my age I get up lots of time in the middle of the night." The audience laughed, but the question was whether they were laughing with the senator or at him.

Although usually in the background, Nancy on occasion played a leading role and demonstrated "presence," that capacity to get people's attention just by entering a room.

Before James Clyburn was elected in 1992 as South Carolina's first black congressman since the post-Reconstruction period, he served for years as executive director of the South Carolina Human Affairs Commission and hosted an annual, bipartisan political "roast." It served as a charitable fund-raiser. When Don Fowler got roasted in the mid-1980s, Clyburn invited Nancy Thurmond to serve as "roastmistress." She accepted, prepared carefully, and presided with just the right bite of humor for political insiders.

Clyburn set the tone for the evening when he introduced the head table. The octogenarian Strom sat next to Emily Clyburn, and Jim Clyburn concluded his introduction of Thurmond with a slight pause, then added, "Now Senator, that's my wife sitting next to you, so you keep your hands on top of the table." Thurmond joined in the howling laughter of a knowing and knowledgeable biracial audience.

Perhaps no politician anywhere can match Strom's legendary image for lechery. Socialite Washington writer Sally Quinn tells of the story from the 1950s of a reception: "My mother and I headed for the buffet table. As we were reaching for the shrimp, both of us jumped and let out a shriek. Sen. Strom Thurmond, grinning from ear to ear, had one hand on my behind and the other on my mother's. As I recall, we were both quite flattered, and thought it terribly funny and wicked of ol' Strom.'" Talking about the incident on a TV talk show at the end of 1997 while promoting her book, Quinn said her mother had grown up in Savannah, knew Thurmond, and said, "Strom, you old devil."[15]

Strom's image for sexual exploits only grew. Just when and where he said it is disputed — some say at the funeral of Florida Congressman Claude Pepper, who championed the cause of senior citizens, and others after Thurmond began siring children — but Sen. John Tower of Texas made the earthy remark, "When he dies, they'll have to beat his pecker down with a baseball bat in order to close the coffin lid."

Word got back to Thurmond, who sent an aide out to buy a Sears Thumper baseball bat and deliver it to Tower. He placed it on permanent display atop the mantel in the Senate Republican cloakroom.[16] Robert Arial, the talented cartoonist for *The State*, sneaks a baseball bat into occasional cartoons about Thurmond.

At least one professional woman from South Carolina, seeing Thurmond on a business matter, suddenly found herself grabbed, groped on the breast, and the recipient of a prolonged kiss on the mouth. Women news reporters have shared the experience.

Another incident involved a female SLED agent, assigned as a driver for Thurmond in the 1980s. Unlike Hollings, who relied on staff to drive him on official trips in South Carolina, Thurmond for decades called upon SLED.

Tales circulated among the agents include one of Thurmond calling a female SLED driver after both had retired to their motel rooms on an overnight trip. The story goes that he asked her to come to his room. She knocked and he said for her to come in. She opened the door and asked what he wanted. He sat on the bed in his underwear, patted the bed, and invited her to come and sit beside him. She closed the door and returned to her room. After her report, SLED quit assigning female agents as drivers.

At least one South Carolina reporter pursued the story, but women agents refused to talk for publication.[17]

At a 1988 Columbia Chamber of Commerce function honoring sixty-year-old Congressman Floyd Spence, Thurmond noted how vigorous and active Spence had become since a double-lung transplant. Thurmond, then eighty-five, quipped he was going to try to find some "different parts" himself to keep going for another twenty years. The audience howled. An editorial in *The State* impishly asked, "Can it be that some parts of the seemingly indestructible Thurmond self-destructed?"[18]

Maureen Dowd noted in a 1994 *New York Times Magazine* article about Strom that although surrounded by colleagues "edgy about gender politics, Thurmond remains blissfully untouched" by such concerns and seemed not to get the point. Back in South Carolina, two female columnists for *The State* retorted, "The day he does, Dowd, the folks at home will know we've got an impostor on our hands."

The Senator once greeted abortion-rights leaders as "lovely ladies." He told one group of witnesses at a hearing: "These are the prettiest witnesses we have had in a long time. I imagine you are all married. If not, you could be if you wanted to be."[19]

He seemed finally to get it, at least in Washington, when a story got out three years after newly elected Senator Patti Murray of Washington state told California Senator Barbara Boxer in 1993 that Thurmond had tried to fondle her on a Capitol elevator. Thurmond denied the charge and Murray's press secretary said she "knows what sexual harassment is and that was not sexual harassment."

Thurmond said he was showing Senator Murray "the same . . . gentlemanly courtesies" he had always made towards women. "That includes assisting them through doors, into vehicles and yes — onto elevators."

Boxer said Murray told her that Thurmond put his arm around her, tried to grope her breast, and said, "Are you married, little lady?"[20]

During Thurmond's 1996 reelection campaign, however,

Thurmond actively fed the image of his virility. In a story playfully headlined, "He Is Slipping — It Was Just Her Arm," *The State* reported him grabbing WOLO-TV reporter Susan Biggers by the arm — in the middle of an interview — and telling her, "You're a good-looking girl."

On the Clemson campus the same day, Thurmond spotted a covey of coeds and asked: "Any of you girls want a hug?" When three complied, the senator looked around and added, "We'll settle for a handshake for you boys."[21]

Strom considered Nancy not only "wholesome, clean, intelligent, and attractive," but an "excellent writer."[22] She wrote two books, *Mother's Medicine*, a parents guide, and *Happy Mother, Happy Child* (1981). In 1988 she hosted a South Carolina Educational Television series, "Parent's Point of View."

Early in 1989, she sought a top job in the Department of Commerce, a $125,000 plum as undersecretary for trade and tourism. It involved travel to many of the world's garden spots. Bandy reported that Secretary of Commerce Robert Mosbacher told a committee staffer, "I don't think she's qualified," but that he was getting "all kinds of pressure from friends of Strom Thurmond." More than twenty senators sent letters of support.

Thurmond had endorsed Senator Robert Dole over Vice President George Bush in 1988, and Bandy initially reported that presidential aides opposed Nancy getting the job for that reason. Strom's top aides believed Nancy influenced him to back Dole because of her friendship with Mrs. Dole, that Nancy would coax ("I hate to say nagging") Strom to get her way.[23]

Former Thurmond protege Lee Atwater, who had managed Bush's campaign, arranged for Nancy to get hired for the Commerce Department job in a consultant's capacity. But she withdrew as a candidate for permanent appointment in mid-April, after a month and a half, citing her husband's reelection plans and her learning of the potential conflict with the Hatch Act, which prohibits federal employees from political activity.[24] At that time, Thurmond had no serious opposition, and a top staff person believed she withdrew because she was in over her head and knew it — and knew that those around her believed she lacked the administrative skills the job required.[25]

Although the problems would not be acknowledged until much later, Nancy had become the subject of Washington rumors, implying she spent an inordinate amount of time with a young male Thurmond aide and other men. Her behavior seemed erratic.

A few years earlier, the Thurmonds car-pooled activities of their teenaged children with their neighbors in Washington's northern Virginia suburbs, fellow Senator Charles "Chuck" Robb and his wife Lynda, eldest daughter of former President Lyndon Johnson. Strom, by then an octogenarian, drove the van one day when Lynda's mother, Lady Bird Johnson, was visiting.

Lynda remarked to him what attractive children he had. Strom leaned over, placed his hand on her shoulder, and said in her ear, "They could have been yours."

As she and Lady Bird exchanged amused glances, Lynda remembered her visit to the Capitol a quarter century earlier, while still in high school a year or so after Jean's death in January 1960, and running into Thurmond, then almost sixty. He invited Lynda to go bike-riding with him that weekend.

She asked permission from her father, the Senate majority leader about to be sworn in as vice president. For the only time in her dating years, Johnson said no.[26]

As relations between Nancy and Strom grew more strained, it became apparent to top staffers there was no longer a real marriage between the two, and in 1991 Nancy announced she was returning to Aiken with her younger children. Their daughter, Nancy Moore, was enrolled at the University of South Carolina, and Strom, Jr., followed her there. Paul later won the state 4-A tennis championship as an Aiken High School student. He accepted a tennis scholarship to Vanderbilt University, playing on the varsity team in the Southeastern Conference, one of America's most competitive leagues for college tennis. Julie enrolled at the College of Charleston.

Lee Bandy heard that Strom told Nancy that if she wanted a divorce she would have to pursue it, that he wouldn't. Although separated, they remained married. Nancy dated other men, but she and Strom still saw one another on his trips home.

A low point in the relationship came at a Washington birthday bash for Thurmond in March 1993, celebrating his ninetieth birthday. Richard Nixon spoke eloquently. President Bill Clinton and Vice President Al Gore dropped in at a reception. Bob Dole served as emcee, keeping the audience in laughter with one-liners. Congressional leaders delivered tributes.

Nancy attended, escorted by Charlie Duell, the socially prominent and wealthy owner of Charleston's Magnolia Gardens. Her efforts to sit at the head table and to speak had been rebuffed by the event's planners as inappropriate.

Bandy reported that after Thurmond spoke, soul singer James Brown led a rendition of "Happy Birthday." As the guests remained standing for the benediction by Sen. John Danforth of Missouri, an ordained Episcopal priest, Nancy took the mike and started speaking. She extolled Strom's virtues. The guests sat back down, sensing she might ramble for awhile.

When she finished, Strom felt obligated to respond. "Not bad for somebody who's separated," he said. Bandy reported that guests left abuzz and discomforted, and he concluded, "The skit writers for 'Saturday Night Live' couldn't have written a more bizarre ending to what otherwise was a perfect evening."[27]

Two months later, Strom and Nancy would be together again in a setting of searing tragedy.

1. Bass interview with Talmadge, June 2, 1998.
2. Bass interview with Lee Bandy, June 24, 1997.
3. *The State*, July 12, 1965.
4. Harry Dent, *The Prodigal South*, pp. 111, 116-117; Bass interview with Dent, June 26, 1967.
5. Thompson interview with Thurmond, December 22, 1981.
6. *The Charlotte Observer*, December 30, 1968.
7. Dent to Bass, telephone interview, 1998.
8. Nina Totenberg, *Parade* magazine, February 15, 1981.
9. *The Charlotte Observer*, January 12, 1969.
10. Ibid.
11. Confidential source.
12. Lee Bandy to Bass.
13. *The Washington Post*, December 22, 1981.
14. Confidential interview.
15. John Monk, *The State*, October 14, quoting *The New Yorker*.
16. *The Washington Post*, April 8, 1996, p. D4.
17. Confidential source.
18. *The State*, October 17, 1988, p. 14A.

19. *The New York Times Magazine*, October 23, 1994, p. 26; *The State*, October 22, 1994, p. B1.
20. Associated Press, *The State*, November 8, 1996, p. A16.
21. *The State*, October 27, 1996, p. D4.
22. Thompson interview with Thurmond.
23. Confidential interview.
24. *The State*, February 5 and April 14, 1989.
25. Confidential interview.
26. Interview with Lynda Robb, July 1997.
27. *The State*, March 21, 1993.

"SEE! I'SE BEEN REPRESENTING YOU FOLKS ALL ALONG!"

CHAPTER TWENTY

✝

Time for Change

Strom Thurmond opened 1969 by defending "freedom of choice" school desegregation plans and saying he expected future support from followers of George Wallace. Those two questions would dominate the next two years of South Carolina politics.

"I haven't changed my philosophy, and they know it," he said of Wallace's supporters. "I've had their support in the past and think I'll get it in the future."

When Thurmond returned to Washington in January, he seemed completely uninformed about the Supreme Court's decision the previous May that effectively struck down "freedom of choice" school desegregation plans. Thurmond said in January 1969 that Richard Nixon came out three times in his 1968 campaign for "freedom of choice" and that he expected the new administration to follow that policy. "What difference does it make if there is desegregation or not if you have freedom of choice and each child has the freedom to choose?" he asked. "That's freedom, isn't it."[1]

Fifteen months later, Assistant Attorney General for Civil Rights Jerris Leonard told South Carolina school officials in Columbia, "Freedom of choice, for all practical purposes, is dead." He said the death came with the Supreme Court's decision in *Green v. New Kent County*. That decision was rendered May 27, 1968, five days before Thurmond's meeting in Atlanta with Nixon, sealing their pact. Rather than finally reading the court's opinion, Thurmond responded to Leonard's remarks by calling for removal of "zealots" in enforcement of school desegregation.[2]

Attention in South Carolina turned that spring to action by

Fritz Hollings forcing his state to confront poverty in its midst. Hollings won a smashing reelection in 1968 to a full Senate term, beating by more than 150,000 votes the same opponent he had defeated by less than 10,000 two years earlier.

Hollings had followed Thurmond's conservative voting line his first two years, even voting with Thurmond against confirmation of Thurgood Marshall as the first black Supreme Court justice. Hollings now moved to the left, often supporting domestic social legislation opposed by Thurmond.

Hollings attracted national attention in 1969 with a series of "poverty tours." He accompanied the Rev. I. DeQuincey Newman, state NAACP field secretary, through littered city alleyways and dusty country roads. Inside weathered shacks, Hollings came face-to-face with hunger and malnutrition, children infested with intestinal parasites, parents who stayed up at night to protect their children from rats. Hollings returned to Washington to tell the disbelievers in a speech in the U. S. Senate, "There is substantial hunger in South Carolina. I have seen it with my own eyes." He acknowledged that as governor he had helped cover up the problem in order to present a better image to help attract industry.

Once acknowledged, the conditions could not be ignored. "South Carolina is undoubtedly being hurt by the publicity," declared old guard state Senate leader Rembert Dennis, "but the situation for action is so serious I think our junior senator should be commended for what he's doing."

Thurmond reacted differently. He suggested that it was all a politically motivated Democratic effort to win black votes. He said "friends" had told him there was no great problem, and added that there have always been those who didn't want to work.

"I would like to lose the argument and that there would be no problems," Hollings said the next week while walking through black slums in Anderson, a textile city of 35,000 that had not a single unit of public housing. "But here it is," he said as he stood on a street of unpainted shacks, wrecked cars, and littered yards, with black children scurrying around.[3]

Testimony by Hollings would lead to a massive expansion of the federal food stamp program and creation of the Women's, Infants, and Children (WIC) food supplement program.

In Washington, attention turned that year to the Supreme Court. After the resignations of Justices Abe Fortas and Earl Warren, Nixon nominated Judge Warren Burger from the U. S.

Court of Appeals for the District of Columbia as chief justice, and he won easy confirmation in the Senate.

Nixon nominated Fourth Circuit Court of Appeals Chief Judge Clement F. Haynsworth of Greenville, S.C., for the slot vacated by Fortas. Although Thurmond readily accepted Haynsworth, he indicated his first choice was Donald Russell. Lyndon Johnson had named him a District Court judge in South Carolina after Russell lost his Senate seat to Hollings in 1966. Insiders disagreed whether Thurmond was being coy — not his usual style — to spare Haynsworth the taint of his baggage among liberals from the Fortas hearings or whether he genuinely preferred Russell.

A highly regarded jurist and Harvard Law graduate, Haynsworth — known for his anti-labor decisions — had been an Eisenhower supporter, but had never been overtly political. Thurmond may have believed that Russell, the protege of Byrnes and a former Democratic senator, would have won confirmation easily and provided a sophisticated conservative vote on the Supreme Court.

Haynsworth ultimately failed to win confirmation after bitter opposition by organized labor. His later record and history's judgment indicate he deserved confirmation. An AFL-CIO regional official in Atlanta said that Greenville lawyer John Bolt Culbertson provided information that the wealthy Haynsworth owned small amounts of stock in several companies involved in lawsuits before his court. The appearance of ethical conflict became a major issue in Senate hearings. "Strom Thurmond got our man," the labor official said, "and we got his."[4]

Unlike Haynsworth, Judge G. Harrold Carswell of the Fifth Circuit Court of Appeals, and Nixon's next choice, proved an inept lightweight with racist baggage. The Senate rejected him, also. He lacked support from the two standout judges on his court, Elbert P. Tuttle of Atlanta and John Minor Wisdom of New Orleans. Although Tuttle and Wisdom were both Republicans and appointed by Eisenhower, they were leaders in fleshing out *Brown v. Board of Education* into a broad mandate for racial justice.

After Carswell's rejection, Nixon declared to the press, "I have reluctantly concluded that I cannot successfully nominate to the Supreme Court any Federal Appellate Judge from the South who believes as I do in the strict construction of the Constitution."[5] When Judge Wisdom's name came up, Attorney General John Mitchell referred to him as "a damn left winger. He'd be as bad as Earl Warren."[6]

Back in South Carolina, the 1970 campaign for governor provided a clear test of the politics of race. Lt. Gov. John West was a moderate who had actively fought the Ku Klux Klan as a state senator and who had stood almost alone in the Senate against repeal of the compulsory school attendance law. As lieutenant governor he had taken an unprecedented bold step by delivering an address at a dinner in Clarendon County in honor of NAACP Executive Director Roy Wilkins. Nevertheless, 1970 was the year of massive school desegregation in the South, and West muted his campaign appeal to blacks and at one point even engaged in a bit of racial rhetoric by attacking the U.S. Department of Health, Education, and Welfare for "social experimentation."

The Nixon administration, while having accepted the reality of the Green decision against "freedom of choice," under pressure from Thurmond initially attempted to slow down desegregation. Justice Department lawyers argued in support of Mississippi school districts for more time to desegregate. The Supreme Court, in the fall of 1970, unanimously reversed a lower court delay and ordered immediate desegregation.

In January, the Supreme Court asserted that every school district was obligated "to terminate dual school systems at once and to operate now and forever only unitary schools."

Thurmond's declarations about "freedom of choice," however, helped create in South Carolina a climate of confusion and hostility. College of Charleston President Alex Sanders, a former legislator, recalled the difficulty he experienced in attempting to counsel people to follow the law and explaining it required much more than "freedom of choice." He vividly remembered, "Someone shot out the rear window of my car!"[7]

In a display of leadership that sharply contrasted with Thurmond's misleading talk about "freedom of choice," Gov. Robert E. McNair — in the midst of an emotional controversy early in 1970 — told a televised audience in Greenville that South Carolina had "run out of courts, run out of time, and must adjust to new circumstances." A mid-year desegregation order involving extensive busing was being implemented for the 58,000-pupil Greenville school system.

Greenville initiated its plan without disorder, with strong leadership coming from state Senator Dick Riley and his father, Ted, who was the school board's attorney. Anti-busing opposition was led by young businessman Carroll Campbell, a Republican who would succeed Riley as a two-term governor.

The crucial event of the year in South Carolina, however, occurred at Lamar, where a mob of angry and frustrated whites in Darlington County attacked school buses carrying black children. Nine days earlier, Congressman Albert Watson had addressed a massive "freedom of choice" rally at Lamar. West and McNair spurned invitations to appear.

Watson told them "<u>Every section</u> of this state is in for it unless you stand up and use every means at your disposal to defend [against] what I consider an illegal order of the Circuit Court of the United States." Lamar wasn't located in Watson's Second Congressional District, and he had drawn applause when he opened his remarks by declaring, "There are some people who said, 'Congressman, why are you coming over here this afternoon to speak to some of those hard-core rednecks over there?' You know my response to them? 'Those citizens are interested in their children, and I'll stand with them.'"

At the state Republican convention, Thurmond nominated Watson for governor. He provided the Republicans a strong candidate with a gift for traditional Southern political oratory that wrapped evangelical religiosity in a patriotic blanket. Watson wore a white tie throughout the campaign to symbolize his outlook on race.

He got all-out support from the Nixon administration in a well-funded campaign. Vice President Spiro Agnew twice and President Nixon's daughter Julie and son-in-law David Eisenhower made trips to South Carolina to join Thurmond in campaigning for Watson.

West's campaign manager purchased billboards saying, "Elect a Good Man Governor." The violence at Lamar, although never mentioned directly by West in the campaign, was a crucial issue that hurt Watson with white racial moderates who had voted for Richard Nixon in 1968. In the fall before the election, two Watson aides were linked to an attempt to stage a racial confrontation at a high school in Columbia.

The State, the largest daily in South Carolina and one with an aristocratic tradition (dating back to its establishment in 1891 expressly to oppose Pitchfork Ben Tillman — his nephew shot and killed the newspaper's first editor), endorsed West, a graduate of The Citadel. The editor of the newspaper was fellow Citadel graduate William D. Workman, Jr., the 1962

Republican candidate for the Senate.[8]

West drew support among Nixon voters, reacting to Watson's redneck appeal and the threat he posed to stability, and from Wallace voters, many of them traditional Democrats reacting against the Nixon administrations's economic and school policies. Despite objections by Thurmond, almost all broadcasters in the state ran the "Broken Promises" ad. With that title, it used a tape of Thurmond in 1968 promising South Carolina voters that Nixon would permit freedom of choice in the school and had pledged to limit textile imports, and there would be a lower cost of living and lower federal taxes.

After Thurmond finished speaking, another voice told listeners, "Don't be misled in '70 as you were in '68." The ad showed Thurmond saying of Nixon on freedom of choice, "He will permit the parent or the child to have freedom to choose any school in the community without discrimination. You, not the government will make the choice."

Thurmond's attorney sent telegrams to radio and TV stations throughout the state a week before the election requesting they not run the commercial "on grounds it would be actionable." Wayne Sawyer, president of the S.C. Association of Broadcasters, said that a majority of them were "resentful" about Thurmond.

Democratic state Chairman Harry Lightsey, Jr., called the ad "both legal and responsible" and said he was "shocked" at Thurmond. "We must conclude the chief reason for his objections is that he now is unwilling for the public of South Carolina to hear his own words and promises of 1968 — which we all realize now have been broken. By using Mr. Thurmond's own words of two years ago, we have avoided the possibility of distortion or misquotation of what he actually said."

Thurmond responded, "I have no objection to being quoted. I do object, however, to the use of my picture and voice without my permission." He called the ad "a last ditch, desperation effort of the Democratic candidate for governor." Thurmond declared the ad "is attempting to convey the impression that I lied . . . when I said that Richard Nixon stood for freedom of choice. His views on this matter have not changed, but it is well known that they have been overridden by decisions of the liberal Supreme Court."

Thurmond added that Nixon has promised to appoint strict constructionists and concluded, "Ultimately, we expect freedom of choice to prevail."[9]

The schools had become integrated, "freedom of choice" was dead, and promised textile import legislation had not yet passed, resulting in layoffs and "short time" for textile workers. West pulled support from both Nixon and Wallace voters to add to his solid black majority and won by 28,000 votes, 53.2 percent of the major-party total.

West lost to Watson 433-410 in the upper-middle-income Arcadia precinct in suburban Columbia, which in 1968 had voted 667 for Nixon , 132 for Humphrey, and 69 for Wallace. West won ten of the twelve counties in which Wallace had received either a majority or plurality in 1968. In Anderson County, which Wallace had carried with a majority of 6,419 to a combined 5,043 for Nixon and Humphrey, West won 10,531-5,362. In Columbia's Ward 9, where all but 24 of the 1,904 registered voters were black, West won 1,006-19.[10]

In a postmortem that Thurmond attended after Watson's defeat, someone said, "Well, it means you can't win any longer just by cussin' the niggers." For Thurmond it meant developing a new "image." A few weeks later, Dent said in a candid interview with an old college buddy, the editor of the newspaper in Aiken, "We're going to get him on the high ground of fairness on the race question. We've got to get him in a position where he can't be attacked like Watson by liberals as being a racist."[11]

Dent advised the senator to hire a black for his staff — at a time when no member of Congress from South Carolina had a black staffer — and Dent recommended Thomas Moss of Orangeburg, forty-three-year-old state director for the southwide Voter Education Project. Moss had invited Dent to represent the Republican Party at a statewide V.E.P. election forum, and Dent was impressed with Moss's quiet competence and the way he dealt with people. He was courteous, patient, and a good listener.

Thurmond called Moss in late December and asked him to come work for him. As a civil rights activist, Moss was a realist who believed changes were needed, patience was necessary, and that "you dealt with the situation as it is."

The unpretentious son of a sharecropper, with parents who instilled strong religious values, Moss attended a couple of terms at Morris College, a Baptist-affiliated school in Sumter, S.C., where he was a running back on the football team before being drafted in the Army and serving as a combat infantryman in Korea. He returned to Orangeburg and worked in a meat-packing plant, becoming president of a biracial union local to which all but a handful of workers paid dues.

He became co-chairman of the voter registration committee for the Orangeburg NAACP chapter in 1968. Under a new state law, he and his co-chairman became deputy registrars. As Republican growth in the state strengthened and became challenging, the still all-white, Democratic-controlled legislature had quietly recognized that expanded black political participation was essential to their remaining dominant as a biracial political coalition.

On evenings and weekends, Moss and his colleague roamed Orangeburg County, which stretches a hundred miles across the South Carolina Lowcountry, registering voters on the spot in scattered villages and crossroads communities.

Moss also served on the national negotiating committee for the meatpackers union, and the next year was offered a $14,000 salary to cover South Carolina, Georgia, and Florida as a union organizer. He was then making between $8,000 and $9,000 as an hourly worker at the meat-packing plant in Orangeburg. Vernon Jordan, then the Atlanta-based executive director of the Voter Education Project, simultaneously asked Moss to become state VEP director in South Carolina for $8,000 a year.

Moss thought about his wife and two children, examined his commitment to the civil rights struggle, and accepted Jordan's offer. In all forty-six counties, he worked with local legislators to expand the number of deputy registrars.

By the time John West had defeated Albert Watson, 229,000 blacks in South Carolina were registered to vote, and Moss knew their turnout made the difference. Moss's predecessor as state V.E.P. director, James Felder, became one of three blacks elected to the legislature in 1970, the first since the post-Reconstruction era. West joined fellow New South governors Reuben Askew of Florida, Dale Bumpers of Arkansas, and Jimmy Carter of Georgia as progressive racial moderates.

Moss felt out black political activists, and they agreed that an opportunity to serve on Thurmond's staff during the Nixon administration would position him to have a positive impact, and his wife approved. He called Thurmond the next day and accepted.

As a meat cutter, Moss had experienced new technology in which automated cutting tools for skinning a cow trimmed a worker's time by two thirds, leaving a single cut that insured top value for the hide. He grasped that new technology would require better educated workers, and he also was aware that financial constraints had forced several of the nation's traditionally black colleges to close.

On Moss's first day on the job in March, Thurmond escorted him to the Senate chamber and introduced him to Senators Walter Mondale of Minnesota, Ted Kennedy of Massachusetts, Jacob Javits of New York, Henry Bellmon of Oklahoma, and Herman Talmadge of Georgia. Moss never forgot Talmadge's red suspenders.

On the walk from the senator's office, Thurmond asked Moss what issues he thought important to blacks. Moss told him about the financial plight of black colleges. Months later, Thurmond invited the presidents of the six historically black colleges in South Carolina to come to Washington. He arranged a meeting with Elliott Richardson, then secretary of the Department of Health, Education and Welfare (HEW).

The spokesman for the six, Harry P. Graham, the president of Voorhees College in Denmark, S.C., explained their financial problems. Richardson agreed to make some discretionary funds available to such colleges. (Subsequent legislation created special funding programs to revitalize black institutions that long had provided access to middle-class opportunity.) Before the meeting broke up, Thurmond asked Richardson how many other senators had brought in black college presidents to discuss their special problems with the Secretary. "You are the first one, Senator," Richardson told him.

Thurmond instructed Moss to help anyone, white or black, who needed help, but told him to give special emphasis to his own people. "They would confide more in him when they needed help," Thurmond later explained. "He tried to remain in touch with the leaders of his race to find out what they needed, and what help he could render."[12]

Before returning to South Carolina, Moss spent almost a month in Washington, where Thurmond set up an orientation program with visits to a wide range of federal departments and agencies. Moss developed a network of contacts and became acquainted with the details of programs, some specifically designed to help minorities. He met black officials in key agency positions who had South Carolina connections. Back home he advised black business owners how to get technical assistance for establishing regional minority enterprise developments centers in the state.

He worked with black mayors, most of whom governed hamlets

with meager resources. Thurmond then helped them get water and sewer grants and funds for other programs, all of which he announced with great fanfare. The mayors responded by collectively endorsing Thurmond in his future election campaigns.

Moss escorted Thurmond on visits to black colleges and ceremonial events. He usually made at least one trip a month to Washington, always spending some time alone with the senator. He never advised Thurmond how to vote on a bill, quietly keeping him informed about black interests and sensitizing him about black aspirations.

For more than a quarter of a century, Moss happily accepted his primary role of helping grass roots constituents, day-to-day requests that he referred to staff specialists for help with Social Security problems, assisting with a son or daughter's military transfer, or resolving a problem with a government agency. He answered all telephone messages before going to bed each night, and he provided a listening post to the state's thirty percent minority group. He never felt that Thurmond let him down.[13]

Thurmond would make dramatic changes in addressing issues important to blacks, and Tom Moss played a quiet role in effectively contributing to that change. But Moss wasn't alone.

Thurmond developed a dramatically different relationship with South Carolina native Armstrong Williams, who was sixteen when he first saw the senator in 1974. After reading that Thurmond was speaking in nearby Mullins, the black teenager convinced his father, a prosperous Marion County farmer who grew a profitable thirty acres of tobacco and annually raised 2,000 hogs, that they should go hear the senator.

"I'll never forget," Williams recalled. "I extended my hand and said, 'I'm Armstrong Williams and I hear you're a racist.' I thought my father was going to smack me."

Thurmond chuckled and said, "You seem like a bright young man. What grade are you in?"

After Williams told him, Thurmond said, "Well, take my card and when you become a senior in high school, why don't you come work for me and find out whether I'm a racist or not."

Williams called a time or two, and Thurmond would take his calls. At the end of Williams's sophomore year at South Carolina College, he didn't want to work on the tobacco farm and called Thurmond. The senator remembered him and offered a one-month internship. "We took a liking to each other," Williams recalled.

"I would tease him about whether he was a racist and anti-black or not. My friends all thought he was a bigot. He said he had some archaic ideas and that even if he changed there would be many people on both sides of the aisle who would not really believe it. He asked if I would give him a chance. I said I was young and that he could manipulate me."

In the fall of 1980, more than a year later and after Armstrong had been elected student body president at S.C. State, he got a call from Thurmond. Nancy would be visiting the campus as part of the Reagan presidential campaign, and Thurmond wanted Williams to escort her. He agreed. As the wife of segregationist Strom Thurmond, she received a less than friendly reception on campus. In the dining hall, there were insulting remarks and some yelled out, "Bitch."

"I was amazed," Williams said. "I never saw such meanness and cruelty in my life. She was in tears. She was really grateful to me, for standing with her. I told her that my father taught me to do what was right."

After Nancy returned to Washington and told Strom what had happened, he called Armstrong to thank him for standing by his wife. "I said, 'It was no big deal, Senator. It was easy. It was the way my parents raised me.'

"And I said, 'There was a time when blacks were treated like chattel and called racial epithets, and people like you did not take a stand to do what was right, but I never drink from that cup of bitterness and anger, because my father taught me better.'

"There was a dead silence. I thought I had lost him."

And then Thurmond told him, "I appreciate your honesty."

Williams recalled, "He said, 'You're different.' I said, 'No, I'm not different.' And I said, 'No matter what may be in your heart, I'm going to always try to do good.' This is when we bonded."

Thurmond put Williams in touch with Lee Atwater, his protege who would soon be working in the Reagan White House, with Congressman Carroll Campbell, who soon would be a two-term Republican governor of South Carolina, and with Floyd Spence, the state's senior Republican congressman. These were all savvy politicians who, like Thurmond, understood that the Republican Party needed to moderate its image on the issue of race. The senator told Williams he should take off the month of January and come to Washington as an inaugural intern for the start of the Reagan administration.

Although he worked on Campbell's staff, he spent time with Thurmond visiting, going to lunch together, sitting in his office and talking. Strom Jr. was then only eight, and Williams believed that he and the seventy-seven-year-old senator developed something of a father and son relationship. "I was different from him and he was different from me. And he'd say, 'You know, son, there's really no difference between black and white people.'" He remembered Thurmond telling him that people reflected what they had learned and how they had been educated.

After Williams graduated, Thurmond got him a job in the Department of Agriculture. After a couple of months, the young man came to see the senator with a complaint. His superiors had him working only on projects involving blacks and minorities. He said, "They're putting me in a box, stereotyping me."

Williams recalled, "He said, 'Son, you just have to prove your worth. Racism is still alive and well, but I'm going to teach you how to deal with those old geezers because I should know.' He said, 'Just trust me.'"

Williams said he learned from Thurmond how to deal with the media, how to use diplomacy, how to use his Southern upbringing to advantage, how to be a Southern gentleman. "I was a country boy and didn't know about that etiquette stuff," he recalled.

When he attempted to bring in black actor Richard Pryor, who had become controversial, for a special Black History Month program for the Department of Agriculture, Williams ran into bureaucratic opposition. "I went to Strom Thurmond and said I could get it to work, that I had creative juices and needed someone to believe in me."

Thurmond told him his idea could backfire and blow up in President Reagan's face. When Williams persisted, however, the senator told him, "If you believe in this so strongly, I'll back you up." Thurmond called Secretary of Agriculture John Block and convinced him to allow Williams to put on his program. He lined up Pryor, drew thousands of people, got good press, and Reagan had a White House reception for Pryor and Black History Month. Pryor told *The Washington Post* it came about because a low-level Department of Agriculture employee invited him.

Clarence Thomas, then head of the Equal Employment Opportunity Commission (EEOC), read the article. He contacted Williams, who recalled, "He told me, 'Boy, they don't know how to take advantage of your skills and your savvy. You should come work for me.'"

When Reagan reappointed Thomas as EEOC chairman, Williams got Thurmond to come over and swear him in. That began a relationship whose climax came several years later when Thurmond emerged as a steadfast supporter of Thomas at his Supreme Court confirmation hearing.

Meanwhile, Williams realized that to move up in Washington, he needed a visible patron. Soon after going to work for Thomas, and while living in a "roach-infested efficiency" on Capitol Hill, Williams decided to throw a housewarming party and invite Thurmond to be his guest of honor. Holly Richardson, the senator's personal secretary, called him and said, "Armstrong, the senator's going to be there."

He told Thurmond the lyrics to a then-popular song that rhythm and blues balladeer Barry White sang: "It's time for change and nothing remains the same. And I've changed." Williams told Thurmond, "You have to learn the words, and it's going to give you some soul." Then he sent out invitations to the house-warming, listing Strom Thurmond as guest of honor. "Nobody believed that Strom Thurmond was going to show up," he recalled, "but I knew he would. And he knew the words for the song."

In the years ahead, Armstrong Williams strengthened his relationship with Thurmond while launching a syndicated radio and TV talk show and a newspaper column that mixed political conservatism with memories of his South Carolina farm boy boyhood. He also developed a profitable and far-ranging public relations business. He traveled widely as a partner of Stedman Graham, a fellow Nixon administration alum and companion of Oprah Winfrey.

He and Thurmond attended events together in Washington. By the mid-1980s, Williams got Thurmond to go with him regularly when S.C. State's football team came up to play rival Howard University, explaining it was an opportunity to meet his home state's black elite who would come up for the game. "I explained that they won't want to shake your hand because they don't like you, that what you've got to do is go out of the way, hug them, ask about their families. This old man would shake their hand and greet them, and they'd just melt. And he'd turn around and wink at me."

Williams took Thurmond to eat soul food at the Florida Avenue Grill, where Strom ate collard greens, potato salad, corn bread muffins, bacon, and dressing — all familiar to him. And Thurmond took Williams to White House receptions. "When he'd put oysters in his pocket, I'd say, 'Senator, those things are leaking.' And he'd whisper, "Well, don't let nobody see it. Protect me.'"

Thurmond staffers knew he could stand in front of oysters on the half shell at receptions and eat until the the platter was empty. Often he would distribute food from his pocket to aides, including after-dinner mints from the Senate dining room that sometimes had pocket lint on them. He loved to give out peanuts from airliners.

In March 1995, the Washington chapter of the Urban League decided to give out awards for special friendships between black and white individuals. Williams was asked if they could honor him and Thurmond.

When Williams called the 92-year-old senator, he responded, "A civil rights orgazniation wants to honor me?" Williams replied, "Senator, they want to honor you." Thurmond cancelled a conflicting event.

But when word got out that the Urban League was going to honor the 1948 segregationist candidate for president, protests began to mount. "The Urban League started calling me to ask if they could give it to us in private," Williams recalled.

"They couldn't deal with the heat. Then they called Strom. He said, 'You talk to Armstrong.' I said, 'Senator, we're not backing down.'"

The event made national news. "The senator and I were walking in, and he said, 'This is like the civil rights movement. And at my age I'm still in the thick of things.'" Williams added, "It was fun. Strom and I got our award, and a few people stood up for him. (*The Washington Post* said Thurmond was as welcome as a "pimple on prom night.")[14]

"I've spent so much time hanging out with him, it's like hanging out with your father."

Williams's mother developed a special affection for Thurmond after her husband died. In the months before his death, he had allowed a Farm Bureau insurance policy to lapse, and company officials wanted to almost triple the premiums to reinstate it. An angry Williams called Thurmond and told him what happened. "He broke down and cried," Williams recalled. "He felt my anguish and said, 'I'm sorry, son, this is happening to you.' And fifteen minutes later the president of the Farm Bureau in Columbia, S.C., called me and apologized profusely and reinstated the policy at the old premium. That's what Strom did. It made my mother love him.

"People tell him negative things about me and he tells me. He whispers, 'Watch him. He's not in your corner.' He looks after me.

"And I don't talk about race, so we talk about so many other things. I'm a third- or fourth-generation Republican. My family never left the party of Lincoln."

Asked about Thurmond and racism, Williams replied, "Of course Strom had racist thoughts and did things absolutely based on race. There's no question about that. But what shocked me was what a good person Strom was. He's a good man. I trust Strom.

"Every saint has a past and every sinner has a future. We all have a past. Strom was what he was. I didn't like it, what happened to American blacks and how he filibustered that legislation. But I'm not so much interested in where he was twenty-five years ago as where he is now. For me Strom has always been there. Our values are so similar."

At President Clinton's first inaugural, Williams met Coretta Scott King and said she was amazed that he was involved in so many things. Thurmond was having a reception and asked Williams if he could get Mrs. King to stop by, that it would mean a lot to him. "I asked Mrs. King. A lot of her advisers said no, but in the end she went by and spent about twenty minutes at the reception at his office. And when Mrs. King had her function at the Conservatory Room at the Washington Hilton, I took Strom with me."

Armstrong Williams's column is widely published in South Carolina newspapers. He actively supported the senator in his tough 1996 campaign when Thurmond received more than fifteen percent of the black vote, a higher percentage than any Republican statewide candidate in the modern era.

Williams recalled Strom once looking back at how their relationship developed. "He said, 'The Lord always gives you what you need.' We both needed something at the time. We just clicked. I'm with Strom, and I get a lot of grief for it."

1. *The Charlotte Observer*, January 10, 1979; January 14, 1969.
2. *The Charlotte Observer*, April 29-30, 1970.
3. Jack Bass and Walter DeVries, *The Transformation of Southern Politics* (Athens, Georgia, University of Georgia Press edition, p. 261.)

4. AFL-CIO official to Bass, 1970.

5. Tom Wicker, *One of Us: Richard Nixon and the American Dream* (New York: Random House, 1991, p. 496-498. Jack Bass, *Unlikely Heroes* (New York: Simon & Schuster, 1981), pp. 318-323.

6. Jack Bass, *Unlikely Heroes*, p. 23, quoting *The Baltimore Sun*, December 14, 1969, p. 12.

7. Alex Sanders to Bass, March 7, 1998.

8. Jack Bass and Walter DeVries, op. cit., pp. 262-263.

9. *The Charlotte Observer*, October 31, 1970.

10. Bass and DeVries, op. cit., pp. 262-263.

11. Ibid., p. 272.

12. Bass and DeVries interview with Thurmond, Washington, D.C., February 1, 1974, Southern Historical Collection, CB#3926, A-166, University of North Carolina at Chapel Hill.

13. Ibid., Dent, Columbia, S. C., June 26, 1997, and Thomas Moss, Columbia, S. C., March 10, 1998.

14. *The Washington Post*, March 9, 1995.

CHAPTER
TWENTY-ONE

✛

Bringing Home the Bacon

When Harry Dent vowed in 1970 to get Strom Thurmond "on the high ground of fairness on the race issue," the second part of that pledge was to make him South Carolina's "indispensable man in Washington."

Ironically, Democrat John West's election as governor made it much easier. His staff included specialists who combed federal programs and wrote grant proposals for state and local projects in South Carolina. A mayor needing federal funds for a water project would call the governor's office. Staff specialists assessed community needs, looked for a federal program that fit, and sent a grant proposal to Washington.

There, with special entree to Nixon's Republican administration, Thurmond guided it through the funding agency and announced its approval. Despite grumbling from the governor's staffers about Thurmond taking credit for their work, West was happy with the arrangement. A top federal official told him South Carolina received more discretionary federal funds than any other state.[1]

Thurmond already had positioned himself with federal agencies. Dent learned this vividly, beginning with his first days of work in the Nixon White House. "One of the first things I did was go to every agency and every department head. I sat down with them to say, 'We're going to need your cooperation.'" Dent made it clear the White House wanted to be informed and credited when appropriate.

"When I walked into a Cabinet nominee's office, they would know I previously had been with Sen. Thurmond. Every one of them said something to this effect, 'Guess who was the first person to pick up the phone and call me when I got here, to say I had his support and ask if there was anything he could do to help? Strom Thurmond.' I just heard that everywhere. The Senator's got a lot of political sense, and what he did meant that he was going to get everything he needed from that Cabinet member or that agency for his constituents in his state."[2]

Lyndon Johnson's Great Society programs continued to operate after Richard Nixon became president, and federal funds from them poured into South Carolina. Although current observers tend to equate L.B.J.'s Great Society with anti-poverty programs, its reach extended much further. Until undermined by the cost and stresses of the Vietnam war, the Great Society aimed to emulate the New Deal by providing federal funds for a broad range of state and local efforts. Many programs sought to stimulate economic development, and others addressed social needs ranging from education and job training to housing and health care. They involved water and sewer grants and highway funds that local communities could use to develop industrial sites.

The Office of Economic Opportunity was the most visible and contentious symbol of L.B.J.'s war on poverty. Its most lasting legacy was the Head Start program. But the Great Society also included the National Endowment for the Arts, National Endowment for the Humanities, and Medicare.

Surprisingly, many of these programs clearly fit the vision that Thurmond had projected more than two decades earlier in his first year as governor, when he supported federal aid to education. He had recognized that the federal government could make a difference in a poor state like South Carolina. But more than twenty years later, with his changed ideology, Thurmond voted against them.

Once these programs were funded, however, he saw to it that South Carolina got its full share. With Nixon's I.O.U. in his pocket, Strom could and did deliver, and he made sure everybody at home knew it. His 1972 Senate opponent, Harvard-educated state Sen. Eugene "Nick" Ziegler, called Thurmond "Santa Claus in South Carolina and Scrooge in Washington."

When South Carolina interests were at stake, Thurmond fought to win. As a Harvard undergraduate, Edgefield native Bettis Rainsford spent the summer of 1971 as an intern for Thurmond and vividly remembers his effort to get a shipload of South Carolina peaches unloaded in Germany. In those days, Thurmond interns worked as staff assistants and performed meaningful tasks while gaining insights into how government worked.[i]

Rainsford arrived as angry peach growers in South Carolina besieged Thurmond with complaints that a Defense Department inspector found their peaches, shipped for use on military bases, deficient. The inspector ordered that they not be unloaded, and the threat of rotten peaches was imminent. Peaches are a major crop in South Carolina, and many growers feared financial ruin.

Rainsford was standing near Thurmond when he told his secretary to get Secretary of Defense Melvin Laird on the phone. Laird apparently insisted the inspectors had a job to do, and Thurmond clearly didn't appreciate the response. "I've never seen him so agitated," Rainsford says. "He said, 'I'm going to send you a letter' and slammed the phone down."

A short while later, Thurmond called Rainsford into his office, handed the tall, young man an envelope, and said, "Take this to the Pentagon and put this in Melvin Laird's hand. Don't give it to anyone else."

A staff driver and car carried Rainsford across the Potomac River to the Pentagon. When he finally got escorted to Laird's office, the Secretary's top aide thanked him and assured him that Laird would get it right away. "No, ma'am," he told her. "Senator Thurmond said I have to deliver it directly to him." He did so. "By the time I got back to the office," Rainsford says, "the inspector had decided they were good peaches."[3]

Never again would Thurmond have the influence in the White House that he had with Nixon. Later, with his man Lee Atwater a key insider in the Reagan and Bush White Houses, Thurmond could get help for projects at home. But with Nixon, he was a player, someone called in to discuss policy. That never happened again.

Except for Ronald Reagan's shoo-in second term, Thurmond never again helped nominate a Republican candidate who got elected president. In 1968 at Miami Beach, he had told Reagan he would support him next time.

The "next time" came in 1976, after Nixon's resignation and with Gerald Ford the sitting president. Dent had taken over Ford's Southern campaign, where Reagan was challenging him for the Republican nomination. Ten days before a crucial North Carolina primary, Dent and top Ford campaign aide Stuart Spencer met

---

i. Thurmond's internships later became patronage offered to children of supporters or those perceived to have political influence — with the interns mostly involved in Washington sight-seeing. In contrast, a senator such as Sam Nunn of Georgia offered four internships a quarter, with the University of Georgia making selections based on merit.

Strom and Nancy for dinner at the Joshua Tree in McLean, Virginia.

"Our suggestion was to have the senator call on Reagan to withdraw," Dent explained, "and if Reagan did not withdraw, then have the senator assist the Ford campaign in North Carolina." Dent apparently was unaware of Thurmond's 1968 pledge to Reagan at Miami Beach, writing that "Thurmond had taken a neutral stance since he had indicated to Reagan in 1971 he would support him in 1976 for the presidential nomination. . . . at my suggestion he had informed Ford and Reagan in January 1976 he would have to be neutral in the nomination contest."

Dent sensed that Thurmond agreed the winning Republican candidate would be hurt in the fall by "fruitless blood-letting" and that Ford, as White House occupant and with years of experience in Congress, would be the stronger candidate. Dent left Thurmond that evening with a request by him "to draw up the appropriate language for a statement by Thurmond to accomplish the end we sought. Two days later the senator dropped the idea."

Reagan's campaign got energized with a 52-46 victory over Ford in North Carolina, close enough that Dent believed Thurmond's intervention would have made the difference.[4]

It isn't known whether Thurmond attempted to intervene with Reagan and was reminded of his pledge or if he simply decided he had made a commitment and therefore felt honor-bound to keep it. Whatever, he remained quietly in the background at the hotly contested 1976 convention in Kansas City.

Many believed that he wanted to support Ford, the sitting president. Reagan had offended many of the most conservative Southern delegates by announcing before the convention that one of the more liberal Republican senators, Richard Schweicker of Pennsylvania, would be his running mate to balance the ticket. In the close contest in which Ford narrowly won the nomination, Thurmond quietly voted for Reagan. Jimmy Carter carried all of the eleven former states of the Confederacy except Virginia in defeating Ford in November — a successful Democratic Southern strategy.

In presidential politics, Thurmond's political judgment appeared to be slipping by 1980. Reagan got elected president that year, while Thurmond supported former Texas Gov. John Connally in the South Carolina Republican primary. Like Thurmond a former Democrat who had switched parties,

Connally served in Nixon's Cabinet, but by 1980 had a sullied reputation after an acquittal in a bribery trial. Reagan overwhelmed him in the South Carolina primary, 79,549 to 43,113. Former Thurmond campaign aide Lee Atwater smoothly managed the Reagan victory in the South Carolina primary and landed in the White House in political operations.

Congressman Carroll Campbell, a future two-term governor, said that Thurmond gave wholehearted support to Reagan after the South Carolina primary. "He and I rode around South Carolina for a week in a camper, visiting thirty-seven communities, and he was out campaigning hard. He gave it everything he could."[5]

In 1988, Thurmond backed Senator Robert Dole in South Carolina against Vice President George Bush, even with his protege Atwater as Bush's national campaign manager. With Gov. Carroll Campbell backing Bush in South Carolina, Thurmond's candidate got wiped out by more than two to one, 94,738 to 40,265. Although Atwater felt betrayed (He confided to an associate, "Strom Thurmond screwed me"), he continued to help Thurmond after the election. After Bush named him Republican national chairman, Atwater died tragically in 1991 of brain cancer. Without his top strategist, Bush lost reelection in 1992 to Bill Clinton.

Thurmond joined Campbell's forces in the 1996 presidential primary for Dole, who got an important win in South Carolina in his race for the Republican nomination. Dole lost the general election.

Whatever his role in presidential politics, Thurmond in 1971 overcame a perception of vulnerability after Albert Watson's gubernatorial defeat. Thurmond tried to get Watson — whom he had nominated in the governor's race — a seat on the U.S. Court of Military Appeals but the effort failed after a Senate discussion of his racial record, sending a further message that racial politics had become a losing hand.

Democrats began to perceive Thurmond as vulnerable. The black vote was growing and almost solidly Democratic. A still lingering Democratic party loyalty remained among Wallace supporters. The new eighteen-year-old voters might view Thurmond as outdated. The "freedom of choice" issue and failure to deliver on curbing textile imports added to his problems.

But not for long. Thurmond moved vigorously, actively pursuing black support. At a reception for him in Charleston in February 1972, a large black woman wearing a turban drew more attention than anyone except the guest of honor. Civil rights activist Victoria DeLee had established credentials as an embattled grass-roots leader with a sense of political shrewdness. (After organizing a voter registration drive among Dorchester County blacks, she met over a kitchen table with the county's white legislative representative. As he made commitments to help the black community, she had a tape recorder hidden beneath the table.) She ran for Congress as an independent in 1970 and received more than 8,000 votes. After she tried elsewhere without success, Thurmond secured her a federal grant to establish a day-care center in Dorchester County. DeLee explained her support for Thurmond, "I'm for the man who can get the job done, and Strom is getting the job done." He greeted her by name in a receiving line at a cocktail party preceding the reception.[6]

Thurmond missed no opportunity to rebuild his political base. With two vacant federal district judgeships in South Carolina, he offended state Republican leaders and puzzled South Carolina political analysts by naming a Democrat, Sol Blatt, Jr., to one of them instead of long-time Republican activist Welch Morrisette. The other judgeship went to Robert Chapman, a former state GOP chairman with impeccable legal and family credentials and personal lawyer to Roger Milliken.

The Blatt appointment was suggested by Judge Charles Simons, Thurmond's friend and former law partner.[7] Simons respected the younger Blatt's legal ability and correctly perceived that it would win Thurmond the undying gratitude and loyalty of Solomon Blatt, Sr., his old enemy. Blatt's word meant the difference of several thousand votes in Barnwell County, and he influenced other small-county Democratic legislators whose local machines could translate into votes for Strom.[ii]

---

ii. Jack Bass, who wrote the foreword to a biography of Solomon Blatt, Sr., ran for Congress as a Democrat in 1978. He got Blatt's support in the Democratic primary, handily winning Barnwell County. Co-author of The Orangeburg Massacre, the definitive account of the 1968 shooting at South Carolina State College, Bass expected solid black support against Republican incumbent Floyd Spence. He got that support everywhere except Barnwell County, where roughly a fourth of the black vote went to Spence. A black undertaker in Williston, totally loyal to Blatt, had built a disciplined political organization. Blatt later explained to Bass his most important goal was the reelection of Strom Thurmond. Because Blatt lacked confidence that the black voters he controlled were sophisticated enough to effectively split their ballots by voting for a Republican for the Senate and a Democrat for the House, he passed the word they should vote for both Republican candidates. For Bass the only difference was losing with forty-three percent of the vote instead of forty-four percent.

By late spring of 1972, Attorney General John Mitchell wanted Dent to serve as President Nixon's national campaign manager. Dent yearned for the job.

White House Chief of Staff H. R. Halderman vetoed it, however, saying that Dent was "too much of a Boy Scout." Dent in fact had been an Eagle Scout. He had refused several assignments of "political dirty tricks" in the process of what became the Watergate scandal of campaign corruption and lawbreaking that ultimately led to Nixon's impeachment and resignation.

Unlike most of his White House associates, Dent spent no time in jail. Watergate prosecutors got a misdemeanor guilty plea from Dent for shared responsibility in the failure to report a 1970 off-year election million dollar campaign contribution. The incident involved a fundraiser depositing the money in an account about which Dent wasn't informed. U. S. District Judge George Hart in Washington sentenced him to 30 days probation and said from the bench, "It does appear to me that Mr. Dent was more of an innocent victim than the perpetrator."[8]

The Watergate-related dirty tricks helped get Nixon the Democratic opponent he wanted in 1972, hapless Sen. George McGovern of South Dakota. Top tier South Carolina Democrats — men like Gov. West, Congressmen James Mann and W. J. Bryan Dorn, or former Gov. Robert McNair — declined to take on Thurmond. Although Nick Zeigler ran a spirited campaign, he ran on a shoestring, with Thurmond outspending him, $666,372 to $167,750.

As their campaign headed down the stretch in late October, a handful of political reporters met Thurmond at 8:15 a.m. in downtown Columbia at Cogburn's Grill on Sumter Street, a few days after the well-publicized birth of Strom, Jr. The senator already had greeted a textile mill shift and talked to a third grade elementary school class.

At breakfast, he downed an eight-ounce glass of prune juice in one long gulp, then drained a glass of skim milk. With a knife and fork, he slashed three eggs over easy, the runny yolks turning yellow the grits on a platter beside whole wheat toast. He wolfed it all down as if on fast forward, wiped his mouth with a paper napkin, and rose to greet and shake hands with every patron and kitchen helper.

At the state's largest shopping center, Strom shook hands non-stop, every third person or so congratulating him on his new baby boy. A young woman, obviously near the end of a pregnancy, recognized him as a family friend. Teetering to maintain her balance and holding a small daughter's hand, she told him, "We're just trying to keep up with the Thurmonds!"

An elderly male bystander nudged a reporter and said, "Ol' Strom, he's sump'n'. Ain't he?"

After cleaning off a vegetable-laden plate in a cafeteria, Thurmond worked the line waiting to be served before heading off to an electronics plant across the Congaree River in Lexington County. Campaign aides handed out brochures and plant workers thronged around to congratulate him on "that fine family." Two black female assembly line workers walked over to get his autograph. When a reporter asked what they thought of Thurmond, one looked at the other, then turned and said, "I think he's fannntastic."

The next morning Thurmond flew to Anderson, the upstate town whose daily newspapers were unique in the state for consistently opposing him. Strom walked through the newsroom, shaking hands with any reporter or editor in sight, and entering uninvited into the editor's office to greet him.

Outside, he brushed aside his campaign manager's entreaty to return to the plane to be on time for his next appointment. "Let's go by the courthouse," he said. Like a vacuum cleaner, he sucked it clean in minutes, shaking hands with everyone in every office, whacking the stooped probate judge almost out of his chair with a slap on the back and telling him, "I remember when you used to room across the hall from me at Clemson."

In magistrate's court, a thin, sallow-complexioned mother stood with clasped hands and head down in front of the judge while her pubescent son squirmed in the witness chair as the defendant in a misdemeanor case. Without slowing down, Thurmond shook hands with the magistrate, the woman, the boy, and moved on. The startled woman turned to the magistrate and said, "Din't know I was gon' get to shake Strong Thurmond's hand when I come here today."

After flying to Greenville and addressing a civic club, Thurmond made the half-hour drive by car to Spartanburg. At Spartan Mills, one of the city's few unionized textile plants, the gate opened and workers streamed out at the end of a shift. Strom positioned himself in the middle, darting sideways back and forth like a crab, reaching out on either side to grab and shake almost every worker's hand.

At the bidding of the state's textile barons, Thurmond had moved earlier in the year to push President Nixon to fulfill a campaign pledge to limit textile imports from Japan and other countries in the Far East. Before Thurmond left Spartan Mills to continue a schedule that stretched until almost midnight, the president of the union local learned that he was on the premises. Because of his record on a broad range of issues supported by the AFL-CIO, the senator had a national image as a hated enemy of organized labor, and his Democratic opponent was the lawyer in South Carolina for the International Ladies Garment Workers Union. The union leader came over to let Thurmond know how he felt.

"Senator," he told him, "I want to thank you for what you've done in saving jobs for us on these textile imports. You've got our support."

Although he crushed Zeigler by winning sixty-three percent of the vote, Thurmond ran nine points behind Nixon in South Carolina.

Edgefield Advertiser editor W. W. Mims, now Thurmond's enemy, got almost no votes as a write-in candidate. But he brought a new issue to the final weeks of the campaign and raised questions about an intriguing chapter in Strom Thurmond's past.

1. Bass interview with John West, January 2, 1998.
2. Bass interview with Harry Dent, June 24, 1997.
3. Bass interview with Bettis Rainsford, Edgefield, S.C., March 12, 1998.
4. Harry Dent, *The Prodigal South Returns to Power*, op. cit., p. 26.
5. Thompson interview with Carroll Campbell, 1982.
6. *The Washington Post*, February 27, 1972, p. 1A.
7. Bass interview with Charles Simons, August 13, 1997.
8. Harry and Betty Dent, *Right vs. Wrong: Solutions to the American Nightmare* (Nashville: Thomas Nelson Publishers, 1992), pp. 5-6.

Essie Mae Washington at South Carolina State College.

CHAPTER TWENTY-TWO

✢

"Colored Offspring"

Deep into the 1972 Senate campaign, editor W. W. Mims of *The Edgefield Advertiser* stripped the following headline in large type down the length of his newspaper's October 11 front page:

SEN. THURMOND IS UNPRINCIPLED-
WITH COLORED OFFSPRING-
WHILE PARADING AS A DEVOUT
SEGREGATIONIST

No story about "offspring" accompanied the headline. But the allegation had long been talked about in South Carolina's African-American community. Mims's headline, which he displayed on paid television spots after announcing as a write-in candidate against Thurmond, suddenly brought the rumor to the attention of white South Carolinians and the state's mainstream press.

The Thurmond campaign quickly asserted that Democratic candidate Nick Ziegler, the erudite lawyer with a classics background at Harvard, was involved. He wasn't, but at Thurmond's campaign headquarters, copies of the *Advertiser* were kept under a counter and displayed to supporters, especially matronly white women, with feigned outrage. His staff would ask, "Have you seen this?" One woman from Anderson told Thurmond's campaign manager, William "Billy" Wilkins (later a judge on the Fourth Circuit Court of Appeals), she was so appalled that he should load the trunk of her car with yard signs, brochures, and other campaign material. She told him, "I'll see that all of it gets distributed!"[1]

Authors writing about Thurmond have treated the subject gingerly, if at all. In her book, biographer Nadine Cohodas dismisses the story of the alleged black daughter as "a legend in the black community" that Thurmond denied.[2] Robert Sherrill included a paragraph in *Gothic Politics in the Deep South* about "one of the most widespread political rumors I ever saw wrapped around a state: that Thurmond had paternal interest in a Negro girl." Sherrill added, "the odd part of it, to me, was that instead of crediting Thurmond with good faith for sending this legendary girl to college, many of the Negroes I talked with somehow seemed to hold it against him that he did not recognize her more authoritatively, although this would of course have been politically fatal."[3] Sherrill called the story "apparently without foundation," but later told a *Penthouse* gossip columnist that he believed it was true, but his publisher wouldn't allow him to write that.[4]

James Felder, who preceded Tom Moss as state Voter Education Project director and won election in 1970 as one of South Carolina's first twentieth century black legislators, explained at the time of Mims's publication the reaction among African-Americans to Thurmond and "the daughter." Felder said, "What black people resent is his messing around with one of our women and then going around knocking us."[5]

When Mims published his headline about "COLORED OFF-SPRING," a group of black men and women in Columbia talked about it. Years before, they had worked nights at the Wade Hampton Hotel, and one of them, Durham Carter, remembered, "We said, 'Damn, he sure got that right.'" While Thurmond was governor, this group remembered him frequently — often two or three times a week — checking into a room at the end of the day after leaving his office in the State House across Gervais Street from the hotel.

Carter, a retired state employee and former schoolteacher, said, "My friends working the freight elevator were told by the night supervisor not to leave until the person visiting the governor came down. We couldn't leave until we brought down his black female guest. About a quarter of eleven, the freight elevator rang." Carter described the governor's visitor as "a light-complexioned, nice-looking woman who appeared to be in her thirties."

He continued, "One of my friends got a job teaching in Edgefield County. He saw her there and knew she was the woman riding the freight elevator."[6]

Jerry Wilson, a politically active leader in Edgefield's black community who operated a cafe and gained a reputation as a reliable plumber despite the loss of one arm, told at least three friends before his death that a car and driver were sent two or three times a week to pick up the woman and drive her to Columbia.

Other African-Americans in Edgefield said that Essie Butler, mother of the child believed to be Thurmond's daughter, maintained a relationship with him that lasted many years. These sources included relatives and neighbors of the child as she was growing up. The child, Essie Mae Washington, was named for her mother.

After the light-skinned daughter was born in October 1925, Essie Butler's neighbors believed that Thurmond was the father, according to taped interviews Mims conducted in the early 1970s in the black community. Modjeska Simkins and others said the mother was destitute when the baby was born, but that young Thurmond initially did not acknowledge the infant or provide support.

Willie Adams, who was born in February 1914 and grew up on a tenant farm on Will Thurmond's land near his home outside Edgefield, knew Essie Butler by her nickname of "Tunch" when she worked as a young teenager in the house for Strom's mother. "Tunch was brown-skinned, with short hair and a pretty face," Adams said.

[After Mims published his "Colored Offspring" headline, a farmer with a problem came into Edgefield to see his lawyer. Before they began discussing the legal matter, the farmer mentioned that week's *Edgefield Advertiser*. He got agitated and denounced the headline as "the most scandalous thing" he'd ever seen. Then he added, "Of course, everyone knew Strom's people had trouble keeping help."][7]

Adams, who moved to town and learned to build houses, said, "Tunch would go to Thurmond's law office late in the afternoon, and the door would then be locked."[8] Simkins said those visits were well-known among blacks in Edgefield.[9]

But the family secret for the Thurmonds would have seemed safe in the first half of the twentieth century. "Back then," Adams said in a succinct summary of the civil rights movement's impact, "a black man couldn't talk about a lot of things, but I've seen the change, and now a black man can talk."[10]

In 1992, after a brief *Penthouse* magazine item about the alleged black daughter, the senator's office first denied any knowledge of

Essie Mae Williams, then acknowledged that she had visited Thurmond on occasion at his Senate office. The two were described as just "friends." Thurmond refused to be interviewed, and his press secretary called the *Penthouse* report "untrue and unworthy of publication." Ms. Williams called it "full of lies."

The Washington Post published a more detailed, 4,000-word story by Marilyn Thompson, based on a lengthy search for Ms. Williams and a reconstruction of her life and its intersections with Thurmond's.[i] Thompson began with the legend, tracking down sources who knew unconnected pieces of Essie Mae's impoverished childhood and her birth in Edgefield's segregated Old Buncombe section, her move northward, or her return to South Carolina as a student at South Carolina State College.

By piecing together fragmented facts and interviewing Essie's neighbors and acquaintances in four states, the story emerged of a close relationship between the girl and Thurmond, at the height of his segregationist years. Thompson uncovered personal correspondence the girl sent to Thurmond as governor, showing that on at least two occasions she turned to him for financial help or acknowledged receiving it. Eventually, when she was located and interviewed, she insisted they were only close family friends.

The evidence in the relationship between Strom Thurmond and Essie Mae strongly suggests that they agreed before she enrolled as a college student that in return for his support she would deflect all questions with a safe response — that the relationship between them was that of "friends." The response, said one of Essie's relatives, shows that "he must know exactly what he's doing not to have had this thing blow up in his face" years ago.[11]

As a child, Essie Mae went north to live with an aunt in Coatesville, Pennsylvania, a grimy steel town near Philadelphia. She lived in the Newlinville section, populated by immigrants and Southern blacks who came north to work for the Lukens Steel Mill, Coatesville's main employer. In the tremendous migration north and west of four and a half million African-Americans from the South between 1930 and 1960, small town blacks tended to follow a trail set by an initial relative or neighbor. The newcomers got help in finding a job and a home, and these new communities developed links to established churches back "home." (In South

---

i. The Washington Post declined to use the married name of Williams, identifying the woman only as Essie Mae Washington, her name before marriage, in order to protect her privacy. Her surname came from a man named Washington, who had retired from a job on the railroad and lived apparently in at least a common law marital relationship with her mother.

Carolina, for example, blacks from Lake City migrated to Patterson, N.J. From Kingstree they went to Rochester, N.Y. And from Edgefield many went to Coatesville.) Although integrated, Coatesville was far from racially progressive. Black children went to an all-black school in the lower grades; most dropped out before high school.

Lillian Carter, a neighbor in Coatesville who knew Essie Mae, said the girl arrived with nothing, but that the family told her Thurmond was the father. She was smart and ambitious. At Coatesville High School, Essie Mae, a poised and well-groomed young woman, was president of the Public Speaking Club, the Bible Club, and the Girl Reserve, a club for "negro" (sic) girls to study famous black Americans. These were happy years for Essie, who in 1995 returned for her fiftieth reunion.

As she was growing up, she returned occasionally to Edgefield to visit family, who lived there on a dirt road of rundown cottages. Mims later quoted a neighbor who said she remembered Thurmond's mother and sister visiting the house one summer to deliver money. But Thurmond's sister who lived in Edgefield, Mary Tompkins, denied it.[12]

Willie Adams said that when Essie Mae visited Edgefield in the years before enrolling at S.C. State, she stayed in town with her aunt, Hattie Smith, who took care of her as a small child and who lived in the same neighborhood as Adams. Essie Mae had friends in the neighborhood, he said, but sometimes accompanied Strom's sisters Mary and Gertrude on trips to the square. "Black people then weren't allowed inside the drug store," Adams said, "but Essie Mae went inside with Mary and Gertrude. She went with them to the picture show and sat downstairs with them." Her black friends all sat in the segregated balcony, which had a separate entrance. "After the picture show, she would walk back home with her friends," said Adams, who had a younger sister the same age as Essie Mae.[13]

Other contemporaries said that Thurmond's sisters came for Essie Mae before she enrolled at S.C. State in the fall of 1946, the year he was elected governor, and bought college clothes for her to wear at the traditionally black institution in Orangeburg.

She was older than most of her classmates, who graduated from South Carolina's then eleven-grade school system. Her individual photograph is missing from the school's yearbooks, but she does appear in a 1948 group photograph of Delta Sigma Theta sorority.

She was attractive and — like most of her sorority sisters — had a light complexion.

She wrote two letters to Governor Thurmond — one after her marriage to Julius Williams, one of the handful of students in the college's newly created law school — that were eventually included in Thurmond's official governor's papers.

The first, a typed message to "Governor J. S. Thurmond" and dated October 31, 1947 — exactly a week before his wedding with Jean — addressed him as "Dear Sir" and stated, "This is to acknowledge receipt of your loan received on Saturday, October 25. "Thank you very much." In carefully rounded, strong penmanship, it was signed, "E. M. Washington."

The second, handwritten in the same script on June 29, 1950, [a time when starting newspaper reporters in South Carolina were being paid less than $40 a week and first class stamps cost three cents] was sent from Coatesville, where the newly wed Essie had returned. It addressed him as "Dear Gov. Thurmond" and stated, "Please let me have a loan of seventy-five dollars. I plan to leave here in about two weeks, so may I hear from you within that time. With best wishes." It was signed, "E. M. Williams."

Essie Mae and Julius Williams had married in a quiet ceremony, his family learning about it afterwards, according to Charlotte Johnson, his sister. Robert Bellinger, a cousin, later recalled, "I used to tease my cousin that he had married the governor's daughter. He'd just laugh and say, 'Well, I wish I could get some of that money.'"

Julius's sister said that Essie Mae never talked about Thurmond, but it was assumed he was her father. "She'd borrow money from my husband," Charlotte Johnson told Thompson in an interview for the 1992 *Washington Post* article, "saying she was going to get the money back from her father. She used him whenever she'd get into trouble."

When Julius returned to Savannah to practice law, other black lawyers understood that Thurmond helped him establish a law office. Julius briefly led the local NAACP branch and worked on a teacher pay equalization case with Aaron Kravitch — a white lawyer who handled civil rights cases few others would touch. (Phyllis Kravitch, his daughter, was appointed by President Carter as a federal judge on the Eleventh Circuit Court of Appeals).[14] That was one of Julius's few big cases, however, and his life and health deteriorated. He died in 1964, leaving Essie Mae — who by then had moved to California — a widow with four children.

When Marilyn Thompson first located Essie Mae Williams in Los Angeles in 1984, she was still teaching. When Thompson showed up unannounced at her school, Mrs. Williams met with her in her office for about ten minutes. She appeared poised and unflustered, acknowledged that she knew Thurmond, and told her consistent story that their relationship was based on family friendship and nothing more.

She acknowledged to Thompson that she had received money from Thurmond "but not a lot." She denied he was her father, calling him "a close friend of my family — a wonderful man who's helped a lot of people."

She added, "He visited me one time [at S. C. State], one time, that's all. He was on campus on other business, and knowing me and knowing my family, he asked to see me. That's all there was to it."[15] She told friends on campus that story at the time, presumably after consultation with him and for the purpose of dousing speculation about the purpose of the visit.

Emma S. Casselberry, who served as executive secretary to S.C. State President M. F. Whittaker (her name then was Dawkins) while Thurmond was governor, remembered it differently: "Gov. Thurmond would come to campus, for some other reason, and ask to see 'this girl from my hometown.' I would call the dean of women and ask that she have Essie come to the president's office, and she and Thurmond and Mrs. Thurmond would meet for fifteen minutes or so in private in an anteroom. He would come once or twice a year."

Mrs. Casselberry recalled, "Essie didn't make any display. She got no special treatment. She dressed well. I heard that anything she wanted, she just called him."[16]

The relationship was known to many students on campus, where Essie Mae moved in the top social strata. M. Maceo Nance, Jr., a student at the time who later served almost two decades as president of S.C. State, recalled, "It was not a big deal. At the time, it was accepted belief on campus that the top assistant to the president of the college was the son of a white trustee. For her to be the daughter of the governor was not viewed as any big deal."[17]

Although Greek life on the S.C. State campus involved both status and social activities, such as dances and parties, there were no fraternity or sorority houses. Sorority sisters engaged in group activities, but shared no living quarters.

Essie Mae's sorority sisters at S.C. State generally regarded her as quiet and a private person, but "willing and cooperative to do what needed to be done," as one of them recalled. Mrs. Curtis Torrey of Fayetteville, N.C., who as Rosa Lee Rainey was vice president of the Deltas in 1948, added that Essie Mae was "an unselfish person" and had "ladylike qualities. We accepted her."

Some of Essie Mae's sorority sisters had heard of her alleged relationship with Gov. Thurmond. Julie Nance, the daughter of the college's business manager whose husband later became the college's president, didn't live in the dormitory, but remembered, "I heard my parents talk about it, who her father was."[18]

Most of the Deltas had some special talent in music or dance or art, but Knoetta Goodwin Judkins remembered, "The sorority was looking for young ladies who had great potential and grade-point averages — the intelligent young ladies."[19] With good grades and an outward display of quiet sophistication, Essie Mae Washington fit the profile of the elite young women of Delta Sigma Theta.

Randall Johnson, the driver who carried Sue Logue to the death chamber and the long-time superintendent of "colored help" at the state Capitol, said Gov. Thurmond had confided that Johnson "was someone he could trust." The governor sent him to pick up Essie Mae several times at the Columbia train station and drive her on shopping trips to Tapp's, then the premier department store on Columbia's Main Street. Afterwards, he said, she would enter the State House through a back door that opened inside the rear of the governor's office spaces.[20]

John McCray, a statewide black leader as the politically active editor of *The Lighthouse and Informer* in Columbia in the 1940s and early 1950s, said that NAACP leaders and Thurmond's white enemies in the Democratic Party arranged for the woman to be secretly photographed for use against him politically. The photographs were made available to Olin Johnston's 1950 campaign staff, but were never made public. Campaign advisers told the authors that such use would have violated a "gentlemen's agreement" not to indulge in smear tactics.[21] Politically, in that bitter campaign, they apparently concluded that use of the photographs could backfire.

The photographs also were available to the campaign staff of Edgar Brown in the 1954 Senate campaign. When the question of using them was presented to Brown, he vetoed it. "I don't believe it's such a good idea to get into matters about illegitimate children," he told his campaign manager, John West, a newly elected state senator.[22] [ii]

Before her courtship by Julius Williams, a handsome World War II veteran from Savannah, Essie Mae dated another law student several times. Matthew J. Perry of Columbia, like Julius a handsome veteran and a class behind him, soon developed his own lasting courtship that forged into a lifetime marriage with another S.C. State coed, Hallie Bacote. In Timmonsville, a small town in the tobacco-growing Pee Dee region, her family maintained friendly relations with white relatives.

During the brief period that Perry dated Essie, "She indicated in some fashion that the then-governor and his family were interested in her welfare and her education at S.C. State. The totality of my recollection, based on my friendship with her during a relatively brief period, was that she knew the then-governor and his family, and they had shown some interest in her. She acknowledged a long-time knowledge of and friendship with the then-governor. She described it as a long-time relationship." Perry had no personal knowledge of her visiting him in Columbia.

Perry recalled his perception at the time that Essie had enrolled late in the summer of 1946, that dormitories were crowded, but that space was made available for her to live on campus at a time when others had to find accommodations off campus.[23]

Perry later became chief counsel for the NAACP in South Carolina. His rich baritone voice, engaging smile, and courtly manner combined with legal skill to win him wide respect. He litigated case after case that desegregated schools, state parks, and other facilities and successfully defended students and others involved in protest demonstrations, in some cases breaking new ground on appeals to the U.S. Supreme Court.

After an unsuccessful race for Congress as a Democrat in 1974, Perry got a telephone call from Thurmond — whom he barely knew at the time — asking that he meet him late that afternoon in Union, a county seat town sixty miles north of Columbia, where the senator would be dedicating a public works project.

Thurmond offered to recommend Perry for a judgeship on the

---

ii. A quarter century later, Brown — once described as a man who treated the state's money as though it was his own — sat in a large chair outside the Senate chamber as an elderly, gray-haired matron with a cane limped past him. She had worked for years as a secretary, a gentle woman who smiled easily and welcomed reporters to committee meetings because she liked to rely on their stories when writing the minutes. Brown nodded toward her and, in a voice tinged with remorse and guilt, told a reporter, "See that girl. I screwed her forty years ago, and it's cost the state of South Carolina a quarter of a million dollars."

U.S. Court of Military Appeals [its name later was changed to the U.S. Court of Appeals for the Armed Services and its membership increased from three judges to five]. The position had six years remaining on a fifteen-year term rather than the lifetime appointment for judges in the national federal court system. Perry understood, however, that Thurmond's initiative in becoming the first senator from the Deep South to recommend a black candidate to any federal court was significant.

After considering the matter overnight and weighing the symbolic importance of his serving on that court, Perry called back his acceptance the next day. A few days later, Thurmond escorted him to the White House to meet top aides of President Gerald Ford.[24]

Lee Bandy of *The State* recalled the swearing-in ceremony in Washington. It seemed "that the entire African-American community from South Carolina was there. The place was packed. Strom was there. It was a big deal. It really was."[25]

Because some of those present had been Perry's college classmates, speculation arose among knowledgeable blacks in South Carolina whether his having dated Essie Mae had anything to do with the appointment.[26] There is no evidence, however, to suggest that Thurmond had any awareness of that past relationship.

Four years later, in 1979, President Jimmy Carter responded to a campaign pledge and began making the first lifetime appointments of black federal District and Court of Appeals judges in the South. He sought to name at least one in every state. Attorney General Griffin Bell found it helpful in persuading Southern senators that such appointments would be politically safe by pointing out Thurmond's role four years earlier.[27]

As the Democratic senator in a Democratic administration, Fritz Hollings happily agreed to elevating Perry to the District Court of South Carolina. He later became chief judge and a new federal courthouse in Columbia was named for him.

In the fall of 1997, Essie Mae Williams, widowed and a retired school teacher, lived in an established, middle-class African-American neighborhood in Los Angeles. She lived in a compact three-bedroom, one-bath home with a pool. Photographs of grandchildren were displayed in the living room.

On a late Saturday morning in November, Bass went to her

home to attempt to interview her. Her oldest grandchild answered the door. A month earlier Bass had written a detailed letter explaining his mission and giving his credentials. He enclosed a copy of *The Orangeburg Massacre*, the definitive account he and Jack Nelson of *The Los Angeles Times* had written about the 1968 tragedy at S.C. State. But — as he expected — had heard nothing. He showed up at her home with a potted plant as a gift.

When the granddaughter told Mrs. Williams the visitor's name, she didn't recognize it. As he explained who he was, she said, "Oh, you want to talk about that Strom Thurmond thing. It's just an old family relationship." Then she paused, and with a stammer said — as she had so many times in the past — "We're just friends. He has lots of friends."

When Bass said it seemed to be a special friendship, she responded, "I don't want to talk to anyone writing any book," then excused herself to run errands. He followed her to her car and commented on the attractive photographs inside. Her voice softened and she spoke with pride, saying she had thirteen grandchildren and a great-grandchild. Before driving off, she said she had retired from teaching a few years earlier after a hip injury. Her granddaughter, the mother of the great grandchild, remained in the house but said she was too busy planning her toddler's birthday to talk.

The relationship between Essie Mae Williams and Thurmond is consistent with patterns of acknowledged parent-child interracial relationships in the South. Justice John Marshall Harlan, who wrote the famous dissent in *Plessy v. Ferguson* — the 1896 Supreme Court case that established the "separate but equal" doctrine and provided the basis for the South's segregated society for the next six decades — maintained some relationship with a half-brother, Robert, whose mother was a slave. Harlan's father attempted to provide the justice's half-brother with a college education, and Robert became a successful businessman.[28]

One of Essie Mae's closest friends at S.C. State recalled another young woman student there, whose white father maintained her family on the edge of a large farm away from the house of his white family. When the young woman became engaged to a fellow S.C. State student, the father insisted on meeting the young man and giving his approval.[29]

The historian Joel Williamson, a South Carolina native who became a leading authority on miscegenation, said the pattern is that the woman tends to be a light-skinned domestic and there has been miscegenation before in the family.[30] In his biography of author William C. Faulkner, *William Faulkner and Southern History*, Williamson tells the story of the "shadow" family that descended from Faulkner's grandfather, the "old colonel," William C. Falkner. (The grandson changed the spelling of the name to Faulkner, and surviving members of his family in Oxford, Mississippi, use both spellings.)

The daughter, Fannie Forrest Falkner, was named by Colonel Falkner, and she attended Rust College in Holly Springs, Mississippi, then the state's most prestigious private black college. It was sponsored by the Northern Methodist Church and provided a quality education. The man she married, Matthew Dogan, later became a college president in Texas, and Williamson reports that family tradition asserted that Colonel Falkner paid Fannie's college bills and frequently came to see his daughter in Holly Springs.

Ironically, Fannie Falkner and her mother had moved into the household of Richard Thurmond in Ripley, Mississippi, before Fannie's enrollment at Rust College in 1885. Thurmond later shot and killed Col. Falkner, ostensibly over a business dispute involving Thurmond's losing investment in Falkner's railroad. An adult sister or half-sister of Fannie's still lived in Falkner's house in Ripley after his wife had left him, and Williamson theorized "that the situations in both Falkner's and [Richard] Thurmond's households had something to do with the obvious hatred of Thurmond for the Colonel" and for the jury's failure to convict Thurmond. Richard Thurmond had moved to Mississippi from North Carolina.[31][iii]

---

iii. The relationship between the Richard Thurmond of Ripley, Miss. and Strom Thurmond's family is remote. Although Strom Thurmond refers to his ancestor, "John Thurmond of Virginia, who fought in the Revolutionary War, then moved to Georgia, and finally established his family in South Carolina," a Thurmond family genealogist in Georgia believes the senator is mistaken. Frank Parker Hudson of Atlanta, while working on the manuscript for *Thurmans and Thurmonds of Early Georgia*, concluded that the Revolutionary War service of the John Thurmond who was Strom Thurmond's great-great-great grandfather consisted of "driving cattle for thirty days" in Albemarle County, Va. Hudson believes the misinformation resulted from a faulty account by an earlier family researcher based on family lore and hearsay rather than on public records. Hudson's research indicates that the John Thurmond ancestor of Strom Thurmond left Virginia in 1784, two tears after the Revolutionary War ended, and moved directly to Edgefield County, South Carolina, purchasing land there in 1784. He had brothers who went to Georgia. His brother Benjanmin's daughter, Nancy Thurmond, married John Thurmond's son William, Strom Thurmond's great-great grandfather. William Thurmond was born in 1761 in Virginia and was the son of John Thurmond and his first wife, Molly (or Mally) Dickerson. Strom's great-grandfather was John Thurmond, the son of William Thurmond. The great-grandfather was born in Edgefield County on May 1, 1794, and his son, George Washington Thurmond, was born November 12, 1819. He had one son, Jasper, by his first wife, and Strom's father, John William (Will) was born twenty-four years later on May 1, 1862, the youngest child of George W. Thurmond and his second wife, Mary Jane Felter of New Orleans. (Jasper Thurmond was the father of Herman Talmadge's mother which made her a half first cousin of Strom, and made Herman and Strom half first cousins, once removed.) George Washington Thurmond died April 11, 1904, when he was eighty-four.

In circumstances that paralleled those of William Faulkner's grandfather in the nineteenth century, Strom Thurmond visited and provided support for Essie Mae Washington during her college years. Although it is widely speculated that Thurmond paid her tuition at the college, there is no known record of her tuition payment. Julie Washington Nance never heard her father, the school's business manager, discuss the subject.[32]

Thurmond lent money to Essie Mae, received letters from her, and, according to eyewitnesses and participants, sent his driver and apparently saw her in Columbia. His office has acknowledged they stayed in touch after he became United States senator.

Such cross-racial relationships under any circumstances in the South were unusual. Without kinship ties or obvious special circumstances — such as the white family of means in Mississippi who knew and recognized the exceptional voice of young Leontyne Price and sent her north for training that led to the Metropolitan Opera — such relationships are virtually unknown.

Because Essie Mae had grown up in Coatesville and had only visited relatives in Edgefield, it is clear that such a close relationship wasn't based, for example, on her having spent considerable time in the Thurmond household as the daughter of a loyal family servant. Even more clearly, it certainly wasn't based on a social relationship between her poverty-stricken black mother and the wealthy white Thurmonds.

Essie enrolled late, but a discreet phone call from the governor-elect, about to become ex-officio chairman of the board of trustees, to the president of South Carolina State College surely could have made a dorm room available.

Two theories flow from the known facts. One is that during the year after Essie Mae's graduation from high school in Coatesville in 1945, either she or her mother made contact with Strom and sought his help. The other, which would explain her enrolling so late, is that after his winning election as governor in the summer of 1946 he saw that helping her get an education would be seen by the family as an act of *noblesse oblige* and also provide a means of protecting him politically. The pact about the "friendship" cover story would insure the relationship's remaining masked from white South Carolinians, then the only ones whose votes counted. The elements of both theories could have come into play.

When *The Washington Post* published its article in 1992, *The State* in Columbia — South Carolina's largest daily and now owned by Knight-Ridder rather than family descendants of Wade Hampton — printed it in full, the first detailed account in a publication widely circulated in the state. Reaction was mixed. Among the larger group who responded was Thurmond's sister Gertrude, who called and angrily told an editor, "How dare you print such trash!"[33]

But Glenice B. Pearson, an African-American, objected to "the hypocrisy gushing forth in reaction to the story." She described how as a child she visited her paternal grandmother's white sisters with her. In a letter to the editor, she wrote about her "sense of shame over the rape that brought my grandmother into the world." But she also told of spending time in the country with white cousins "reared by kind, loving and decent human beings."

She concluded, "Americans need to grow up and mature with respect to their racial attitudes. A part of this racial maturing is to acknowledge the fact that the much feared 'race mixing' used by hatemongers to incite conflict has been and continues to be an integral part of the fabric of life in this nation. . . . Perhaps if we can accept this truth about ourselves, we can take another step forward."[34]

When Jim Clyburn, after his election to Congress, was asked about the reaction among fellow African-Americans in South Carolina when the *Post*'s story was published in the Columbia newspaper, he said, "I don't think there was any impact. Ever since I was a child I often heard that he had black children — under the definition that this country gives to what makes one black. The thing that was news is that it was told to white South Carolinians in a public context."[35]

Armstrong Williams at times has teased Thurmond about the story of the black daughter. Strom told him, "They really give me a lot of credit, don't they?" He didn't deny it, however. "When I talk to him about it," Williams said, "he smiles."[36]

1. Bass interview in 1972 with William Wilkins, Thurmond campaign manager.
2. Cohodas, op. cit., p. 481.

3. Robert Sherrill, *Gothic Politics in the Deep South*, p. 244.
4. Sharon Churcher telephone to Jack Bass, spring 1992.
5. Felder to Bass, fall 1969.
6. Bass telephone interview with Durham Carter, July 21, 1998.
7. Confidential interview.
8. Bass interview with Willie Adams, August 9, 1998.
9. Simkins to Bass, circa 1982.
10. Willie Adams interview, op. cit.
11. Thompson telephone interview with Charlotte Johnson, July 22, 1998.
12. *The Washington Post*, op. cit.
13. Willie Adams interview, op. cit.
14. Bass telephone interview with Superior Court Judge Eugene H. Gadsden, December 30, 1997.
15. *The Washington Post*, August 9, 1992.
16. Bass interview with Emma Casselberry, Orangeburg, S.C., October 4, 1997.
17. Bass interview with Maceo Nance, Orangeburg, S.C., October 4, 1997.
18. Bass telephone interview with Julie Washington Nance, April 25, 1998.
19. Bass telephone interview with Knoetta Goodwin Judkins, April 19, 1998.
20. *The Washington Post*, op. cit.
21. *The Washington Post*, op. cit.
22. Bass interview with John C. West, January 1, 1998.
23. Bass telephone interview with Matthew J. Perry, July 20, 1998.
24. Bass interview with Matthew J. Perry, Columbia, S.C., June 24, 1997.
25. Bass interview with Lee Bandy, Columbia, S.C., June 24, 1997.
26. Nance interview, op. cit.
27. Bass interview with Griffin Bell, Jacksonville, Florida, August 3, 1979.
28. Tinsley E. Yarbrough, *Judicial Enigma: The First Justice Harlan* (New York: Oxford University Press, 1995), p. 10-14, 141.
29. Confidential interview.
30. Bass telephone interview with Joel Williamson, February 2, 1998.
31. Joel Williamson, *William Faulkner and Southern History* (New York: Oxford University Press, 1993), pp. 64-71.

32. Bass telephone interview with Julie Washington Nance, July 20, 1998.
33. Bass interview with Harry Logan, Columbia, S.C., June 24, 1997.
34. *The State*, p. 14A, August 26, 1992.
35. Bass interview with James E. Clyburn, July 11, 1997.
36. Bass interview with Armstrong Williams, February 2, 1998.

CHAPTER
TWENTY-THREE

✝

Mainstream Senator

Beginning about 1970, Strom Thurmond seemed to change in response to new realities. With race no longer the defining element in Southern politics, Thurmond began to seek maximum acceptance. He abandoned the harsh rhetoric that generated controversy and made many hate him. Unlike George Wallace, Thurmond never admitted he was "wrong." But the code words of "states rights" began disappearing from his vocabulary. This new Thurmond reflected the diminishing sense of historic Southern grievance as the region turned its energies away from defending the social institutions that had held it back and toward economic growth and national political influence. Thurmond sought to become part of the consensus — at least the new Republican consensus of reducing the role of government (except when it meant announcing federal dollars for South Carolina). How history would judge him began to matter.

In the summer of 1973, a full year before Richard Nixon resigned as president because of the Watergate scandal, Strom Thurmond asserted at the Hampton County Watermelon Festival at Estill, "If the president and all those people working for him up there don't get their story straight and explain it to the American people, they're all through." Don Fowler remembers hearing Strom say it. "I almost dropped my teeth. And he was right. The most amazing of all of Strom's abilities is to read people and sense the public will. I think he has some sort of counter inside his soul and intuition that is arithmetic. It's astounding."[1]

Thurmond in 1977 gave up his position as ranking minority

member of the Senate Armed Services Committee to become rank-ing Republican on the Judiciary Committee. At the suggestion of other conservatives, he yielded on Armed Services to his good friend and fellow conservative Barry Goldwater and moved to block liberal Republican Sen. Charles "Mac" Mathias of Maryland on Judiciary. If Republicans gained a Senate majority, it would mean Thurmond as chairman of Judiciary and Goldwater as chairman of Armed Services.

The next year Thurmond at seventy-five met his most serious reelection challenge. He faced Charles D. "Pug" Ravenel, who in 1974 made one of the most spectacular political launches ever in South Carolina before being tripped up at the finish line. Growing up in modest circumstances in Charleston, Ravenel had returned home at thirty-six with political ambition and a financial stake after a record as star quarterback at Harvard, White House Fellow, and Wall Street investment banker.

He brought sizzle and fresh ideas to the 1974 Democratic pri-mary for governor, with good looks, youthful vigor, and a message of governmental reform that he articulated with conviction. He took his message directly to the voters with the most sophisticated TV campaign South Carolina had seen. His campaign echoed the progressive themes of Thurmond's 1946 race for governor, taking on the political establishment.

But unlike Strom in 1946, already an experienced politician whose father had served as mentor, Ravenel was like a beautiful cut of wood not yet seasoned. He generated excitement in derail-ing two political veterans, Lt. Gov. Earle Morris and Congressman Bryan Dorn, to win the Democratic nomination. When Ravenel referred to the overwhelmingly Democratic state Senate as a "den of thieves," however, even its honest members took offense. Ravenel seemed not to understand that it was honor he attacked. He soon learned he was dealing with the pit bulls of South Carolina politics.

Those inside the state's political establishment operated with their own unwritten rules, and they didn't tolerate attacks on per-sonal honor. Ravenel found himself in a court fight over whether he met the state constitution's five-year residency requirement.

Although the judiciary clearly is a separate branch of govern-ment in South Carolina, the state is unique in that the legislature elects judges. And, like Thurmond when he campaigned among colleagues forty years earlier to become circuit judge, legislative service still provided the usual path to a judgeship. The challenge came in a lawsuit filed by Milton Dukes, a part-time fundamentalist preacher who cooked and sold pork barbecue for a living and once provided comic relief as a candidate for governor. Funding for the lawsuit apparently came from undetermined political opponents, with speculation centering on Dorn supporters and on Republicans.

The case came before state Circuit Judge Julius B. "Bubba" Ness, a former state senator and future state Supreme Court chief justice. He disqualified Ravenel for failing to meet the requirement on residency — a legally vague issue that a person's intent helps determine. A judge has room for wide discretion.

Ravenel had sought and gotten an earlier ruling that seemed to clear that hurdle, but Judge Ness ruled definitively. Ravenel appealed to the five white men on the state Supreme Court — former legislators all. They upheld Judge Ness, and the U. S. Supreme Court declined to overrule them.

The state Democratic Party's convention then reconvened and nominated Dorn in a squeaker over reform state Sen. Dick Riley. In the confusion that followed, the Republican sacrificial lamb, Charleston oral surgeon and first-term state Sen. James B. Edwards, got fifty-two percent of the vote to win election as governor.

Riley gave Dorn his full support. Although Dorn had developed a progressive record in Congress, he was linked politically and by style to the Democratic old guard that Ravenel had challenged. Facing this dilemma with his supporters, Ravenel said he would vote for Dorn, but not endorse him, a move that further alienated the Democratic political establishment. Riley then became state campaign chairman in 1976 for Georgia Gov. Jimmy Carter. For Riley's plans to run for governor in 1978, Ravenel presented a major obstacle that the White House helped remove.

The story is told in South Carolina that Pug Ravenel rode in from the Charleston airport in 1977 with Vice President Walter Mondale, who was making a ceremonial visit. When Mondale suggested that he challenge Strom Thurmond in 1978, Ravenel said he planned to run again for governor, that he believed he had a lot to offer the people of the state. The story goes that Mondale then said, "But what about the people of the United States?" And Ravenel replied, "I never thought of it like that."

Ravenel did run against Thurmond, and Riley ran for governor — nosing out Dorn for second place in the first primary and getting his support for a runoff victory against Lt. Gov. Brantley Harvey, Jr. Lee Atwater helped run Thurmond's campaign. A few days before the election, he confided that polls indicated Thurmond's age made him vulnerable, but most people didn't know he was seventy-five. "Pug tried to be coy by saying he wouldn't make age an issue," Atwater said, "but that didn't cut it."[2]

Strom moved his family to Columbia for the fall campaign and looked vigorous with his young children photographed with him on the campaign trail wearing tee shirts that said, "Vote for my Daddy." Thurmond combated the age issue by projecting vim, vigor, vitality, and virility.

Strom, as usual, didn't debate his opponent. At one joint appearance with Ravenel, however, Thurmond asserted he would be embarrassed to ask people to vote for him for the United States Senate if had never even been elected to a town council.

Ravenel's handling of his 1974 dilemma also worked against him. County courthouse Democrats — the sheriffs, clerks of court, and other elected local officials who influenced their friends and neighbors and who had been loyal to Bryan Dorn four years earlier remembered Ravenel's failure to endorse Dorn. And they ridiculed Ravenel as a liberal New Yorker.

Riley got sixty percent of the gubernatorial vote against Republican Congressman Ed Young. But in the Senate race, Thurmond, who outspent Ravenel $2,013,000 to $1,134,000, got fifty-six percent of the vote.

Unlike Edwards, who developed important skills and personal relationships as a state senator after a losing race for Congress, Ravenel seemed unwilling to serve a political apprenticeship. After losing to Thurmond, he ran for Congress from the Charleston area and lost.

He later helped organize a federally insured savings and loan and got help from Thurmond in cutting through bureaucratic red tape in Washington.[3] His business ventures, however, developed serious financial difficulties, and his political dreams flamed out.

Back in Washington, Thurmond served as ranking Republican on the Judiciary Committee as Chairman Edward M. "Ted" Kennedy expanded its staff with young liberal lawyers after taking over in 1979 following the retirement of Sen. James O. Eastland of Mississippi. Kennedy had learned a decade earlier of Thurmond's little-known capacity for repartee.

In an exchange in 1969 that made the front page of *The New*

York Times, Kennedy interrupted Thurmond's attack on the Senate floor of Justice William O. Douglas. It occurred less than a month after the resignation of Abe Fortas and on the day the Senate confirmed Warren Burger as chief justice. Thurmond called for Douglas to resign because he had served at $12,000 a year as chairman of the Parvin Foundation. It helped fund a South American institute to train what Thurmond called "leftwing radicals under the tutelage of such leftist Latin politicians as Juan Bosch and Jose Figueres."

This exchange followed:

Mr. KENNEDY. Mr. President, will the Senator yield, or does he wish to continue? I have some familiarity with the individuals about whom he is talking.

Mr. THURMOND. I will be glad to. One of Mr. Figueres' supporters, are you?

Mr. KENNEDY. No. I am able to pronounce his name correctly, and I would think that when you are using it in making charges about an individual, it is helpful to pronounce his name correctly, with due respect to an individual.

Mr. THURMOND. Some pronounce it "Figueres" and some "Figueres" [placing the accent on different syllables].

Mr. KENNEDY. How?

Mr. THURMOND. Some pronounce it "Figueres" and some "Figueres." Are you trying to correct my pronunciation in English, or are you holding yourself up as an English teacher? Are you an expert because you went to Harvard? What was your record at Harvard?

Mr. KENNEDY. All I was trying to get——

Mr. THURMOND. I will not show up your record at Harvard; that is all right.

Mr. KENNEDY. I was trying to get the way Mr. Figueres pronounces his name.

Mr. THURMOND. *I will not go into your record at Harvard.*[4]

The news accounts pointed out the apparent allusion to Kennedy's expulsion from Harvard during his freshman year in 1951, after he had a classmate take a Spanish exam for him.

Kennedy spent two years in the Army as an enlisted man, then returned to Harvard, graduating in 1956.

The Washington Post reported only two other senators were present when the heated exchange took place. One of them, Russell Long of Louisiana, whom Kennedy beat for the majority whip job earlier that year, sat smiling throughout the encounter.[5]

Kennedy's chairmanship lasted only two years as Ronald Reagan swept in a Republican majority in his crushing defeat of Jimmy Carter in 1980. Thurmond had supported John Connally in the South Carolina presidential primary, but he campaigned actively for Reagan in the fall. When Strom introduced him at an overflow rally in the Clemson University field house, Reagan got a glimpse of the Thurmond mystique.

Retired head football coach Frank Howard first introduced Thurmond, then seventy-seven. A legend in the state for both his coaching record and his dry rustic humor, Howard paid tribute to Jean Crouch Thurmond and spoke of her connections to Clemson. Then he alluded to Strom's virility and spoke of his winning the heart of young Nancy Moore.

Howard then deadpanned, "And I'm proud to announce that this morning in Edgefield, a very important event took place — Strom's third wife was born." The audience howled, Thurmond beamed, and Reagan looked puzzled — then sensed it was politically safe to join in the fun.[6]

Thurmond was in his glory as Judiciary chairman. As both president pro tem of the Senate and chairman of the Judiciary Committee, he proclaimed himself to a South Carolina reporter "the third most powerful man in the world."[7] He slashed Judiciary's budget by more than a million dollars and pared the staff from 207-134, dismissing much of the liberal staff Kennedy had hired. The committee's respected chief counsel, Emory Sneeden, contended that an oversized staff felt compelled to "justify its existence with needless hearings and legislation."[8] Thurmond placed two conservative non-lawyers, Jeremiah Denton of Alabama and Charles Grassley, on the committee, making Denton chairman of a new Security and Terrorism subcommittee.

The title of president pro tem of the Senate was a largely hon-
orific position, but it did indeed put Thurmond third in the line of
presidential succession, behind the vice president and Speaker of
the House. Thurmond understood that the title and imposing
office in the Capitol that went with it provided the power of public prestige; he formally opened the Senate each day and made special key chain souvenirs for visitors, decorating them with his
name and title, "President Pro Tempore."

Still, Thurmond was not an insider in the Reagan White
House. He got no advance notice when Reagan picked William
Rehnquist as chief justice to succeed Burger, but Thurmond happily presided over the confirmation process for Reagan's conservative jurists. As Judiciary Committee chairman, he guided Sandra
Day O'Connor, the first woman nominated to the Supreme Court,
like the father of the bride, shielding her from tough questioning
and escorting her to receptions. On September 25, 1981, the
Senate confirmed her unanimously.

As Thurmond's relationships with blacks and behavior toward
them changed to conform with new political realities, so did his
attitudes. During the Carter administration, when about forty
blacks were nominated to the federal district and appellate courts,
Thurmond voted for every single one. When Kennedy had accused
him in November 1979 of holding back approval of several liberal nominees in an attempt to speed approval of some conservative
appointees, Thurmond warned that Kennedy had better not bring
up Thurmond's position on black nominees. "I have leaned over
backward to approve every one of the black judges," he told the
Judiciary Committee."[9]

Harry Dent and Lee Atwater, respectively, had hand-picked a
pair of bright, young, and self-confident staff assistants, and
Thurmond hired them. U.S.C. law school honor graduate Dennis
Shedd and newspaper reporter Mark Goodin melded together as a
one-two team rivaling in influence that of Dent and Buzhardt two
decades earlier. With Thurmond's higher visibility, they replaced
his gaudy plaid jackets with distinguished-looking dark suits. They
moved him in the direction of measured moderation and sensitized
him that addressing professional women at committee hearings as
"pretty ladies" offended them. Although Thurmond always had
supported the Equal Rights Amendment, he had difficulty understanding that female professionals wanted to be treated the same
as male counterparts, whom he didn't welcome to the committee

as "handsome men."[10]

Shedd and Goodin grasped that South Carolina itself had been transformed in the half-century since Thurmond first ran for political office. It was now part of the booming South Atlantic region, with economic growth spurred by progressive leadership from governors such as Hollings, Russell, McNair, West, and Riley, who improved public schools, raised technical skills, and enhanced state universities while actively courting higher paying skilled industries. Freed by the civil rights revolution, they included blacks in their new equation, resulting in an expanded work force that created broader markets for goods and services.

Between 1965 and 1988, South Carolina's population grew by forty percent, from 2.5 million to 3.5 million, compared with twenty-seven percent for the United States as a whole. The newcomers included retirees and service workers at the coastal developments that followed the lead of Hilton Head, as well as upwardly bound younger people who migrated with the expanding economy. Natural growth occurred among native African-Americans, who no longer left after high school in search of better jobs and more freedom. Younger people remained single longer, and women expected to work — many in white-collar jobs away from the traditional textile and apparel industries.[11]

Shedd and Goodin recognized that to attract new voters, Thurmond needed to demonstrate that he accepted new realities. Despite his reaching out to blacks, Thurmond seemed not to understand that aside from his segregationist past, blacks saw a large and interventionist federal government as their agent of change. Although they understood his votes against programs and policies that helped them, he no longer aroused their determined opposition. As it melted he began attracting a trickle of black votes.

Thurmond's defining moment during his six years as Judiciary Committee chairman came in the 1982 debate over extending the Voting Rights Act. Thurmond said after Reagan's sweep that he wanted to abolish it. He had bitterly opposed it in the past and still resented that Section Five, the preclearance section, applied only to states with a history of discrimination.

A 6-3 Supreme Court ruling in the spring of 1980, a case from Mobile, Alabama, mobilized civil rights organizations across the country. The Supreme Court decided in the Mobile case that plaintiffs in Section Two cases, which outlawed discriminatory election systems nationally, must prove a discriminatory "purpose" rather than effect. From Thurmond's perspective, he had reason to be pleased with the record of Richard Nixon's Supreme Court appointments. All four Nixon appointees — Warren Burger, Harry Blackmun, William Rehnquist, and Lewis Powell — voted with the majority in the Mobile case. To prove discriminatory intent would be almost impossible. A Birmingham, Alabama, newspaper quipped editorially that perhaps dead legislators could be subpoenaed to testify.

Nowhere did the Mobile decision hit more directly than Edgefield County. Black leadership there came from Thomas C. McCain, an Edgefield County resident for thirty years with a masters degree in math from the University of Georgia. When he paid his filing fee in 1974 to run for county council, the Democratic Party refused to put his name on the ballot. He filed a complaint with the Justice Department.

He and others already had filed a lawsuit protesting the name "Rebels" as the mascot for Strom Thurmond High School and the waving of the Confederate battle flag and playing of "Dixie" at school events. They also sought to rename the school. The case was resolved with a compromise to stop waving the flag and playing "Dixie," practices that almost all public high schools across South Carolina discontinued after integration. McCain filed other suits to end discrimination in selecting grand juries and to end segregation of prisoners on chain gangs.

Under Section Two of the Voting Rights Act, McCain in 1975 challenged the at-large system of electing county council. He got help from the American Civil Liberties Union (ACLU) regional office in Atlanta. Finally, in April 1980, District Judge Robert Chapman issued a strongly worded opinion that found "racial discrimination in all areas of life, with bloc voting by whites on a scale that this court has never before witnessed." In striking down the at-large system and replacing it with single-member districts, Chapman said "the law requires that black voters and candidates have a fair chance of being successful in elections."

When the Mobile opinion came down weeks later, Chapman withdrew his order. Over the next year, Thurmond moderated his opposition, saying he could vote for a watered-down version of the Voting Rights Act if all provisions were applied nationally. It was an impractical solution. In practice it would mean every election law change from every state, including those with no history of discrimination, would have to be reviewed by the Justice

Department, overwhelming the enforcement mechanism.

On June 28, 1981, as a strong bill was working its way through the Democratic-controlled House, South Carolina native Jesse Jackson joined hundreds of black protesters at a rally in Edgefield, telling them, "We don't want to dominate, we want to participate."[12] In perfect harmony, the crowd sang "Ain't Gonna Let Strom Thurmond Turn Me 'Round" as it marched, gaining national publicity designed to hurt Thurmond's image.

Two days later, a group of South Carolina blacks met with Thurmond in Washington. They included Jackson, McCain, and state Rep. James Felder. Thurmond asked McCain, "What church do you pastor?"

McCain answered, "This is Tom McCain, Senator."

Thurmond replied, "I thought you were in Ohio." McCain, who was completing a doctorate in educational administration at Ohio State University, smiled that Strom was keeping tabs on him.

Jackson pleaded with Thurmond to commit his support for the Voting Rights Act, but the group found Thurmond more interested in talking than listening, telling them how he got rid of the poll tax as governor and defending his record as someone who always supported any qualified person's right to vote.[13] Whatever Thurmond was thinking, he kept it to himself.

Civil rights groups mobilized an all-out effort both to extend the Voting Rights Act and to strengthen it. They especially wanted to overcome the Supreme Court's ruling in the Mobile case. The Reagan administration indicated opposition to the bill, but displayed little interest in shaping it.

By early 1982, Thurmond indicated a willingness to reconsider his position. He talked to Armstrong Williams and agreed to meet with a group of black Republicans who supported the Voting Rights Act. They included Art Fletcher, Elaine Jenkins, and Clarence Pendleton. Williams remembers, "Strom showed me all these letters from racists, using the 'N' word and everything. He said, 'I want you to convince me I should support it.'"

The chief lobbyist for the Voting Rights Act's extension was Armand Derfner, a top civil rights lawyer who had moved to his wife's hometown in Charleston. She was related to Judge J. Waties Waring. Another key draftsman for the bill was Laughlin McDonald, the ACLU's Southern regional director in Atlanta and a South Carolina native. He and Derfner had been involved in McCain's civil rights litigation in Edgefield County.

Meanwhile, Thurmond's staff quietly advised him that politically, the hardliners writing the letters would be with him whatever he did, that the bill was going to pass anyway, that a vote for the bill would improve his image with moderate white ticket-splitters, and that his vote would help shape how history would judge him.

By the time McDonald appeared as a lead witness before Sen. Orrin Hatch's subcommittee on the Constitution, Thurmond's public position opposing the bill remained unchanged. He had opened the hearing by asserting that his past opposition to the voting rights law had been based on the mechanics of the statute. That position, he emphasized, "must not be interpreted as opposition to the right to vote itself." As committee chairman, Thurmond led off the questioning of the man challenging the at-large election system in Edgefield County. Knowledgeable observers expecting a thorough grilling got a surprise:

"Mr. McDonald," Thurmond asked, "do you live in Atlanta?"

"Yes, I do, Senator."

"I know the McDonald family in South Carolina," Thurmond continued. "They originally came from Winnsboro. Some moved to Chester, some to Greenwood, some to Columbia. Heyward McDonald is a state senator down there now."

"Yes sir, he's my cousin," McDonald said.

"Who was your father?"

"Tom McDonald from Winnsboro."

"Tom is your father?"

"Yes sir."

Thurmond told him that Tom McDonald had been a good friend.

"I know he was, Senator."

"We've tried cases together. And I had the pleasure of appointing your mother to the state hospital board. She is a very lovely woman."

"And nothing has ever pleased her any more in her life, I might add, Senator, than that appointment. She speaks about it often to me."

"I just wondered if you were connected with the McDonalds there," Thurmond said, "because they are all very fine people and friends of mine."

"Well, I appreciate that, Senator Thurmond."

"I have no questions," Thurmond added. "Thank you."

With that, Hatch turned on his microphone, commenting, "I

knew Senator Thurmond was a legend in his own time, but I didn't realize he knew everyone in the South." The audience laughed, and it got louder when McDonald commented, "I think he just got my vote when I move back to South Carolina."

Tom McCain testified that Edgefield County's at-large election system and record of voting on racial lines provided a textbook example of why the Voting Rights Act was still needed and why the Supreme Court ruling in the Mobile case needed easing. It wasn't proportional representation he was seeking, McCain explained, but a plan that gives blacks "a chance of electing someone."[14]

While Thurmond was holding out for a weak bill, Republican Majority Leader Robert Dole got interested in passing something stronger. He seemed to have only one concern, asking if Rowan County, N.C. (where Elizabeth Dole grew up) was among the 40 (of 100) North Carolina counties that the Act covered. The answer was "No," and it was full speed ahead for Dole, who believed in fairness and the right to vote, had a vision of the Republicans still being the party of Lincoln, and was thinking about running for president.[15]

Dole and Kennedy worked out compromise language for Section Two, essentially incorporating the language the Supreme Court used in an earlier case, *White v. Register*. It outlawed election systems that had a discriminatory result, but provided specific criteria based on "the totality of the circumstances."

As the compromise neared final agreement, Dole asked Ralph Neas, the head of a Washington civil rights coalition, to meet with Thurmond and two other reluctant Republicans. Thurmond mentioned that South Carolina's black mayors had not taken a position on the bill and that he planned to meet with them in a few days.

With that tip, Neas alerted Armand Derfner. He spoke to several black leaders back home, including Mayor Charles Ross of Lincolnville, an almost all-black community near Charleston whose roots dated back to Reconstruction. The dozen or so mayors almost all represented hamlets of well under 1,000 population.

When Thurmond met with them to make the case for his weakening amendment, he faced a barrage of questions from fully briefed inquisitors. Although Thurmond and three of the other seventeen members opposed the compromise in the Judiciary Committee, he agreed to send it forward to the full Senate.

There, Fritz Hollings took on North Carolina Republican John East, a former college professor who grew up outside the South. East attacked the bill for treating one state differently from another and claimed he'd never seen a bill come before the Senate "so ill-conceived and so badly flawed."

Hollings said that East's remarks against the bill "completely disregard the historical practice and experience of his backyard and my backyard over the many years." He spoke passionately, telling East that it wasn't a case of the law treating the states differently — the essential Thurmond argument. "The states treated the people differently," Hollings asserted. "That is where you cannot understand and see what I see."

He continued, "If this debate is going to continue on as though a bunch of technical nuts got together in the Judiciary Committee and reported an ill-conceived and so badly flawed law, someone has to give the hard, bitter experience of the past thirty years, and even years before that, where the official policy, practices, conspiracies, societal habits, customs, mores and what-have-you said, 'No, you're not going to come in the door.'"

Hollings cited the Edgefield case. He pointed out Judge Chapman's finding that white bloc voting prevented black candidates from being considered on their merits. He called Chapman "a pedigree Republican, not a white-flight Republican." To Hollings it was "not easy or a happy thing to get up and tell of this particular history, but unless we can speak honestly and realistically and objectively of what we have learned from our experiences, then we are not going to be ale to vote intelligently on this particular matter."

South Carolina Gov. Riley had written to the Judiciary Committee supporting the House bill. He pointed to the South Carolina's progress, with fifteen blacks in the legislature and another fifty-eight in "significant county offices." Riley then asked, "Should we pat ourselves on the back for a job well done? I think not. That we have achieved great strides is without question; that we have met the task of eradicating the blight of discrimination from our election process is just not true."

The next day, Thurmond expressed resentment about Hollings's singling out Edgefield with no mention of "the positive and decent character of its citizens." Even if true, he said, the allegations no more indicted "all the people of Edgefield County" than a school discrimination case in Boston, Detroit, or Cleveland "is a comment on all the citizens who live in these cities."

He proudly pointed out South Carolina's progress and criticized Hollings for focusing "almost entirely on negative aspects of our state and its citizens in the past. . . . The implication that we in South Carolina are dealing with the issue of voting rights in any way other than a proper manner is simply inaccurate and without foundation."[16]

At bottom, the Thurmond-Hollings debate reflected the same themes that would reverberate within the Supreme Court as it moved further to the right, the conservatives arguing that any individual case of discrimination should be remedied, but overlooking the historical background of discrimination against African-Americans as a class. The focus would fall in the 1990s on the issue of affirmative action, the idea of a judicial remedy or a public policy designed to overcome the effects of past discrimination.

In the end, Thurmond expressed "concerns" about the bill, but said, "I must take into account the common perception that a vote against the bill indicates opposition to the right to vote and, indeed, opposition to the group of citizens who are protected under the Voting Rights Act." When his turn came to vote on the legislation, Thurmond answered, "Aye."

By late summer of 1983, Thurmond had eliminated any serious opposition for his reelection in 1984. President Reagan came to South Carolina and helped raise $300,000 in one night. Thurmond got endorsements from the black mayors, from progressive Democratic Mayor Joe Riley of Charleston (Thurmond had helped secure $14 million for Riley's revitalization of the city's business district), and fund-raising help from former Democratic Gov. McNair. Riley and Congressman Butler Derrick, Thurmond's two potential Democratic challengers, bowed out.

Stories were beginning to appear suggesting Thurmond's age had caught up with him. But Thurmond at eighty-one faced only nominal opposition in 1984 and got two-thirds of the vote, a pattern he essentially repeated in 1990. Each time he spent more than $1.5 million against political unknowns who spent less than $10,000.

He was still "taking exercise" every day, a routine of calisthenics that emphasized stretching, working with weights, and riding a stationary bicycle — and swimming once or twice a week. And he maintained his healthy diet. "I don't think it's a question of age," he said, "as it's a question of what kind of shape you're in."[17]

Back in Edgefield, blacks finally got single-member districts, elected a 3-2 majority on county council, and appointed Tom McCain as county administrator. One of his first goals was to get the county Department of Social Services out of the courthouse basement. Naturally enough, he went to Thurmond, who got a $100,000 grant for a new building from discretionary funds in the Department of Health and Human Services.[18]

On the Armed Services Committee, Thurmond played a key role in passage of the Department of Defense Reorganizations Act of 1986. Committee Chairman Barry Goldwater and ranking Democrat Sam Nunn of Georgia faced determined opposition from the Joint Chiefs of Staff and the Department of Defense. The military services opposed a unified defense structure. The Navy especially sought to retain an independent status.

The committee was split 10-9 in favor of the legislation, with Republicans opposing it 7-3 and Democrats supporting it 7-2. Among Republicans, only Thurmond and William Cohen, who would become Secretary of Defense under President Bill Clinton, supported Goldwater.

The Department of Defense expected Thurmond, given his conservatism and long history of support, to oppose reform and attempted to recruit him to their side. Thurmond had long supported the concept of military unification, however, and his years of friendship with Goldwater promoted trust and loyalty.

Although the Department of Defense was targeting Thurmond, Goldwater never doubted he would keep his commitment, but Nunn was concerned that he might waiver. Nunn later said the battle within the committee during its first days "was as fierce as it gets." He called the rock-solid nature of Thurmond's support under enormous pressure absolutely critical. One scholar concluded, "After the first week, when Senator Thurmond's support did not waiver and their majority held, it was clear that Goldwater and Nunn would be able to report some kind of bill out of committee."[19]

Nunn later said, "I had learned not to rely on every senator's commitment, but Strom Thurmond was solid."[20]

When Democrats regained control of the Senate in 1987, Thurmond gave up the Judiciary chairmanship to Democrat Joe Biden of Delaware. Forty years younger than Thurmond and a man whose interest in politics was sparked in large part by the civil rights movement, Biden as ranking Democrat had forged a good relationship with Thurmond by promising never to do anything to undercut him. Thurmond reciprocated.

In a tribute to Thurmond upon his breaking the record on May 25, 1997, as the longest serving senator, Biden said, "His word is his bond, and each of us — even the most partisan of political opponents — knows that through the heat of political debate, regardless of the intense pressure that may be upon him, Strom Thurmond can be trusted to keep that word; not when it's politically possible or expedient, but always."

Although the tributes paid by many senators seemed perfunctory, Biden's was longer than most and contained more passion. He asserted that Thurmond's "political longevity lies . . . deep within Strom Thurmond himself. It lies in his strength of character, his absolute honesty and integrity, his strong sense of fairness, and his commitment to public service. None of those things are skills which you learn; they are qualities deep within you which, when people know you well, they can sense. That is the secret to Strom Thurmond's success."[21]

Thurmond intimates insist that although he has a biting wit that shows itself in repartee, at times he displays a childlike curiosity that reflects a quality of innocence. Unknowing sophisticates tend to question his innocence and intelligence in such questions.

At the confirmation hearings for Justice Rehnquist as chief justice, the executive director of the National Gay and Lesbian Task Force, Jeffrey Levi, testified in opposition. He appeared at a late night hearing with representatives of Americans United for Separation of Church and State and the chairman of the National Abortion Rights Action League.

Under questioning from Biden, then ranking Democrat, Levi expressed special concern about Rehnquist's vote in *Bowers v. Hardwick*, a 5-4 decision that upheld Georgia's sodomy statute.

Thurmond asked about Levi's claim that ten percent of American adults are predominantly homosexual, the senator saying he was "shocked to hear that if that is true." Levi attributed the figure to the Kinsey Institute (other studies suggest a much lower number), and then the following colloquy:

The CHAIRMAN. Does your organization advocate any kind of treatment for gays and lesbians to see if they can change them and make them normal like other people?

Mr. LEVI. Well, Senator, we consider ourselves to be quite normal, thank you. We just happen to be different from other people. And the beauty of the American society is that ultimately we do accept all differences of behavior and viewpoint.

To answer the question more seriously, the predominant scientific viewpoint is that homosexuality is probably innate; if not innate, then formed very early in life. The responsible medical community no longer considers homosexuality to be an illness but rather something that is just a variation of standard behavior.

The CHAIRMAN. You do not think gays and lesbians are subject to change? You do not think that they could change?

Mr. LEVI. No more so, Senator, than heterosexuals.

The CHAIRMAN. You do not think that they could be converted to be like other people in some way?

Mr. LEVI. Well, we think we are like other people with one small exception. And, unfortunately, it is the rest of society that makes a big deal out of that exception.

The CHAIRMAN. A small exception? That is a pretty big exception.

With that, other senators tried to suppress laughter, and Levi gamely replied, "Unfortunately, society makes it a big exception. We wish it would not, and that is why our organization exists."

The witnesses and a handful of supporters left stunned at Thurmond's remarks, which seemed to ridicule a witness at a hearing. One of them told Levi, "You should have said, 'Thank you, Senator,' then go kiss him on the lips."[22]

Thurmond was then eighty-three, and a staffer insists the senator was not baiting, that like others of his generation, he knew little about homosexuality and his questions were only an effort to learn more. It was reminiscent of what law clerks said about Eleventh Circuit Court of Appeals Judge Frank M. Johnson, who wrote the lower court opinion that the Supreme Court reversed in *Bowers v. Hardwick*. The law clerks detected a generational gap as he talked about "finding a cure" for homosexuality before ruling the Georgia sodomy statute unconstitutional.[23]

Examples abound of this "childlike curiosity" quality of Thurmond. For example, he decided in 1983 to support making

Martin Luther King's birthday a national holiday after gauging audience reaction during a speech at Voorhees College, an Episcopal-related, traditionally black institution in Denmark, S.C. Tom Moss set up the appearance and accompanied Thurmond.

Thurmond initially opposed the bill because of the cost of adding another recognized national holiday. By the time he got to Voorhees, his doubts centered on whether Dr. King was the right black leader to honor. In his remarks, Thurmond mentioned George Washington Carver and Booker T. Washington — whom Strom as a child had heard speak in Edgefield — but cheers and applause filled the auditorium when he mentioned the name of Martin Luther King, Jr. For Thurmond — fifteen years after King's death — it was genuine revelation. His knowledge of King had come primarily from FBI Director J. Edgar Hoover and his notorious effort to discredit the civil rights leader. Thurmond absorbs reality through his pores, and he told the Voorhees audience he would support the King holiday. Back in Washington, he told his staff about mentioning King's name and the auditorium "going wild."[24]

On another occasion a woman leaving his staff was a Mormon, and she explained to Thurmond the belief that God had written the Book of Mormon and presented it as divine revelation to a tribe of North American Indians. Thurmond asked, "Could they speak Hebrew?" She accepted it as a serious question. It was — Thurmond associating God with the Hebrew Old Testament and asking how the tribe that received the Book of Mormon was able to read it.

When Morris Amitay directed the American-Israel Public Affairs Committee (AIPAC), the so-called Jewish lobby, Thurmond in conversation referred to Israelis as Israelites.[25]

Earlier, Thurmond had been justifiably upset when, on the weekend his engagement to Nancy was announced, someone on the news desk at *The State* scurried to find a photo and ran on the front page a shot of Nancy in a bathing suit at a beauty pageant. Thurmond called publisher Ambrose Hampton, who called the general manager, who called executive editor Charles Wickenberg — and appropriate apologies were made. (Someone later came in and removed all swimsuit photographs of Nancy from the newspaper's files.)[26] Thurmond said years later the news editor should have been "horsewhipped."[27]

Thurmond then believed there was a conspiracy in *The State* newsroom because Lee Bandy wasn't writing stories on each of the senator's press releases. This time Thurmond traveled to Columbia and showed up at publisher Hampton's weekend lake cottage to complain. Strom brought copies of all his press releases and of Bandy's stories to prove his point.

Hampton turned the material over to Wickenberg, who had known Strom for a long time and was furious that Thurmond didn't come to him with his concern. Wickenberg flew to Washington, met with Strom and Nancy and the senator's press secretary and bluntly explained, "Mr. Bandy doesn't work for you, Senator. He works for *The State*, and it's interested in news, not publicity." He made it clear that if the handouts were printed, they would be rewritten as news "in some not-so-self-serving form." Thurmond then understood.

"He wanted credit for every nickel the federal government turned over to South Carolina," Wickenberg said. "I was steamed when I got there, but I cooled off. Nobody raised their voices."[28]

Most experienced politicians develop either a forthrightness with the press that serves them well or a glibness that offers protection. But Thurmond's earnestness seemed to scare his staff into overprotecting him, especially around savvy national reporters. Because Thurmond in fact generally has been well-informed about issues he cares about, this overprotection hasn't served him well.

For example, when *The Washington Post* assigned Robert G. "Bob" Kaiser to cover the Senate, he set out immediately to meet and interview all 100 senators. It took almost a year to get to see Thurmond. Four aides sat in. The interview lasted about ten minutes. Kaiser felt the aides were clearly there to get rid of the reporter for *The Washington Post* as quickly as possible. Thurmond was nonresponsive and to Kaiser, who went on to become managing editor, "he seemed out of it, even then."[29]

But Nina Totenberg, Supreme Court correspondent for National Public Radio, got a far different impression of Thurmond in a 1981 interview. For a magazine profile as he was taking over as Senate Judiciary Committee chairman, she wrote, "A personally delightful, courtly Southern gentleman, Strom Thurmond is often misunderstood. People who don't know him often underrate his intelligence, his political canniness and his energy."[30]

Congressman Butler Derrick's home office in Aiken was located next door to Thurmond's. They had agreed to ride over together to Barnwell, roughly a half hour away, for a 10 a.m. ceremonial reception, with Thurmond furnishing the car and driver. As the hour approached, Derrick went to the senator's office to say it was almost time for the event itself to get started. "If you don't get there late and leave early," Thurmond told him, "they think you don't have anything else to do."[31]

As South Carolina's first black congressman since 1897, James E. "Jim" Clyburn went to Washington after his election in 1992 with a priority goal. He intended to name a new federal courthouse in Columbia for Judge Matthew J. Perry, the state's first African-American federal jurist. Clyburn got a seat on the Public Works and Transportation Committee, with an assignment to the Public Buildings and Grounds subcommittee.

Clyburn introduced his bill. "It didn't cross my mind that anybody would object to this," Clyburn says. "Everybody liked Matthew Perry." He soon found himself in a clash with Thurmond.

The existing federal courthouse in Columbia was attached to the Strom Thurmond Federal Building, and someone told Clyburn, "The old man is upset." He found out that Thurmond was blocking the bill to name the new courthouse for Perry.

Clyburn then heard objections raised about naming the building for Perry while he was still on the bench, that it could cause a problem if any kind of scandal arose. "We just named the federal building in Aiken for Judge Charles Simons, Thurmond's former law partner," Clyburn said. "Nobody said a word about that. I was fit to be tied."

He resolved the matter when John Napier, a Republican and Thurmond loyalist who once had represented Clyburn's Sixth District, came by one day to ask for help on a matter. Before leaving, Napier asked if there was anything he could do for Clyburn.

Clyburn said "yes," then issued a not-so-subtle threat. Based on his research, he explained that the current Strom Thurmond Federal Building was named by administrative edict of the Governmental Services Administration (GSA). Bills twice introduced in the House to name the building for Thurmond by statute had failed.

Clyburn told Napier that anything done by administrative edict can be undone by statute. Unless Thurmond removed his objection, Clyburn said he planned to introduce a bill to rename the current Strom Thurmond Federal Building for Perry.

Clyburn told Napier, "It may not pass the Senate, but it will pass in the House. If the Senator can stand that embarrassment, it's all right with me.' He said, 'Oh, you wouldn't do that.' I said, 'Yes I would. Just watch me.'"

Clyburn asked Napier to pass that information to Thurmond and get a response over the weekend because Clyburn planned to introduce his bill on Monday. Clyburn got a call from Napier on Saturday, saying that Thurmond would remove his objection, provided the new courthouse was going to be a free-standing building.

"It always was a free-standing building," Clyburn says. "Anyway, that's how we got the building named." Construction on the Matthew J. Perry Federal Courthouse began in 1998.

In fighting the battle to name the courthouse, Clyburn's research found twenty-three different entities in South Carolina named for Strom Thurmond. The official "Tributes" to Thurmond printed by the U. S. Government Printing Office lists these: Thurmond Hall at Winthrop College (1939); Strom Thurmond High School, Edgefield County (1961); Strom Thurmond Student Center, Charleston Southern University (1972); Strom Thurmond Federal Building, Columbia (1975); The Strom Thurmond Center for Excellence in Government and Public Service at Clemson University (1981); Strom Thurmond Chairs and Scholarships (1981); Strom Thurmond Auditorium at University of South Carolina School of Law (1982); life-sized statue erected on Edgefield town square by people of Edgefield County (1984); streets in several South Carolina cities; Strom Thurmond Lake, Dam, and Highway, Clarks Hill (1987); Strom Thurmond Mall, Columbia (1988); has endowed fifty-two scholarships at forty-five colleges and universities, established the Strom Thurmond Foundation, which assists in educating 80 to 100 needy, worthy students annually; Strom Thurmond Soldier Service Center, Fort Jackson, Columbia (1991); Strom Thurmond Room, U.S. Capitol, 1991; Strom Thurmond Highway (Interstate 20 from the Georgia Line to Florence, S.C. (1992); Strom Thurmond Biomedical Research Center, Medical University of South Carolina (1993); Storm Thurmond National Guard Armory (1994). The list hasn't stopped, including the 1997 act of the legislature for a Strom Thurmond statue on the State House grounds.

After Clyburn did his research, he grew more determined about naming the courthouse for Judge Perry. "I don't think every damn building in the state has to be named for Strom Thurmond," Clyburn said. "I think the state has a real sickness about it."

Alone among South Carolina's congressmen, Clyburn has

demonstrated a willingness to challenge Thurmond. Thurmond had become the patron of South Carolina's six traditionally black colleges, but all six were located in the boundaries of the new black majority Sixth District after the 1990 census.

When a bill that provided funds for those institutions came up in the House, a colleague told Clyburn to leave it alone. Thurmond wanted to amend it in the Senate to increase funding for the South Carolina schools. "All six are in my district," Clyburn told him, "And you're telling me that I've got to wait for the great white father? Why don't you wait for your senator to do it? I said, 'Hell, I'm not going to do that. I'm going to amend this bill right here.' And I did, and we got it passed."

Clyburn continued, "I don't mind Strom Thurmond getting his just credit. But my staff works just as hard, and I think they deserve credit, too."

1. Bass interview with Donald L. Fowler, Columbia, S.C., February 6, 1998.
2. Atwater to Bass, October, 1978.
3. Thurmond help for Ravenel, confidential source; "Thurmond outspent," *1980 Almanac of American Politics*, p. 794; other information, Bass as participant-observer (public affairs coordinator for 1974 Bryan Dorn for governor campaign; Democratic candidate for Congress in 1978.)
4. Congressional Record – Senate, June 9, 1969, p. 15203.
5. *The New York Times* and *The Washington Post*, June 10, 1969.
6. Interview with Howell Raines, who covered the event for *The New York Times*, May 14, 1998.
7. Thompson interview with Thurmond, 1981.
8. Thompson interview with Emory Sneeden, March, 1981.
9. *The American Lawyer*, January 1981, p. 21.
10. Cohodas, Strom Thurmond and the Politics of Southern Change, p. 461.
11. *1988 Almanac of American Politics*, p. xxxix; *1990 Almanac of American Politics*, p. xxv.
12. Cohodas, pp. 463-466.
13. Bass telephone interview with Thomas C. McCain, July 15, 1998.

14. Ibid. 470-472.
15. Bass telephone interview with Armand Derfner, July 12, 1998.
16. Cohodas, pp. 473-78.
17. Cohodas, pp. 484-485.
18. Bass interview with McCain, July 15, 1998.
19. Colleen Marie Getz, "Congressional Policy Making: The Goldwater-Nichols Defense Reorganization Act of 1986," dissertation at Yale University, May 1998, pp. 202-207.
20. Nunn to Bass, May 1998.
21. Strom Thurmond, *Tributes, in the Congress of the United States* (Washington, U. S. Government Printing Office, 1997), pp. 43-44.
22. Confidential source.
23. Jack Bass, *Taming the Storm* (New York: Doubleday, 1993), p. 424.
24. Confidential source.
25. Bass telephone interview with Morris Amitay, July 28, 1998.
26. Bass telephone interview with Charles Wickenberg, op. cit.
27. Thompson interview with Thurmond, December 22, 1981.
28. Bass telephone interview with Charles Wickenberg, March 5, 1998.
29. Bass interview with Robert G. Kaiser, July 14, 1997.
30. *Parade*, February 15, 1981.
31. Bass telephone interview with Butler Derrick, op. cit.

The Thurmond family:
(back row, l-r) Strom Jr., Nancy Moore, Julie, and Paul,
(front row) Nancy and Strom.

CHAPTER
TWENTY-FOUR

✛

"My Baby is Dying"

On the evening of April 13, 1993, Democratic Lt. Gov. Nick
Theodore was reading the directions on some medication as his
highway patrolman driver pulled out of the Eckerd's drug store park-
ing lot — onto Harden Street in Columbia's busy Five Points area.
With its restaurants and coffee shops, the spot is a place of heavy
evening foot traffic near the University of South Carolina campus.

Theodore heard a dull thud. He looked toward the street and
saw a car stop. A distraught woman driver got out, ran toward his
car, and shouted through the window, "I didn't mean to hit her.
She stepped in front of my car."

Theodore's driver, James Peppers, had looked directly at the
accident, less than twenty feet away, as the speeding northbound
car struck a young woman walking — not running — across the
street. Her head smashed into the windshield and then she pin-
wheeled into the air, limbs flying, and crashed down again on her
head.

As his driver called for help, Theodore jumped out of the car,
dashed over to the still body, and removed his jacket to place it
over the unconscious young woman for protection against shock.
She had been walking across the street from a boyfriend's apartment to buy a chess set at Eckerd's.

The northbound car seemed to come from nowhere, the patrolman later estimating its speed at forty-five miles per hour. The driver, Corrinne Koenig, called her lawyer, Henry McMaster. He was
chairman of the South Carolina Republican Party and a former
United States Attorney for the state, a patronage job arranged by

Strom Thurmond. McMaster lived only a few blocks away and interceded for his client with the police, who waited almost two hours before administering a blood alcohol test.

A wallet in the victim's purse identified her as Nancy Moore Thurmond, the senator's oldest child. Theodore had gotten to know her as his favorite waitress at Al's Upstairs, a pasta restaurant across the Congaree River, and had attended her 22nd birthday party a few weeks earlier. He knew Strom Thurmond was in Columbia because both men had attended a ceremonial event earlier in the day.

Within ten minutes, Theodore and his driver followed an ambulance that rushed the unconscious victim to Richland Memorial Hospital. A few minutes later, Theodore located her father and told him there had been a serious accident, then called the senator's estranged wife, Nancy, in Aiken. Ninety-year-old Strom Thurmond arrived quickly. "He had his faculties," said Theodore, who remained at the hospital until 2 a.m., after the distraught mother had arrived. Strom, Jr., a twenty-year-old student at U.S.C. who was close to his sister, learned of the accident soon after it happened and rushed to the hospital.[1]

Hours later, Thurmond called Chris Simpson, a former press aide then working in media relations for the University of South Carolina, and asked him to take charge. He closed off the hospital floor, called in two of the senator's Columbia office secretaries to man phones, and set up press briefings. Upon learning who the victim was, McMaster joined the Thurmonds at the hospital and withdrew from the case.

Early the next morning, Vice President Al Gore called Thurmond. Gore's own son was almost killed a few years earlier when hit by a car after a Baltimore Orioles baseball game. Soon afterwards, President Bill Clinton called and asked about Nancy Moore's condition. A grieving Strom Thurmond told him, "My baby is dying."[2]

She died within hours without regaining consciousness. A beauty queen like her mother, she was only a month away from graduating with honors from the university.

Nancy Moore had quit the waitress job two weeks earlier to prepare for the upcoming Miss South Carolina pageant, where she was to represent Aiken. She intended to pursue a career in law, championing children's causes. She had been modeling for years and was an instructor for a local modeling agency. She was sole proprietor of Designs by Nancy, a business specializing in designer jewelry.

Tests showed Koenig, thirty-six, had a blood alcohol count of .16 almost two hours after the accident. Anything .10 or higher in South Carolina is enough for a driving under the influence conviction.

Koenig, a native of Spokane, Washington, was a consultant for people seeking alcohol permits. She previously had worked for a private attorney who was former chairman of the state Alcoholic Beverage Control Commission.

For Thurmond, a teetotaler for much of his life, the accident was a grim prophecy come true. From his earliest days as a school-teacher, he had railed against the danger of alcohol, preaching abstinence as a key to healthy living. In the Senate, he pushed for higher taxes on alcohol and stronger warning labels on bottles. In 1982, during a spirited floor debate in the Senate on his proposal to increase the tax on alcoholic beverages, he concluded that "drunk driving is responsible for the most common form of violent death in the Nation."[3] [There was a sad irony in alcohol's powerful impact on his family's story the next few years.]

When young Nancy's body was brought to the funeral home in Aiken, Strom Thurmond joined her mother to view the battered face of their precious first child in her coffin. They already had agreed to donate her organs to help others, a way of honoring her before the burial in the Thurmond family plot in Edgefield.

Both felt a special closeness to her. Nancy Thurmond later described how her namesake "called me sometimes ten or twelve times a day. We looked alike. We talked alike. She was my best friend in this world."[4] When Strom held his first-born in his arms in 1971, photographs showed him beaming, his usually gruff demeanor transformed. He was almost always like that in her presence.

The State published a letter to the editor memorializing the young woman. "Not Nancy, the daughter of a prominent U.S. senator," wrote one of her professors, Gene Stephens at the U.S.C. College of Criminal Justice. "Not Nancy, the dazzling beauty queen. But Nancy, the wonderful, caring, concerned human being.

"I knew Nancy as a student and as a friendly, easy-to-talk-with young lady whom I recommended for law school a few weeks ago.

"To my knowledge, Nancy never sought special consideration, as she well might, but instead used the opportunities prominence brought to serve others. While maintaining a high grade point average and enjoying the best of college life, she gave tirelessly of her time to the sick and needy — particularly children — and to countless community service projects.

"Whereas I feel that the privileged and wealthy have an obligation to serve others with a portion of their time and money, I'm sure Nancy never saw it as an obligation. She saw it as a pleasure and gained enormously from the experience.

"While we are deeply saddened, there is one thought that should give us all comfort: Nancy Thurmond packed a lot of quality living into her twenty-two years on this earth."[5]

The morning after the accident, Circuit Solicitor Richard "Dick" Harpootlian, the state prosecutor, personally went out and began interviewing witnesses. Clearly, Koenig had been drinking heavily, but he needed details to present a strong case to a jury.

"She'd been to four bars that night, and I interviewed every bartender as to how much she had to drink. I had her obtaining nine to twelve beers over a three-hour period prior to getting into the car and hitting her.

"I found that one of the national experts on blood alcohol extrapolation happens to be at the Medical University of South Carolina in Charleston, so we were going to use him. Sixteen is what she read two hours after the accident." The expert was prepared to testify it would have been a minimum of twenty-two at the time of the accident.

"She did not appear to be drunk," Harpootlian continued, "but our expert would testify that somebody who drinks a lot every day can mask it, especially when the adrenaline hits from having this kind of trauma."

The investigation put Harpootlian in an ironic role. More than two decades earlier, as 1972 editor of Clemson's student newspaper, *The Tiger*, Harpootlian had written scathing editorials about Thurmond and run every humiliating picture of him that he could find, especially one with Thurmond's mouth full of barbecue. He and a handful of like-minded Clemson student journalists — Marilyn Thompson and her brother, Jim Walser, among them — then descended on Columbia and launched an alternative weekly, *Osceola*. Modeled after *The Texas Observer*, it likewise reviled Thurmond while providing laudable depth reporting on politics and public affairs.

"Politically, I've never been on the same side of the fence as him and did not know him except in the political context," said Harpootlian, who in 1998 became state Democratic chairman in South Carolina. "You know, in my perspective he was a segregationist, pro-war, very conservative, all those sorts of things that didn't mesh with my idea of what we ought to be doing in this country.

"I probably talked to him no more than ten minutes in my life up until the point at which he and Nancy came to me to decide whether the woman that hit and killed his daughter should be prosecuted.

"Immediately it was a sort of sentiment out there that this woman would not have been prosecuted had she not hit Strom Thurmond's daughter. Rumors started flying that this Thurmond girl was jaywalking, that she was drunk, that Koenig had been roughed up. I mean it was just awful. It was amazing how public opinion shifted to Koenig. I was shocked that it shifted that way. Koenig did a masterful p.r. job. I've got to give her credit."

Harpootlian ordered an autopsy so there would be no dispute over whether Nancy Moore had been drinking. The report revealed a zero blood alcohol content. Several months passed before the solicitor's first in-depth meeting with Strom and Nancy Thurmond. Strom was then ninety and Nancy forty-six. "What amazed me about him," Harpootlian said, "was that he was alert, that he was articulate, that he had a grasp of some of the more arcane legal principles and the difference between felony D.U.I. and reckless homicide.

"I forgot he was a state court judge back in the 30s and 40s. The elements of crime haven't changed much, so he knew a lot more than any other victim's parents knew that I've dealt with on these kinds of cases.

"As we went through the process, it became obvious to me that we were going to have a hell of a time getting a jury that would be fair to me. Koenig was just very adept in promoting the concept that she was somehow being strung up because she had killed Strom Thurmond's daughter."

Because Harpootlian declined to comment on details of the accident to insure a fair trial, the press had limited information that did not include Koenig's high speed at the time of the accident. Although the .16 blood alcohol content was reported, it was placed in the context of drinking "several beers" instead of the nine to twelve that Harpootlian confirmed. What the public read after the accident implied that the speed of the car may have been less than twenty-five miles per hour, that the victim was jaywalking, and that the driver didn't see her until too late.

"I don't promote my cases," Harpootlian said. "I think that's unethical. As we began to draw a jury, a number of them said they think she's being singled out. I was shocked.

"Thurmond and Nancy for a couple of weeks were in and out of my office every day. They acted just like any other victim's father and mother I ever dealt with except they were much more understanding, more willing to get the thing resolved than most parents. And Strom — Nancy had to be a little firm with him from time to time because he was used to the 30s and 40s where people got twenty-five years. Reckless homicide carries five years. Felony D.U.I. carries up to twenty years.

"It took him a while to grasp the fact that public opinion wasn't in his favor. Initially, he wanted to hang her. If it had been my daughter, I would have wanted to hang her."

Harpootlian had doubts about getting a felony D.U.I. conviction because it would have required proof that Koenig also was speeding. Harpootlian wasn't sure whether he could prove with legal certainty that the speed limit in the dense shopping area at Five Points technically was only twenty-five miles per hour — as posted a block north of the accident — rather than forty-five miles per hour, the limit by state law for unposted areas in a municipality. There was also the jaywalking by the victim, which Koenig's trial lawyer, John Hardaway, would have stressed in arguing that the wreck was an "unavoidable accident."

In addition to the high speed and drinking, an examination by the solicitor's office of Koenig's car indicated that the front beam lights were aimed too low, giving limited forward vision. Police were ready to testify that Koenig told one of them she drank a beer before the accident, another that she drank two, and another that she drank three — compared with the nine to twelve that the bartenders said they saw her consume.

But the real problem, Harpootlian thought, was the sympathy Koenig had generated. If the victim weren't Strom Thurmond's daughter, Harpootlian was convinced he could have convicted the driver on felony D.U.I., with at least a fifteen-year sentence. "Being Strom Thurmond's daughter cut against us," he said. "Jurors were telling me that. All it takes is one juror to hang it up."

Harpootlian located personal records relating to past behavior by Koenig, and Judge Ralph Anderson considered, in a closed hearing, whether they could be admitted as evidence. "If these records came in," Harpootlian later explained, "our job would be much easier."

When Anderson ruled them admissible, the parties negotiated a plea bargain that sealed the records. The Thurmonds discussed the plea issue and finally agreed. "They did not want to be perceived as using his stature in the state as somehow to punish somebody more than they would be punished normally," Harpootlian said. "They wanted Koenig to be punished in some way, and the fact was that she was going to jail. Thurmond just looked at me and said, 'You do what you think is right.'

"I said, 'Well, Senator, I think my best estimate of the right thing to do is to show some mercy and get it over with right now. She's going to jail.' Mercy meant to me to put an end to it."

Koenig entered a guilty plea to involuntary manslaughter, but not until after testimony on September 1 in open court and an offer by Harpootlian to accept a guilty plea with no sentencing recommendation to the judge. In the courtroom, Harpootlian routinely followed his practice of inviting the family to sit in a row of chairs behind the prosecutor's table. Strom and Nancy were joined by Strom, Jr., and Julie. The youngest son, Paul, was at a tennis academy in Florida. The senator's twin younger sisters, Mary Tompkins and Martha Bishop, also joined them.

Thurmond rejected any notion he was there to pressure the court. "That's not the purpose at all," he told reporter Lee Bandy. "Here is a father whose daughter was killed by a drunk driver exceeding the speed limit."

Bandy could see "the hurt and pain in their eyes as they were forced to relive that horrible night of April 13." But Thurmond, the war hero, tried to minimize the emotional toll. "Of course, this is a tough time. But it hasn't gotten me down," he told Bandy. "All through life, you have matters that come up you have to deal with. And this is one of them."

The family showed little emotion as a sobbing and remorseful Koenig entered the guilty plea and said, "I'm so sorry." Nancy Thurmond bit her upper lip. A letter from her, read to the court, said, "The silent and vicious killer in this case was alcohol" and expressed hope it would serve to educate others about alcohol's dangers.[6]

After agreement on the guilty plea, Judge Anderson asked the sobbing Koenig, "Do you still want to go forward?"

"Yes, sir."

"In your heart and soul, are you guilty of involuntary manslaughter in the death of Nancy Thurmond?"

The courtroom fell silent.

"Yes, sir."

Harpootlian told Anderson that agreeing to a plea bargain was not an easy decision. "There is no joy in what we do here today," the solicitor said. "There is no feeling that the Thurmonds will leave here satisfied, happy, with what occurred. . . . What we hope we leave the courtroom with is a sense that justice was done."

The judge imposed a sentence of two years in prison plus five years probation. He also required that she receive substance abuse counseling.[7] Columbia's most influential TV station, WIS, broke in live and transmitted it live to other NBC affiliates statewide.

Thurmond had told Bandy he would be relieved when the trial ended. It would allow him to look forward again. "I believe in the Bible, in God, in the future, in eternal life. And that's what keeps us all going," he said.[8]

Looking back four years later, Harpootlian said, "Strom was taken aback that his stature didn't cut for him in this case, that it cut against him. I still shake my head about it. I mean here's Strom Thurmond, the beloved Strom Thurmond's daughter killed by a drunk driver and the perception out there was that somehow this woman was being prosecuted because she killed Thurmond's daughter rather than being guilty. It was the weirdest thing I've ever seen.

"He was just a stand-up guy, and I can't say enough good things about him. I still don't agree with much of what he does politically, but I know there is a guy that has a sense of values. He really agonized over what's the right thing to do, and the relationship between him and Nancy was fascinating.

"He actually listened to her, took her advice. He initially said she's got to get at least ten years. Nancy said, 'Strom, that's not what's important. What's important is that something positive come out of this. If she'll plead guilty and goes to jail, then we ought to live with it.' She felt Nancy's death could be used for something positive, against drunk driving; it shouldn't turn into a political circus.

"I left and when I came back she and Strom were sitting on the couch together and holding hands. It wasn't 'Senator and wife' or 'Senator and estranged wife;' it was mom and dad figuring out what to do. That was just it. Not what I expected.

"They were like any other family I ever dealt with except they were a lot calmer and a lot nicer and a lot more considerate of me and what I have to go through than any other family I have had to deal with.

"Strom, Jr. just wanted to kick somebody's ass. What do you expect of a twenty-year-old? His sister is dead, and she was very close to him. Again, that's natural. That's what you see with every one of these families. I've dealt with too many people whose families are in trauma and who don't have a good foundation; you watch them disintegrate.

"That's what I figured would turn into a nasty scene—with Nancy and Strom separated and the daughter dead and the political overlay, but it never did. They really behaved like champs.

"And I think it was real. I think whatever their relationship is, it's a real one. I don't know why they are separated. I don't know why they are not living together, but they got along very well. They worked it together. They had the kids come in to talk to them for awhile about what was going to happen. There was a mom and dad trying to get through this thing together, and that was sort of amazing to me."

At one point before the trial, Harpootlian said, "Thurmond and I were having a very back and forth, two-lawyers-talking about elements of crime. . . . That particular moment I came to the realization that this guy got where he got because he's a smart son-of-a-bitch. He's like a young guy in an old guy's body."[9]

At the funeral service at First Baptist Church in Aiken, Strom Thurmond broke down crying. Many staffers had never seen him cry before. Now they saw Strom, Jr., stretch his arm around his father to comfort him. Later, the three surviving children stood with their parents, shaking hands with hundreds who came to express condolences. To an intimate of the senator, the children displayed an adult understanding of their role in a public family. The event seemed to him — with much of the Senate and Vice President Al Gore, the Senate's presiding officer, there — almost like a dress rehearsal for Strom Thurmond's funeral.[10]

At Willowbrook Cemetery in Edgefield, a family friend arranged the purchase of adjoining land from a neighbor's back yard to add to the Thurmond family plot, making it the largest there. On either side of the daughter's grave sit pink marble benches. On one of them is inscribed:

"Suffer the little children
to come unto me,
for of such is the kingdom of heaven."

Inscribed on the other is:

Precious Nancy Moore
Our love for you endureth forever
Mommy and Daddy
Nancy and Strom Thurmond

Nancy visits the grave almost daily when she's at home in Aiken.

Koenig, paroled after serving almost a year in jail, later was charged with violating parole. After a hearing on August 29, 1996, that called for her to undergo four months of daily drug testing, she said she wanted to leave South Carolina. "I'm a spectacle for the state," she told a reporter, complaining she could get nothing more than a minimum wage job. "People think I've forgotten. I live this accident every day."[11]

Two days after Koenig's hearing, and a little more than three years after the daughter's death, Nancy Thurmond was charged with drunken driving and speeding by an Aiken police officer. Her first response, when asked for her driver's license, was to pull out a wad of money and arrange it in front of the officer. The incident was videotaped from the arresting officer's patrol car.

After losing her balance during a sobriety test and refusing to stand on one foot or take the Breathalyzer test, she was arrested and spent the night in the Aiken County Jail. The next morning, she posted a $418 bond.

The senator issued a statement a few days later, saying, "My family and I deeply regret this and pray she will handle it in a responsible manner."[12]

Nancy immediately entered an out-of-state treatment center. She forfeited the bond, losing her license and getting sentenced to perform community service. Roughly a year after her daughter's accident, she had acknowledged her problem with alcohol in letters to friends, including Bandy. He quoted from it a month after her arrest: "In an effort to face this issue openly and honestly, and hopefully to strengthen my own journey toward sobriety and recovery, I wish to acknowledge this progressive and fatal disease with all of its ramifications, beginning with my powerlessness over alcohol and the unmanageability of life around it."

She asked for prayers and "God's grace, not just for myself, but for all those who continue to suffer in silence from addictive disease."[13] Some language in her letter is almost identical to that found in Alcoholics Anonymous literature.

Three months after her arrest, Nancy spoke out publicly for the first time, acknowledging a twenty-year battle with alcoholism and prescription diet pills and being "clean and sober" for the three months since her arrest. She went public after a speech at Clemson by former Sen. George McGovern. He talked about his daughter, Terry, who died after a long struggle with alcohol. Nancy told reporter Dottie Ashley of *The Post and Courier* in Charleston, "I want people to know how I feel about my alcoholism and how I know that I, too, could have killed someone just as my own child was killed."

Nancy had never tasted alcohol until soon after marrying Strom, who had begun drinking an occasional glass of wine on the advice of his doctor. Curious, Nancy decided one night to have her own glass of wine. After her first sip, she said, "I immediately threw up in my plate, right there in front of everyone. [Her allergic reaction was symptomatic of a certain type of alcoholism.] Strom, always the Southern gentleman, covered my plate with his napkin and just pretended nothing had happened!

"Strom was always very busy and he did not confront me per se with my addiction. But when I told him I needed some help, he was very receptive.

"But, of course, Strom was famous as a health advocate and as a teetotaler and for him to be saddled with a drunken wife just didn't make sense — it just didn't add up."

She talked about the stress as a senator's wife who had four children in less than five years. She said Strom was a devoted father, but his career kept him busy. Nancy found herself staying home alone with the children more often at night.

"I was a very quiet drunk," she told Ashley. "I never felt that I caused any trouble or got loud or obnoxious or embarrassed anyone."

In the 1970s, she began taking diet pills prescribed to help lose weight after the births of her children and became dependent on amphetamines. "Because I was so hyper from the pills, often I just couldn't get to sleep, and so I would have a glass of wine to block out tiredness."

She became despondent and her self-esteem diminished. "Sometimes I was lonely, although I would work on my two books, *Mother's Medicine* (1979), and *Happy Mother, Happy Child* (1981), when the children were napping or sleeping.

But I was using wine as a sleeping potion, and over the years I became more and more clandestine about my drinking. . . . My most deeply felt sense of loss is that I have to realize that I was not the mother I intended to be, or that God intended for me to be."[14]

After the Associated Press distributed the story statewide in South Carolina, *The State* editorialized, "This is a brutally harsh self-assessment — probably much too harsh. It would have taken an unusually strong person to navigate a marriage with a huge age gap (forty-four years) in the glare of national media and with constant demands on a husband whose public life she had to adopt as her own — not to mention raising four children born close together. But the Nancy Thurmond South Carolinians remember so well and appreciate is a gracious woman who gave generously of her time to public fund-raising efforts by multiple organizations throughout the state. . . . We admire her for her openness and her courage."[15]

If a mother is judged by reputation of her children, Nancy Thurmond was quite successful. Strom Jr. was described by a former Thurmond staffer as "sensitive and intelligent." A law school staff member said young Thurmond never sought special consideration, and others there characterized him as "quiet and reserved." He was an undergraduate English major. In the spring of 1998, he announced his engagement to marry Heather Gail Holland, who graduated a year behind him at both Aiken High School and U.S.C. They married in September.

When it was diagnosed that Julie, the second daughter, suffered from a severe form of diabetes, family associates said both parents responded with attention and concern. Julie graduated from the College of Charleston and returned to Washington. She worked in the private sector, saw her father regularly and sometimes accompanied him at official functions. She joined him in 1997 on a trip he made to China as president pro tem of the Senate just before his ninety-fifth birthday.

Paul Thurmond was captain of the Vanderbilt University tennis team in 1998, his senior year, with plans to enter law school. As an athlete he was an academic all-SEC (Southeastern Conference) selection all four years. He made the Dean's List majoring in Human and Organization Development. He was also involved off the court with such activities as tutoring public school first graders in reading.

The two sons have told a close family friend they ultimately want to practice law together, with offices in Aiken and Edgefield. Thurmond, in response to an interviewer's question, once said he would like his sons to enter politics "only if that's what they want."[16] A family friend said both young men "handle themselves well" around people and had the qualities to succeed if they ever chose to seek elective office.

In the year after Nancy's arrest, she had begun to see Strom a bit more often, even attending Washington events with him. In the fall of 1997 she let friends know that she had been "clean and sober" for a year.

1. Bass interview with Nick Theodore, July 1, 1998.
2. Confidential source.
3. *Congressional Record*, July 22, 1982.
4. *The Post and Courier*, December 1, 1996.
5. *The State*, April 18, 1993.
6. *The State*, September 2, 1993.
7. *The State*, September 2, 1993, p. 1A.
8. Ibid.
9. Bass interview with Richard Harpootlian, June 25, 1997.
10. Confidential interview.
11. *The State*, August 30, 1996.
12. *The State*, September 8, 1996.
13. *The State*, October 5, 1996.
14. *The Post and Courier*, December 1, 1996.
15. *The State*, December 4, 1996.
16. Banks interview, 1976.

The permanent fixtures of Washington :

THE WHITE HOUSE | THE WASH. MONUMENT | STROM THURMOND

CHAPTER
TWENTY-FIVE

✛

Constituent Service

At a 1996 fund-raiser for Elliott Close, the Democratic challenger to Strom Thurmond, one slightly devilish contributor asked the candidate how he planned to deal with the issue of Strom's record of constituent service.

For several minutes, one Close supporter after another swapped stories of getting help from Thurmond. It is reasonably estimated that his Senate office since 1955 has handled roughly 700,000 requests from South Carolinians with a problem.

And it seems as though in 699,999 of those cases, good service was rendered. For Thurmond it is politics at its best, building a reservoir of goodwill from which votes flow at election time.

A top staffer says Thurmond obviously realizes the political payoff, but also has a sincere belief that somebody has to look out for the people. Thurmond once told the aide, "If the bureaucrats would do what they are supposed to do, I wouldn't have to do it. I could do what people think a legislator more typically does."

The aide explained that the staff got results, not because they're exceptional, but because they used Thurmond's name. "His name moves people in Washington because the agency workers know his staff is speaking for him and that if Senator Thurmond gets exercised enough, he'll call the head of the Social Security Administration for that woman in Duncan, S.C., concerned about not receiving her death benefit after her husband died. The implied threat that he would do it carried weight. That's exactly how it worked.

"He understood that you had to get the bureaucrats to move.

His philosophy permeated the staff that if some constituent called about something, you did your best to accommodate that person to get them some relief."

All requests get a response within twenty-four hours. If the individual assigned to a matter can't provide a result, the section chief handles it. If that doesn't work, the matter goes to the administrative assistant, the top staffer in a Senate office. If after all that, a South Carolinian insists on talking to Thurmond about his or her problem, he returns the call. And it may be to someone he's never met.

The aide added, "It's unbelievable what people would call about. He would say, 'Look, I know that might not sound important to you. That might not sound important to me. But to that person, especially if they take the time to write or call about it, that's the single most important issue in their life.' We had to deal with it that way.

"Another characteristic I've never seen in anybody else in my life is that he really didn't have gradations of importance. If he was working on the Fortas nomination, that was important, but getting Mrs. Smith in Duncan her Social Security check was important, too. An amazing thing. And he was the most energetic person I've ever known at any age."[1]

Strom seems to get genuine pleasure from helping others and an inner satisfaction in showing that he can help. It all bundled together with his role as politician — someone who knows how to deal with people, who likes to deal with people, and who helps people and relates to them positively. In that sense, Thurmond is "incomparable," says Don Fowler, a political scientist by training who, as a state and national Democratic Party leader, spent decades observing him in South Carolina, as well as many years of lining up opposition at election time.

After Fowler became commanding officer of the 360th Civil Affairs unit as an Army Reserve colonel, Thurmond in 1981 attended the unit's thirtieth anniversary of its founding. Thurmond had organized the 360th after completing his term as governor.

It was summer and the seventy-eight-year-old senator — by then a retired major general in the Army Reserve — stood on the hot asphalt in Columbia and spoke for almost twenty minutes, denouncing the Communist menace as the troops sweltered. Afterwards, he met Col. Fowler's son, Donnie, and said, "My, my what a fine young man. If you ever want to be my page in Washington, let me know and I'll make sure it happens."

Fritz Hollings never made such an offer, and Thurmond called

Fowler back a few years later, renewing it. Donnie as a high school senior went up and became a Senate page for Thurmond in January 1985.[2] Fowler by then operated his own public relations and lobbying firm, and Thurmond was always happy to be helpful. He also had only token opposition in 1984 and 1990, winning reelection handily at the ages of eighty-one and eighty-seven.

Neill Macaulay, a Columbia dentist's son and adventurous graduate of The Citadel, first met Sen. Thurmond in 1956 while hitchhiking home from Central America. Thurmond, driving his Cadillac, thought the hitchhiker had "an honest face." He picked him up on Highway 78 west of Augusta, Georgia, then stopped at his brother's house in North Augusta for Cokes and cookies before dropping Macaulay off on the highway to Columbia. Macaulay found Thurmond "sincere and gracious, and although I disagreed with him on almost every question of the day, I couldn't help liking him."

Four years later, Thurmond interceded when the State Department threatened to take away Macaulay's American citizenship. He had moved to Cuba and fought in the early days with Fidel Castro. The issue was whether he had done so voluntarily after January 1, 1959, in violation of American policy. Macaulay, already disenchanted with Castro, had submitted his resignation on January 1 to comply with the American edict, but the embassy in Havana charged otherwise.

Travis Medlock, a young lawyer who later became South Carolina's attorney general, represented Macaulay and called on Thurmond for help. Thurmond set up and attended a meeting in his office with Medlock and two State Department attorneys, saying only that he once picked up Macaulay as a hitchhiker and thought him a "nice fellow." After Medlock presented the evidence, the State Department allowed Macaulay to retain his citizenship.[3]

As the full effect of the civil rights revolution transformed the American South into a far more open society, Lonnie Hamilton of Charleston found the second relationship he had with Strom Thurmond far different from the first. A trumpet player as a child for the touring jazz band of the Jenkins Orphanage, Lonnie couldn't study music as an undergraduate at South Carolina State College in the late 1940s because the subject then wasn't taught at the all-black institution.

He majored instead in industrial arts, and one of his jobs was working with a team in a tailoring class to make a two-piece suit for Gov. Strom Thurmond — a traditional goodwill gesture to each new governor. Correspondence exists in which Thurmond sent the suit back for alterations. Historian William Hine at S.C. State says Thurmond wasn't unique among governors in getting the alterations, but he was the only one who offered to pay for them.[4]

Hamilton's next contact with Thurmond came in 1987. By then, in his second term as chairman of Charleston County Council, Hamilton needed Navy approval for a solid-waste incinerator for the county. The contract agreement was stalled on the Secretary of the Navy's desk.

Someone told Hamilton, "Lonnie, why don't you talk to Strom Thurmond about it?" Hamilton remembered, "I had the county administrator call his office, and I spoke to Senator Thurmond." When Hamilton said he wanted to come to Washington about the matter, Thurmond said he would be in Charleston that Friday and to meet him at a Marriott hotel near the Charleston Naval Station. Hamilton walked in with the county's public works manager and attorney, explained the problem, and asked Thurmond if he could help.

Hamilton remembers, "He said, 'Get me the Secretary of the Navy on the telephone.' I didn't know how to get the Secretary of the Navy on the telephone. I said, 'Senator, you're going back to Washington. It can wait until Monday.' He called me back on Tuesday and said, 'It's signed.'

Charlton deSaussure, Jr., the young bond attorney handling the project's financing and scion of an old aristocratic Charleston family, said, "Mr. Hamilton, that's some kind of power."[5]

After Charles Wickenberg retired as executive editor of *The State*, his grandson Ben Cobb decided, for a third-grade assignment, to report on a biography of Sen. John Glenn, the former astronaut. The odyssey that followed included a trip to Washington to meet with Glenn, who unexpectedly had to return to Ohio. Strom Thurmond stepped in, found out who the youngster was, and escorted him to meet Utah Sen. Jake Garn, who had flown aboard a space shuttle. Ben then had his picture taken with Thurmond. In his thank-you note, Ben on his own initiative invited Thurmond to visit his school. He came in the fall of 1992, speaking to Ben's class and then to all the students. After that, Ben Cobb was never afraid of meeting anyone. Thurmond told Ben's father, "For thirty years, I've been trying to get Wick to put up a picture of me in his office, and now he will."[6]

Thurmond didn't always get the desired results. A politically active South Carolina lawyer got Thurmond to accompany him in 1980 to meet with the director of the Environmental Protection Agency to consider a request to waive a regulation for a steel mill in Georgetown. Thurmond brought along a package of shelled South Carolina pecan halves as a token gift. The EPA official listened to a presentation of projected economic benefits for the community, but refused to grant the waiver. "We've got a new administration coming in," Thurmond told him, "and we'll replace you." With that, the senator picked up the pecans and left.[7]

The one case of Thurmond providing "help" that proved genuinely embarrassing involved seventy-seven-year-old twin sisters from Barnwell County who called in 1971 to complain that Edgar Brown, the local political kingpin, was trying to take their land. The sisters never understood that Brown's office was routinely handling a legal matter for the state.

South Carolina law then required any recipient of public welfare owning real estate to give the state a lien on the property. The state took legal action after the person's death to recover the amount of aid received. The objective was to discourage poor people from seeking public assistance if they owned land they wanted to leave to heirs.

In this case, the sisters had inherited from an aunt 160 acres with a small house in which they lived. The aunt had received $4,955.72 in old-age assistance from the state — eighty percent of it federal funds. The acreage included a family cemetery and had been owned by the family for generations.

Brown's office got involved by chance. The state attorney general's office rotated such cases in Barnwell County between the law offices of Brown and House Speaker Solomon Blatt. It was Brown's turn this time, and a young lawyer from his office, Thomas Boulware, went to see the two women and explain the situation. He pointed out there was twenty acres of virgin timber on the property, and the trees, if cut and sold for lumber, were worth enough to pay off the lien. He offered other suggestions, but the women were suspicious and believed that, somehow, Edgar Brown was attempting to take their land. They valued the trees and didn't want them cut. They explained their predicament to a relative, who suggested they contact Thurmond for help.

Strom was more than willing to assist them. Nancy, too. One of the sisters later wrote a cousin in Florida, "A very prominent person will own our famous place some day — U.S. Sen. Strom Thurmond paid the debts in full and gave us the privileges we asked for — what a friend."

The women, clad in ragged clothing, told Jack Bass and a fellow reporter that they had willed the property to Strom and Nancy Thurmond. But the reporters had a copy of courthouse records showing that, with payment of the lien, title had passed to Nancy Thurmond, and the two sisters retained a life estate. In other words, they could continue living in the house until they died. Thurmond's lawyer included a provision that the women could not cut or sell any timber. They insisted to the reporters, however, that they still owned the land, that they paid the taxes.

The women lived off the highway from Blackville to Barnwell, and the reporters drove to the county courthouse to check the tax records. Those records also listed Nancy Thurmond's name as owner after the deed was recorded. Her name was typed on the tax books, but then scratched through with a pen and the names of the two sisters handwritten in above it.

When asked about it by the reporters, the county treasurer explained that the women had sent him a "right nasty note" about not getting the tax notice and told him they also called the senator about it. The treasurer said someone in Thurmond's office returned the tax notice with directions "that it should be sent to the ladies." The taxes amounted to $78.30. The ladies paid them even though Nancy held title to the property.

Thurmond said he didn't take advantage of the women, that he offered to help them get a loan, but they didn't want that. He paid the cost of installing running water and indoor plumbing in the house. The Thurmonds' purchase price amounted to $4,955.72, slightly more than $30 an acre. He acknowledged that no independent appraisal was made of the value of the property. Boulware estimated that comparable land in Barnwell County then was selling for $225 to $250 an acre.[8]

A cousin of the sisters, a large peach farmer in Edgefield County and a contemporary of Thurmond's, told the reporters, "Ol' Strom's a rascal."

Soon after a story about the transaction was published in *The Charlotte Observer*, the South Carolina legislature quietly repealed the lien law. Thurmond announced publicly an offer to sell the property back to the two sisters, for what Nancy paid. The sisters, however, had no money.

Less than a year later, after one sister died, the timber was cut under a contract between Nancy Thurmond and the surviving sister, who received a payment of $2,000, $1,000 for herself and $1,000 to be applied to debts of the deceased sister's estate.[9] There is no further public record related to the timber sale.

When Bass and his colleague met with Thurmond to ask him about the land purchase from the two sisters, he responded angrily about their "making something out of that" when he had an election coming up the next year. Thurmond told them he didn't have any money, but that Nancy had some that she had saved from her year as Miss South Carolina.[i] He already was unhappy with articles Bass was writing about his changing image and outreach to black voters, a politically sensitive issue, and he called Bass "a skunk." But in keeping with Thurmond's philosophy of keeping no enemies, he wrote Bass a friendly "Dear Jack" letter a week or so later that accompanied an official book of testimonials and tributes to "our good friend Mendel Rivers," the Charleston congressman who had died earlier that year.

A decade later, when Bass was developing a television course, "The American South Comes of Age," he interviewed Thurmond in the President Pro Tem's Senate office. An aide asked if the senator could be helpful while Bass and his camera crew were in Washington. Bass, who had been repeatedly rebuffed in efforts to schedule an interview with U. S. Trade Ambassador William E. Brock, asked for assistance. Bass wanted to interview Brock, a former Tennessee senator and chairman of the Republican national committee, about the party's "Southern strategy," which Brock viewed as a mistake. Thurmond made a telephone call.

The next morning, while a cameraman was attaching a microphone to Brock's lapel, he looked at Bass, smiled, and said, "You fellows know how to play the game."

i. Thurmond had received national attention in 1969 when *Life* magazine disclosed that he and Charles Simons had received higher payments than neighboring land owners for acreage condemned for I-20 near Aiken, but they were accused of no illegality. Thurmond also had purchased two lots across the Congaree River from Columbia adjacent to a site that the South Carolina Highway Department later announced as location for a new bridge across the river. Thurmond later sold the land to the Highway Department for what he paid, plus the prevailing rate of interest for the period he owned it. Four days after publication of the *Life* story, Thurmond purchased 1,668 acres in York County about sixteen miles from a proposed $60 million nuclear fuel reprocessing plant, but immediately transferred the deed to the Strom Thurmond Foundation. (By 1992, a year in which Thurmond gave $398,000 in campaign funds to the Foundation for scholarships, one of its officials reported it had provided 3,709 scholarships during thirty years of existence.) In 1989, Thurmond purchased thirty-nine acres near Columbia from South Carolina Electric & Gas Co. (SCANA) for $23,300 ($599 an acre), but sold it back later in the year to avoid an appearance of a conflict of interest after several real estate developers said the land was worth more than $100,000 and after an aide reminded the senator of a meeting he attended with federal highway officials and power company representatives to discuss a nearby proposed interstate highway interchange.

✝ ✝ ✝

1. Confidential interview.
2. Bass interview with Donald Fowler, February 6, 1998.
3. Neill Macaulay, *A Rebel in Cuba* (Chicago: Quadrangle Books, 1970), pp. 182-194.
4. William Hine to Bass.
5. Bass telephone interview with Lonnie Hamilton, December 21, 1997.
6. Bass interview with Tom Cobb, Ben's father, June 1998.
7. Bass telephone interview with James Moore, July 12, 1998.
8. *The Charlotte Observer*, May 23, 1971.
9. See Recording Book 13-H, pp. 338-339, Barnwell County Courthouse, Barnwell, S.C.

CHAPTER TWENTY-SIX

+

Grand Old Man

Shortly after the November 1996 election in South Carolina, Strom Thurmond called Harry Dent at home. "Harry, I won, didn't I?" the senator asked rhetorically. Less than a month before his ninety-fourth birthday, his voice had a special satisfaction.

Dent replied, "Yes, Senator, you sure did."

"Guess what I'm doing."

"What?"

"I'm writing a $250 check for your ministry."

Dent had tried to talk Thurmond out of running and did no work in the campaign. With his wife Betty, Dent had been a born-again Christian for almost two decades. Associates of the Rev. Billy Graham, the Dents devoted themselves to their own lay ministry, "Laity: Alive and Serving." They wrote an inspirational book, *Right vs. Wrong: Solution to the American Nightmare*. Even Strom, who has acknowledged he almost never reads a book, read this one.

When Thurmond was contemplating seeking an eighth term at the age of ninety-three, he was already the oldest person ever to serve in the Senate. Dent thought Thurmond's age made him vulnerable and told him the reasons he shouldn't run.

In the fall of 1995, Thurmond had lunch with a trusted and able former press secretary, Mark Goodin, who agreed with Dent. Goodin told him, "You don't have to prove anything. You have served well and admirably. I would hate to see your career end with a bitter campaign waged over the age issue that might be a squeaker that you could lose." Goodin recalled, "He thanked me, but it was clear he wasn't happy." Another trusted associate, however, advised that a majority of South Carolina voters would prefer he not run, but would vote for him if he did.

Thurmond decided to run, and he met again with Goodin, this time asking him to go to South Carolina and take a look at his campaign situation. Because of loyalty, Goodin reluctantly agreed to go.

"Strom Thurmond is the most exceptional person I've ever known," he said. "He is a remarkably uncynical man for having been in this business. Patriotism, honor — it's not hokum for him. He's the most unvenal, uncynical person I've ever known. I've seen him angry and furious — never vindictive."

One of Lee Atwater's savvy proteges, Goodin was a political realist who had worked for Vice President Dan Quayle after seven years in the 1980s with Thurmond. He returned from South Carolina with grim news. "Do you want the unvarnished truth?" he asked Thurmond.

"Give it to me straight."

"I've seen better campaigns for a high school student council race. There's no organization." A long pause followed.

"Will you run it? Will you fix it?"

Goodin agreed to go down on a volunteer basis to set up the campaign, provided he had absolute control, and to find a competent manager. He knew Thurmond balked at placing that much control in one person, but Strom agreed.

Goodin found at the end of 1997 that the campaign had raised barely $100,000, a "ridiculously low amount." Within two weeks he raised a couple of hundred thousand dollars from his corporate clients and by working the phones. He kept Cindy Carter, "the best political organizer I ever knew. She helped bring the campaign back to life." He hired Maxie Haltiwanger, a savvy political fund-raiser, as finance director for $8,000 a month — an unheard of amount for a Thurmond campaign — and told her she would work for every penny.

After asking Goodin how much he was paying Ms. Haltiwanger, Thurmond said, "Eight thousand dollars a month!"

"You said I would have full authority."

Thurmond bit his lip, then said, "We have a lot of confidence in you."

Goodin understood. "He meant, 'You better deliver.'"

In Atwater fashion, Goodin moved to bump Secretary of State James Miles from challenging Thurmond in a GOP primary. Among statewide Republican office-holders, only Miles hadn't endorsed Thurmond. Goodin believed Miles was running a nascent campaign and played political hardball to dry up Miles's campaign contributions.

On a day when Miles was out of state, Goodin denounced him at a press conference for not endorsing the senator, stressing that giving money to Miles was opposing Thurmond. He said that anyone who had contributed to Miles thinking they were contributing to a future campaign against Fritz Hollings should ask for their money back.

Goodin encouraged people to write letters to the editor. In Miles's home town of Greenville, Goodin brought Dan Quayle in for a fund-raiser and set up a huge Thurmond rally at Bob Jones University, where more than 7,000 people packed the assembly hall. At the annual Silver Elephant dinner in Columbia, the GOP major fundraiser, Young Republicans at each door pasted "I'm for Strom" stickers on the several thousand attendees.

Goodin recalled, "Thurmond made good remarks. The crowd naturally responded very well, and Strom said nice things about Miles — classic Strom Thurmond." Soon afterwards, Miles endorsed him. Goodin landed a solid campaign manager in Tony Denny, former executive director of the state Republican Party.

Republican state Rep. Harold Worley, a Myrtle Beach developer, spent $600,000 of his own money challenging Thurmond in the Republican primary, calling him "simply too old." Worley got thirty percent of the vote, carrying only his home county of Horry, and a third Republican candidate got nine percent.

In the general election, no established Democrat came forward. Clinton's Secretary of Education Dick Riley, the former two-term governor, considered and rejected the idea, as did Fifth District Congressman John Spratt. Thurmond ended up facing Elliott Close, forty-three, a wealthy but politically inexperienced great-grandson of textile magnate Elliott White Springs, founder of Springs Industries. Although he avoided mentioning it in his campaign, Close also was a brother-in-law of Clinton's White House chief of staff, Erskine Bowles.

Thurmond hasn't debated an opponent since Olin Johnston in 1950, and he followed Goodin's strategy. "I told him," Goodin said, "We're making history. Nobody your age has run before. We have to keep excitement out of this race. That means no mistakes, and that means, 'Don't take chances.' I make a mistake and it's because I'm tired; you make a mistake and it's because you're old."

As the 1998 *Almanac of American Politics* summarized: "Thurmond campaigned actively, shaking hands and speaking from note cards . . . He got a bit tough with Close. 'It might have been more in order for him to run for the town council of Fort Mill,' he said. 'It would take my opponent sxity years to catch up with what I can do in the next six years.' And 'I'm a conservative and he's a liberal, from all I hear about him. He's got the money, but I've got the experience.' Close spent $944,000 of his own money on a stumbling campaign that had three different managers. He boasted that his family's mill never laid off workers during the Depression, just one week before it closed three mills and laid off 850 workers. Close focused on Thurmond's age and alleged infirmness [sic]: 'Is Strom Thurmond still up to the job? . . . Vote for our future, not for our past.' Thurmond supporters like [former Governor] Carroll Campbell bellowed in rage, but the attacks on age didn't seem to have a huge impact. During the fall Thurmond was running in the low fifties in polls, and on election day he won fifty three percent to forty-four percent. He carried all the bigger metropolitan areas and lost mainly low-income rural counties. He has said he will not run again, and if he serves out his term he will turn 100 one month before he retires."[1]

In one of his few direct encounters with Close, Thurmond engaged in chitchat, telling the younger man that he had attended the 1928 Democratic national convention with his grandfather. Close said afterwards, "Actually, it was my great grandfather."[2]

Goodin says Thurmond "is still a great campaigner. There's still nobody better at pressing the flesh." Reporter Kevin Sack of *The New York Times*, after two days on the campaign trail with Thurmond, wrote: "Polls show that the vast majority of South Carolinians believe it is far past time for him to retire. . . . But the polls cannot accurately measure the profound affection felt in this state for Mr. Thurmond. . . . Despite their concerns about his abilities, many South Carolinians just cannot bring themselves to turn the old man out."

Another image featured Esther Hunter, an eighty-one-year-old black woman who showed up at a campaign stop at Gene's Restaurant in the town of Union "to thank Mr. Thurmond for the condolence letter he sent when her husband died in 1993.

"It mattered little that it was a form letter, no different from thousands of others sent to survivors over the years by Mr. Thurmond's staff. Nor did it matter that Mr. Thurmond was once one of the South's staunchest segregationists.

"'He sent me this fine letter when my husband died,' Mrs. Hunter said, clutching a wrinkled page. 'You can't pay attention to everything you hear. People say, you know, he didn't like black people. But he knows I'm 100 percent black and he sure did pay me respect. You have to praise the bridge that carries you across.'"[3] He received between fifteen and twenty percent of the black vote, a record for any Republican statewide candidate in modern South Carolina and almost enough to make the difference between winning and losing.

In addition to almost a million dollars of his own money, Close raised almost another million, which to Thurmond's strategists meant the wealthy challenger lacked confidence because he apparently was unwilling to invest more of his own fortune. Including the primary, Thurmond outspent Close $2,632,682 to $1,913,574.

On election night, Thurmond joined Goodin for dinner. "If they turn me out, they turn me out," the senator said as they waited for returns. "I think he would have been hurt," Goodin says, "Heart-broken."[4]

Thurmond apparently survived because no qualified Democratic challenger came forward. In a post-election analysis concluding that Thurmond had "dodged the bullet," Lee Bandy indicated that Thurmond campaign aides privately conceded that Riley or Spratt could have beaten him.[5]

On May 25, 1997, Thurmond became the longest serving senator in United States history, breaking the record held by Democrat Carl Hayden of Arizona, who died in 1969. Thurmond returned to Edgefield County, where he gave the main speech for the town of Johnston's centennial celebration eight miles from his birthplace. His sister Mary sat in the front row. "People often ask me how I want to be remembered," he said, "honest, patriotic and helpful."

Speakers from across the spectrum praised him, including Tom McCain and black state Rep. William Clyburn, whose House district included Johnston. If their presence on the program represented change, the bare smattering of black faces in the audience reflected continuity, a feeling that this Sunday afternoon function somehow didn't really include the African-Americans who make up more than half of Johnston's population.

Thurmond's niece, Mary T. Freeman, wrote a poem for the occasion that reflects his family's pride and affection for him:

STROMMY

Your life is one of service.
Your good influence has reached wide and far.
Today you set a new record
as you capture that highest star.

For the longest senatorial service ever
you humbly take your bow.
To the record books you now go
For folks to read about and think, "Wow!"

Your family takes much pride in you.
We love you for who you are.
The warm and caring "Strommy"
who's most always "up to par."

"Strong in mind and body
determined to succeed,
mingling with other folks of fame
you didn't neglect your neighbor's need.

God bless you now and always
for the many achievements you have made
and give you grace and more time to serve
as you continue to "make the grade."

Back in Washington, a staffer accompanied Thurmond anywhere
he went at the Capitol. But he said he was still riding his exercycle
every morning and swimming weekly. To ease lonely weekends at
home, Administrative Assistant R. J. "Duke" Short and his wife
usually had Thurmond come over for at least one meal.[6] A fellow
senator on the Armed Services Committee complained that Short
"gets him up in the morning and puts him to bed at night and basically guides him through the day. Everything is sort of in the area
of protecting Senator Thurmond."[7]

Although national media often noted that Thurmond in his
nineties seemed heavily scripted, Lee Bandy of *The State* said,
"When Strom was much younger, I would go to the committee
hearings and Strom always read what was written for him on the
4x5 cards. He didn't ask a question that wasn't already written for

him."[8] Thurmond returned to Washington as chairman of the Senate Armed Services Committee [He announced early in 1998 that he would step down as chairman at the end of the year and in September he cast his 15,000th vote, only the second person to reach that milestone]. His stewardship of that committee, which he inherited from lawyerly Democrat Sam Nunn of Georgia, came under fire. One witness said that in private meetings Thurmond alternates from being "the slickest politician I ever saw" to appearing overwhelmed by details, totally dependent on his aides and focused on the funding of South Carolina military installations to the exclusion of weighty national security issues.[9]

A few years earlier, after the fiftieth anniversary celebration and memorial of the D-day landing at Normandy in 1994, Sen. Paul Coverdell of Georgia told the Senate that Thurmond didn't attend because it conflicted with the high school graduation of his youngest son. Some members chuckled at the nature of their ninety-one-year-old colleague's dilemma. A much younger fellow senator who had attended the memorial events at Normandy came up afterwards to Thurmond to tell him what a wonderful occasion it had been and that it was unfortunate he had been unable to attend. Thurmond, jabbing a forefinger in his younger colleague's chest, said, "Son, I was there when it counted."

A half century after his July 1948 Dixiecrat speech, declaring "there's not enough troops in the Army to force the Southern people to . . . admit the Negro race into our theaters, into our swimming pools, into our homes and into our churches," Strom Thurmond said, "I don't have anything to apologize for. I don't have any regrets.

"I may have said some things that I could have left off, because I favor everybody receiving equal treatment. Race should not enter into it. It's merit that counts.

"The States' Rights Party addressed a legitimate issue in 1948 America — whether our states should surrender power to the federal government."[10]

George Wallace, Thurmond's rival as a symbol of segregationist resistance, had said, "We were wrong."[11] Thurmond has never been willing to say that, denying that he even ran a racist campaign. Yet, defense of white supremacy was the heart of the

Dixiecrat movement. His campaign poster in South Carolina, with a huge headline, NOW IS THE TIME TO FIGHT, at the top, proclaimed, "Join the fight to defeat the FEPC and the abolition of segregation . . . and to protect States Rights."

Thurmond seemed to want it both ways — "no regrets" and "I may have said some things that I could have left off." Wallace had far more for which to apologize. But he did apologize and he did it forthrightly. Thurmond hasn't done that. It leaves him with Tom Turnipseed's characterization as "a racist in denial."

In defending the Dixiecrat campaign on the issue of "whether our states should surrender power to the federal government" — in this case the power to end legally-mandated racial segregation and make real the idea of equality under law — Thurmond missed an opportunity to explore the larger historical significance. His 1948 campaign provided a historic turning point in transforming the American South from a political backwater to a major force in American politics. As the United States faces the twenty-first century, the South drives presidential politics (every twentieth century Democratic president after John F. Kennedy came from a former Confederate state), and shapes conservative ideology and Republican strategy. Thurmond's 1948 campaign provided the first step on this journey, and his 1964 party switch and 1968 kingmaker role for Richard Nixon blazed new trails along the way.

Thurmond has come a long way in overcoming his racist past, but he hasn't yet overcome denial of it. But hardly had he said he didn't "have anything to apologize for" than he took action that gave the appearance of repudiating his Dixiecrat speech.

It involved a confirmation vote on the Senate Armed Services Committee for a new Air Force Secretary on July 22, 1998, the 50th anniversary week of the Dixiecrat speech. After a nine-hour public hearing followed by an executive session after ten months consideration, the committee rejected the nomination of Daryl Jones, who would have been the first black Air Force Secretary. On a 9-9 vote refusing to send the nomination to the full Senate without a recommendation, Thurmond was the lone Republican to support Jones. Two Democrats who opposed confirmation, Robert Byrd of West Virginia and ex-marine Charles Robb of Virginia, voted with other members of their party to submit the matter to the full Senate. An honors graduate of the Air Force Academy, Jones was a jet pilot, lawyer, and Florida legislator.

Critics, including a former Air Force Reserve squadron commander, accused him of lying about why he stopped flying jet fighters. They charged him with attempting to pressure enlisted reservists to buy Amway products from him and collecting flight pay after he stopped flying.

During Jones's portion of the nine-hour hearing, broadcast on C-SPAN, his responses in some cases were clearly troubling. Although grounded by his squadron commander over safety-related issues, which left Jones an option of appealing or accepting a non-flying position, he first said he voluntarily decided to take a desk job. He exaggerated his amount of flight time.

Supporters, including other squadron members, said racial animosity motivated at least some of the complaints, that a number of white pilots had resented him, suspecting that he had won a spot in the unit because he is black. Jones denied encountering racism in the squadron.[12]

In a staff-written statement he read before the final vote, Thurmond cited "media accounts, rumor campaigns, and personal attacks" in an effort to "raise doubts about the integrity, character, and ability of Daryl Jones." But, he continued, "In each and every matter, Mr. Jones offered a plausible, credible, and believable explanation concerning the matters in question."[13]

Others disagreed. But Thurmond, based on his questions that failed to probe the issues troubling his colleagues, appeared committed to vote for Jones no matter what. At one point, Thurmond questioned the nominee's wife, who sat behind her husband, about whether she really wanted him to have the job and did she love him. Other senators shifted uncomfortably or looked straight ahead.

One might argue that Thurmond appeared intuitively to understand from his own background that racial motivation did lurk behind some of the criticism, that he appreciated the nominee's refusal to charge racism, and that he seemed to recognize the exceptional achievement by Jones in overcoming an unprivileged background to compile what Thurmond called an "admirable" record.

In contrast to his assertion a half century earlier that even the Army lacked the force to break down segregation, Thurmond stood alone among fellow Republicans in supporting a black Southerner as civilian leader of the Air Force. This interpretation would also mean that Thurmond, a committee chairman unable to persuade a single fellow Republican to vote with him, had lost all influence.

The outcome allowed Thurmond to have it both ways politically. He could get credit for supporting the black nominee, but no blame from racial conservatives for getting him confirmed. The questions left hanging for skeptics were these: Had Thurmond, with his record of political slickness, simply positioned himself for history's evaluation? Had he done so without acting to change history itself? Or had he become powerless in the Senate? Or all of the above? On the matter of race, the appearance of having crossed back over the Rubicon seemed a mirage. Thurmond seemed to want to cross over, but without getting his feet wet.

Thurmond had once told Harry Dent that he wanted him to give his funeral eulogy, adding, "unless I have to give yours."

In terms of South Carolina, Dent places Thurmond historically on a par with James F. Byrnes and John C. Calhoun. "He's the most unusual person South Carolina has ever produced," Dent says. "He had the courage and the guts to take the risks for what he believed. That's the essence. My wife hates politics and hates politicians, but she reveres Strom Thurmond. She saw him helping any and everybody, and that's where that extra vote came in down here in this last election. The average person in this state believes that Strom Thurmond is a straight shooter and not a politician. It's not going to be hard."[14]

The only question is who will be eulogizing whom.

1. *The Almanac of American Politics 1998*, p. 1,271.
2. Confidential source.
3. *The New York Times*, October 24, 1996, p. 1.
4. Bass telephone interview with Mark Goodin, July 30, 1997.
5. *The State*, November 10, 1996, p. D4.
6. R. J. "Duke" Short to Bass, July 1997.
7. *The Washington Post*, April 8, 1996, p. D4.
8. Lee Bandy to Bass.
9. *The Washington Post*, April 8, 1996, p. D4.
10. *The State*, July 12, 1998, p. D1.
11. *American South Comes of Age* video, University of South Carolina and South Carolina Educational Television, 1987, program 14, "The Emerging South."

12. *The New York Times*, July 23, 1998, p. A13.
13. Opening Statement by Senator Strom Thurmond (R-SC),
    Senate Armed Services Committee, July 22, 1998.
14. Bass interview with Dent, op. cit.

INDEX

News and Courier, The, 127, 130-131, 139, 144, 145, 146, 193, 194

Nicholson, B.E. III, 68

Nixon, Julie, 251

Nixon, Patricia, 151

Nixon, Richard, 2, 13, 43, 104, 149, 190, 209, 216, 219-233, 243, 247-249, 250-252, 263-265, 271, 289, 297

"Parent's Point of View," 242

Normandy, 73, 93, 225

nuclear weapons, manufacture of, 135

Nunn, Sam, 265, 303, 341

O'Connor, Sandra Day, 295

O'Hara, Scarlett, 17

Oakley Park Redshirt Shrine, 17, 20

Oberdorfer, Don, 230-231

Office of Economic Opportunity, 264

Official Detective Stories, 69

oil, ownership of in coastal areas, 114

Oklahoma, McLarin v., 129

Orangeburg Massacre, 196

Orangeburg Massacre, The, 268, 283

Osborne, Sammie, 59-61

Osceola, 316

Painter, Sweatt v., 129

Palmetto Federal Savings and Loan, 135

Parker, John J., 99

Parvin Foundation, 216, 293

Pastore, John O., 197

Patterson, Eugene (Gene), 94, 99, 108

Patton, George, 77

Peace, Roger, 201

Pearl Harbor, 69

Pearson, Glenice B., 286

Pendleton, Clarence, 298

Pepper, Claude, 126, 240

Peppers, James, 313

Percy, Charles, 225

Perry, Matthew J., 281-282, 308-309

Peters, James S., 105

Pickens, Andrew, 7

Pickens, Francis, 7, 14, 15, 16

Pickens, Lucy Holcolme, 15

Plessy v. Ferguson, 157, 283

Plume, David, 20

Plume, Emily Mansfield, 20

police power, 107

politics
beginnings, 37-51
governor of South Carolina, 82-88
mastery of, 3
personal, 12
run for president, 97-115
run for U.S. senator, 119-131, 139-147
switch from Democratic to Republican Party, 189-205

"Politics of 1948, The," 100

poll tax, 88, 98, 100, 105

Pope, Thomas A., 53-54, 84

Popham, John, 105

Populist movement, 19

Porter, Paul, 207, 215

Post and Courier, 323

Powell, Lewis, 297

Powell, Roy, 47, 121

prayer, 190. See also religion.

President's Committee on Civil Rights, 86, 88

presidential campaign, 97-115

presidential candidate, 2, 144

presidential nomination, 104

presidential primary, New Hampshire, 122

Presley, Elvis, 238

Price, Leontyne, 285

Prioleau, William F. (Buddy), 141, 142, 145, 146

Pryor, Richard, 258

public accommodations law, federal, 196, 197

Quayle, Dan, 336, 337

Quinn, Sally, 240

race relations, 12, 107

racial politics, 79, 250

racial violence, 17

racism
"aristocratic," 129
"democratic," 128

Rainsford, Bettis, 8, 11, 12-13, 264-265

Ramage, Carroll Johnson, 49